PRAISE FOR *THE GOOD RETREAT GUIDE*:

'This fascinating book is not just a guide to the idyllic
retreats of northern Europe, it's a guide to living.'
Daily Express

'I feel rested and refreshed after reading
this calm, come-hither compendium.'
Christina Hardyman, *Telegraph Magazine*

'An inexpensive way of finding peace.'
Guardian

'Spiritual sustenance without being force-fed.'
The Sunday Times

'The definitive guide.'
Marie Claire Health & Beauty

'If you are on a quest for inner harmony,
the guide might have the answer.'
Woman's Journal

'Vital breaks from the pace of work.'
Time Out

'A flip through its pages is an eye-opening experience.'
The Sunday Telegraph

'Deservedly popular and a very helpful book.'
Yoga & Health

'Some retreats concentrate on prayer and meditation,
others combine spiritual guidance with a physical activity
such as yoga, music and dance, icon painting or gardening.
Useful sections on Ireland, France and Spain.'
The Independent on Sunday

'*The Good Retreat Guide* is indispensable.'
Traveller

'To find peaceful retreats read this guide.'
Top Santé

'An excellent publication
you dozens of ideas in
London

'Europe's best-selling book on retreats.'
The Softback Review

'Whether you fancy a music or yoga retreat, meditation workshop or
simple solitude, this guide will help you choose your sanctuary.'
Zest

'Lists more than 400 different European retreats.'
Red

'Retreats and how to choose the best one
for you, read *The Good Retreat Guide*.'
Home & Life

'Stafford Whiteaker encourages us to step
off the world at least occasionally.'
The Universe

'Most notable is the inner-faith emphasis.'
The Tablet

'Choose from Anglican, Buddhist, Roman Catholic or
non-denominational with retreats in complete silence or interactive.'
Sunday Mirror

'More and more people are visiting Britain's retreat houses
in search of civilised tranquillity and solitude.'
The Times

'The first comprehensive guide of its kind.'
Methodist Recorder

'Describes what you are likely to encounter at
New Age centres, healing retreats or prayer retreats.'
Daily Telegraph

'Isn't peace and quiet a luxury these days? *The Good Retreat Guide*
details hundreds of Christian, Buddhist and non-affiliated
retreats both here and on the Continent.'
Tatler

'Charges your batteries to such an extent, you won't want to leave.'
New Dimensions

'We all need a private sanctuary where we can wind down
away from the pressure of modern life.'
Options

THE
GOOD
RETREAT
GUIDE

STAFFORD WHITEAKER

RIDER

LONDON · SYDNEY · AUCKLAND · JOHANNESBURG

1 3 5 7 9 10 8 6 4 2

First published in 1991 by Rider
Revised editions 1994, 1997, 2001

This edition published in 2004 by Rider, an imprint of
Ebury Press
Random House
20 Vauxhall Bridge Road
London SW1V 2SA

Random House Australia (Pty) Limited
20 Alfred Street
Milsons Point, Sydney
New South Wales 2061, Australia

Random House New Zealand Limited
18 Poland Road, Glenfield
Auckland 10, New Zealand

Random House South Africa (Pty) Limited
Endulini, 5A Jubilee Road
Parktown 2193, South Africa

The Random House Group Limited Reg. No. 954009

Papers used by Rider are natural, recyclable products
made from wood grown in sustainable forests.

Typeset by seagulls
Printed and bound in Great Britain by Mackays of Chatham plc, Kent

A CIP catalogue record for this book is available from the British Library

ISBN 1 8441 3228 5

Please Note: Whilst every effort has been made to ensure that
the information in this guide is accurate at the time of going to press,
readers are advised that details and prices may be subject to change.
We therefore strongly recommend that readers contact retreat centres
directly in order to confirm the details of their stay and discuss their
requirements, especially with respect to the availability of disabled facilities.

ACKNOWLEDGEMENTS

With thanks for research to Anna Howard, Ann Barlow Carr, Ros Frecker, David Gadsby, Emma Baddeley, Gary Fisher, Adrian Scott and Ingrid Palairet, and to the many readers who sent in opinions and information. GuideWebsite design by Nicky Trulsson (nicky.t@telia.com). With special appreciation to Judith Kendra at Random House for being my editor over many editions of this guide.

For Gregory van der Kleij OSB

Contents

Preface   xi

Introduction   1
   Is this all there is to life?   1
   Do you want to discover your true self?   1
   Are you fighting for some peace in your life?   1
   Finding calm and getting to know yourself   2
   What is a retreat?   2
   A retreat is not an escape from reality   3
   Do you have to be religious or belong to a faith or church?   3
   Spiritual practices   3
   Christian spirituality   4
   Buddhist spirituality   4
   Mind Body Spirit spirituality   5
   Who goes on retreats?   6
   The people you may meet on a retreat   6
   Going on retreat for the first time   6
   Going on retreat with people with disabilities   7
   Different kinds of retreat   7
   A typical day on retreat   17
   Obtaining spiritual help   18
   Staying in a monastery   18
   So what do monks and nuns actually do?   18
   General guidelines on being a monastery guest   19
   Staying in a Christian monastery   19
   Staying in a Buddhist monastery   20
   What is prayer?   20
   What is meditation?   21
   Spiritual guides and spiritual direction   21
   Yoga today   21
   Going on a retreat abroad   22
   How to get the retreat you want   22
   How the guide is organised   23
   Telephoning in Britain   23
   Highly recommended places of retreat   23
   Your opinion is wanted   24
   Setting out on the interior journey   24

Retreat Centres by Region

England	25
London	25
South-west	43
Avon	43
Cornwall	46
Devon	51
Dorset	62
Somerset	68
Wiltshire	80
South and South-east	83
Berkshire	83
Hampshire	86
Kent	92
Middlesex	99
Surrey	103
Sussex (East)	110
Sussex (West)	112
Isle of Wight	118
East and East Anglia	120
Bedfordshire	120
Cambridgeshire	123
Essex	127
Hertfordshire	131
Lincolnshire	134
Norfolk	137
Suffolk	143
Central	147
Birmingham and West Midlands	147
Buckinghamshire	148
Derbyshire	151
Gloucestershire	155
Herefordshire	159
Leicestershire	162
Northamptonshire	165
Oxfordshire	166
Shropshire	173
Staffordshire	178
Warwickshire	179
Worcestershire	180
Northern	185
Cheshire	185
Cumbria	188
Durham	191
Lancashire	192
Manchester	194
Merseyside	195
Northumberland	196
Yorkshire (South)	203
Yorkshire (North)	204
Yorkshire (West)	213
Wales	219
Scotland	240

Channel Islands   269
Ireland and Northern Ireland   270
    Introduction   270
    Antrim   270
    Cavan   272
    Clave   273
    Cork   273
    Donegal   277
    Down   280
    Dublin   281
    Galway   284
    Kerry   286
    Kildare   288
    Limerick   289
    Mayo   290
    Sligo   291
    Tipperary   293
    Waterford   294
    Wicklow   295
France   298
    Introduction   298
    Retreat centres by Department of France   300
    Evangelical churches and centres   343
    Yoga in France   344
    Creation spirituality   345
    Hermitage retreats   346
    Buddhist facilities   346
    Further information on France   346
Italy   349
    Introduction   349
    Retreats by place   349
Spain   354
    Introduction   354
    Retreats by place   356
Yoga centres   363
    England   373
    Wales   373
    Scotland   373
    Ireland and Northern Ireland   374
    France   375
    Spain   376
Open centres   377

Appendix: A Spiritual Notebook   379

Helpful addresses   384

Helpful publications   389

Travel organisations   391

Selected reading   393

Glossary   395

Preface

For some fifteen years years, I have watched the retreat movement grow from a mostly Roman Catholic tradition into a multi-million-pound industry. The popularity of retreats has spread across Western Europe, embracing not just one religion but many. From Christ and Buddha to Shamanism and reiki healing, spirituality today has become broad and open, inviting everyone to explore the mysterious inner world of the self. Retreats are now so much part of our ordinary lifestyle that they are acclaimed by the media as essential for healthy living in the modern world.

NEW DEVELOPMENTS

One of the major developments in the modern retreat movement is the guest house provision now made by many male monastic communities for women. Another is the huge growth in the use of alternative healing techniques, such as massage, aromatherapy, reiki and reflexology, as forms of spiritual help. These are increasingly being incorporated into Christian retreat house programmes. A similar trend is the use of arts and crafts, usually coupled with prayer or meditation. Icon painting and prayer from the Orthodox Christianity tradition has become widely popular. Silence has become the gold of retreat houses, with the result that mobile phones and tape and CD players are increasingly being forbidden.

FUTURE AREAS OF RETREAT GROWTH

It is likely that in the future retreats will become more specialised, catering for discrete groups in terms of gender, age and sexual orientation. Heralds of this change are the current rapid growth in women-only retreats (often in retreat houses designated for women only), masculine spirituality and male rites of passage retreats, and new concepts such as reading retreats.

Retreats based on Sufi spirituality and those rooted in a revival of the desert spirituality of the early Christian hermits will enter the scene. Buddhism, already a rapidly growing religion in the West, will continue to spread its teachings and meditation methods through retreats and courses.

Although it will be slow, an increase in retreats for lesbian and gay men is on the cards, in spite of homophobic pronouncements on doctrine by various Christian denominations and the hysteria of the media.

While in the West its spiritual dimension continues frequently to be overshadowed by its fitness aspects, yoga has swept Europe and America, reaching even into rural backwaters. The yoga retreat business is sure to go on flourishing, with an increased number of yoga courses for children and therapeutic yoga courses.

As to youth retreats, American teenagers are turning their backs on traditional holiday fun, such as hiking and camping, and going for health centres, where inner discovery, meditation, yoga and tai chi are all part of a package that includes losing weight and having your fingernails painted. It is only a matter of time until youth retreat centres in Britain start such programmes.

Fashionable management development courses have now taken a leap into the spiritual with retreats based on the wisdom of the Rule of Saint Benedict, twelfth-century guidelines for living devised for Christian monastic communities. This new trend is all about the art of understanding how people tick. Such retreats will grow in number, with proven spiritual methods and philosophies increasingly used as tools for commercial goals.

There has been a steady growth in eco-spirituality retreats in all programmes. These use walking, gardening, woodland renewal, water conservation, nature discoveries and the visiting of sacred sites as a way to increase our awareness of the intimate inter-connection of all aspects of our world. Nothing, we learn, is separate. These types of retreat are bound to increase as the problems of Gaia become more acute.

RISING STANDARDS

On the accommodation front, retreat houses are continuing to upgrade, putting in ensuite facilities to meet guests' constantly rising expectations. Still there but definitely on the way out is the monastic cell with its minimal and uninviting furnishings. Maximum comfort is the key concept, because it is seen as a way of enabling guests to relax and rest. It also helps with repeat business. Vegetarian and special diets are almost always available, and many places are including vegan dishes on the menu as well. Food in general is lighter, more appetising and better prepared.

THE COST OF RETREATS TODAY

Costs in general have not risen very much, although most monasteries have become more commercial in their charging levels. They and other centres who ask only for donations have made the suggested levels more realistic. Costs today vary widely from the very modest to a goodly sum.

THE NEW ADAM AND THE NEW EVE

Church attendance, baptisms and religious marriage vows may be on the decrease, but the Holy Spirit is at work, with a great spiritual awakening in Europe that goes beyond institutional structures. There is in general an increased awareness that we are spiritual beings with an invisible dimension that demands our exploration and understanding. The yearning for the sacred is universal, and love, the highest of all human and divine expressions, is the crown jewel of spiritual life.

Stafford Whiteaker

Introduction

IS THIS ALL THERE IS TO LIFE?

What happens when one day you wake up and – in spite all those many signs of a successful lifestyle: the good job, the right relationship, even the children you always wanted – you ask yourself: 'Is this all there is to life?'

Such a question usually brings with it a sense of discomfort and unease. Some people cope by ignoring it or finding new roles or activities to boost their confidence, but many more today are accepting the challenge and searching for their own answers.

DO YOU WANT TO DISCOVER YOUR TRUE SELF?

This search can lead to an increased awareness of self that may be both exciting and rewarding.

Although the self is always with us, all too rarely do we take the time to look deep within and discover this inner being that so dominates our nature. Yet everything we feel and do is filtered through our sense of self. Even sleep offers no escape. Call it self-awareness, self-identity or consciousness, the sense of self is intrinsic to being human. If you find yourself actively seeking this interior journey towards the true self, you have already begun the search for something more in life.

ARE YOU FIGHTING FOR SOME PEACE IN YOUR LIFE?

How can we begin to explore this question of our humanity until we have first found some peace and quiet, in a place where distractions of every kind are at a minimum? Our usual holidays cannot provide this kind of sanctuary. Most church services are filled with the business of ritual and sound. Even a quiet day alone at home is likely to end in the performing of some long-postponed domestic task. Many people today feel as if they are being swept along by a tide of events beyond their control without ever having a chance for a bit of peaceful living. There is no denying that the impact of the pace of the world, the economic imperative to succeed and the demand that we be goal-orientated all help to erode our sense of individuality and self. However, most people cannot simply drop out and go to live on some remote mountain because that would entail leaving behind the relationships and responsibilities that play an enriching role in their lives.

FINDING CALM AND GETTING TO KNOW YOURSELF

So it is not surprising that more and more people are seeking special places where they can start their quest for the spiritual by temporarily withdrawing from their ordinary existence. These special places are called retreats, and going on one has become a popular solution to the dilemma of finding a time and a place to discover the self.

Retreats have taken their rightful place alongside all the other modern tools that we employ in the desire to lead a full and healthy life in which we come to realise our true self. Millions of people, many of whom never go to church and do not profess any religious belief, now go on retreat. Going on a retreat is today so much a part of the way many of us live that even the popular media regularly gives coverage to retreat centres.

We all have a need for spiritual experiences and reflections – the ones that make us stop and think, 'I remember now why I am here,' 'I can see what my life is about,' 'This is how I want to change my life,' 'This is what love is about for me.'

Going on a retreat is a contemporary way of finding out more about where we really are on our life's journey. We can stop and find out not just what we want but also what we need. We can begin to answer that vital question: Is this all there is to life?

WHAT IS A RETREAT?

A retreat is a time away from our ordinary living in which we reflect on ourselves, our relationships, our values and our lifestyle. It is a deliberate attempt to step outside our ordinary life.

Retreats are not a new phenomenon. Throughout the ages and in all the world's great spiritual traditions men and women have at times needed to withdraw temporarily from daily living in order to nourish their spiritual life. Moses retreated to Mount Sinai. Jesus went into the desert. Buddhists make an annual retreat. Moslems go for a day of prayer and fasting within the mosque. Hindus withdraw to the temple or wander alone across the land. Native Americans travel into the hidden realms of Mother Earth. Sufi Dervishes dance until they leave behind all visible worlds. Zen Buddhists meditate on the wall until the wall disappears. The hermit sits in the desert silence meditating on holy words. All have withdrawn temporarily from the world to live in the garden of the soul.

Being on a retreat is an inward exploration that lets our feelings open out and gives us access to both the light and dark corners of our deepest feelings and relationships. When we are able to reflect upon the discoveries we have made about ourselves, we grow in personal knowledge, opening ourselves to the adventure of living and to a greater consciousness of others. For most this will be a movement away from the ego and towards peace. For many, it will be an awakening to the presence of the sacred in their lives.

A RETREAT IS NOT AN ESCAPE FROM REALITY

Silence and stillness are a very great challenge in this age of noise, diversion and aggression. Our lives are filled with preoccupations, distractions, illusions, desires, and too much useless information and gratuitous sound. Even after a few hours of stillness, an inner consciousness opens up within ourselves, and for those who are unaccustomed to taking silent time out, this may be an unexpected and perhaps rather startling experience.

In opening up your interior self, you may find a surprising void – an empty inner space you never knew existed. Suddenly there are no radios, televisions, friends, children or pets, and no constant background of human activity. There is no gossip, no grumbling, no meetings, no decisions, no responsibilities and no limits on the time you can spend dwelling in your inner space. You slip into a slower physical, mental and emotional gear. You relax, and your spirit says: 'Hey! This is great!' It is at this moment that your retreat truly begins.

This happy state of consciousness may well initiate a meditation on the giving of undivided attention to the spiritual in you. Many wise men and women have said that this is the moment of opening the door to timelessness and to the inexplicable and invisible force that is so often simply called 'God'.

However, going on retreat is not necessarily about having some kind of sudden spiritual awakening – although this can happen. More than anything else it is about refreshing yourself, relaxing and taking a journey into the deeper self.

DO YOU HAVE TO BE RELIGIOUS
OR BELONG TO A FAITH OR CHURCH?

In most cases, absolutely not! Men and women of all faiths and those of none go on retreat. You do not have to believe in God. You do not have to be a Christian or Buddhist to go on a retreat even in a monastery. The important factor is your positive decision to take this time for the nourishment and enrichment of your spiritual life.

Access to places of the Islamic faith is a different matter and you must enquire first as to the position regarding non-Muslims. In general, retreats as we understand them today are not a tradition of Islam, but pilgrimages are. You should also enquire first at places of Hindu worship and study. If you go on an event or course retreat for Jews, it is generally understood that you are of that religion. However, you should enquire, as there are also some study courses for people of other faiths. The Inter-Faith Network, for example, whose address is in Helpful Addresses, may be able to assist you in these matters.

SPIRITUAL PRACTICES

There are many paths to spirituality, in many different traditions and religions. The use of ritual, formal prayers, spiritual exercises and meditation are all common practices. No matter what form they take, spiritual practices are essentially to be pursued in a spirit of *letting go and letting happen* rather than as an intellectual exercise.

In a Christian retreat place you are likely to encounter spiritual practices that derive from Anglican, English, Franciscan, Augustinian, Dominican and Benedictine traditions, to name but a few. Some practices, such as those of Black spirituality or from the Orthodox tradition may be less familiar. The Charismatic Movement and Pentecostalism continue to foster a reawakening of the spirituality of the early Church and have developed an increasingly popular approach. The scripture-based approaches of Evangelical churches have also grown in popularity.

CHRISTIAN SPIRITUALITY

Christianity is a religious faith based on the teachings of Jesus Christ which had its origins in Judaism. Its believers hold that Jesus is the Messiah prophesied in the Old Testament. The tenets of Christianity are based on the New Testament; the doctrines of the Trinity of God the Father, the Son, and the Holy Spirit; and the incarnation and resurrection of Christ. Christ's role is seen as that of redeemer of all humanity.

While there is a basic shared belief system throughout Western Christianity, approaches to it may differ. For example, the approach of the twentieth-century philosopher and theologian Pierre Teilhard de Chardin is quite different from that of the sixteenth-century mystic Saint Teresa of Avila – and different again from that of sixteenth-century reformer Martin Luther or modern Christian thinker Hans Kung. Yet all these people belong to a common Christian heritage. Included in the many ways of Western Christian spirituality is also the rich treasury of Orthodox Christian traditions.

BUDDHIST SPIRITUALITY

Buddhism began in India some 2,500 years ago and its teachings spread throughout Asia. There is no doctrine and no need to hold to any particular beliefs. There are, however, different Buddhist traditions. The aim of Buddhism is to show us how to develop our capacity for awareness, love and energy to the point where we become *enlightened* or *fully awake to reality*. Indeed, the word *Buddha* means 'one who is awake'. Buddhists do not believe in a Supreme Creator, since they hold that the world rises and declines in an eternal and timeless cycle; nevertheless, Buddhism, like all the major religions still contains elements of worship at the centre of its practice. There is a liturgy and scriptures that are chanted, physical acts of reverence, and inner contemplation of the Buddha – which is often compared to contemplative Christian prayer.

Much of the current interest in Buddhism in the West is due to its being non-exclusive and non-dogmatic. To be a Buddhist you do not have to wear strange robes, adopt Eastern customs or reject Western culture. Buddhism is often called 'a way of harmony'. This is because the Buddha's teachings offer a set of tools for finding inner peace and harmony by working with your own feelings and experiences of life. By learning to look closely and honestly at your thoughts, emotions and physical feelings, you arrive at a new perspective from which to understand your frustrations and discontent. Then you can start to deal effectively with them. From such insights you may develop a joyful, kind and thoughtful attitude to others and to yourself. This should lead you onwards to a state of compassion and peace. This inner examination and insight is a direct method of transforming consciousness and is termed 'meditation'.

There are many different forms of Buddhism, the two major ones being Theravada and Mahayana. When you receive literature from a Buddhist centre, it will probably state which form is followed. The Theravada doctrine prevails in Southeast Asia, including Sri Lanka, Burma, Thailand, Kampuchea and Laos. Mahayana doctrine predominates further north, in China, Tibet, Korea, Japan and Vietnam. There are traditions and schools within these two major divisions, so, in a sense, Buddhism is similar to Christianity in having many different groups and divisions around the world. Yet all spring from a single spiritual inspiration.

MIND BODY SPIRIT SPIRITUALITY

It is easier to describe the Mind Body Spirit movement than it is to define it, for it is a collection of many ideas and practices aimed at personal growth, self-development, and healing of the whole person. The majority of these ideas, techniques and methods spring from well-established traditions of healing and self-discovery, some of them thousands of years old. Others are a combination of different methods brought into a single practice originated by the person who is running the retreat. The movement has no established dogma or leaders and is very much a phenomenon of our time.

The retreats, courses and workshops offered by Mind Body Spirit centres offer an approach to self-growth that is helpful to many people who do not want to enter an established way as offered, for example, by Buddhism or Christianity. The aspect that appeals to most people is the great emphasis placed on a holistic approach to mind, body and spirit, which are regarded as inseparable. This approach is hardly new, as it is part of all the major faiths, but this awareness has been a rediscovery for many Christians.

It is fair to say that the Mind Body Spirit movement draws on some of the most ancient healing traditions in the human history and that it is mainly through the growth of this movement that a general awareness of this great spiritual and healing inheritance has been raised. The alternative approaches to health, healing and self-discovery that the Mind Body Spirit movement has to offer are increasingly part of our everyday living. They influence much of our thinking and culture. There is now hardly anyone who has not heard about such practices, for example, as aromatherapy, reflexology and acupuncture.

What is included in this kind of broad and wide-sweeping spirituality ranges from spiritualism, past-life therapy, environmentalism, telepathy, healing, astrology, rebirthing, work with crystals, paganism and shamanism, reflexology and Reiki to elements of Eastern religions and spiritual practices. Psychological methods and personal counselling also play a part in this kind of spirituality. It embraces a wide range of philosophical, social and ecological thinking, and includes the work of prominent scientists whose discoveries – particularly in such disciplines as sub-atomic physics, psychology, parapsychology and geology – bring a new validity to ancient teachings.

There are literally hundreds of Mind Body Spirit centres. The criterion for including such places in this guide has been that their approach is holistic, that there is a genuine interest in helping people and that the spirituality offered is of substance – perhaps based on an established spiritual tradition or a new development that has become of interest to a large number of people. Mind Body Spirit centres do not share a common central basis of belief in the way that established religious places do, so you will find each one different from the other. Most centres have very extensive programmes and will be happy to provide details. If you are looking for silence, you may find there is rather too much personal sharing and discussion, so enquire about the nature of the event or workshop before you book.

Although certain Mind Body Spirit methods and approaches are increasingly being incorporated by Christian retreat centres, many Christians may wish to make certain before attending a Mind Body Spirit retreat that the course content or ideas put forward are not in conflict with their religious beliefs and doctrines. For Roman Catholics the Vatican has recently issued a document on the subject.

WHO GOES ON RETREATS?

At a retreat centre you will meet people of all ages and from every kind of background – students, housewives, grandparents, businessmen and women, the millionaire celebrity and the unknown poor. It is a kind of spiritual club with membership open to all. A group retreat can be fun and a time for making new friends. Even on a private retreat you are likely to meet interesting people.

THE PEOPLE YOU MAY MEET ON A RETREAT

At a retreat you are placing yourself amongst strangers. You will probably meet people you like at once, people you do not want to know better and people who make a nuisance of themselves – perhaps the kind of person who has some problem and cannot help talking about it to everyone they meet. You may also encounter the kind of person who persists in hammering away about God and salvation or the greening of the planet or why vegetarianism or raw juice is the key to a better life. This is apt to annoy even the most virtuous and polite. If cornered by this sort of person, don't be embarrassed about cutting it short. You are there for another purpose, so excuse yourself without hesitation and go away at once to your room or for a walk. On the other hand, you may find it both charitable and instructive to *really listen* to what the person is saying – even if at first you do not believe a word of it. Spiritual truths may hide in all manner of thoughts, words and deeds.

GOING ON RETREAT FOR THE FIRST TIME

If you have never been on retreat before, you will be venturing into unknown territory. There may be a lot of questions floating around in your head: 'How should I behave?' 'What will actually happen?' 'Suppose I have to go to the toilet when we are meditating?' 'Will people expect me talk about God?' Rest assured, you can just be yourself; nothing embarrassing is likely to happen –

and if you have to go to the toilet, you just go to the nearest one. And you do not have to discuss any of your beliefs or feelings unless *you* want to. It is a common notion that people on a retreat have to be quiet all the time. This is not true. Many retreats have little or no silence, and some retreat houses are quite noisy. If you are not staying at one of the latter and the silence and stillness become too much for you, which may happen to people who have just dropped in from a hectic lifestyle, then find a pleasant activity such as walking or reading. This is often a good way to relax into your new environment. You have decided on a retreat to get some peace and calm, so keep focusing on that goal and everything will fall into place.

GOING ON RETREAT FOR PEOPLE WITH DISABILITIES

Unfortunately, many retreat centres have still not been updated to the national standard set for the disabled. Too many places still believe that a wheelchair ramp or a ground floor toilet is all that is needed. But change is taking place, if slowly, and increasingly when they refurbish and rebuild retreat houses are including high-standard accommodation and access for the disabled. However, even these facilities are often for independent people with disabilities and do not necessarily offer the kind of facilities necessary for those who need to be accompanied by a carer. The Pastoral Centre at Holton Lee in Dorset is one exception, offering a retreat place for people with disabilities and for their carers (See Dorset section). Hopefully, the future will bring more such facilities so that the retreat movement is truly inclusive, as it always ought to be.

Wherever possible this guide tries to indicate whether a retreat centre has facilities for the disabled and if these are limited. You should always double-check before booking so that you are certain of exactly what is on offer.

DIFFERENT KINDS OF RETREAT

Most retreats fall into the following main groups: conducted retreats, individually guided retreats, theme retreats, private retreats, awareness workshop retreats, day retreats, alternative therapies, healing retreats, ecological and nature retreats, and retreats based on shamanism and other Native Peoples' spiritualities. The choices grow by the year and are becoming ever more imaginative and exciting. The following are just a few of the many kinds of retreats on offer.

Art and craft retreats Art and craft retreats are theme retreats that focus on awakening personal creativity through a craft or other art form. This may be anything from embroidery, calligraphy and painting to making pots and building a wall. The art themes are just as diverse – ranging from music making, singing and drumming to creative writing and dancing. The point is to discover new ways to increase and express your awareness of the eternal. Talent or skill is not a requirement for such retreats. They should be approached with an expectation that you are going to enjoy yourself.

Beginners retreats Beginners retreats are for those who are trying some special or particular techniques for the first time. They are usually offered by Buddhist centres where different types of meditation are used. For Christian and most Mind Body Spirit retreats you usually need no prior experience.

Business Retreats with Saint Benedict Fashionable management development courses have taken a leap into the spiritual with the development of retreats for executives based on the wisdom of the Rule of Saint Benedict, a twelfth-century rule of living for Christian monastic communities. It is all about art of understanding how people tick. Douai Abbey has pioneered this kind of retreat (see Berkshire section).

Celtic spirituality retreats There has been a recent emergence of retreats based on Celtic spirituality. The outstanding feature of this Christian spiritual heritage is the overwhelming sense of the presence of God in the natural world. Rich in poems and songs, Celtic spirituality can bring an understanding of the depth of God's presence in his own creation. It is an ancient inheritance that has become newly appropriate in a time when we are concerned for the environment and the future of our planet.

Chardinian spirituality retreats Chardinian spirituality retreats confront the question of how to be in the world but not of it. They are based on the approach of Pierre Teilhard de Chardin (1881–1955), who did not try to present an ordered way to spiritual progress although he was a Jesuit and follower of Saint Ignatius. His spirituality has a cosmic focus that eventually leads to a person's love of the world coinciding with his or her love for Christ.

Dance retreats Dance retreats may be Christian or Mind Body Spirit in focus. Sacred dancing is common to most spiritualities. It helps to release physical and emotional tensions, brings to the surface deep feelings, and increases self-awareness. The Sufi's remind us 'to dance with joy!' The Christian psalms tell us the same thing.

Day retreats Day retreats can be very flexible. They can take the form of a day of silence, a theme- or activity-centred day, a day for group discussion, a day based on a special talk, or a day of lessons in meditation technique. The day retreat is like a mini-retreat. It has the advantage of allowing you to explore a number of different types of retreat during the year without taking a great deal of time away from your ordinary life, while at the same time giving you a real *day away*.

Directed or guided retreats Directed or guided retreats are often based on the spiritual exercises of St Ignatius (see page 11) and can last for six, eight or thirty days. The Buddhist tradition offers directed retreats of several weeks, thirty days, six months and even three years. Any retreat that offers a spiritual director with guidance for the individual on his or her spiritual progress through a structured retreat routine may be said to be a directed or guided retreat.

Drop-in retreats Drop-in retreats are non-residential. The idea is that you live at home or stay elsewhere and drop in to take part in the resident community's regular pattern of prayer or for a series of talks and other activities planned around a short and simple programme. This is an increasingly popular type of retreat for those who have neither the time nor the resources to go away or whose commitments may prevent them from being away from home overnight. Regular visitors to a Buddhist or Christian monastery or centre often attend on such a basis.

Enneagram retreats Enneagram retreats make use of a method (the Enneagram) intended to help you see yourself in the mirror of your mind, with particular emphasis on elucidating aspects of your personality that have become distorted by your basic attitudes to yourself. The Enneagram has a long history. It is reputed to have originated in Afghanistan some 2,000 years ago, or perhaps in the early years of Christian influence in Persia. It then moved to the Indian subcontinent, where it remained an oral tradition known to Sufi masters. Representing a journey into self, the purpose of the Enneagram is self-enlightenment. According to this system, there are nine types of human personality. These have a basic compulsion to behave in a certain way, and this behaviour is maintained through a defence mechanism that avoids any change. For example, there are personality types who avoid at all costs anger or failure or weakness or conflict. The Enneagram technique leads to self-criticism, which, in turn, leads to self-discovery. As a result, we may gain freedom from the negative aspects of self, and this may open the way to deeper faith. Advocates of this spiritual exercise believe its careful study results in a new self-understanding and provides practical guidelines for healing.

Family retreats These retreats, held at places that have suitable facilities, give a family the experience of going on retreat together. These retreats need to be well planned so that each member of the family, from the youngest to the oldest, has a real chance to benefit from the experience. It would be difficult to find any convent, monastery or temple in which children would not be welcomed with love and joy – but many such places simply have no facilities for children. Like it or not, restless children and crying babes are a distraction for those at prayer and for anyone seeking interior stillness. So take your children to a centre that clearly states it has facilities – then you can relax and so can everyone else. Buddhist centres and monasteries often have a children's *Dahampasala*, which is a school study-session held each Sunday. Otherwise family retreats are often organised by larger Christian retreat and holiday centres who specialise in this type of event. These are intended to be joyous family occasions.

Gardening and prayer retreats Gardening and prayer retreats generally involve some practical work in the retreat house garden in combination with the study of plants, trees and shrubs. There are also talks and time for rest and prayer. This kind of retreat helps to develop your awareness of the world around you and can bring the benefit of working happily and productively with others – not something that many people today experience in their ordinary daily job.

Gay and lesbian retreats Gay and lesbian retreats (either mixed gender or gender-specific) can address and offer support in relation to the problems gay and lesbian people often experience in gaining access to established church life and to various spirituality groups. Such retreats may have themes that bear directly on living as a gay or lesbian person within society and which link into spiritual matters. On the other hand, they may simply take traditional retreat themes. The only difference between this kind of retreat and any other is that the group happen to be gay or lesbian. Gay and lesbian retreats are very few as yet, no matter what the spiritual tradition. In spite of legal and social advances and the wide-spread change in European attitudes towards same-sex orientation, the majority of retreat houses refuse to put such retreats on their programme – and if they are prepared to do so, they are often forced to withdraw them under pressure. The news media and the religious institutions continue to be homophobic and this, of course, affects developments in the retreat movement. The Lesbian and Gay Christian Movement (LGCM) is trying to improve this situation (see Helpful Addresses section). The LGCM holds annual retreats for lesbian, gay and bisexual women and men. The main one is usually held in Scotland at the Macleod Centre (see Scotland section). Some places we have listed in the guide where gay men's retreats have been or are being held include Winford Manor (see Somerset section), Loyola Hall (see Merseyside section), St Katharine's (see London section) and Podere Fiorli in Italy (see Italy section). If you are a lesbian, a gay man or a transsexual person do not go to a place that sends out mixed signals about your sexuality orientation. If in doubt, ask them exactly where they stand on issues that concern you as a lesbian, gay, bisexual or transsexual person.

Healing retreats Healing retreats may use prayer, meditation, chanting or the laying on of hands. Inner healing and healing of the physical body through prayer and the laying on of hands have become prominent features of many Christian ministries today. They are also often a feature of Mind Body Spirit retreats and workshops. Healing may be concerned with a physical complaint or with the healing of the whole person in order to eliminate obstacles to personal and spiritual growth. It can help us realise our own potential as healers and reconcilers. For the Christian this always involves the inspirational power of the Holy Spirit. A healing retreat is not usually for a specific illness (although it can be) but for healing the whole person.

Healing therapy retreats Healing therapy retreats make use of one or more of the many alternative healing therapies and techniques now available. These may be modern, such as aromatherapy, or ancient, such as Ayurveda or herbal medicine. There are many healing therapies on offer today, including massage, reflexology, shiatsu, and Reiki. All are designed to relax and to bring about holistic healing of the person.

Hermitage and solitude retreats Hermitage and solitude retreats, and desert experience retreats are personal and private silent retreats in which you stay in a hermitage alone, perhaps joining others for prayer or a religious service. Otherwise it is a time alone with God in the tradition of the Early Desert Fathers of Christianity and the ancient Hindu sages. Hermitages for this kind of retreat are becoming more common among all retreat centres and have always been a feature of Orthodox Christian monastic life. Many people today are called to a life of solitude for spiritual purposes. Further information and support on this way of living can be obtained from the Fellowship of Solitaries, Coed Glas, Talgarth Road, Bronllys, Powys, Wales LD3 OHN or at **www.solitaries.org.uk**.

Icon and icon painting retreats Icon and icon painting retreats are about creating and/or using a religious work of art as a form of prayer. This is an established Christian spiritual tradition, particularly in the Orthodox Church, and a very popular activity retreat. You do not have to be an artist to enjoy and benefit from such an experience. Similar to this but in the Hindu tradition is *yantra* painting, offered by a number of yoga centres. In addition, there has been an increase in interest and courses in Tibetan sacred art.

Ignatian retreats Ignatian retreats are based on the spiritual exercises originated by the founder of the Jesuits, Saint Ignatius of Loyola, in the sixteenth century. A full retreat can last thirty days but shorter versions are available. The retreat director assigned to you works with you on a one-to-one basis, providing different material from the Gospels for daily contemplative meditation. You then have an opportunity to discuss what response this has provoked from you. In the course of the retreat, you are led with some vigour to review your life in the light of Gospel teachings and to seek God's guidance for your future. Ignatian spirituality has been described as 'finding God in all things'. It is a way of spirituality that is designed for anyone, whether Christian or not. The satisfaction of these exercises is found not in knowledge of the Gospels but in greater understanding of the most intimate truths of self and God. The number of Ignatian retreats and courses built around Ignatian spirituality has increased greatly in the last few years. They are now widely popular and are used much more frequently in Roman Catholic spiritual counselling.

Individually guided retreats Individually guided retreats are often structured around a particular system of spiritual exercises, such as those of St Ignatius (see above), or based upon a defined form of meditation such as Vipassana, one of India's most ancient forms of meditation. Your guide is a spiritually informed or trained person who acts as a kind of soul mate during your retreat. Mind Body Spirit centres also give individually guided retreats; however, these generally make use of approaches to spiritual direction based not on a religious tradition but derived from schools of self-development, psychological processes and self-realisation.

Inner child retreats Inner child retreats seek to bring you into contact with the most real and innocent part of yourself to renew and foster a greater sense of your true nature and inner being. This kind of retreat continues to enjoy enormous popularity.

Insight retreats Insight retreats are especially good for people who have had no prior contact with a church or religion. They can introduce you to a new vocabulary of spirituality and helps to de-mystify spirituality. They can be helpful for young men and women who are seeking access to forms of spirituality and asking questions about the possible spiritual or religious paths they might take.

Journalling retreats Journalling retreats introduce you to the concept and practice of keeping a journal as a spiritual exercise. In a busy life it is often hard to see where and how the spiritual dimension of ourselves or of God is at work in us. Keeping a daily journal helps us to remember and to reflect. The aim is to become more sensitive to the content of your life and to see the continuity of your spirituality.

Labyrinth retreats These retreats make use of the labyrinth as a little pilgrimage of the soul. Walking the labyrinth is a symbolic journey to the centre of the self, which belongs to the spiritual world, and a journey back again into the ordinary world. The labyrinth often has places to stop and reflect or pray, all of them spiritually symbolic. For example, there may be a small pool and a pile of pebbles. You pick up a pebble and throw away your worry or fear. There may be a place where you light a candle in hope and thanksgiving. The labyrinth is an ancient and respected spiritual technique that predates Christianity but has also has been part of the Christian tradition for many centuries.

Meditation retreats While all retreats allow, to a greater or lesser degree, time for individual meditation, there is a growing demand for retreats specifically aimed at the study and practice of meditation. The Buddhist response to this has been excellent, resulting in many opportunities for learning how to meditate. In addition to weekly classes, most Buddhist centres and monasteries hold a monthly meditation retreat that is open to both beginners and the more experienced, enabling them to participate in what is considered to be an all-important spiritual practice in Buddhism. In Christianity, meditation was long felt to be discursive, and the approach was to reflect in a devout way on some theme, often a biblical one. While this practice remains, there has been a world-wide revival of earlier Christian approaches to meditation which share much in common with those found in the religious traditions of the East. There is now an international Christian Meditation Centre (see London section).

Men's work retreats and rites of passage for men retreats This is not just another Catholic or Christian inspired retreat exclusively for men, but five days of formal male initiation. These teachings on the mysteries and the accompanying rituals of Passover have met with a very strong response in recent years. Some 1,500 men have now been initiated in these retreats, which started at Ghost Ranch in northern New Mexico; however, they are now held in Britain and other European countrie. After six years of facilitating these life-changing rites, Richard Rohr, the founder of this movement, has now trained a team of men to do the same. They will continue to hand on the experience to new groups of men, with Richard Rohr in a supervisory role. These retreats are best suited to those who have already done some men's work or male empowerment courses and are on a serious spiritual journey. It is important to make this experience as a lone seeker. Fathers and sons are normally not initiated together, nor is it a buddy experience. You may come with friends, but expect to be assigned to a home group where you will be anonymous and start from scratch together. An application is required, and places are awarded not on a first-come-first-serve basis but according to an applicant's readiness and who else will profit from his attendance. There is now a very large number of applications each year, and the number on any one retreat is limited to 115 men. See Richard Rohr's article in the appendix for more information. UK contacts are James Fahey, Winford Manor Retreat, tel: 01275 472262, e-mail:

omegatrust@aol.com, website: www.winfordmanorretreat.com; Adrian Scott, The Listen Centre, tel : 0114 251 7679, e-mail: thelistencentre@aol.com. See also www.cacradicalgrace.org and www.malespirituality.org.

Mind Body Spirit retreats These retreats go under a great many titles. Some examples are *Soul Journeying, Whole Person Retreat, Holistic Retreat, Awakening the Inner Self* and *Awareness of the Inner Man/Women*. They are usually structured around rest, relaxation and inner discovery. A wide range of practices may be used in such a retreat, including drumming, voice and song, Ayurveda, shamanism, nutritional therapy, alternative healing therapies and human encounter groups. If you are interested in going on a Mind Body Spirit retreat, check the relevant centre's brochure for what is involved. You may want to follow up with a phone call to ask any questions you may have and clarify terms that may be new to you. Christian monasteries now often include such diffuse themes as well as some alternative therapies (for example, Reiki and massage) in their programmes.

Mother and baby retreats, and busy mums retreats These retreats offer that rare opportunity for a mother to have a little time to pray, be alone, and share her spiritual feelings with other mothers. This is a retreat designed for mothers and not for the babies, who are carefully looked after for much of the day. The nuns at Turvey Abbey (see East and East Anglia section) often offer such retreats. The day's programme looks like this: mothers and babies arrive at about 9.45a.m. and babies are taken to the crèche. At 10a.m. coffee is served and everybody meets each other. Then there is a talk focusing on the spiritual dimensions of life and motherhood. At Turvey Abbey the topic is often *Motherhood and God*, followed by a group discussion. Then there is time for prayer and meditation without interruptions. If there is a midday service of worship, such as Mass, the mothers can join in if they want. At lunch the mothers feed their babies, then go to their own lunch. In the afternoon, there is free time until about 2.15p.m., when there is a reflective and prayerful session. After that, the mothers collect their babies and go home. This is a great retreat idea that needs to be taken up by more retreat places.

Music retreats Music can express our deepest spiritual sentiments, while singing and dancing can bring a gladness of heart that surprises and delights. The Old Testament psalms call for Jews and Christians to bring forth their songs, trumpets, lutes, harps, timbrels, and to dance. Music retreats may be based on music only, or on music and dance, on singing, on song and dance, or on the playing or learning of a musical instrument. Music in all forms is the most ancient aspect of religious worship and the praise of the sacred. Don't worry if you can't sing very well, don't play a musical instrument or have never danced. That is not important. Your efforts have a spiritual purpose; what you do is not about performance.

Myers-Briggs retreats Isabel Myers-Briggs spent forty years investigating personality types, building upon the research into personality done by Carl Jung. She set out eight qualities or characteristics found in each person. Myers-Briggs believed there were sixteen personality types, all of which are either introverted or extroverted, and either perceiving or judging. By discovering which Myers-Briggs personality type you are, you select the form of spirituality that best suits you. The idea is that some personalities respond better and more easily to one way of spirituality than another. For example, an intuitive personality might do better with a spirituality of hope, while a thinking personality might do better with a spirituality centred on reason. Myers-Briggs and Enneagram retreats (see above) are very popular, and a great many retreat centres offer them.

Nature and prayer, and Ecospirituality retreats Both these types of retreat link care for the environment to your life and help you gain an increased awareness of the unity of all things in creation. Time is spent observing flowers, birds and trees. These are active retreats, but ones in which stillness, meditation and prayer also play their part. They may well include awareness walks, in which you concentrate on seeing things afresh and learn to appreciate colour, shape and texture in order to heighten your awareness of creation at work all around you. Walking meditation in the Buddhist tradition may also be done. Such retreats may involve working in a woodland or meadow, or in an organic garden to focus you on the world and nature around you. This awareness of the inter-connection between all of creation is now very much part of Buddhist, Christian and Mind Body Spirit retreat and course themes. Christianity, Celtic and Creation Spirituality retreats in particular focus on it, and it is a theme of many of the psalms sung during chapel or oratory services.

Open door retreats Open door retreats enable you to make a retreat in your own home while having the direction and support of a group. The idea is for a trained leader or a team of two religious or lay people to go to a private house, conference room or local church to lead such a group. The group then meets for a few hours each week over a number of continuous weeks. The group members make a commitment to pray individually during their days back in their own home and to hold regular prayer meetings. The leader provides guidance, materials and talks to help all the members of the group in their meditation and reflection.

Preached retreats Preached retreats are traditionally conducted Christian retreats which may be limited to a group from a parish or other organisation, or may be open to everyone. The retreat conductor may be a clerical, religious or lay person. Sometimes such retreats are led by a team rather than one person. Usually the retreat is planned around a series of Bible-based talks designed to inspire and encourage a Christian lifestyle, and to provide material for individual and group meditation and prayer. There may be opportunity for silence, but not always. Sharing together is a feature of these retreats.

Private retreats Private Retreats are undertaken alone as an individual. They are usually a silent time in which you find solitude in order to reflect, rest and meditate. In many monasteries and retreat houses you may arrange to take your meals in your room or separately from others so that you can maintain this framework of silence. Private retreats have the aim of enabling you to hold yourself open to God from the very core of your being. This spiritual state is often referred to as 'contemplation' or 'contemplative prayer'. Such contemplation is not an intellectual exercise, yet it is demanding and searching, even painful on occasion – as the lives of numerous saints and holy men and women bear testimony. A convent or monastery devoted to a contemplative way of life is probably the best place for you if you want to make this kind of retreat. There you will find strong spiritual support through joining the community in their daily round of prayer and worship. Contemplation as a way of spiritual awareness is not confined to Christianity but is part of the practice of other faiths as well.

Quiet garden, and quiet space retreats These are neither organised retreats nor residential but are a private and personal retreat into a peaceful sanctuary space for sacred purposes. The idea is part of the vision of The Quiet Garden Movement (see Central section) to initiate a network of gardens and spaces that will be open to the public for prayer, silence, reflection, the appreciation of beauty and 'experiencing creativity and healing in the context of God's love'. The movement is now international and has proven a great blessing in many people's lives, giving them opportunity and space in which to find hospitality and prayer.

Renewal retreats These retreats are almost always Christian. Renewal for a Christian means a new awareness of the presence of Christ, a deeper experience of the Holy Spirit and a clearer understanding of his or her mission in the Church. If you think this kind of retreat is for you, discuss the matter first, if you can, with your priest or minister. Then decide where you want to go.

Salesian spirituality retreats Francis de Sales (1567–1622) believed that a person need not enter a convent or monastery to develop a deep spirituality. In his famous work *Introduction to the Devout Life*, he suggested five steps for spiritual growth. These make a progression from a desire for holiness through the practice of virtue to methods for spiritual renewal. His methods are gentle and have always enjoyed wide appeal among people living ordinary lives.

Silent retreats Silent retreats are an adventure into stillness. Silence is one of the most powerful of all spiritual aids. A time of total silence for spiritual reasons is often called a 'desert experience' because you have withdrawn from the world to an inner place which you may find at first to be barren like a desert. In this interior world, silence helps to focus you on your true inner self. Then, in this seemingly empty interior landscape, inner realities about yourself and your life may arise. For a little while you may listen with the heart and not just your ears – perhaps even listen a little to God. Some silent retreats are especially designed to provide you with techniques to help you lose your dependence on noise, distractions and the necessity for constant talking. On a private retreat (see above) you can remain in silence.

Swimming with dolphins retreats To enter into the world of another creature is to go to a place of magic and wonderment. It is a rare and amazing human experience to swim with a dolphin, and one that people describe as deeply spiritual. To swim with a dolphin is a way to discover how intimately we are connected to every other creature and to promote inner renewal and healing. It is an inexplicable event in which we are released from the bindings of our human need for power and control and placed safely in the realm of another life-form. It is a lesson in hope, humility and joy.

Teresian spirituality retreats Saint Teresa of Avila (1515–82) wrote *The Interior Castle* in order to lead individuals from the beginnings of spiritual growth to the heights of mysticism. The steps she describes in this work are viewed as mansions, and we progress in our spiritual pilgrimage from one to the next. The seven mansions are self-knowledge, detachment, humility and aridity, affective prayer, the beginning of our union with God, the mystical experience or the prayer of quiet, and, finally, peaceful union with God. Teresian spirituality is at once both logical and mystical.

Theme and activity retreats In the last few years the growth in awareness of the intimate connection between mind, body and spirit has produced a wide range of courses and study retreats that combine body and spiritual awareness in methods that spring from modern knowledge or that are based on rediscovering traditional forms of spiritual awakening. You enter an activity, such as painting or dance, through which you bring together your feelings, senses and intuition into a greater awareness of self, of others and of God. There are a great number of themes and activities available in this form of retreat, which is often called after the particular activity or theme. Examples are *Pottery and Prayer, Walking and Creation, Painting and the Inner Child* and *Clowning for God.* (See also Art and Craft Retreats, and Nature and Prayer Retreats above.)

Volunteer and working retreats The experience of living in a community or being a volunteer in a monastery, lay community, retreat centre or charitable residence can bring a personal and spiritual growth through sharing in the highs and lows and life of others. To live in a spiritual community is to help a place of compassion and love. It is a wonderful retreat and especially suitable for young people or those who want a period in which to reflect on the next step in their life.

Weekend retreats This is the most popular form of retreat. It usually has a particular theme or is centred on a particular spiritual approach. A weekend retreat is a break away from busy days and duties, and the demands of modern living. You leave mobile phones, tape and CD players, and radios at home. There is no TV, and someone else makes your bed and prepares the meals. The aim is to have an emotional detox and find some peace. Such a retreat is likely to run along the following lines: you arrive on Friday evening, settle your things in your single room (most often ensuite nowadays) and go down to meet the retreat leader and the other guests. After supper you meet for a short talk about the weekend and are given a timetable. From that time onwards you will cease most talking unless it is to the retreat conductor or unless a group discussion or shared prayer is being held. During Saturday and Sunday there will be religious ceremonies of some nature and probably a short talk on a subject that will help you to meditate and pray or just get you to unwind. There will be times for walks, reading, cat-napping and just resting. It is all simple, easy and peaceful. Millions of people from bus drivers to celebrity pop stars take this kind of retreat on a regular basis.

Wisdom retreats Wisdom retreats are intended for people in the third age or the last part of their life. Such retreats are based on subjects such as the aging process, death, separation from loved ones, and transitions and changes in lifestyle. These are explored in a positive manner and viewed as part of the spiritual journey as understood in various religious traditions. Prayers, rituals, biblical references, meditations and exercises may be used. Sometimes such retreats are entitled *Moving On Retreats*.

Women's spirituality retreats These retreats are on the increase now as more retreat houses see that gender-orientated spirituality has a special and important role in serving both women and men. Women's spirituality retreats are an opportunity for women of all ages to discover and explore common spirituality issues together, often with pastoral and tutorial support. Sharing with other women through discussion, reflection, prayer, meditation and creativity can help women to discover a new richness in their personal lives and relationships. For Christian women it can deepen the understanding that there is neither male nor female in God and help in transcending the patriarchal nature of Holy Scripture and hierarchical Church structures. Subjects that may be covered in these retreats include *Women's Spiritual Experience*, *Women Mystics*, *Women of the Bible*, *Women's Spirituality and Language*, *Women's Spirituality and Healing*, *Introduction to Feminist Theology*, *Women's Spirituality and the Arts*, *Women's Spirituality in Contemporary Issues* and *Women's Spirituality and Embodiment*. Warmth, support, acceptance and generosity are key features of women's spirituality retreats. Such retreats are on offer at Christian, Buddhist, and Mind Body Spirit centres (see The Grange and Taraloka in the Central section and Holy Rood House in the North section).

Yoga retreats Yoga is not just a form of exercise for physical fitness. It is an ancient spiritual tradition and sacred practice. Yoga retreats are based on yoga practice sessions, and rest and relaxation, sometimes with spirituality-based talks. They employ postures and breathing exercises to achieve greater physical balance and mental stillness as an aid to meditation, physical fitness, and de-stressing body and mind. Yoga classes are now so widely popular in Europe that there is hardly a town or even a village that does not have a regular one (see Yoga section). Many yoga retreats now take place in sunny holiday resorts in countries such as Spain (see Spain section).

A TYPICAL DAY ON RETREAT

Nothing is obligatory on a retreat. When you arrive, you can expect to be welcomed and made to feel at home. Don't worry about what to do next – someone will tell you what the arrangements are for all the basics such as meals.

The timetable for a simple Christian day retreat might be as follows: you arrive at your destination – say, a convent. The sister who is the Guest Mistress shows you to a quiet room where you meet a few other people who form a small group. Coffee is followed by a short introduction by one of the sisters or the retreat leader telling you about the place and the day's programme. From that moment until after lunch you and the other retreatants maintain silence. There will perhaps be a morning talk followed by worship or a group prayer. You are not obliged to attend these if you choose not to. At lunch, you eat in silence while someone reads aloud from a spiritual work – or you may all talk, get acquainted and exchange views. Then you may take a walk alone through the garden or into the nearby countryside, before a talk is given by the retreat leader with a group discussion. The day ends with a sharing of thoughts and prayer.

A typical Buddhist day retreat may have more silence and certainly more formal meditation times. But, again, you will be sharing with others in a new and gentle way.

At a Mind Body Spirit centre the day may well include more active sessions and draw on the spiritual practices of Eastern or tribal cultures. If you want to have time to yourself, check in advance that no sound-orientated workshops such as drumming, sacred dancing or chanting will be going on.

OBTAINING SPIRITUAL HELP

Many retreat centres offer time for personal interviews to talk to someone about your life or your personal problems. However, such talks are intended to lead to some spiritual benefit. Those with over-riding emotional and psychological problems should seek help elsewhere unless this kind of counselling by professionally trained and qualified people is specifically offered. But if you need to talk to someone about your spiritual life and could do with some guidance, most places of retreat will have someone who can help you. A directed or guided retreat, an Ignatian retreat or any retreat with a spiritual director or facilitator will usually offer opportunities for personal talks. Meditation, shared prayer, group discussions and directed reading are all alternative ways of obtaining spiritual help.

STAYING IN A MONASTERY

Monasteries are busy places with a day divided into prayer and work. They have but one goal, which is the experience of God, the Universal, the Eternal. All the prayer, meditation, study of sacred scriptures, fasting, charity, chastity and poverty that are hallmarks of a monastery are but tools to accomplish this great spiritual goal.

So if you have never been to such a place, do not expect to see the monks and nuns sitting around looking holy or otherwise, for they follow a tough and active daily routine. Having said that, you are likely to be able to find someone for a little chat, and – even when silence reigns – the atmosphere is a positive one.

SO WHAT DO MONKS AND NUNS ACTUALLY DO?

The basics of life within a monastery are in most ways like those of the outside world. Monks and nuns must eat and sleep. They have emotional ups and downs like all of us. There are health complaints and moans about changes that take place. The religious life is supposed to make you more human, not less, and even saints have been assailed with doubts. One of the most famous modern monks, Thomas Merton, expressed anxieties about his life with his monastic community until the end of his days – yet no one could doubt his great personal spirituality or unwavering faith. So remember that monks and nuns are just as human as you are.

The difference is that monks and nuns feel they have been called by God or the sacred life to devote themselves to the practice of prayer, praise, meditation and contemplation of the spiritual and the sacred realm. This life is generally lived in community with others who have also heeded such a spiritual calling. The spiritual practices take many forms, but essentially the day's activities are centred around them.

We would make the point here that there are millions of men and women who feel called to a life of prayer and who do not chose to live in a monastery but rather to live an ordinary life in the world. Their lives can be as filled with spiritual truth and personal holiness as any monastic life and, in many cases, perhaps more so.

GENERAL GUIDELINES ON BEING A MONASTERY GUEST

Many people who are staying for the first time in a convent or monastery are afraid that somehow they will feel awkward and uncomfortable. The question is always, 'How should I behave?' The short answer is: be yourself. If in any doubt about what to do next, just be quiet and wait, because someone will show you how things are done, whether it is taking your meal with the community or going into the chapel and sitting down. Once you understand that the daily monastic routine revolves around a life of prayer, that there are traditional ways of doing things and that the monks and nuns are just ordinary human beings like yourself, it all becomes simple and relaxed.

As a monastery guest you may expect to be received with warmth and affection. Everyone will try to make you feel comfortable as quickly as possible. You get up when you want to, and if you do not feel like attending any of the prayers or meditations – or even the retreat programme if you are on one – no one is likely to demand that you do so. However, you will probably find that joining the daily life of prayer and worship, helps enormously to sustain and nourish your mind, body and spirit during your time with the community.

Having said that, there are some – both Christian and Buddhist – monasteries where you will be expected to come to all the prayers, services or meditations. If this is the case, we try to mention it in our listings for the place. Actually, even in such places, if you do not feel up to going, no one is going to make a fuss. The option is usually there to just stay in your room and rest if you want to.

In any case, just stay calm. The point is that you are supposed to be enjoying yourself on a retreat and becoming still and peaceful. This is often called 'opening the heart to God'.

STAYING IN A CHRISTIAN MONASTERY

Christian monasteries structure their life around prayer and praise. This is usually taken from what has come to be known as Divine Office (see Glossary) – set prayers from the Psalms with scripture readings from the Bible. The exact form may differ between, say the Roman Catholics and the Anglicans, but it will nevertheless be centred on the Psalms. While the Divine Office may take the form of private prayer, it is usually sung or chanted by the monastic community together in a chapel or oratory at designated hours of the day and night. By and large, monks and nuns do not go outside their cloisters very much. Some communities are enclosed, for example those of the Carmelite nuns. This means that the community members remain in the monastery separate from the world. There is usually a special room in which you may meet members of the community from time to time, but you will not mix with them. The Guest Monk or Guest Sister will normally meet you and see to your arrangements and needs. Guest accommodation in monasteries is usually in a guest house where there are single rooms. Often nowadays the rooms are ensuite. Guest lounges and libraries are usually provided too. Meals are taken either in the guest house dining room or in the refectory with the community. Food is traditional and rarely strictly vegetarian, although meat does not rank high on the menus. Provision for vegetarians is now made almost everywhere.

STAYING IN A BUDDHIST MONASTERY

Buddhist monks and nuns live much as Christian ones do. The life is centred on meditation and spiritual practices. Such monasteries are often also places of training for monks and nuns, although they still welcome guests. Traditionally, Buddhist monks and nuns are dependent on the generosity of their friends and visitors for all their material requirements, including food. Such places are run as simply as possible. It is normal for guests to have had some practice of meditation in the tradition of the monastery but there are now plenty of Buddhist beginner's meditation retreats to get you started. Guest accommodation in Buddhist monasteries and retreat houses can be in single rooms, but dormitories, doubles and triples are still common. Vegetarian food will be provided, and you will usually eat with the community.

WHAT IS PRAYER?

Each faith has its own tradition of prayer. The Christian 'Our Father' prayer and the opening prayer of the Koran, in which God is praised and His guidance sought on 'the Straight Path' are examples of outstanding and important single prayers to which all may turn. The number of books about prayer and manuals on how to pray are legion. They burden the shelves of libraries and religious institutions. Yet the question remains for most men and women: 'How should I pray?'

If there were a single way to begin, then perhaps it might be the request, 'Grant me a pure heart.' This involves the surrender of self and the offering of your vulnerability and trust up to God. A pure heart brings forth charity, hope, trust, faith and reconciliation. Here, love may be discovered and we may hold fast to that which is best in ourselves and in others. Perfect love is not possible, since we are human and therefore fallible. But a pure and willing heart, prepared to view all things through love, is constantly possible for anyone. We may fail from time to time to hold ourselves in this state because we are so human, yet it returns and we can go on again.

For those who have faith in God, divine love secretly informs the heart.

Such faith makes prayer more instinctive than intellectual, and this prompting of the spirit may occur at any time and in any place. For the Christian, God is both the instigator and the object of such prayer.

WHAT IS MEDITATION?

Meditation is a stillness of body and of mind. There are many different meditation techniques to help you attain this state of being. They range from Insight or Vipassana meditation practice from the Buddhist tradition to Christian meditation such as that set out by the monk Dom John Main (1926–82), which now enjoys a world-wide following among Christians.

Meditation begins by relaxing the body into a state of stillness, then the mind into inner silence. Many of the techniques that achieve this start by establishing a particular breathing pattern. (It is claimed that the breath is a bridge from the known to the unknown.) This approach is widely employed to marshal the body and mind and is used also in yoga, tai chi and shiatsu.

A single word or phrase, sometimes called a *mantra*, is often used to help the regularity of breathing. For example, in John Main's approach to meditation, the word *Maranatha* is repeated in a slow and rhythmical fashion. This word means 'Come Lord' in Aramaic, the language Jesus himself spoke. It is used by both Saint Paul and Saint John in their writings.

Many people, including Christians, still believe that meditation is some strange mental state in which they may lose control of themselves. Nothing could be further from the truth, for meditation is not concerned with thinking but with *being*. In such a state of consciousness, you are at peace. This peace could not exist if you felt insecure. Millions of men and women of all faiths or none find in meditation a method for reaching through deep, inner silence to an experience of self that leads to a more loving response to life.

SPIRITUAL GUIDES AND SPIRITUAL DIRECTION

A spiritual director or guide is someone who helps you in your spiritual journey by being a good listener and *soul companion*, and by making suggestions for meditation, reading, study or prayer. Such directors and guides are often religious men or women, clergy or lay people who have had special training and experience in helping people with spiritual matters. The important thing is that the person helps you with spiritual discernment and is someone with whom you feel very comfortable and to whom you able to entrust your confidences. If you ask in advance, there is usually someone at a Christian or Buddhist monastery with whom you can have a personal talk. If you go on a group retreat, it is likely there will be sharing of personal spiritual experiences, and the retreat leader is usually prepared to help you.

YOGA TODAY

One of the most significant developments in European spirituality over the past few years, has been the wide-spread popularity of yoga. From local adult education classes in village halls to centres and organisations devoted exclusively to yoga, this ancient way to stillness, spiritual openness and better health has been adopted by people of all ages and from all walks of life. Recently people in the West have also caught on to the idea (recognised for thousands of years in the East) that yoga is also a form of healing therapy and is particularly useful in medical conditions and diseases involving breathing, such as asthma.

Yoga is one of the six main schools of Hinduism, and yoga philosophy regards both spirit and matter as real, and traces the whole of the physical universe to a single source. In modern practice, especially in the West, some elements of yoga are emphasised more than others. For example, hatha yoga, which is concerned particularly with yoga postures and breathing, is often taught as a complete system of self-improvement. The calm and deliberate movements of yoga can lend themselves to deep relaxation and a peaceful harmony between mind and body which can become a framework for prayer.

In addition to the yoga centres listed in this guide (see Yoga section), you will find that many retreat centres offer yoga in their programmes for spiritual development and self-development. For a comprehensive listing of yoga places and retreats both in Britain and abroad, see *Best Yoga Centres and Retreats* by Stafford Whiteaker, published by Rider Books, London 2003. Details can be found at **www.thegoodretreatguide.com**.

GOING ON A RETREAT ABROAD

The Good Retreat Guide now covers retreats in France, Spain and Italy. In the section on yoga centres we also mention a few centres in these and other countries outside Britain. Going on a retreat abroad can also be a holiday, as most centres are in sunny climates with swimming or the sea near at hand. The retreats most often combine spirituality with having fun and getting rested and relaxed. Many in France and Spain are run by British people either from Britain or the country concerned, and the retreat is conducted in the English language. Often the retreat is an all-in package, with travel, accommodation, day trips, and spirituality and healing sessions included. Always make certain exactly what is part of the package and what is extra before you confirm a booking.

HOW TO GET THE RETREAT YOU WANT

Having made the decision to go on retreat, here are four steps to finding the right one for you:
1. Select a centre from this guide that strikes you as interesting, is in an area of the country you would like to visit or is convenient for travelling to.
2. Write, telephone, fax or e-mail for more information and details of the retreat programme – or if you just want a private retreat, go on to step three.
3. Visit the centre's website if they have one.
4. Book, giving the dates you want to stay and explaining the retreat you want to do. Ask if you need to bring anything like towels, soap or special clothing and what time of arrival is best. Some retreat places have separate facilities for men and women, so it is helpful if you make clear your gender.

You do not need to say anything more about yourself. Never mind your age, your beliefs or lack of them, or your personal circumstances – unless you are a student or unemployed, in which case mention the fact as you may qualify for a concession.

HOW THE GUIDE IS ORGANISED

After the preface and introductory chapters, the guide is divided into 15 sections: England, Wales, Scotland, Ireland and Northern Ireland, France, Italy, Spain, Yoga Centres, Open Centres, Appendix, A Spiritual Notebook, Helpful Addresses, Helpful Publications, Travel Organisations, Selected Spiritual Reading and Glossary.

The section covering England is sub-divided according to geographical region of the country. For example, South West. In that region you will find counties or major metropolitan areas, and after that the name of the city, town or village where the retreat centre is located. In Wales, Scotland and Ireland, centres are listed first by the town or place.

After the name, address and telephone/fax/e-mail/website of the retreat centre, the guide specifies the tradition to which it attaches. For example: Roman Catholic, Ecumenical, Mind Body Spirit, Buddhist, Scottish Churches, Quaker, etc. Many places have no definitive term for their form of spirituality so we have either called them 'Open spirituality' or tried to give other words that indicate the kind of spirituality you will find there.

In the majority of cases, a short description then follows which tells you something about the place. After that, detailed information is given as to what is on offer in terms of situation, accommodation and retreat programme. Most centres will send you a brochure about the place, activities, retreats and costs.

For France, the listing is by department and then by city, town or village. For Spain and Italy, the listing is by place. Yoga Centres are listed by counties for Britain. Open Centres are listed by name of place.

TELEPHONING IN BRITAIN

A British Telecom 0800 number is a freephone number from any landline phone in Britain. A British Telecom 08445 number is a local rate charge number and works from any landline in Britain. If the listing in this guide gives only one of these two numbers and no other then you cannot connect with that number if you are calling from outside Britain or from a mobile phone. There are hundreds of telephone codes in Britain. If the code you dial proves incorrect, call Operator Services or Information Services at British Telecom to find the current code and number.

HIGHLY RECOMMENDED PLACES OF RETREAT

Those places which it is felt can be highly recommended are marked at the start of the entry with a star symbol. ✪

YOUR OPINION IS WANTED

The Good Retreat Guide welcomes reports on places of retreat whether your opinion is favourable or not. There is a Report Form at the end of the Guide or you may send an email via **www.thegoodretreatguide.com** or to **staffordwhiteaker@compuserve.com**.

SETTING OUT ON THE INTERIOR JOURNEY

No one can give us the final answers to our spirituality, for it is intimately connected with who we are. Wisdom always gives the same advice if we want to live a sacred life and find God: know thyself. This is the paramount task of our life. The fruit of our labour is the discovery of our true self, and there we find God waiting. This journey transcends all human events and creations and gives profound meaning to our lives. Until we make this journey we remain in exile from the deepest meanings of our own being because these are not obtained by reason but by faith. Set out on the road then, brothers and sisters, and peace be with you forever.

England

Alternatives
St James's Church
197 Piccadilly
London W1J 9LL

Tel: 020 7287 6711
Fax: 020 7734 7449
e-mail: alternatives@ukonline.co.uk
Website: www.alternatives.org.uk

Inter-denominational – Open Christian – Ecumenical
The intention of Alternatives is to provide a space in the heart of London where people can explore new visions for living in a spirit of openness and community. It is a non-profit-making organisation which has run talks and workshops with great success since 1982. All events are offered in a spirit of service and are open to all. The programmes are wide-ranging and cover diverse approaches to living and spirituality. To give you an idea of what is likely to be on offer, recent talks and workshops have included *Sacred Sounds, Creating Harmony with Time, The Power of Now, Drawing from the Heart* and *Living Magically and Writing from the Soul*. Talks are at the Church and usually start at 7p.m. The cost is around £8, £5 concessions. Workshops are held at different venues around London.

Bethlehem House of Prayer
Convent of Mercy
McAuley Close
Glenure Road
Eltham, London SE9 1UF

Tel: 020 8850 1877

Roman Catholic
Seven single rooms, chapel, spiritual direction by arrangement.

Benedictine Centre for Spirituality
Bramley Road
London N14 4HE

Tel/Fax: 020 849 2499
e-mail: benedictine_centreN14UK@compuserve.com
Website: www.church-of-christ-the-king.com

Roman Catholic
The Centre is above the Benedictine Parish Church of Christ the King and adjacent to the modern monastery. You may join the monastic community at prayer for the Divine Office and at Mass each day. A full programme of retreats and events, with residential courses on Benedictine monastic spirituality, is on offer. Examples include an *Open Door Spirituality Workshop, Women and Ministry, Coping with Change, Yoga Practice, Carmelite Spirituality for Modern Times,* and *Rethinking Your Values and Vision*. The retreat leaders and speakers are among some of the most experienced and may include the writer Lavinia Byrne, Rev Angela Tilby, Fr Timothy Radcliffe

(former head of the Dominicans) or Dom Laurence Freeman (director of the World Community of Christian Meditation). There is a healing ministry for the sick, available to anyone, offering prayer and the laying on of hands. One of the monks, Br Benedict Heron, has written a clear and informative book, *Praying for Healing: The Challenge*, which explores the subject of Christian healing. It is gives examples of testimonies to the healing power of prayer. The guesthouse offers extra space for those guest retreatants who just want B&B accommodation. When you go on retreat here, the community tries to welcome you into the daily Benedictine monastic life, and so you are welcome to pray with the monks and to join them for the mid-day meal in the monastery. There are several Masses daily and lots of parish activities going on. Trent County Park is only a few minutes walk away for some meditative time with nature. The community works to improve all the facilities on the site, with new projects going on most years. The monastery itself is full of light and has a sense of privacy and space. With facilities up to modern expectations and active religious and lay communities involved, as well as retreat facilitators of national and international note, this is a retreat centre of outstanding excellence. **Highly Recommended**

Open: All year except Christmas week. Receives men, women, young people, families, groups and non-retreatants.

Rooms: 5 singles, 3 doubles.

Facilities: Chapel, prayer room, conferences, garden, roof garden, nearby park, library, guest lounge, payphone (020 8449 1604). French, Italian, German and Dutch are spoken by various monks.

Spiritual Help: Meditation, personal retreat direction, healing ministry. An Ecumenical Charismatic Prayer Group meets in the church. Spiritual direction with both male and female spiritual directors available. Yoga on offer each week, plus therapies, which vary according to the retreat programme.

Guests Admitted to: Everywhere including chapel, prayer room.

Meals: Self-catering. Enquire about what is provided and what you need to bring yourself. Vegetarian and special diets available.

Special Activities: Planned programme. Send for brochure.

Situation: On the edge of a north London suburb with walks near by and opposite a large country park in the green belt. Usually quiet but can be rather busy, especially in summer.

Maximum Stay: 2 weeks.

Bookings: Letter, e-mail, telephone during office hours.

Charges: £30 full board, £20 B&B. £12 quiet day rate.

Access: Underground: Piccadilly Line to Oakwood. Bus Nos: 307 and 299. Road: M25 exit 24, A111.

Brahma Kumaris World Spiritual University
Global Co-operation House
65 Pound Lane
London NW10 2HH

Tel: 020 8459 1400
Fax: 020 8451 6480

Non-religious – Open spirituality
Founded in 1937 in Karachi, the Brahma Kumaris University is an interna-

tional organisation working at all levels of society for positive change. The University offers a wide range of educational programmes for the development of human and spiritual values through its 3,000 branches in 62 countries. It is a non-governmental organisation affiliated to the United Nations department of Public Information, and the recipient of seven UN Peace Messenger Awards. Courses, workshops, seminars and conferences covering a wide range of topics are on offer, including self-development, stress-free living and self-management, creating inner freedom, soul care, women's development, and meditation. Activities are held at all levels of the community to help people cope more positively with everyday living and to find greater harmony within themselves and their relationships. All courses, events and activities are free of charge. The University operates the **World Global Retreat Centre** at Nuneham Courtney near Oxford (see Oxfordshire entry) and **Inner Space**, an information Centre at 528 High Road, Wembley, Middlesex HA9 7BS, Tel: 020 8903 1911. Brochure of events and courses available.

Buddhafield Retreats
PO Box 27822
London SE24 9YZ   Tel/Fax: 020 8671 7144
                                          Website: www.buddhafield.org
Buddhist
Buddhafield is a non-profit-making organisation that offers a range of retreats to suit all ages. These take place under canvas in beautiful West Country locations. Vision and transformation are main themes, and retreats titles include *Single Sex Retreat, Spring Retreat, Open Meditation*, and *Meditation Retreat*. Qi Gong and yoga are on offer too. Call for the current year's programme

---

Buddhapadipa Temple   Tel: 020 8946 1357
14 Calonne Road   Fax: 020 8944 5788
Wimbledon   e-mail dhammacaro@yahoo.co.uk
London SW19 5HJ   Further info: The Lay Buddhist Association
                               Tel: 020 8946 7410/020 8870 2072
         Appointments for further discussion: Venerable PM Sangthong
                            Dhammacaro at dhammacaro@yahoo.co.uk
Buddhist (Theravada)
This active Buddhist temple has up to eight monks in community. On offer are various forms of study and meditation courses, including a one-week meditation course, and meditation four days a week, plus there are meditation classes four evenings each week. A summer retreat is usually held in September. Chants, which are usually in Pali, can be followed by the use of an English/Pali book, which is collected before entering the Uposatha Hall. Sometimes a monk may not be fluent in English, so be patient when seeking information by telephone. There are some Dharma talks and discussions in English on the programme. **There is no accommodation for visitors to the temple except for those guests who come for the meditation retreat held three times a year.**

Open: Most of the year. Receives men, women.
Rooms: The temple itself has no facilities for guests except during the thrice-annual retreats, but arrangements can be made for accommodation elsewhere.

Facilities: Shrine room, study room, meditation garden. Sometimes part of main garden.
Spiritual Help: One-day retreats, personal talks, meditation, directed study.
Guests Admitted to: Temple and most areas except community private ones.
Meals: Everyone eats together. Thai/whole food.
Special Activities: Telephone for information (See note above) or you may telephone the Lay Buddhist Association (Tel: 020 8946 7410/020 8870 2072). Thai festivals and New Year celebrations.
Situation: Urban.
Maximum Stay: For duration of meditation period, class or course only.
Bookings: Letter, fax, telephone.
Charges: On request.
Access: Underground and bus: regular service.

Centre for Jewish Education
Leo Baeck College
Sternberg Centre for Judaism
80 East End Road   Tel: 020 8349 5620
London N3 2SY   Fax: 020 8349 5639
                                                        e-mail: info@lbc.ac.uk

Judaism
The Centre for Jewish Education is dedicated to promoting the intellectual, spiritual and professional development of Progressive Judaism in Britain and Europe and stimulating Jewish religious thought and values. There are no Jewish retreat centres as such, but there are teachers of Jewish spirituality who address themselves to Jewish people. However, in the past the Centre has organised Family Retreats to provide Jewish educational, social, and spiritual enrichment for participating families, to strengthen and deepen relationships between families and synagogue staff, and to create a positive environment free of distraction in which every participant can thrive within a context of Judaism. Other events, not organised by the Centre, are held at Ammerdown (see Southwest/Somerset section), such as Jewish–Christian text studies day, inter-faith days and on occasion other courses, which are centred on opening Jewish–Christian dialogue. In the past there has been a ten-day Jewish–Christian summer school retreat

---

Christian Meditation Centre
St Mark's
Myddelton Square   Tel: 020 7833 9615
London EC1R 1XX   Fax: 020 7713 6346
                                                        Website: london@wccm.org
Christian – Inter-denominational
This is a new centre for the practice and teaching of meditation in the Christian tradition, following the method of John Main. It is under the auspices of the World Community for Christian Meditation. Other themes here are world peace and inter-faith dialogue. There is a programme, so send off for details.

Community of the Word of God
90–92 Kenworthy Road
London E9 5RA

Tel: 020 8986 8511
e-mail: cwg@fish.co.uk

Inter-denominational

The Community of the Word of God was founded in east London in 1972. The pattern of the Community's life is rather like that of a Christian family whose members seek to share the love of Christ and to encourage each other in their witness and work. Some follow secular occupations while others are home-based. The present community is made up of a small groups of women who form a small evangelical lay community living in two terraced houses, with a third, Emmaus House, for guests. Although in the inner city, Emmaus House offers a place for people who are looking to get away from their daily routine. Retreats, which are usually of the traditional, preached kind, are organised during the year. This is a place of quiet and deep Christian faith where the community hopes guests will meet with Christ in some way during their stay. A house of peace.

Open: February to December. Receives men, women, young people, families, and non-retreatants.
Rooms: 1–2 singles, 1 double. A non-smoking house.
Facilities: Chapel, garden, small library, guest lounge.
Spiritual Help: Personal talks, spiritual direction, personal retreat direction.
Guests Admitted to: Everywhere except community living quarters.
Meals: You may eat with the community or alone in the guesthouse (self-catering facilities are limited). Traditional, simple food. Vegetarian, special diets for medical reason, e.g. diabetic, low fats.
Special Activities: Retreats are organised during the year. Ask for details.
Situation: Inner city.
Maximum Stay: 1 week. Longer stays negotiable.
Bookings: Letter, e-mail, telephone 7–9:30p.m.
Charges: Donation towards costs if possible. Suggested £20 pp/pn.
Access: Train, bus and car all possible, but parking can be a problem.

Eagle's Wing Centre for Contemporary Shamanism
BM Box 7475
London WC1N 3XX

Tel: 01435 810233
e-mail: eagleswing@shamanism.co.uk
Website: www.shamanism.co.uk

Mind Body Spirit (Shamanism, North American Indian spirituality)
Our ancient human roots are shamanic, and whatever our culture we share in this spiritual heritage. All of us come from shamanic cultures because humans have always sought understanding and knowledge of the wider universe using a variety of experiential methods and tools. These practices are still in use in a surprisingly large number of places in the world, and many shamans of indigenous cultures are now teaching Westerners. The shamanic journey, the trance dance, the vision quest and the purifying ceremony of the sweat lodge are ancient but still relevant ways to contact the timeless reality that exists, hidden at first from our eyes and senses. Hidden, that is, until we open the

doors and begin to see with the expanded vision that shamanism brings. Eagle's Wing is a well-established and widely respected central resource for information and courses on shamanism. Leo Rutherford, who runs the Centre, has been a leading practitioner of this spiritual way for many years and is well-known and respected for his work. Chanting, drumming, dancing, instruction in the use of the medicine wheel, ceremony and celebration are all part of the Centre's teaching. While **there is no residential accommodation at the Centre**, there are a number of interesting day courses and workshops, which explore this rich and ancient tradition of spirituality. These are held at various venues around the country, with some in Greece. Examples of what is on offer include *Shaman Dance, Sweat Lodge, Dance and Ceremony Weekend, Shaman Wisdom, Shaman Healing and Soul Retrieval* and a trance dance training group. An example of what a retreat may be like is *Shamanic Divination*, with Howard G Charing (Tel: 01273 882027). This is a residential workshop weekend in which there is an introduction to the ways and means of divination. Divination is not fortune telling; it is a way into a deeper understanding of events, influences and circumstances surrounding a situation or person.

Other recent workshops at the Centre include *Divination with Rocks, Divinatory Shamanism Trance Postures, Drum and Rattle Talking* and *Sunbeam Divination Journey*. Course fees are about £140, which includes accommodation and meals at the venue where the course is being held. **Highly Recommended.**

Open: According to programme. Receives men and women.
Rooms: Not at Centre but on courses elsewhere.
Special Activities: Send for brochure.
Bookings: Letter or telephone.
Charges: Vary according to event/course. See brochure.
Access: See individual events.

Ealing Abbey
Charlbury Grove
Ealing, London W5 2DY   Tel: 020 8862 2100

Roman Catholic
The monks serve a large parish so this is a busy place, well and truly integrated into the world at large. Yet guests are welcome to share in the liturgy and community prayer, which help sustain all the various activities of the Abbey.

Open: September to July. Men, women, young people, families, groups, non-retreatants.
Rooms: 4 singles, 3 doubles.
Facilities: Chapel, garden, guest lounge.
Spiritual Help: Personal talks, directed study.
Guests Admitted to: Abbey church.
Meals: Meals eaten in the guesthouse. Traditional food.
Special Activities: Planned programme of events and regular retreats. Send for brochure.
Situation: Rather busy, in a city.

Maximum Stay: 1 week.
Bookings: Letter.
Charges: By arrangement.
Access: Train, underground: Ealing Broadway station 1 mile away. Bus: No. E2

Gatekeepers Trust
154 South Park Road
Wimbledon, London SW19 8TA

Tel: 020 8540 3684
e-mail: secretary@gatekeeper.org.uk
Website www.gatekeeper.org.uk

Eco-spirituality – Mind Body Spirit
The Gatekeepers Trust works to increase awareness of how to walk on the Earth in a simple and sacred way. These methods follow in the ancient footsteps of the sacred walking of Hindu, Christian and Islamic pilgrimages; Australian Aborigine walk-abouts; and Native American Great Father journeys. Courses, events and journeys are held in Britain and abroad. New landscapes often bring new understandings. In them are hidden spiritual truths, which emerge on your journey. The company of other seekers and pilgrims is enriching and also spiritually enlightening. The Gatekeepers Trust has an excellent and wide-ranging programme. To give you an idea of what is on offer, events may include the following: *A Day in Epping Forest, Heart of Scotland Pilgrimage, Spirit of the Himalayas, Midsummer Walk, Zodiacs in the Landscape.* Send for a brochure with information and the current year's programme.

Greenspirit – Centre for Creation Spirituality
St. James's Church
197 Piccadilly
London W1V 9LF

Tel: 020 7287 2741
e-mail: admin@greenspirit.org.uk
Website: www.greenspirit.org.uk

Judaic-Christian tradition
Creation spirituality finds support in the writings and life of some of the most distinguished religious thinkers and mystics over the last thousand years, including Hildegard of Bingen, Meister Eckhart, Julian of Norwich and St Francis. The Creation Spirituality movement is closely linked to ecological concerns and to a holistic view of living. Matthew Fox, a world leader in Creation Spirituality theology, has written a number of books, which have had a significant influence in the development of this particular spirituality approach. These include *Original Blessing* and *The Coming of the Cosmic Christ.* The Centre does not offer retreats as such, but there are various local groups and an annual programme of events, some national. Check out the website for further information on what may be currently available. Creation spirituality has had an international impact and it may offer you a new way of looking at your understanding of spirituality and God.

> In you, O Lord, I take refuge. Let me never be put to shame. In your justice, set me free, hear me and speedily rescue me.
> PSALM 30

ICCS Retreats
St Giles Church (ICCS Oasis Days)
Cripplegate
Wood Street, Barbican
London EC2Y 8BJ

Tel: 020 7739 1500
Fax: 020 7251 9384

Christian

Quiet days for prayer and reflection are held on the **second Tuesday** of every month from 10a.m. to 4p.m. at St Giles Church in the Barbican. Costs are £15 for the waged and £10 for the unwaged, which includes lunch and coffee, plus handout materials. Send for annual programme with the subjects of each day. The programme currently includes *What does the Lord Require of You?*, *The importance of Being Silent* and *The God who Surprises*. If you cannot get away for a few days' retreat and can manage a day at the Barbican, then try one of these events to nourish your spiritual life and give yourself some time out to think about eternal values.

Kairos Centre
Mount Angelus Road
Roehampton
London SW15 4JA

Tel: 020 8788 4188
Fax: 020 8788 4198
e-mail: info@thekairoscentre.co.uk
Website: www.thekairoscentre.co.uk

Roman Catholic – Inter-denominational

Kairos is a Greek word meaning 'favourable time' or 'graced moment'. Retreats, conference and business meeting facilities, and various courses are all on offer at this centre located near beautiful Richmond Park and only a few miles from central London itself.

Open: Almost all year. Receives everyone.
Rooms: 17 singles. 12 doubles. No smoking. No alcohol except taken with meals.
Facilities: Disabled, conferences, garden, guest lounge, TV.
Spiritual Help: Spiritual direction, personal retreat direction, meditation.
Guests Admitted to: Chapel, oratory.
Meals: Everyone eats together. Traditional and simple food. Vegetarian and special diets.
Special Activities: Planned programme. Send for information.
Situation: Calm and peaceful centre.
Maximum Stay: 1 month
Bookings: Letter, fax, e-mail, telephone 8.30a.m.–4p.m.
Charges: Different rates apply. These range from £16 up to £95.
Access: Rail, underground, bus. Car: via M4 or A3.

> What the heart wants from God, is God himself; nothing less than that can satisfy it.
> A CARTHUSIAN MONK

Kagyu Samye Dzong London
Carlisle Lane
Lambeth
London SE1 7LG

Tel: 020 7928 5447
e-mail: london@samye.org
Website: www.samye.org/london

Tibetan Buddhism – Karma Kagyu Tradition
Within walking distance of the Houses of Parliament, Lambeth Palace and Archbishop's Park, this centre is an unexpected find in an old and historical part of London. A former Victorian primary school, the buildings have been converted to provide a large shrine room, library, tearoom and simple dormitory accommodation. Away from the busy streets of Westminster, in the centre's gardens, you can find peace and quiet most afternoons when Kagyu Samye Dzong is open to the general public. The centre opened in 1998 and is part of Samye Ling in Scotland. It is run by Lama Zangmo – a fully ordained nun and the first person in Britain to be given the title of Lama (which means 'teacher') – and a small, often transient community of Buddhist monks, nuns and lay people. There are regular classes in meditation, basic Buddhism, Tibetan language and Tibetan thanka painting. Evening meditation is open to the public most days. See the programme for details of other courses and teachings, often led by experienced and eminent teachers from Britain and abroad. Additional premises within the grounds offer space for workshops, yoga and tetsudo (Tibetan martial arts), and a treatment room where consultations in Tibetan medicine are available.
The centre is closed on Mondays and Tuesdays and is open between 2p.m. and 9p.m. every other day. No meals are provided. The nearest underground stations are Westminster and Waterloo.

Lesbian & Gay Christian Movement
LGCM
Oxford House
Derbyshire Street
London E2 6HG

Tel/Fax: 020 7739 1249
e-mail: lgcm@lgcm/org.uk

Christian
The Lesbian & Gay Christian Movement holds annual retreats for lesbian, gay and bisexual women and men. The main one is usually held in Scotland at the Macleod Centre (see the Scotland section). Such retreats are led by internationally known men and women in the field of theology with concerns in lesbian, gay and bisexual Christianity and spirituality such as James Allison, Susy Brouard, Urs Mattmann and others. There is a small but growing number of retreats for lesbians, gays, bisexuals and transsexuals in Britain, and more retreat houses are including such events in their programmes. *The Good Retreat Guide* **welcomes this development and hopes that an increasing number of religious houses and retreat centers will become aware and inclusive of the spiritual needs of lesbian, gay, bisexual and transsexual men and women.**

London Buddhist Centre
51 Roman Road
Bethnal Green
London E2 0HU

Tel: 0845 458 4716
Fax: 020 8980 1960
e-mail: info@lbc.org.uk
Website: www.lbc.org.uk

Buddhist – Friends of the Western Buddhist Order

The Friends of the Western Buddhist Order (FWBO) strives to put Buddhism's essential teachings into practice in the West through identifying core Buddhist principles and values and making them relevant to men and women living in the modern world. The London Buddhist Centre is at the heart of a thriving spiritual community in the East End of London and an essential part of the international and rapidly expanding FWBO movement. Buddhist practices and classes are offered as well as retreats for people of all levels of experience and of all ages. Evening and lunchtime meditation classes are available. There is no residential community in London as such, so people can only visit by attending one of the organised retreats. You may, of course, call into the Centre for a brief visit. However, a sort of Buddhist village has evolved around the Centre. There are small shops and restaurants, which share common values and are run co-operatively. The Natural Health Centre, **Bodywise (Tel: 020 8981 6938)**, offers a wide range of yoga classes, alternative treatments and therapies. On the retreat side of things there is a wide variety of retreats and special spiritual events on the programme, which may include gay men's retreats; people of colour retreats; family retreats; parents and children's retreats; a summer open retreat of nine nights; a working retreat, which combines meditation, study and work; and seminars on ancient wisdom, which may include the Buddha's advice on relationships and the practice of the Dharma in everyday life. Regular retreats are held at Vajrasana, the retreat centre in Suffolk, all year around. If you are interested in Buddhism, this is a great place to get started. **Highly Recommended.**

Open: All year Monday to Friday, 10a.m.–5p.m. Receives everyone.
Rooms: Discuss accommodation with the Centre when you decide what interests you on the programme. Singles, doubles, dormitories and camping available depending on the retreat.
Facilities: Disabled, garden. Other facilities available at Vajrasana.
Spiritual Help: Personal talks, group sharing, spiritual direction, personal retreat direction, meditation, directed study.
Guests Admitted to: Everywhere.
Meals: Everyone eats together. Whole food, vegetarian, special diets.
Special Activities: Programme of events. Brochure available and information on FWBO.
Situation: In a city but very quiet. Other FWBO retreat locations outside London are also quiet and peaceful.
Maximum Stay: By arrangement.
Bookings: Letter, fax, e-mail, telephone 10.a.m.–5p.m.
Charges: Charges vary, but introductory meditation weekend retreat is about £95 or £55 concessionary rate. Longer retreats run at different rates, but there are concessionary rates for these too.
Access: Underground: Bethnal Green and then a walk. Buses: Nos. 253 and 8.

Other FWBO Centres in and around London:

Covent Garden
Neals Yard Meeting Rooms
Neal's Yard, London   (Enquiries through the London Buddhist Centre)

North London Buddhist Centre
St. Mark's Studies
Chillingworth Road   Tel: 020 7700 3075
London N7 8SJ   e-mail: nlbc@cwcom.net

West London Buddhist Centre   Tel: 0845 458 5461
94 Westbourne Park Villas   e-mail: info@wlbc.co.uk
London W2 5EB   Website: www.westlondonbuddhistcentre.com

Croydon Buddhist Centre
96–98 High Street   Tel: 020 8688 8624
Croydon CRO 1ND   e-mail: croydonbc@lineone.net
Through the Croydon Centre reservations can be made and a copy of the
year's programme obtained for the **Rivendell Buddhist Retreat Centre in
Surrey**. Rivendell has an excellent programme of retreats and courses, includ-
ing arts-related retreats, yoga retreats and meditation retreats. Such topics as
follows are often found in the annual programme: *Meditation Retreat for
Men, The Way of Non-Duality, The Wheel of Life, Amitabha – Entering the
Inner World*, and *Vairocana – the Quest for Illumination*.

Buddhist Meditation in Brixton
Brockwell Lido
Dulwich Road
London SE24   (For details contact London Buddhist Centre)

London Buddhist Vihara
Dharmapala Building   Tel: 020 8995 9493
The Avenue, Chiswick   Fax: 020 8994 8130
London W4 4JU   e-mail: London.vihara@virgin.net
                        Website: www.londonbuddhistvihara.co.uk
Buddhist (Theravada)
No residential facilities are available here. There is a resident community of
monks at the Vihara, which is open daily from 9.00a.m. to 9.00p.m. Evening
classes explore a wide range of subjects: Bhavana (meditation) instruction and
practice, Beginner's Buddhism, Dharma study, Buddhist psychology, the
Sinhala language and Pali, which is the language of the Buddhist canon. A
Buddhist discussion group meets monthly in an informal atmosphere. There
are monthly retreats and a children's Sunday school. The Vihara also caters for
the needs of expatriate Buddhists from Asia – mainly Sri Lanka.

Open: All year. Receives everyone. Children welcome.
Rooms: None.
Facilities: Conferences, shrine room, garden, library, payphone, bookstall.
Spiritual Help: Personal talks, meditation, directed study.

Guests Admitted to: Everywhere except monks' rooms.
Meals: Traditional food – monks eat separately, everyone else together.
Special Activities: See programme.
Situation: Quiet within the house.
Maximum Stay: One day.
Bookings: Letter, fax, e-mail, telephone.
Charges: By donation.
Access: Underground or bus.

Marie Reparatrice Retreat Centre
115 Ridgway
Wimbledon   Tel: 020 8946 1088
London SW19 4RB   Fax: 020 8947 9820
       e-mail: smrwim@gn.apc.org

Roman Catholic
A modern house close to parks and Wimbledon Common, run by sisters of
Marie Reparatrice, an international congregation whose main work has been
retreats and whose spirituality is Ignatian.

Open: All year except Christmas and New Year. Receives men, women,
 young people, groups, non-retreatants.
Rooms: 31 singles, 1 double.
Facilities: Disabled, conferences, garden, library, guest lounge, TV, guest
 telephone (020 8946 3391).
Spiritual Help: Personal talks, spiritual direction, personal retreat direction,
 group sharing, meditation.
Guests Admitted to: Unrestricted access.
Meals: Meals taken in guesthouse. Whole food. Vegetarian, special diets.
Special Activities: Programme of one-day events and six-day retreats, which
 may include Holy Week retreats, individually guided retreats and preached
 retreats.
Situation: Quiet but in a town.
Maximum Stay: 1–2 weeks.
Bookings: Letter, fax, telephone.
Charges: £34 per night per person for 24-hour stay.
Access: Underground, train, bus, car.

Neal's Yard Workshops and Courses
Neal's Yard
Covent Garden   Tel/Fax: 0870 442702
London WC1N 3XX   e-mail: info@nealsyardagency.com
       Website: www.nealsyardagency.com

Open spirituality – Mind Body Spirit
A wonderful organisation which has hosted and helped any number of
courses and workshops to take place – a few at Neal's Yard itself and others
elsewhere in London, around the country or abroad. Topics covered include
arts and life skills, bodymind, tai chi, yoga, healing, spiritual healing, meditation, holidays, getaways and retreats. **Highly Recommended.**

North Bank Centre
Chester House
Pages Lane
Muswell Hill, London N10 1PR

Tel: 020 8883 7850
Fax: 020 8883 8042
e-mail: admin@northbank.methodist.org.uk
Website: www.northbank.methodist.org.uk

Ecumenical – Christian
This is a Methodist residential and non-residential centre with ecumenical staff. The Centre is set in some ten acres of garden and offers accommodation for about 16 guests. There is a good programme on offer based around Christian scripture and prayer.

Open Centre
Third Floor
188 Old Street
London EC1 9FR

Tel/Fax: 020 7251 1504
e-mail: info@opencentre.com
Website: www.opencentre.com

Mind Body Spirit – Self-development
Now running for over twenty-five years, The Open Centre offers a programme to increase your awareness of yourself and others and to help you take a look at your relationships, your assumptions and your decisions about life and work. The key ideas are centred in therapy, movement, healing and growth. Courses on offer usually include primal integration, deep bodywork, Feldenkrais method and bioenergetics. **There are some residential intensives, including one in Devon and one in south-west France.**

Open: All year. Receives men, women and groups.
Rooms: None except group rooms used for courses.
Facilities: See above.
Spiritual Help: Group sharing.
Guests Admitted to: Course areas.
Meals: None unless on residential course.
Special Activities: Programme of courses and events. See brochure.
Situation: In city.
Maximum Stay: For course or programme.
Bookings: Letter, fax, e-mail, telephone.
Charges: Vary according to course or intensive but range is from £48 to £395.
Access: Train/underground: Old Street.

Royal Foundation of St Katherine
Retreat and Conference Centre
2 Butchers Row
London E14 8DS

Tel: 020 7790 3540
Fax: 020 7702 7603
e-mail: michael@stkatharine.co.uk

Anglican
St Katherine serves people living in the area through teaching, spiritual ministry and social work. The interesting retreats and conferences offered here in the past have been wide-ranging and relevant to modern living. Ask

for the current programme as the Centre is undergoing major rebuilding and will reopen during 2004. All rooms will then be ensuite.

Open: All year. Receives men, women, young people, groups.
Rooms: Lots, and all ensuite when Centre re-opens. No smoking.
Facilities: Disabled, conferences, garden, library, guest lounge, guest telephone.
Spiritual Help: Personal talks, spiritual direction.
Guests Admitted to: chapel, gardens.
Meals: Everyone eats together. Traditional food. Vegetarian and special diets.
Special Activities: None.
Situation: Reasonably quiet in a city.
Maximum Stay: By programme or arrangement.
Bookings: Letter, fax, e-mail, telephone.
Charges: Ask for rates when you contact or see new programme. They will be probably between £40 and £50 per 24-hour period full board.
Access: Two minutes from Limehouse DLR Station, which connects to London Underground.

Sacred Heart Priory
The Dominican Sisters
38 Hyde Vale
Greenwich
London SE10 8QH   Tel: 020 8692 3382

Roman Catholic
Overnight accommodation with self-catering facilities for women only. There are opportunities for quiet days, Christian meditation and scriptural sharing, and there is a monthly retreat day with quiet prayer. There are some Open Door and guided prayer events too. Programme available.

Spirit Horse Nomadic Circle
19 Holmwood Gardens
Finchley   Tel: 020 8346 3660
London N3 3NS   e-mail: indraerika@hotmail.com
                                  Website: www.spirithorse.co.uk

Mind Body Spirit
Nearly all events by the Spirit Horse Nomadic Circle are held in Powys, Wales, in the summertime under canvas. This ranges from personal tents you bring with you to Turkoman gers, yurts and tipis. There is a large Celtic roundhouse. The structured courses on offer cover shaman practice, ceremony, meditation, sexuality (uninvited intimacy is not part of the process) and aspects of both Buddhism and Celtic mythology. What is offered here is an archaic, ceremonial environment, close to nature with a variety of different courses enabling a rediscovery of self through spiritual practices, healing and mythology. Sources used are Tibetan Buddhism, and Celtic and North American Indian traditions. Sweat lodge, stone medicine healing, storytelling, Arabic dancing, song and voice work, Buddhist visionary instruction and much more can be involved in the programme. The website is interesting and informative about the organisation.

Open: Summer only. Receives everyone.
Rooms: Special tents.
Facilities: Conferences possible, camping.
Spiritual Help: Personal talks, group sharing, meditation, directed study.
Guests Admitted to: Unrestricted access.
Meals: Traditional food. Vegetarians catered for.
Special Activities: See brochure for programme.
Situation: In peaceful countryside.
Maximum Stay: 5–10 days.
Bookings: Letter.
Charges: In range of £125 to £500 for 3-, 5-, and 10-day courses. See the programme for the current rates.
Access: Car. Some events via train.

Society of St John the Evangelist
St Edward's House
22 Great College Street
London SW1P 3QA

Tel: 020 7222 9234
e-mail: frpeterssjeuk@talk21.com
Website: www.ssje.org.uk

Anglican

The Society of St John the Evangelist is the oldest monastic community for men in the Anglican Church. Guests stay with the community and not separately. There is silence from 9p.m. until 9a.m. the next morning. You will receive a traditional monastic welcome here by a men's religious community open for short-stay breaks, particularly geared to Christians and charity groups who want to live and share in the community's life. The Society is located in central London. The guest rooms are simple but comfortable and neat, and the guest lounge, or Common Room, is filled with comfortable chairs and is a light and airy space. There is space to sit outside during good weather. The Society holds conducted retreats, some preached, and provides quiet days by arrangement. If you are called to explore the monastic life, or feel that a deeper Christian commitment is necessary in your life, the Superior of the community is happy to discuss these matters with you.

> Oh, God grant unto men to see by some small example the elements in common between small things and great.
> SAINT AUGUSTINE

Open: All year except August, Christmas, Easter. Receives men, women, families, groups.
Rooms: 17 singles. No smoking, radios or mobile phones.
Facilities: Chapel, library, garden, guest lounge, payphone.
Spiritual Help: Personal talks, meditation, spiritual direction, personal retreat direction, directed study. Guests do not have to attend religious services but may if they want.
Guests Admitted to: Church, chapel, refectory, library, garden.
Meals: Everyone eats together. Food is simple and traditional. Vegetarians can be catered for but advance notice must be given. No special diets.
Special Activities: Quiet days.

Situation: In a city. Rather busy, but near all London attractions if need these on hand.
Maximum Stay: 7 days.
Bookings: Letter, e-mail, on-line. If you have to telephone do it after 9.30a.m. and before 9p.m.
Charges: £30–£35, depending on meals taken.
Access: Underground to St James Park. Bus to Westminster Abbey.

St Marylebone Healing & Counselling Centre
St Marylebone Parish Church
17 Marylebone Road
London NW1 5LT

Tel: 020 7935 5066

Ecumenical
This centre has been operating for many years now. There is an ecumenical team of spiritual directors, with professional counselling offered by Christian therapists. Days of prayer and courses are on offer too. Send for detailed information and the current programme.

St Saviour's Priory
18 Queensbridge Road
Haggerston
London E2 8NS

Tel: 020 7739 6775
Fax: 020 7739 1248

Anglican
There are no conducted retreats and groups are received only for the day facilities, but this is a good place for a private retreat, especially if you live in or near the Greater London area. Such traditional Anglican convents as this one, which do not offer any programmes only traditional private retreat, have recently grown in popularity, especially among women with busy careers. St Saviour's may be booked up well in advance, so do not be disappointed if there is no room for you when you want it. Most spiritualities claim patience as a virtue!

Open: Most of the year. Receives men, women, young people, families. Groups for the day only.
Rooms: 6 singles, 2 doubles.
Facilities: Chapel, garden.
Spiritual Help: Personal talks, spiritual direction, Reiki. There is not always someone immediately available, so appointments have to be arranged for guidance and treatment.
Guests Admitted to: Chapel, garden.
Meals: Traditional. self-catering available. If vegetarian, discuss when booking.
Special Activities: None.
Situation: In a city.
Maximum Stay: 2 weeks.
Bookings: Letter, fax, telephone 10.30a.m.–12.30p.m. and 6.30–8.30p.m.
Charges: Donations according to means – to give you an idea, a stay costs the community about £20–£25 per 24 hours per guest.
Access: Bus: Nos. 26, 48, 55. Car parking is difficult here.

Swaminarayan Hindu Mission and The Shri Swaminarayan Mandir
105–119 Brentfield Road
Neasden   Tel: 020 8965 2651
London NW10 8JP   Fax: 020 8965 6313
                               Website: www.swaminarayan-baps.org

Hindu
The Swaminarayan Hindu Mission is a branch of the worldwide
Bochasanwasi Akshar Purushottam Sanstha of India, which is a prominent
and charitable Hindu organisation with a wide spectrum of activities including a medical college. It strives to promote social, moral, cultural, and spiritual values among all ages within society and has some 3,000 centres and 300
temples around the world. The inspirer and spiritual leader is His Holiness
Pramukh Swami Maharaj. The London centres have now opened the largest
traditional Hindu Mandir (temple) in Europe and they welcome people from
all faiths. The Mandir has transformed the north London district of Neasden.
It took three years to build and employed 1,500 sculptors, 2,000 tons of
marble and 3,000 tons of limestone. Among those who have visited this
temple with its nine shrines and marvelled at its design and craftsmanship
have been the Prince of Wales; Diana, Princess of Wales; the Duke of
Edinburgh; and Tony Blair. Facilities include a community and social centre,
a cultural centre, a school, sports and recreation facilities, a library, a health
clinic and a programme of various activities for men, women and families.
There is a permanent exhibition on Hinduism and a video presentation on
the construction of the Mandir. **This is a remarkable and marvelous place,
well worth a visit.**

Open: All year from 9a.m. to 6p.m. **Please note dress code: Shorts, skirts
and dresses above the knee are not permitted except on children
under 10 years.**

Tyburn Convent
8 Hyde Park Place
Bayswater Road   Tel: 020 7723 7262
London W2 2LJ   Fax: 020 7706 4507
                              Website: www.tyburnconvent.org.uk

Roman Catholic
Just opposite Hyde Park, Tyburn Convent is right in the heart of London.
Amid the busy outside world the sisters preside over the perpetual exposition
of the Blessed Sacrament – the chapel is open all day and retreat guests may
go there at night. Nearby was Tyburn's place of execution, which operated
from 1196 to 1783. Over one hundred officially recognised martyrs died
there for their faith and the Convent's Martyrs' Altar is a replica of the
Tyburn tree, erected in honour of the memory of its victims. Try the
Convent's tour, taking in the prayer book and chapel. The Convent's website
is one of the best. **Highly Recommended.**

Open: All year. Receives women who wish to make a private retreat and men
only occasionally. Tyburn Convent is the National Shrine of the Martyrs
of England and Wales, so all are welcome to visit the crypt itself. Groups
received.

Rooms: 5 singles. Guests are usually expected to be in by 8.30p.m., when the Convent is locked.

Facilities: Chapel, small patio, library, garden, Hyde Park at hand, payphone. Facilities for day groups and conferences.

Spiritual Help: Retreatants are left to spend their time as they wish, but are welcome to share in the Divine Office, Mass and the Adoration of the Blessed Sacrament. If anyone feels the need, a talk with a sister can be arranged.

Guests Admitted to: Chapel, shrine room. A sister is available three times a day or by appointment to give individuals or groups a guided tour of the Martyrs' Crypt.

Meals: Everyone eats together in the guesthouse. Traditional simple food, with provision for vegetarian and special diets (within reason) by prior arrangement.

Special Activities: The perpetual exposition of the Blessed Sacrament in the chapel, which is open to the public all day, a sung Divine Office, and the Shrine of the Martyrs.

Situation: Hyde Park is across the road but the Convent is in the very heart of busy London.

Maximum Stay: 1 week.

Bookings: Letter, fax, telephone.

Charges: Usually arranged with the Guest Mistress. £25 per night.

Access: Underground to Marble Arch. Central London buses. Parking difficult.

**The Well
90 Suffolk Road
Tottenham
London N15 5RH**

Tel/Fax: 020 8802 2450
e-mail: lynneosm@waitrose.com

Roman Catholic

Open to everyone on a spiritual journey. Home of the Community of Servite Sisters. They welcome guests for a day or longer. Meals can be taken with the community and there is a programme of themed retreats. Individual spiritual direction is possible on request.

> The will of man is a brass wall between him and God and a stone of stumbling. When a man renounces it, he is also saying, 'By God, I can leap over the wall.'
> ABBA POEMEN, DESERT FATHER

South West

Bristol

Emmaus House Conference & Retreat Centre
Clifton Hill ★
Clifton
Bristol BS8 1BN

Tel: 0117 907 9950
Fax: 0117 907 9952
Restaurant: 0117 907 9954
e-mail: emmaushouse@msn.com
Website: www.emmaushouse.co.uk and www.laretraiute.co.uk

Roman Catholic – Inter-denominational
Set in Clifton Village on the outskirts of Bristol, Emmaus House welcomes guests to workshops or simply to stay, have a meal and enjoy the view. Facilities are continuously upgraded and include award-winning gardens and a restaurant serving food of a high standard. There are plenty of places to pray, an art room and spiritual companionship available for those that want it. The community here is noted for teaching the Enneagram in Helen Palmer's narrative tradition. This is an oasis in the midst of a busy world. **Highly Recommended.**

Open: All year except Christmas, Easter. August retreats only. Receives men, women, groups, non-retreatants.
Rooms: 11 Singles, 11 twin doubles. No smoking.
Facilities: Conference facilities including TV, video camera and most necessary equipment; a rather special small garden; library; art room; bookshop; payphone.
Spiritual Help: Spiritual direction, personal retreat direction, personal talks, massage, Reiki.
Guests Admitted to: Chapel, guest areas, gardens.
Meals: Taken in dining room. Southern Mediterranean cooking which is very good indeed. Vegetarian and special diets.
Special Activities: Full programme of courses and retreats. Send for brochure.
Situation: In town. Amount of noise depends on group in house at any given time. Lovely views and pleasant neighbourhood.
Maximum Stay: Negotiable.
Bookings: Letter, fax, e-mail.
Charges: Retreats £40 per 24 hours. Weekend workshops residential £95, non-residential £75. Quiet days of prayer with lunch per person £20. Spiritual direction is available over a period of time – discuss donation fee arrangements for this service.
Access: Train to Bristol Temple Meads. Bus: No. 8 from station to W.H. Smith in Clifton Down Road. Car: from north take M5, Exit 17, then A4018; from London take M4, Exit 20, then M5, Exit 19, followed by A369.

Elsie Briggs House of Prayer
38 Church Road
Westbury-on-Trym
Bristol
BS9 3EQ   Tel: 0117 9507242

Christian
Self-catering accommodation consisting of two rooms with a meditation hut
and a garden house for creative activities. All are welcome here.

Bath

Ammerdown Centre
Radstock
Bath BA3 5SW   Tel: 01761 433709
                                               Fax: 01761 433094
                                         e-mail: centre@ammerdown.org
                                         Website: www.ammerdown.org
Ecumenical
Ammerdown, which has now been operating for thirty years, is an outstand-
ing retreat centre. It offers one of the most extensive and broadly spiritual
ranges of retreats and courses on offer anywhere in Britain. Some of them
may include *A Taste of Buddhism*, *A Taste of Hinduism*, *Prayer Weekend*,
Circle Dancing, *Dreams*, *The Four Faces of the Moon*, *Art of Living*, *Healing
Breath Workshop* and *The Beatitudes and Colour*. Among other subjects
covered are ecumenical dialogue, interfaith dialogue, Christian ethics,
Christian Jewish Bible study and meditation skills. The Centre also provides
accommodation for those who wish to spend time alone on a prayer retreat.
The Centre occupies various attractive old buildings in and around the stable-
block of Ammerdown House, the private residence of Lord Hylton and his
family. Some of the parklands and gardens are open to residents. While
predominantly Christian, the governing body also represents other religious
communities. For example, one of the governors has been the well-known
Rabbi Lionel Blue. The Ammerdown Centre is an open Christian community dedicated to peace, reconciliation and renewal. It makes provision within
a secure, welcoming and prayerful atmosphere with respect for all regardless
of beliefs. There is plenty on offer for both the first-time private retreatant
and for those who attend religious retreats regularly. Course leaders are experienced and informed and include such people as Dr Karen Jankulak from the
University of Wales at Lampeter, Hal French from the USA, Gerald
O'Collins, Joyce Rupp and Rabbi Mark Solomon from Leo Baeck College in
London. Guests are welcome to join the resident community at prayer times
during the week. **Highly Recommended.**

Open: All year except Christmas. Receives men, women, young people, fami-
    lies, groups, non-retreatants.
Rooms: 31 singles, 11 doubles (including 5 family rooms), 1 self-catering
    flat, also the self-catering Peace Cottage with various accommodations.
Facilities: Disabled – 2 ground-floor rooms, specially designed bathrooms,
    loop system. Conference rooms, garden, park, library, guest lounge with
    bar, TV, payphone (01761 433708), chapel, prayer room, religious book-

shop, craft shop, woodland and parkland walks, heated summer swimming pool, various games such as badminton.

Spiritual Help: Personal talks, group sharing, meditation, directed study, spiritual direction, personal retreat direction, community prayer twice a day.

Guests Admitted to: Unrestricted access.

Meals: Everyone eats together at big tables – very jolly and friendly dining room. Self-catering facilities. Traditional food and there is always a vegetarian option. Special diets.

Special Activities: A very extensive programme – see brochure.

Situation: Very quiet, in the countryside, with access to large and lovely parkland.

Maximum Stay: By arrangement or by duration of course.

Bookings: Letter, fax, e-mail, telephone 9a.m.–5p.m.

Charges: Price range £36 to £51 per person per 24 hours. Each course is individually priced, so consult the programme for the current year. £80–£175 gives you some idea of range, but it can be less or more than this.

Access: Train: Bath Spa. Buses: to Radstock. Car: Centre is just off A362.

Winford

Winford Manor Retreat
Winford
Bristol BS18 8DW

Tel: 01275 472262
Fax: 01275 472065
e-mail: info@winfordmanorretreat.com
Website: www.winfordmanorretreat.com

Ecumenical

This is one of *The Good Retreat Guide*'s favourite retreat houses. Founded in 1980, the Omega Order at Winford Manor Retreat takes its title from the words of Christ: 'I am the Alpha and the Omega, the first and the last.' The Manor has gone from strength to strength over the years and guests are welcome at all times, either to attend courses and retreats or to find space for rest and reflection and to join the resident community of men and women in the rhythm of a life of prayer, well-being, and peace. The welcome here is warm and friendly, with caring hospitality shown by everyone living in the house. This makes the atmosphere relaxed and happy. The administration is excellent but low-key and there is no feeling of the institutional about Winford Manor. Courses may include retreats to enhance insight through the study of calligraphy, contemplative dance, Christian and Buddhist spirituality or new and scientific concepts of God. A few retreat titles will give you a good feel of what is on offer here *Enneagram, Spirituality Beyond Religion, St. John's Gospel, Angels and Our Lives, The Gospel of Falling Down, Being a Man* (based on Rev Richard Rohr's *Rites of Men's Passage* retreats), *Becoming Men of Love – Discovering, Exploring and Growing in the Spiritual Life for Gay Men* (lead by Urs Mattmann, leader of a church community in Switzerland). There are also traditional courses on contemplative prayer and meditation. Creativity and the holiness of a heart and spirit open to God are encouraged in many ways here. The Prior and Founder, Canon Peter Spank, has written a number of thought-provoking spirituality books, and Winford Manor Retreat has produced a series of cassettes and offers a correspondence course to help participants develop their own perceptions and insights. In short, Winford Manor Retreat offers silence in which to reflect and studies in which to expand and develop consciousness of the spirit. This is a good location for those who may not want their first retreat to be in a church setting that is overwhelmingly traditional. It is a place where you will be taken seriously if you ask why God is referred to as masculine – and you will get a considered answer. The Omega Offices, which are used as a daily liturgy, are delightful. If you are invited to join in with circle dancing in the chapel as part of the service, do participate, as the dances are easy and very much an act of praying together. As you dance, recall that King David in the Old Testament *danced* for joy before the altar of the Lord God. Winford Manor Retreat will help you to feel the presence of the Universal and Cosmic Christ perhaps more strongly than many other places of Christian religious or church life. **Highly Recommended.**

Open: All year. Receives everyone. Children welcome.

Rooms: Up to 30 – single, double, twin-bedded.

Facilities: Disabled, conferences, garden, park, excellent library, very spacious and comfortable guest lounge, payphone, direct dialing.

Spiritual Help: Personal retreat direction, meditation.

Guests Admitted to: Chapel, shrine room, work of the community.

Meals: Everyone eats together. Food is well prepared and excellent, with provision for vegetarians.

Special Activities: A wide-ranging and exciting planned programme of events and retreats. Send for information. Meditation techniques, yoga, reflexology, massage, aromatherapy, Reiki, peace-making, **assistance in recovery programmes, respite care and counselling.**

Situation: Quiet, in the countryside. An old house standing in 7 acres of wooded grounds.

Maximum Stay: None

Bookings: Letter, fax, telephone 9a.m.–5p.m. weekdays.

Charges: Full Board £35 per 24 hours. Three-night mid-week break £90. Weekend course £130. Therapies from £25–£30 per session.

Access: Train: Bristol Temple Meads (7 miles away). Buses: Central Bristol Bus Station, Car: via A38 from Bristol to Exeter Road. Air: Bristol Airport down the road.

CORNWALL

Bodmin

Lanuah Retreat Centre
Treskilling
Luxulyan
Bodmin
Cornwall PL30 5EL   Tel: 01726 851502

Christian – The Quiet Garden Trust
Lanuah means 'come and rest'. This retreat house is a bungalow with 2 twin rooms, a double, a hermitage, a large conservatory, and an ancient granite

Cornish cottage integrated into the retreat situation. There is even a small wooden chapel on the property. There are retreats and quiet days, and the Centre is near the Eden Project. A very peaceful and welcoming place of peace and prayer. Discuss your retreat needs with the organisers.

Bude

The Eye of the Sun
Beeston Farm
Marhamchurch
Bude
Cornwall EX23 OET

Tel: 01288 381638
e-mail: jane@eyeofthesun.com
Website: www.eyeofthesun.com

Open spirituality – sacred space
Eye of the Sun is in a secluded corner of Cornwall and is dedicated to helping people find and experience sacred space and to feel harmony within themselves and with the universe. Organic vegetarian food from the garden is served. Accommodation is limited to four in two double rooms but is comfortable. B&B, full board and self-catering are all possible. Meditation, prayer and alternative lifestyles are central here, and individual guided retreats are available. The studio, land and woodlands are all open to adult guests.

Helston

Trelowarren Christian Fellowship
Mawgan in Meneage
Helston
Cornwall TR12 6AD

Tel: 01326 221366
Fax: 01326 221834

Inter-denominational
Located in an ancient manor house buried in the heart of the countryside, the Fellowship is open to Christians of all denominations, whether in groups or as individuals, who want to spend time away from it all. Healing, teaching and renewal conferences are held here, and prayer, counselling and ministry in the power of the Holy Spirit are available by arrangement. This is very much a place for those who are already Christians and not for those who feel that they may find their spirituality through exploring other faiths. It is a sanctuary of peace where you may deepen your spiritual awareness and perhaps find a fuller understanding of the Christian Gospel.

Open: February–mid-December. Receives men, women, young people, families, groups, non-retreatants, Christian religious. Children welcome.
Rooms: 1 single, 1 double, 8 twins, 2 family rooms.
Facilities: Conferences, garden, library, park, guest lounge, TV, payphone, direct dialing.
Spiritual Help: Personal talks, group sharing, directed study, spiritual direction, prayer ministry.
Guests Admitted to: Chapel, work of the community.
Meals: Everyone eats together. Traditional food. Vegetarian and special diets.
Special Activities: Planned programme of events, including monthly healing service. Send for brochure.

Situation: Very quiet.
Maximum Stay: 2 weeks.
Bookings: Letter, telephone 9a.m.–6p.m.
Charges: By donation – guideline: £23 per day.
Access: Consult the brochure map, which details travel arrangements.

Penberth

Shell Cottage
Penberth
St Buryan
Near Penzance
Cornwall TR19 6HJ

Tel: 01736 810659
Fax: 01736 810941
e-mail: bridget@shellcottage.net
Website: www.shellcottage.net

Christian

Just a few yards from the water's edge and fishing boats, Shell Cottage provides an unusual and rather idyllic location for a private or group retreat, quiet days or simply space for rest and prayer. Although principally catering for those in ordained ministry, Shell Cottage is a place where all may come on retreat.

Open: All year. Receives men, women, religious, groups. No families for holidays, no children, no pets.
Rooms: 2 singles.
Facilities: Garden, guest lounge, payphone, chapel.
Spiritual Help: Anglican priest is available.
Guests Admitted to: Unrestricted access.
Meals: Self-catering facilities.
Special Activities: Regularly led quiet days. Complete silence in part of the house at all times.
Situation: Cottage is on the cliff overlooking a small fishing cove with sea views.
Maximum Stay: Open.
Bookings: Letter, fax, telephone – best time evenings.
Charges: Suggested donation £10 per person per night. £5 for the day only.
Access: Train: Penzance. Car: not far from Land's End. Ask for details of route.

Pendoggett St Kew

Cornish Tipi Holidays
Tregare
Pendoggett St Kew
Cornwall PL30 3LW

Tel: 01208 880781
Fax: 01208 880487
e-mail: info@cornish-tipi-holidays.co.uk
Website: www.cornish-tipi-holidays.co.uk

Non-religious – Open spirituality

Cornish Tipi Holidays combines an ancient and traditional lifestyle with the lovely Cornish countryside. The tipis are in an old valley, which is full of local flora and fauna. Nearby, a large freshwater lake offers swimming, fishing and boating. Tipi accommodation consists of both medium and large tipi fully equipped for four to six people. Families and children have found holiday fun and relaxation in taking a tipi retreat this way. *Evening Standard* and *Observer* writers have praised these holidays.

Penzance

Sancreed House
Sancreed
Penzance
Cornwall TR20 8QS

Tel: 01736 810409
e-mail: claredyas@madasafish.com
Website: www.sancreedhouse.com

Mind Body Spirit – Eco-spirituality
This is an old vicarage full of spiritual history and with lovely gardens. There is a little well nearby, where a hermit once lived, Saint Credan, after whom the village was named. It is all very romantic. The self-catering accommodation is in separate bungalows and there is an art studio and indoor space for workshops.

Open: All year. Receives men, women, young people, groups, non-retreatants.
Rooms: 2 singles, 3 doubles, hermitage. Tapes, mobile phones and radios discouraged.
Facilities: Garden, library, payphone.
Spiritual Help: Personal talks, meditation, shiatsu, kinesiology, past life regression, reflexology, astrology.

> Practise random acts of kindness and senseless acts of beauty.
> X̞ᴛɪɴᴇ Hᴀɴᴋɪɴsᴏɴ

Guests Admitted to: Chapel, garden, work by arrangement.
Meals: B&B in guest house, self-catering, full board possible. Traditional and vegetarian food.
Special Activities: Planned programme of events.
Situation: Quiet in a rather remote village in the countryside.
Maximum Stay: 4 weeks.
Bookings: Letter, telephone.
Charges: B&B about £20 single – ask for current charges when you contact them.
Access: Train: Penzance. Car: A30 to Penzance. Ask for further travel details when booking.

Stoke Climsland

Hampton Manor
Stoke Climsland
Callington
Cornwall PL17 8LX

Tel: 01579 370494
e-mail: hamptonmanor@supanet.com
Website: www.hamptonmanor.co.uk

Inter-denominational
Set in two acres of land in the Tamar Valley, Hampton Manor is a quaint old Victorian house, which is now a place of Christian prayer, teaching and witness. All who are seeking spiritual and physical refreshment are welcome. Morning and evening prayer is held in the chapel and there is a programme of quiet days as well as other retreats.

Open: All year except Christmas. Receives men, women, young people, families, groups for the day only, non-retreatants. Children welcome.

Rooms: 1 single, 6 twins.

Facilities: Disabled, garden, guest lounge, TV, conference facilities for up to 35 people in separate building.

Spiritual Help: Personal talks, prayer ministry, counselling.

Guests Admitted to: Unrestricted access everywhere.

Meals: Taken in the guest house. Traditional food. Vegetarian, vegan and special diets.

Special Activities: Planned programme – send for brochure.

Situation: Very quiet in the countryside

Maximum Stay: No limit.

Bookings: Letter, fax, e-mail, telephone.

Charges: £20 bed (+ £5 single supplement), breakfast £3–£5, lunch £5, evening meal £8–£10

Access: Consult the brochure map, which gives detailed travel arrangements with directions. Train station 5 miles – pick-up available.

Zennor

**Boswednack Manor
Zennor
St Ives
Cornwall TR26 3DD**   Tel: 01736 794183

Non-denominational – Ecospirituality/Buddhist orientation

Boswednack Manor is set in three acres of organic meadow and vegetable, fruit and flower gardens, with great views from the guest rooms. There is a detached meditation room and a Yoga Barn, which can also be used by groups. Guest comments include: 'Peaceful and wild – really enjoyed being here', 'Felt reborn – thank you', 'Idyllic! I'll be back soon', 'A calm and refreshing home', 'Peaceful!'. The programme here is a small one but events may include Tibetan Buddhism retreats in the lineage of the Nyiingma Tradition, yoga retreats and *A Boswednack Yoga Week* with two to three sessions daily, led by experienced and qualified teachers. The latter week-long retreat is restricted to 14 people.

Open: Easter to October. Receives everyone. No pets.

Rooms: 1 single, 4 doubles, self-catering cottage. All rooms in house have tea-making facilities.

Facilities: Garden, library, guest lounge, Yoga Barn, meditation room. No smoking. (Mobiles do not work here.)

Spiritual Help: Meditation.

Guests Admitted to: Unrestricted access.

Meals: Vegetarian only. Vegan by request. Full board or B&B.

Special Activities: Programme of courses and retreats – send for leaflets. Guided nature walks also available.

Situation: Quiet, in countryside, with sea views.

Maximum Stay: None.

Bookings: Letter, telephone 6–10p.m.

Charges: B&B from £19 per person per night, cottage (sleeping four people) from £215 per week. Rates do vary according to season, summer being high season. Special group rates.

Access: Train: Penzance. Bus: No. 8. Car route: B3306, 1 mile west of Zennor, 6 miles from St Ives and Penzance.

DEVON

Ashburton

The Ashburton Centre
79 East Street   Tel: 01364 652784
Ashburton   Fax: 01364 653825
Devon TQ13 7AL   E-mail: stella@ashburtoncentre.freeserve.co.uk
                               Website: www.ashburtoncentre.co.uk
Inter-denominational
The Ashburton Centre for Holistic Education and Training was founded in 1994 to provide personal development, spiritual, healing, environmental and related residential courses within a supportive community. Guests join the community during their stay so that a feeling of belonging and family is generated. The programme on offer covers a wide variety of modern approaches to spirituality – for example, meditation, qi gong, shiatsu as a spiritual practice, choice and transformation seminars, healing, yoga, and voice workshops. The centre is in the town, but there are many good country and woodland walks nearby. **The Centre is also the home of The Carers Trust, offering a range of bursary-funded retreat breaks for carers in the community and for professional carers such as nurses and social workers.**

Open: All year. Receives men, women, groups
Rooms: 4 singles, 3 twin doubles, 2 triples. No smoking. No outside shoes worn in the house.
Facilities: Garden, guest lounge, TV, payphone.
Spiritual Help: Meditation, yoga, body exercises, tai chi.
Guests Admitted to: Unrestricted access.
Meals: Everyone eats together. Vegetarian whole food.
Special Activities: Planned programme – send for brochure. Courses and holidays in France and Spain are offered, and self-catering retreats are possible.
Situation: In a small town adjoining Dartmoor National Park.
Maximum Stay: By arrangement.
Bookings: Letter, fax, telephone 9a.m.–6p.m.
Charges: £25 B&B, weekend retreats about £115, weekend courses £155, holidays only from £345.
Access: Train: Newton Abbot Station is 10 minutes away. The Centre will collect you. Car route with easy access from M5.

Ashprington

The Barn Rural Retreat Centre
Lower Sharpham Barton
Ashprington
Totnes
Devon TQ9 7DX

Tel: 01803 732661
Fax: 01803 732718
e-mail: barn@sharphamcollege.org
Website: www.sharpham-trust.org/barn.htm

Buddhist tradition – Non-denominational
The underlying purpose of The Barn, which has been running for some thirteen years, is to create a working retreat centre – a place where you come not only on temporary retreat from the world at large, but also to work on the land. The atmosphere is contemplative and there is much silence. During your stay here, you will be expected to be fully involved in the daily schedule of activities and to take your turn preparing vegetarian meals for everyone. The daily schedule includes four to five hours' work on the land and regular periods of group silent meditation. No previous experience of farm work is necessary. One evening a week is devoted to discussing personal matters as well as broader issues that relate to the community's life together. You are encouraged to pursue those activities – such as Buddhist study classes, yoga mornings and listening to cassettes of Dharma talks – that support a contemplative way of life. The Barn Community is based on the Buddhist meditation tradition but is non-denominational and does not require people to follow any prescribed methods of practice. Regular talks at Sharpham College nearby and instruction from Buddhist teachers, as well as yoga sessions, are sometimes on offer. **Highly Recommended.**

Open: All year. Receives men and women – you do not have to be a Buddhist, but some established background in meditation helps.
Rooms: 7 singles, 1 double.
Facilities: Garden, library, payphone, woodworking equipment, woodland huts for more advanced meditation practitioners who want a three-day silent meditation retreat.
Spiritual Help: Personal talks when a teacher is available, group sharing, spiritual direction, meditation, personal retreat direction if required.
Guests Admitted to: Unrestricted access to all areas, including shrine room and work of the community, which consists of gardening, woodland maintenance, household care and upkeep, cooking, preserving, looking after poultry and other smallholding chores.
Meals: Everyone eats together. Meals are vegetarian. Special diets possible but vegetarian food only.
Special Activities: Daily schedule followed 6 days a week.
Situation: Very quiet, in the countryside. Beautiful location on the Sharpham Estate, on a hillside overlooking the River Dart – no roads visible. Fantastic views.
Maximum Stay: 2 week *minimum* if possible, 6 months maximum.
Bookings: By letter, e-mail, online, telephone. You will be asked for some personal details about your experience of retreats and meditation.
Charges: £120 week. Low income week £76. Bursary possible after first week of stay.
Access: By car is best, but enquire if you want to walk from the nearest place served by public transport.

**Sharpham College for Buddhist Studies
   and Contemporary Inquiry**
Ashprington
Totnes
Devon TQ9 7UT

Tel: 01803 732542
Fax: 01803 732037
e-mail: college@sharpham-trust.org
e-mail: colinmoore@dial.pipex.com

Buddhist

Sharpham College for Buddhist Studies and Contemporary Enquiry occupies a beautiful English Palladian house with views stretching down to the River Dart. It is here that the Sharpham Trust strives to create a new way of education, aiming to achieve a balance between the practical and the spiritual. Although the approach is Buddhist, the College

> **Fame is nothing but an empty name.**
> CHARLES CHURCHILL

does not adhere to any particular school. The Buddhist studies include Theravada, Indo-Tibetan Mahayana, Zen and Chinese Buddhism, plus Buddhist history, philosophy, and psychology, including courses such as *The Psychology of Awakening*. 'Contemporary Enquiry' means studies on right livelihood, ecology and the environment, Western philosophy and psychology, the new sciences, and arts and culture. The teachers come from a broad spectrum of backgrounds and have long-standing commitments to Buddhism. The college cannot accommodate short-term guests because the programme course students occupy all the living accommodation. However, there is also a programme of day educational events. They are very interesting and have excellent teachers and speakers. Participants in the year and three-month programmes need to be familiar with one of the Buddhist traditions and have an established meditation practice. If you are thinking of an in-depth study of Buddhism, this is a very good place to go.

Open: September to July for students. Closed January and August.
Receives: men, women.
Rooms: 10 singles. Silence until 10a.m.
Facilities: Garden, library, student lounge, TV, payphone. No smoking.
Spiritual Help: Personal talks, meditation, group sharing, directed study, personal retreat direction, yoga, chi gung.
Guests Admitted to: Shrine room, work of community.
Meals: Everyone eats together. Meals consist of vegetarian whole food.
Special Activities: Send for programme brochure and information on the college.
Situation: A busy and active place.
Maximum Stay: The programmes are 3-month and 1-year. Short-term guests are not received.
Bookings: Letter.
Charges: 1-year programme fee currently £5,500, 3-month course £2,200. See programme brochure for cost of other courses.
Access: Car route best.

Buckfastleigh

Southgate Retreat Centre
Buckfast Abbey
Buckfastleigh
Devon TQ11 OEE

Tel: 01364 645521
Fax: 01364 645520
e-mail: gusta@buckfast.org.uk
Website: www.buckfast.org.uk

Roman Catholic
Nearly a million people come to visit Buckfast Abbey every year – to walk through its grounds by the River Dart and to admire the work of these monks whose history here has been so remarkable. The monastery was founded in 1018. It experienced centuries of peace, followed by ruin when Henry VIII dissolved the monasteries and, finally, restoration in 1907, when the monks returned to rebuild their Abbey. The great church was finished in 1937, largely restored to its original form and filled with beautiful artefacts from the enamelled and bejewelled Stations of the Cross to the glorious marble mosaic floor of the nave. The Lady Chapel has one of the most impressive stained glass windows of Christ in Europe, designed and made by one of the monks. It is justly famous. Outside the silence of the monastic enclosure and the church, this is a top tourist attraction, with shops, walks and throngs of visitors – a very busy and perhaps too crowded a place in the summer. There is a restaurant and even a separate modern shop selling the products made by religious of other Benedictine Communities in Europe. Still, this is a place for seeking God, where the Rule of St Benedict remains in force, so you will find hospitality. There is a constant flow of retreat guests staying in this very popular place. You must book well in advance if you want to come on retreat here.

> " One of the most important gifts of a retreat is to help make us aware that the life we are living may not be entirely our own, or that it is not as authentic as we would like it to be or that we are not getting as much out of our lives as we feel we should be. Such discoveries are never easy. "
> LESLIE KENTON

Open: All year except early January. Receives men, women, groups.
Rooms: Singles, doubles.
Facilities: Church, large garden, guest lounge, library, payphone, direct dialing, gift shop, book shop, monastic products centre, restaurant.
Spiritual Help: Personal talks.
Guests Admitted to: Church.
Meals: Taken in guest house. Traditional food. Vegetarian and special diets.
Special Activities: Some organised retreats – ask for details.
Situation: Beautiful location, but many tourists around during the day.
Maximum Stay: By arrangement.
Bookings: Letter to Guest Master.
Charges: Please enquire.
Access: Train: Newton Abbot Station 11 miles away. Bus: Devon General No. 188 from Newton Abbot. Coach: National Express, Exeter–Plymouth. Car: via A38.

Combe Martin

The Wild Pear Centre
King Street
Combe Martin
Devon EX34 OAG   Tel: 020 8341 7226 / 01271 883 086
                                                    Fax: 020 8341 7226

Mind Body Spirit
The Wild Pear Centre is situated in the north Devon seaside village of Combe Martin, a gateway to Exmoor National Park. While no garden or grounds exist at the Centre, you can treat the whole area as a wild garden on your doorstep. The Centre is available for both residential and non-residential use and hosts different workshops, including yoga, meditation, bodywork, voice work, movement and dance. It also runs personal growth courses.

Open: All year for bookings. Receives everyone – individuals and groups.
Rooms: Accommodation for about 25 in rooms and dormitories.
Facilities: Guest hall, meeting room, payphone.
Spiritual Help: None.
Guests Admitted to: Unrestricted access.
Meals: Everyone eats together. Whole food/vegetarian food. Special diets. Self-catering facilities, full board, B&B.
Special Activities: None.
Situation: Quiet, in countryside.
Maximum Stay: Short stays only.
Bookings: Letter, fax, telephone.
Charges: £15 per day self-catering, £30 per person per day for full board.
Access: Ask for travel information – which is excellent.

Dunsford

The Sheldon Centre
Society of Mary and Martha
Sheldon
Dunsford   Tel/Fax: 01647 252752
Exeter EX6 7LE   e-mail: smm@sheldon.uk.com
                                                Website: www.sheldon.uk.com

Ecumenical Christian
This fifteenth-century farmhouse and buildings were converted some years ago to provide modern facilities for retreats, quiet days, day conferences, celebrations and quality events drawn from a broad base of Christian traditions. A resident community of laymen and women runs the Centre. Retreats on offer may be individually guided or on Celtic spirituality, some of the saints (with a monk from Buckfast Abbey or a sister from the Community of St Francis as leader), Myer Briggs basics or beginners massage. There are also reading weeks, and quiet weeks. There has been some misunderstanding about arrangements in the past, particularly regarding meals and self-catering, so here is what the community themselves say in their brochure: '[There are] opportunities to come to Sheldon for quiet space, whether you need to read, relax, unwind, recuperate or simply have some time out in beautiful surroundings with good company. We will feed you well and make you welcome, but give you plenty of space to do your

own things.' According to the administrator, if you come on a private retreat not in the programme, it is self-catering. If you come on a programmed retreat, you get meals. Major conversion work has begun on a barn and building which will provide more facilities when opened. This development has been named the Courtyard.

Open: February–December. Receives everyone.
Rooms: 6 singles, 14 doubles. New facilities are being constructed, so check out what is available at the time of your visit.
Facilities: Garden, library, guest lounge, TV, payphone.
Spiritual Help: None.
Guests Admitted to: Chapel.
Meals: Traditional food. Vegetarian and special diets.
Special Activities: Planned programme – send for brochure.
Situation: Usually quiet, beautiful views, 18 acres of fields and woods.
Maximum Stay: 7 nights.
Bookings: Letter, fax, telephone.
Charges: £23 per night accommodation, £11 per day food.
Access: Train station within 10 miles. Bus service poor. Car best. Ask for details.

Honiton

Heartridge Buddhist Monastery
Devon Vihara
Upottery
Honiton　　　　　　　　　　　　　　　Tel: 01404 891258
Devon EX14 9QE　　　　　　　　　　Fax: 01404 890023

A Buddhist monastery with occasional meditation days and a few retreats for lay visitors. It is in a lovely spot.

St. Rita's Centre　　　　　　　　　
Ottery Moor Land
Honiton　　　　　　　　　　　　　　　Tel: 01404 42601
Devon EX14 8AP　　　　　　　　　　Fax: 01404 42635
　　　　　　　　　　　　　　　　　　e-mail: StRitas98@aol.com

Roman Catholic
The Friars, Augustinian Recollects, have done a complete refurbishment and upgrade job at this Centre, which is in a beautiful setting in East Devon. There is now a new conference room, day course rooms and chapel. As if all that was not enough, they have made all the bedrooms as comfortable as possible and all ensuite. You can join the community in Divine Office and there is a daily Mass. Group retreats, youth retreats and personal retreats for the individual are available. This is a place to get away from the daily routines of life, wind down and be at peace with God. **Highly Recommended.**

Open: Open most of year. Receives everyone.
Rooms: 2 single, 11 twin, 2 family rooms. All rooms ensuite.

Facilities: Conference room, chapel, garden, library, guest lounge, book shop.
Spiritual Help: Guided retreats, spiritual counselling.
Guests Admitted to: Chapel. Invitation to take part in Divine Office.
Meals: It all depends on the event or retreat and what suits you. For example, those who come on a private retreat may want to take meals alone; if so, ready-cooked meals can be provided. Meals can be taken with others or not as the mood suits – a very flexible arrangement. Traditional food. Vegetarian and special diets.
Special Activities: Group and youth retreats, individual or guided retreats for weekend or a single day.
Situation: Quiet.
Maximum Stay: By arrangement.
Bookings: Letter, fax, e-mail, telephone.
Charges: By suggested donation.
Access: Ask for directions when you book.

Kingsbridge

Shepherd's House
East Prawle
Kingsbridge
Devon TQ7 2BY   Tel: 01548 511247

Roman Catholic – The Quiet Garden Trust
This is a barn sleeping two people in self-catering accommodation, suitable for those who are looking for quiet time and retreat in the Benedictine and Ignatian traditions. It is a simple place with a little private patio. There is a daily Mass and Divine Office in a nearby small chapel. All are welcome at Shepherd's House, which is a place of prayer and peace.

Lynton

Lee Abbey Fellowship
Lynton
Devon EX35 6JJ   Tel: 01598 752621
                                                          Fax: 01598 752619
                                          e-mail: relax@leeabbey.org.uk
                                          Website: www.leeabbey.org.uk
Inter-denominational
Recently voted one of the top ten spiritual places in England by BBC listeners, Lee Abbey is a very large country estate in the Exmoor National Park. Originally Anglican, it is today ecumenical, inter-denominational and international, sharing Christ through relationships and existing to glorify God. In addition to planned retreats, there are Breakaway weeks or weekends for those wishing to benefit from the accommodation and facilities without joining in an organised activity. The programme of events is quite extensive over the year with a wide range of Christianity-based subjects and themes. A happy and fruitful place of God. **Highly Recommended.**

Open: All year except some weeks for events – see programme. Receives everyone.

Rooms: Some 20 singles and 15 doubles (some ensuite), plus other multi-
ples, adding up to a total capacity of 135. For retreats all rooms are treated
as single. Mobile phones do not work here.

Facilities: Disabled, conferences, library, guest lounges, TV, chapel, shop,
laundry, playroom for children, tennis courts, sports hall, mini-golf,
private beach, 280-acre estate for walking, payphone.

Spiritual Help: None.

Guests Admitted to: House and grounds, chapel.

Meals: Everyone eats together. Traditional food. Vegetarian and special diets.

Special Activities: A programme of retreats and events including bible study
and group retreats, but individuals are welcome on Breakaway retreats at
other times – send for details.

Situation: Quiet. The house is set in a 260-acre coastal estate in the Exmoor
National Park.

Maximum Stay: 2 weeks.

Bookings: Letter, fax, telephone.

Charges: See programme, but range is about £90 full board for a weekend
retreat, £140–£178 for a 1-week programmed retreat.

Access: By car is best.

Monastery of Poor Clares
Lynton
Devon EX35 6BX

Tel: 01598 753373
Fax: 01598 753878

Roman Catholic

Those who wish to share the quiet, prayer and worship of the Franciscan way
of life will find a warm welcome from the sisters, whose convent in this small
seaside resort is near many beauty spots on the edge of Exmoor. It is an ideal
and simple place for a private retreat or for those who need a very peaceful
and modest base. There are lovely walks by the sea. Guests stay in self-catering facilities in their own accommodation, which includes small kitchens. The
doubles are really two self-contained small flats, one with dining room and
bathroom, and one with shower. Female religious who come as guests may
eat with this enclosed community of women in their refectory, and two single
rooms are set aside for such guests inside the private enclosure. Such guests
may use the monastic library and are free to come and go as they please.
**There is also one single room for a woman guest inside the community's
quarters. If you feel you may have a calling to this kind of spiritual life
with God, discuss it with the sisters and perhaps come and share a little
in their life.** All guests are welcome to join the community for Mass and the
Divine Office. Some sisters are available to meet guests who wish to see them
for individual spiritual guidance in the form of a personal talk or to be joined
in accompaniment in prayer, but the sisters do not give spiritual direction as
such. The Monastery of Poor Clares is a traditional monastic house with all
the rich spiritual inheritance and daily life of prayer that this implies. It is a
place to put aside your expectations about personal comfort and material
things – for a while at least – and get down to some serious time with God.
Highly Recommended.

Open: Most of year except the Christmas period and Holy Week. Receives men, women, non-retreatants, religious on retreat.

Rooms: 2 doubles – two separate guests flats with twin beds and self-catering facilities. No smoking.

Facilities: Nearby beaches and moor for walking, TV.

Spiritual Help: Personal talks by arrangement.

Guests Admitted to: Church, choir.

Meals: Self-catering. Meals served for visiting religious sisters in the refectory.

Special Activities: None.

Situation: A delightful area in which to retreat from the world at large. On the edge of Exmoor National Park in very beautiful countryside by the sea.

Maximum Stay: 2 weeks.

Bookings: Letter, telephone 9–10a.m. and 4–5.30p.m.

Charges: No fixed charge but a minimum donation of £5 per person just covers costs. With most retreat houses charging around £25–£30 per day, we feel most guests will want to dig deeper in their pockets than that and give at least £20.

Access: Train and buses to Barnstaple, about 18 miles away. National Express coach. Car via A39.

Newton Abbot

Gaia House
West Ogwell
Newton Abbot
Devon TQ12 6DY

Tel: 01626 333613
Fax: 01626 352650
e-mail: gaiahouse@gn.apc.org
Website: www.ga.apc.org/gaiahouse

Buddhist

Gaia House was founded in 1984 to provide a setting for the teaching and practice of ethics, meditation and wisdom learning. The Centre, which is new and roomy, is set in quiet countryside and offers a full programme with facilities for individual practice, meditation retreats and personal retreats drawn from the Theravada and Mahayana traditions of Buddhism. Retreats cover such topics as *Breathing like a Buddha, Freedom of the Heart, Serenity, Wisdom, Compassion* and *Making Friends with Life*. The environment here is a silent one and there is opportunity to enjoy solitude. Work retreats are also available. **Highly Recommended.**

Open: All year. Receives men, women, young people. Families on family retreats once a year. Groups and non-retreatants only on a 1-day retreat basis.

Rooms: Space for 20–30 people but no guarantee of a single room. Some doubles, dormitory, hermitage wing for long retreats.

Facilities: Meditation room, park, garden, library, guest lounge, payphone.

Spiritual Help: Meditation, personal talks, interviews with teacher of retreat.

Guests Admitted to: Unrestricted access.

Meals: Everyone eats together in the house or in the garden – or wherever it happens. Vegetarian whole food, and very good. Medical diets only catered for.

Special Activities: Group and personal retreats offered. Send for detailed annual brochure.

Situation: Very quiet, in the countryside. Gaia is a silent house.

Maximum Stay: No limit, depending on meditation experience.
Bookings: Letter.
Charges: About £12–£20 per day.
Access: By car is best.

Sidmouth

The Old Kennels
Boswell Farm
Sidford
Near Sidmouth
Devon EX10 0PP

Tel: 01395 514162
e-mail: dillion@boswell-farm.co.uk
Website: www.oldkennels-boswell.co.uk

Non-religious
Just 16 miles from Exeter, The Old Kennels is a group of buildings that are available for a variety of retreats and workshops. The facility includes two excellent studios with a professionally sprung floor for dance, yoga and other floor-based activities. There are seven very comfortably furnished cottages with modern kitchens, which together can accomodate 36 people. Tennis courts, spring water, trout pond, and abundant wildlife all about you, make this a cosy, attractive and up-to-date place to use for a group retreat or course. Send for the excellent brochure and for a list of current rates.

Whitestone

The Beacon Centre
Cutteridge Farm
Whitestone
Exeter EX4 2HE

Tel/Fax: 01392 811203
e-mail: ceri@beacon-centre.com
Website: www.beacon-centre.com

Mind Body Spirit
Personal and planetary healing and transformation are the aims of the Centre. A variety of workshops, training courses, retreats and therapies are on offer. The Centre, which has been running for many years, is part of a larger farm and there are a number of buildings, including several private apartments. The heart is a courtyard around which are the farmhouse, the Centre, and the residences. Programmes on offer may include such courses as *Focusing and Experiential Listening, Gestalt Basics, Mindfulness Meditation for Health Care Workers, The Hakomi Method of Psychotherapy, Core Therapy Energetics* and *Living Art Workshop*. The rooms are comfortable and many have ensuite facilities. On the other hand, if you want to try a real hermit's existence, you can stay in the Retreat Hermitage down in the fields, where there are no modern facilities – including no water. The resident directors are very welcoming and helpful, and one is a working therapist. Group and private retreatants will find a supportive space for spiritual growth.

Open: All year. Receives everyone.
Rooms: 3 singles, 7 doubles, dormitory, camping site, hermitage. The hermitage is away from the other facilities for a back-to-nature retreat – there is no water and no indoor toilet facilities.

Facilities: Conferences, camping, garden, library, guest lounge, TV, house phone. There is a meditation sanctuary in the garden which is a quiet place for meditation and prayer.

Spiritual Help: Personal talks, group sharing, meditation, counselling, healing.

Guests Admitted to: Unrestricted access to all areas except private residential areas.

Meals: Wholefood. Taken in guest house. There is also a self-catering kitchen. Vegetarians and vegans catered for.

Special Activities: Daily schedule followed 6 days a week. Planned events each year.

Situation: Quiet, in the countryside. Traffic on the busy major road nearby can be heard but it is not too intrusive.

Maximum Stay: Depending on course. No upper limit.

Bookings: Letter, e-mail, telephone.

Charges: See programme.

Access: By car is best – 3 miles from Exeter. Train (Exeter St Davids) and bus are possible. Ask for detailed travel directions when booking.

Yelverton

Grimstone Manor
Jordan Lane
Yelverton
Devon PL20 7QY

Tel: 01822 854358
e-mail: enquiries@grimstonemanor.co.uk
Website: www.grimstonemanor.co.uk

Mind Body Spirit – Personal development

Programmes run throughout the year, so space for personal and private retreats is not on offer here. You must join a specific group programme run either by the resident community or visiting groups. Workshops have included *Healing Tao Retreat, Vortex Healing, Gestalt Workshop* and *Yoga – Sharing the Quest*. See the website for the current programme. A brochure is available with information on travelling to the centre, what to bring and so on. Grimstone has been running successfully for many years now, and its courses are popular and well-established. People come and join the regular community as volunteer workers, helping out with courses and celebrations.

Open: All year except January. Open to men, women, families, groups – but it depends on which course you want to attend. No pets.

Rooms: Accommodation for up to 40 people – 1 single, 4 doubles, 8 dormitories. Bring towel, soap, slippers for the house. Brochure gives useful details about your stay.

Facilities: Disabled, conferences, guest lounge, garden of some 30 acres with pond, swimming pool, jacuzzi, sauna, guest phone (01822 854824), book shop, walking on moor.

Spiritual Help: Meditation.

Guests Admitted to: Group rooms.

Meals: Everyone eats together in the dining room, doing their own washing up. Vegetarian food.

Special Activities: Planned programme – see website.

Situation: Very quiet, in the countryside.

Maximum Stay: As long as the group is staying.
Bookings: By telephone is best for the Manor's own events.
Charges: About £35–£45 per night full board.
Access: Train to Plymouth. Bus to Horrabridge. Car route shown on map in brochure.

DORSET

Bournemouth

**Hamilton Hall
1 Carysfort Road
Boscombe
Bournemouth
Dorset BH1 4EJ**

Tel: 01202 399227
e-mail: Hamilton.hall@virgin.net
Website: www.en-light.net/hamiltonhall

This is a big comfortable old place dedicated to people of all ages who just want to relax and do whatever takes their fancy in a quiet place in the centre of town. It is a broad-minded place where you can do something or nothing. There is plenty of privacy if you want it. The *Regeneration by Inaction Personal Retreat*, on which you make up what you do or don't do as you go along, sounds like a good get-away weekend to have here. Check the website, telephone and discuss what kind of break you are hoping to have.

**St Boniface Retreat House and Prayer Centre
Doveshill Crescent
Ensbury Park
Bournemouth
Dorset BH10 5BS**

Tel: 01202 513555
Fax: 01202 513965

Christian – Ecumenical
The Centre offers individually guided retreats, with weekend retreats of prayer and spiritual direction available on request. There is acommodation for about 20 guests. Meals can be provided.

Bridport

**Othona Community House
Coast Road
Burton Bradstock
Bridport
Dorset DT6 4RN**

Tel: 01308 897130
Fax: 01308 898205
e-mail: mail@othona-bb.org.uk
Website: www.othona-bb.org.uk

Ecumenical – Christian community living
The community live in a large stone house on an unspoiled stretch of heritage coast. They have a chapel and a separate arts and crafts building. The grounds are designated a site of special nature conservation interest and the beach is just a few minutes walk away. There is that good mixture here of a sense of

community combined with stillness and peace. Othona explicitly extends a welcome to all, regardless of background, creed, status or sexual orientation. Othona is about people and has an aproach to spirituality that understands the great and intimate mystery we call God as being surely beyond dogma. This is an open Christian community in which learning comes from people of all faiths and none. There is no pressure to conform in religious terms. All guests are considered to be in community with the regular members for as long as they stay. There is an extensive range of retreats and courses on offer. Some examples are *Introduction to the Enneagram, Simply Community, Encountering Creation, Changing Images of God, A New Vision of Christianity, Spirituality in the Workplace* and *Jewish Spirituality*. There is a summer programme aimed at families including activities for children. Othona has been offering a three-month internship, which involves living in the community, learning more about spirituality and gaining in personal awareness. There is another community in Essex (see the Essex section). **Highly Recommended.**

Open: Most of year. Receives everyone. Children welcome.
Rooms: 3 singles, 8 doubles, 4 dormitories. No TV. Radios/Tapes softly if at all. Mobile phones are discouraged.
Facilities: Disabled, 6-acre informal garden, library, guest lounge, payphone. Guests are expected to join in a a few daily chores such as washing up or preparing some vegetables.
Spiritual Help: Varies with the programme course. Chapel services of an informal nature.
Guests Admitted to: Unrestricted access, including to the work of the community.
Meals: Everyone eats together. Whole food, home-cooked, using local and home-grown produce where possible.Vegetarian. Special diets within reason
Special Activities: Planned programme including work projects, concerts, music-making and a studio for arts and crafts including spinning and weaving – send for brochure.
Situation: Quiet, near a village, set in an area of outstanding natural beauty overlooking the sea.
Maximum Stay: Usually 1 week.
Bookings: Letter, fax, e-mail, telephone.
Charges: Usually about £26 per person per night full board, £19 concessionary rate. Additional course fees which range from about £5–£45. Weekly rates also available.
Access: Car route best – but enquire as to train, taxi, bus service to Burton Bradstock.

Pilsdon Community
Pilsdon Manor
Bridport
Dorset DT2 9QS

Tel: 01308 868308
Fax: 01308 868161
e-mail: pilsdon@lineone.com
Website: www.lineone.net/~pilsdon

Christian
Started more than forty years ago, the community, based in this seventeenth-century house in Dorset, has welcomed thousands of visitors. There is also a

smallholding, on which help is always welcome. Daily prayer and meditation and the offering of hospitality are key spiritual practices here. There is no limit on the length of your stay.

Charmouth

Monkton Wyld Court
Charmouth,
Bridport
Dorset DT6 6DQ

Tel: 01297 560342
e-mail: monktonwyldcourt@btinternet.com
Website: www.monktonwyldcourt.com

Mind Body Spirit – Holistic education
Eleven acres of grounds surround this large Victorian rectory that is situated in a secluded valley on the Devon–Dorset border, providing a green, healthy space for people to find inner awareness. Monkton is a leading centre for holistic education run by a community with their children. It has welcomed many visitors and enjoyed good media coverage of its activities. The emphasis is on encouraging personal and spiritual growth, combined with a firm commitment to ecology, green issues and self-sufficiency – for example, on the farm the cows are hand-milked. There are walks to the sea, peace for meditation and yet the comforting buzz of a community with a family life. There are plenty of courses that reflect these approaches to the art of living, many of them exciting and challenging, and offering real potential for-self development and spiritual growth. Some examples include: *Sweatlodge*, *Trance Dance and Ceremony*, *Positive Comedy*, *Deepening Love and Sexual Union*, *Yoga and Meditation*, *Non-violent Communication*, *Affirming the Female Body*, *Celebrating Nature*, *Healing and Evolving Men's Sexuality* and *Women's Drumming*. Weekend retreats in peace with the community itself can be arranged and there is tai chi, devotional singing, a work camp, body-mind centring, stained-glass-making, drawing, circle and sacred dancing and chanting, shaman dancing, and qi gong as well. A broad and generous programme from which to chose a weekend or longer retreat or course.

Open: Most of the year. Occasional closures. Receives men, women, young people, families, groups, non-retreatants. Children welcome
Rooms: 3 doubles, 8 dormitories, barn, camping. A single by arrangement.
Facilities: Camping, garden, library, guest lounge, crafts shop, arts and crafts facilities, meditation room, massage and healing room, guest phone.
Spiritual Help: Through the courses and retreats on offer, meditation.
Guests Admitted to: Everywhere except community living areas, including work of the community.
Meals: Everyone eats together. Organic vegetarian wholefood. Special diets.
Special Activities: Planned programme of events – send for excellent brochure.
Situation: Very quiet, in the countryside.
Maximum Stay: Depending on course being attended or by arrangement.
Bookings: Letter, e-mail, telephone 10a.m.–1p.m. Monday to Friday.
Charges: £150–£300 per person, per workshop/course, which are 2–6 days.
Access: By train: station 3 miles away – take taxi. Car via A35.

East Holton

The Barn
Holton Lee
East Holton, Near Poole
Dorset BH16 6JN

Tel/Fax: 01202 631063
e-mail: holton@lds.co.uk
Website: www.lds.co.uk/holtonlee

Inter-denominational
Lying between Poole and Wareham, The Barn at Holton Lee is a centre for people with disabilities and for carers. Here can be found relaxation, respite, care, retreats, education activities and courses. There is full personal care by staff and personal care assistance when needed. Everything is purpose-built. The Barn provides residential accommodation for up to eight people. The Pavilion is a multi-purpose building providing space for a wide variety of workshops and courses, including pottery, painting and sculpture. Gateway Cottage offers separate residential accommodation with its own meeting room. Farm Cottage provides a separate quiet building with facilities for counselling, spiritual direction and massage, as well as two guest rooms. The programme on offer is small but interesting and may include such topics as *Enneagram and Spirituality, Living with Stress, Take Time to Grow* and *Feminine Creativity.* **Highly Recommended.**

Open: All year. Receives men, women, young people (if under 16 must be accompanied by a guardian), families, small groups, non-retreatants. Children welcome, guide dogs accepted.
Rooms: 9 singles, 6 doubles. Modern, comfortable and clean.
Facilities: Small conferences, garden, sometimes camping, park, guest lounge, TV, payphone, chapel.
Spiritual Help: Personal talks, meditation, directed study, spiritiual direction and personal retreat direction, reflexology, aromatherapy.
Guests Admitted to: Unrestricted access everywhere.
Meals: Everyone eats together. Self-catering also available. Traditional/ vegetarian food. Special diets.
Special Activities: Planned programme of events – send for brochure.
Situation: Quiet, in the countryside. 350 acres of beautiful land with paths. Bird hide overlooking a pond.
Maximum Stay: 2 weeks.
Bookings: Letter or telephone.
Charges: Various rates – ask for tariff list.
Access: Train, bus, car all possible.

Hilfield

Society of St Francis
The Friary
Hilfield, Dorchester
Dorset DT2 7BE

Tel: 01300 341345

Anglican
It is up to each guest to decide how best to use his or her time at the Friary, but all are welcome to join the community in chapel for prayer. Set in peaceful surroundings, this is a quiet place where you will find space for thinking

things through. Many guests have busy and active careers and find that the Friary is just the place they need for rest and reflection. Hospitality is offered to all, so the man at prayer next to you could equally well be a successful industrialist or a wayfarer who tramps the road. **Highly Recommended.**

Open: All year except August, from Tuesdays to Saturdays. Receives men, women, young people, groups.
Rooms: 11 singles, 1 double. Radios/tapes discouraged. No mobile phones in refectory or chapel, or where they could disturb silence and peacefulness.
Facilities: Disabled – ask what the arrangements are when booking. Chapel, oratory, choir, garden, library, book and craft shop, guest lounge, payphone. Bring a towel.
Spiritual Help: Personal talks, spiritual direction, personal retreat direction, meditation.
Guests Admitted to: Chapel, choir and work of the community.
Meals: Everyone eats together. Traditional food. Vegetarian and special diets with advance notice.
Special Activities: None.
Situation: Very quiet, in the countryside.
Maximum Stay: 5 nights.
Bookings: Letter.
Charges: By donation – £20 per person per 24 hours suggested.
Access: Train: Dorchester. Guests are met when possible. Car route easy.

Gillingham

The Osho Leela Centre – Foundation for Joyous Living
Thorngrove House
Common Mead Lane   Tel: 01747 821221
Gillingham   Fax: 01747 826386
Dorset SP8 4RE   e-mail: info@osholeela.co.uk
          Website: www.osholeela.co.uk

Mind Body Spirit
Osho Leela is a commune of people welcoming all spiritual seekers and visitors for group and celebration events. Disciples of Master Osho are welcome, but it is not necessary to be a follower of Osho to come here as a guest. The commune has a calendar of courses, which may include dance, an energy ecstasy weekend, a shaman gathering for women, a celebration of woman as goddess, a men's group, cranio-sacral balancing training, chakra training or a nature-art-meditation retreat. The Osho Mystic Rose Meditative Therapy Course is a three-week intensive in which laughing and crying are used to cleanse the heart, then follows a week of silent meditation. There is a four-year therapist training programme and a nine-month personal education course.

Open: All year. Receives everyone.
Rooms: 40 bed spaces divded into singles, doubles and shared rooms, camping site with spaces for caravans.
Facilities: Disabled, camping, caravan site, garden, park, library, guest lounge, TV, payphone, healing centre (aromatherapy massage).
Spiritual Help: Personal talks, group sharing, meditation, directed study, personal retreat direction, aromatherapy, Reiki, reflexology.

Guests Admitted to: Unrestricted access.
Meals: Everyone eats together. Vegetarian whole food. Special diets.
Special Activities: Planned programme – send for brochure calendar.
   Working weekends, evening classes, music festival, forestry programme to
   which guests can contribute time and work.
Situation: Quiet, in a joyful atmosphere, near a town.
Maximum Stay: No limit.
Bookings: Letter, fax, e-mail, telephone 10a.m.–6p.m.
Charges: Weekends £70–£195 all inclusive, weeks £70 all inclusive.
Access: Train and bus to Gillingham. Car: M3/A303 West

Poole

Green Pastures
Christian Centre of Pastoral Care and Healing
17 Burton Road
Branksome Park   Tel: 01202 764776
Poole   Fax: 01202 768144
Dorset BH13 6DT   e-mail: admin@green-pastures.org
                              Website: www.green-pastures.org
Christian – Inter-denominational
Professional counselling and a variety of healing therapies are on offer here as
well as single and double accommodation, mostly ensuite. There is full-board
catering, a programme of events, a chapel, a garden and swimming pool, and
the Centre is only a mile from the sea. This is a peaceful place just to be and
to find healing and renewal.

Wimborne

Gaunts House
Wimborne   Tel: 01202 841522
Dorset BH21 4JQ   e-mail: courses@rgf-gaunts.demon.co.uk
                         Website: www.rgf-gaunts.demon.co.uk
Non-denominational – Spiritual
Run by the Richard Glyn Foundation and part of the Gaunts estate, Gaunts
House is dedicated to growth within a life lived on a spiritual basis. It offers
space for and help with spiritual and personal development among a support-
ive community, all set in beautiful parkland. The facilities are wide-ranging,
from a sanctuary to healing rooms. There are many different programmes on
offer – for example in the past there has been an *Easter Yoga Retreat* (which
included inter-faith multicultural programmes), *Gospel Choir, Sanskrit
Mantra Chanting, Native American Traditions, Storytelling – the Art and
Craft, Women and the Sacred, A Celebration of Sound and Sound Healing,
Druid Traditions* and *Celtic Music*. The programme is always broad and
interesting – a brochure is available or see the website. Young people, aged
17 to 29, can come here for an experience of community for a minimum of
one month up to a maximum of six months. Older adults start as paying
guests initially but after a period of time may be able to join the community.
The community also has many friends who come to do volunteer work.
Gaunts House runs a regular *Community Experience Weekend* to give people
a taste of community life here.

Open: All year. Receives men, women, young people, families, groups. Children welcome. No pets.

Rooms: Can accommodate up to 160 people at one time. Singles, doubles, camping, dormitories.

Facilities: Conferences, camping, garden, library, guest lounge, TV, payphone.

Spiritual Help: Personal talks, group sharing, meditation, support and advice. Therapies available on request.

Guests Admitted to: Unrestricted access to all areas including sanctuary, work of the community.

Meals: Vegetarian – guests can share in the cooking. Food may be brought or purchased at the centre. Special diets.

Special Activities: Planned programme of events – send for brochure, issued twice yearly.

Situation: Very quiet, in the countryside.

Maximum Stay: Unlimited.

Bookings: Letter or telephone.

Charges: These vary so ask for rates. An example would be a private retreat for two days at about £80 or a week's stay for about £180.

Access: Train to Poole or bus to Wimborne, then taxi or telephone for a lift. Car.

SOMERSET

Cleveden

Community of the Sisters of the Church
St Gabriel's
27a Dial Hill Road
Cleveden
Somerset BS21 7HL   Tel/fax: 01275 872586

Anglican
A quiet house of prayer for anyone looking for time out from a busy life, direction in their lives or just a good break from routines. Silence is kept until late morning each day.

Open: All year.

Rooms: 4 singles.

Facilities: Garden, guest lounge, TV.

Spiritual Help: Personal talks, spiritual direction, personal retreat direction.

Guests Admitted to: Unrestricted access.

Meals: Taken in room. Vegetarian catered for.

Special Activities: None.

Situation: Quiet, overlooking Bristol channel.

Maximum Stay: 10 days.

Bookings: Letter.

Charges: £20 per night.

Access: Train: Yate, and then collected. Bus and car good – ask for details.

Compton Durville

Community of St Francis
Compton Durville   Tel: 01460 240473
South Petherton   Fax: 01460 242360
Somerset TA13 5ES   e-mail: comptondurvillecsf@franciscans.org.uk
                                        Website: www.franciscans.org.uk

Anglican

The pretty little hamlet of Compton Durville has the community house, church, and guest facilities on either side of the entrance street like welcoming portals. The hospitality here is cheerful and very friendly. The main house is handsome inside and out, the garden walks are remarkably peaceful and lovely, and the church is intimate and light with a nice liturgy. The oldest building on the site is a grade II listed seventeenth-century manor house with public access to a sitting room. A small quiet chapel can be entered through the rear of the house. The community library is good and guests are free to wander around the grounds, which include a wild garden area and an orchard. In the nearby modern building are the chapel, refectory, conference and other rooms. The community tries to upgrade and improve its guest accomodation with each passing year. They run a modest but good retreat programme which is usually led by members of the community. Options for your retreat include silence and solitude in a single-person hermitage where you can self-cater, or alternatively a working stay, as periods of manual work may be helpful on, for example, a silent contemplative retreat.

Open: All year from Monday afternoon to after lunch on Sundays. Sometimes closed for short periods only. Receives everyone. Children welcome by prior arrangement.

Rooms: 14 singles, 2 twin doubles, dormitories, self-catering cottage for 6, hermitage.

Facilities: Conferences, large garden, library, guest lounge, TV, guest phone (01460 240473).

Spiritual Help: Personal talks by arrangement, chapel services, spiritual direction, personal retreat direction.

Guests Admitted to: Unrestricted access except to community private areas. Work of community sometimes.

Meals: Everyone eats main meals together. Simple food. Vegetarian and special diets by prior arrangement. Self-catering available.

Special Activities: Quiet days, individually guided retreats – send for information.

Situation: Very quiet, in a small village.

Maximum Stay: Normally 6 days unless on an 8-day Ignatian retreat or in self-catering accomodation.

Bookings: Letter, fax, e-mail, telephone 9.30–11.45a.m., 2–5p.m., 7.15–8.15p.m.

Charges: £20 per day, hermitage £12 per day, day visitors £5 per person plus meals, cottage £175–£225 per week according to season.

Access: Train or by bus to Taunton or Yeovil, where you can make arrangements to be picked up. Car route easy – good directions brochure available.

Glastonbury

Abbey House
Chilkwell Street
Glastonbury   Tel: 01458 831112
Somerset BA6 8BT   Fax: 01458 831893
                                    e-mail: abbeyhouse@easinet.co.uk
Anglican
This busy, lay-run, retreat house is owned by the Diocese of Bath and Wells, and it welcomes all who are on a spiritual journey. It caters mainly for groups and tries to fit in individuals when and where possible. Situated at the east end of the Abbey ruins, the house has stunning views into Abbey Park and the surrounding countryside. Food is prepared using as far as possible local ingredients and suppliers. Home-grown vegetables are also used whenever possible. A peaceful beautiful place.

Open: All year. Receives men, women, groups.
Rooms: 18 singles, 9 twin-bedded rooms.
Facilities: Conferences, garden, park, library, guest lounge, payphone.
Spiritual Help: None.
Guests Admitted to: Unrestricted access.
Meals: Traditional simple food – local produce where possible.Vegetarian, vegan, and special diets by prior arrangement.
Special Activities: Planned programme – see brochure.
Situation: In town but quiet, within grounds of Abbey.
Maximum Stay: 10 days.
Bookings: Letter, fax, e-mail, telephone daytime hours.
Charges: £70 per person per weekend, £120 Monday to Friday per person full board.
Access: Train:Castle Cary (15 miles). Bus: Badgerline No. 376 travels hourly at 5 minutes to the hour from Bristol coach station; National Express coach runs daily from London Victoria.

Berachah Colour Healing Centre
Berachah House
Well House Lane   Tel: 01458 834214
Glastonbury   Fax: 01458 835417
Somerset BA6 8BJ   e-mail: Jan@facetsofavalon.com
                                       Website: www.facetsofavalon.com
Mind Body Spirit
Just ten minutes walk from Glastonbury High Street, this house, now a colour healing centre, was built on the site of the first known ashram in Britain and the former location of one of the most influential occultists of recent times, Violet Firth. Today, Berachah offers a programme of astrology, aura soma readings, life path readings, massage and colour healing.

Open: All year. Receives everyone.
Rooms: 1 single, 3 doubles.
Facilities: Library, guest lounge, TV.
Spiritual Help: Massage, colour healing.
Guests Admitted to: Unrestricted access.

Meals: Guests eat together. Vegetarians catered for.
Special Activities: Planned programme.
Situation: Quiet.
Maximum Stay: By arrangement.
Bookings: Letter or tel/fax.
Charges: £25 per person per night. Therapies and readings separate rates –
see brochure.
Access: Rail, bus: Glastonbury. Car.

Chalice Well
Chilkwell Street   Tel: 01458 831154
Glastonbury   Fax: 01458 835528
Somerset BA6 8DD   e-mail: info@chalicewell.org.uk
                               Website: www.chalicewell.org.uk

Ecumenical – Inter-denominational
As you enter the Chalice Well Gardens, you leave behind the hustle and
bustle of the busy world and all its distractions. Here, under entwining
branches, you enter a shrine that is timeless and sacred. In the gardens is a
well or perhaps a spring (who knows? – it is so ancient) the waters of which
are said by many to be very healing. Certainly it is pure water with a high iron
content tested for drinking on a regular basis. The water has been taken by
visitors at least since the Middle Ages. You may take a picnic to have in the
Meadows. At Little St Michaels, the retreat house for Companions of the
Well, there six rooms (available for individuals or groups), each named after
a tree: The Holy Thorn, Yew, Oak, Willow, Rowan, and Elder. You can
become a Companion and you will probably want to after your initial visit to
this lovely and most unusual sanctuary of peace.

House of Prayer
2 Parkfields
High Street
Butleigh, Glastonbury
Somerset BA6 8SZ   Tel: 01458 851561
                         e-mail: Elizabethrees_ocv@hotmail.com

Christian
A small House of Prayer in a village south of Glastonbury where you can find
spiritual direction, counselling and individually guided retreats.

Retreat House
33 Hillhead
Glastonbury
Somerset BA6 8AW   Tel: 01458 830434
                          e-mail: drsuejennings@hotmail.com

Christian
A small retreat house where creative group work, Ignatian spiritual guidance,
and quiet days are on offer. Accommodation consists of two singles. Contact
Dr Sue Jennings on the above number.

> There is grief that is useful
> and grief that is destructive.
> AMMA SYNCLETICA, DESERT MOTHER

Shekinashram
Dod Lane, Glastonbury
Somerset BA6 8BZ

Tel: 01458 832300
e-mail: info@shekinashram
Website: www.shekinashram.org

Eco-spiritual – Non-dualistic
Shekinashram is a newly formed community and dedicated sacred space, situated at the base of Chalice Hill, on a pilgrimage route to Glastonbury Tor. There are currently five permanent residents at the ashram. Open all year round, the essential vision of the Shekinashram is to follow a way of life that is both conscious and selfless, and which deeply honours the Divine One in all its miraculous forms. The community lives according to a set of holistic principles and keeps the ashram free from unnecessary distractions. This way of life is intended to reflect freedom of being. Meals are organic vegan raw food, and meditation, yoga and the singing of devotional songs together are among the various regular activities. A group room is available for hire, and up to ten guests on residential workshops can be accommodated at the ashram. The programme is a developing one of events and workshops.

Open: All year. Receives men, women.
Rooms: 10 bed spaces. Shared ashram-style accommodation. No smoking or alcohol in house or garden.
Facilities: Group room for hire, sauna, office use, small shop, therapies, yurt.
Spiritual Help: Meditation, therapies, vortex healing, reiki, sharing, yoga, Eckhart Tolle practice, group and inner process.
Guests Admitted to: Everywhere except private community areas.
Meals: Exclusively vegan raw food.
Special Activities: Planned programme of events – see website.
Situation: Quiet. Nice garden with a yurt.
Maximum Stay: By arrangement.
Bookings: Letter, fax, e-mail, telephone.
Charges: B&B £15 multiple occupancy room, £25 single, £45 twin/double, £65 double ensuite. Full board also available. Daily buffet lunches £5.
Access: Train: Castle Carey, then taxi (20 minutes). Local bus from Bath or Bristol to Glastonbury. 5-minute walk from Glastonbury town centre.

Tordown Healing Centre
5 Ashwell Lane
Glastonbury
Somerset BA6 8BG

Tel: 01458 832287
Fax: 01458 831100
e-mail: torangel@aol.com
Website: www.Tordown.com

Mind Body Spirit
A quiet place for a B&B type retreat, with really good views from some of the bedrooms (the Centre is on the slopes of Gastonbury Tor). Two Reiki masters are in residence, so treatment is available. The facilities are very

comfortable, with a welcoming atmosphere in a family environment, and the whole place is designed around healing and health. This is a helpful place for those wishing some rest.

Open: All year. Receives everyone. Children welcome. Pets by prior arrangement.
Rooms: 2 singles, 2 doubles, 3 twins. No smoking anywhere.
Facilities: Garden, library, guest lounge, TV, payphone.
Spiritual Help: Personal talks, personal retreat direction.
Guests Admitted to: Unrestricted access.
Meals: Taken in guest house. Vegetarian food. Vegan, special diets by prior arrangement.
Special Activities: No planned programme. Activities include Reiki teaching, healing, and sessions concentrating on higher self-awareness which include multi-dimensional cellular healing.
Situation: Quiet.
Maximum Stay: 1 month.
Bookings: Letter, fax, e-mail, telephone.
Charges: From £22 B&B per person per day – maximum of £35 per person per day.
Access: Train: Castle Cary, then taxi. Bus: Glastonbury town hall. Car: off A361 to Frome.

Langport

St Gilda's Christian Centre
The Hill
Langport
Somerset TA10 9QF

Tel: 01458 250496
Fax: 01458 251293
e-mail: ccngildas@aol.com
Website: www.chemin-neuf.org

Roman Catholic – Ecumenical
This is a big white eighteenth-century house in the middle of Langport which has been called The Light on the Hill. There is a very good library, a fine but simple chapel with much light, and a five-acre garden. The Chemin Neuf Community, who run the Centre, are a Catholic community with an ecumenical vocation that started in France in 1973. It currently has over 900 members in eighteen countries. The brothers and sisters of the Community (who continue as members of their own churches – Catholic, Orthodox, Anglican, French Reformed, Lutheran, Evangelical and Pentecostal) have chosen to live together without giving up their own indentity and remain in communion with their own churches. The retreat programme, which includes quiet days, is not overly ambitious. It encompasses retreats for beginners, inner healing retreats, weekend retreats for couples and families, retreats for young adults and teenagers, six-day retreats for married couple (of which the goal is the strengthening of marriage bonds), individually guided silent Ignatian retreats and days of prayer. **Highly Recommended.**

Open: All year except over Christmas. Receives everyone. Children welcome.
Rooms: 4 singles, 19 doubles, 2 dormitories.
Facilities: Disabled, conferences, garden, park of 5 acres, library, guest lounge, TV.

Spiritual Help: Personal talks, group sharing, spiritual direction, personal retreat direction, meditation.
Guests Admitted to: Unrestricted access.
Meals: Everyone eats together. Traditional food. Vegetarian and special diets.
Special Activities: Planned programme of events – send for information.
Situation: Quiet, in a large village.
Maximum Stay: 1 week.
Bookings: Letter, fax, e-mail, telephone.
Charges: Price range, including meals, £180–£220 for 1 week. Different weekly rate for youths and children. 24-hour stay, including meals, about £30–£35, again with lower rates for youths and children.
Access: Train, bus and car all possible – ask for directions. The Centre is about a 1-mile walk from South Petherton and 2 miles by car from the A303.

Minehead

Croydon Hall
Felons Oak, Minehead
Somerset TA24 6QT   Tel: 01984 642200
Website: www.croydonhall.co.uk
Mind Body Spirit – Holistic healing
Croydon Hall offers workshops and holistic healing breaks in an environment which is meditative and peaceful. You can also join the resident group here for a community living experience, which costs about £95 a week all in. There is a two-day *Body and Being* course for around £195. Check out current offers on the website.

Porlock

Halsecombe Retreat Centre and Place for Healing
Parsons Hill
Porlock   Tel: 01643 862621
Somerset TA24 8QP   e-mail: halsecombe@aol.com
Website: www.interfaithministers.org.uk

Interfaith
Halsecombe is high up above Porlock, overlooking the bay and set in its own thirty-acre estate. Run as retreat centre for individuals and small groups, the house is manged by a small community of people connected to the Interfaith Seminary (see website above). They share in a vision of person-centred spirituality. There is an organic garden supplying much of the food served, which is vegetarian. In addition to a library, conservatory, therapy room, and meeting rooms, there is a large meditation room overlooking the sea. Rooms are comfortable and spacious. The community can provide qualified complementary therapists and conducts regular interfaith fellowship ceremonies. Therapies include Alexander Technique, aromatherapy, counselling, hypnotherapy, reflexology, Reiki, shiatsu, and nutrition and lifestyle advice.

Open: All year. Receives everyone.
Rooms: Sleeps 12 people in the house. 2 caravans situated near house also.
Facilities: Meditation room, therapy room, guest lounge, meeting room, conservatory, library, gardens.

Spiritual Help: Weekly programme of silent meditation, prayer, chanting, art and study. Therapies available.
Guests Admitted to: Everywhere.
Meals: Vegetarian, mainly local produce.
Special Activities: Weekly programme of meditation and prayer.
Situation: Very quiet, lovely spot.
Maximum Stay: By arrangement.
Bookings: Letter, e-mail, telephone.
Charges: There are a number of combinations available. For example, B&B £17.50, Lunch £5, weekly B&B rate £110, full board £180, day use of facilities £10, caravans £100–£135 per week.
Access: Train, coach and car all possible. Single track to house. Travel details in brochure.

Street

Creative Arts Retreat Movement
182 High Street
Street
Somerset BA16 ONH

Ecumenical
Painting, calligraphy, embroidery, creative writing, poetry, pottery, music and art are all creative retreats under the umbrella of this organisation. Each retreat has a chaplain and a tutor, who coordinate all the various elements. The spiritual is focused on during times of worship, and there can be a daily Eucharist, night prayer, meditation or a talk. The retreats are held at centres throughout Britain, many listed elsewhere in this guide. Sometimes retreats are on offer overseas in such attractive places as Bruges in Belgium. The Creative Arts Retreat Movement is a clever and timely idea that has much appeal. The programme brochure is an excellent starting point for those thinking about going on such a retreat. There are some forty tutors and forty chaplains now involved who give their services free, and the membership is almost 1,000. For those less financially well off, there is the possibility of a bursary to help cover costs. Officers of the organisation change from time to time; therefore there is not a telephone number and all enquiries should be by letter in the first instance. Chairman of the Movement, Preb Geoffrey Sunderland, says: 'Whatever inspires you to take a retreat, I hope you find it an imaginative and peaceful experience.'

Bath

Bainesbury House
Downside Abbey
Stratton on the Fosse
Bath
Somerset BA5 4RH

Tel: 01761 235161
Fax: 01761 235124

Roman Catholic – Ecumenical
This retreat guest house, owned by Downside Abbey, is open to all Christian individuals and groups and is self-catering.

Open: All year. Receives everyone. Children welcome.
Rooms: 1 single, dormitories. Check when booking on exact arrangements.
Facilities: Abbey church, garden, park, library by arrangement, guest lounge, payphone.
Spiritual Help: Groups usually arrange their own programme; however, members of the monastic community are usually available to Roman Catholics for sacramental needs.
Guests Admitted to: nearby Abbey church.
Meals: Self-catering.
Special Activities: No planned programme – groups arrange their own.
Situation: Very quiet, near the village, in the countryside, about 12 miles from Bath.
Maximum Stay: By arrangement.
Bookings: Letter, fax, telephone.
Charges: About £5 per person per night, about £4 students and unemployed.
Access: Train: Bath Spa. Bus: from Bath Spa to Stratton on the Fosse. Car: via A367.

Downside Abbey
Stratton on the Fosse
Bath
Somerset BA5 4RH   Tel: 01761 232295

Roman Catholic
This is the home of a famous boys' public school, with an abbey church of cathedral proportions. The community welcomes men who wish to share in monastic prayer and quiet or who may just want a peaceful private break. This is very much a hard-working place with a busy schedule, but the guest master is usually available for a personal talk and to help with spiritual guidance.

Open: All year except Christmas and mid-July to mid-August. Receives men only.
Rooms: 10 singles.
Facilities: Abbey church, garden, library (by permission), guest lounge, TV, guest phone.
Spiritual Help: Personal talks, directed study.
Guests Admitted to: Chapel. Guests are not to enter the school area.
Meals: Everyone eats together. Traditional food. Vegetarians catered for.
Special Activities: None.
Situation: Quiet, near the village, about 12 miles from Bath.
Maximum Stay: 1 week.
Bookings: Letter or telephone.
Charges: By donation.
Access: Train: Bath Spa. Bus: Bath Spa to Stratton on the Fosse. Car via A367.

Coursing Batch

Shambhala Health and Healing Retreat
Coursing Batch
Glastonbury
Somerset BA6 8BH

Tel: 01458 831797
e-mail: findyourself@shambhala.co.uk
Website: www.shambhala.co.uk

Mind Body Spirit
Relaxing and healing breaks, spiritual growth experiences, regeneration and development, and physical and emotional healing – these are the core aims behind your stay at this Mind Body Spirit centre. It is located on the ancient sacred site of Glastonbury Tor – indeed, there is a ley line straight down the middle of the separate hermitage in which Isis Livingstone, the leader of Shambala, sleeps. At Shambhala you can receive a massage, healing therapy or Reiki. There is a jacuzzi inside a small Oriental type building hidden away in the garden, and a wood-burning sauna. The therapies on offer concentrate on healing, stimulating, cleansing and dynamic balancing. They are charged extra and cost from about £40 up to £80. The Centre does not occupy a lot of ground, yet once you walk through the gate and cross the crystal star set in the stones, it seems to be set away from the world. You will find all sorts of people with widely differing spiritual beliefs staying here. They may be concerned with reincarnation, the lost civilisation of Atlantis or channelling guardian angels. The accomodation is comfortable. There is a high degree of informality in the house and activities during the day are not usually structured into a programme. Some people who have stayed here adore the place, others are not so keen – but Shambala has enjoyed very positive media coverage over the years.

> The rule of life for a perfect person is to be the image and likeness of God.
> CLEMENT OF ALEXANDRIA

Open: All year. Receives everyone.
Rooms: 5 rooms. No smoking, no alcohol.
Facilities: Sanctuary, sauna, jacuzzi, healing massage room, water garden, guest lounge, books, TV, payphone.
Spiritual Help: Spiritual healing, sanctuary for silence.
Guests Admitted to: Unrestricted access.
Meals: Everyone eats together. Vegetarian food.
Special Activities: Spiritual healing, Reiki – see brochures and if you have questions then telephone and ask.
Situation: On the side of Glastonbury Tor.
Maximum Stay: 5 days
Bookings: Letter, e-mail, telephone.
Charges: £36 per day per person includes breakfast, buffet, use of jacuzzi, sauna and meditation sanctuary. Therapies are extra, charges from about £40–£80.
Access: Train: Castle Cary. Coach: Bath/Bristol. Car: On A361 between Shepton Mallett and Glastonbury. Be sure to follow the directions for parking.

> Nothing on earth consumes a
> man more completely than
> the passion of resentment.
> FRIEDRICH NIETZSCHE

Queen Camel

Self-realisation Meditation Healing Centre
Laurel Lane
Queen Camel
Near Yeovil   Tel: 01935 850266
Somerset BA22 7NU   Fax: 01935 850234
      e-mail: info@selfrealizationcentres.org
      Website: www.selfrealizationcentres.org

Mind Body Spirit – Non-denominational
The Centre is a charitable trust run by a team of counsellors and healers living
and working together as a unit and using the guidance of yoga, meditation, and
healing self-development in their work and courses. The seventeenth-century
house has extensive grounds of some 3½ acres. There is plenty of space and facilities, including a therapy pool. The Centre is near the River Cam and open countryside, and the ancient spiritual centres of Glastonbury and Wells are within easy
reach. Meditation is a central feature here. There is meditation twice daily,
usually in the morning and evening, and all guests are welcome to join in – no
need for previous meditation experience. The Centre prides itself on the warmth
of its welcome and its atmosphere of harmony. Many people who come here for
their first experience of a retreat away from their ordinary life and looking for a
new approach to their spirituality have been pleased with the comfort of the
Centre and the thoughtfulness of the resident community. There are sister
centres in Australia, New Zealand and Canada. **Highly Recommended.**

Open: All year. Receives men, women, young people, groups, non-retreatants.
Rooms: 7 singles, 7 twins, 2 family rooms for 3–4 people, hermitage.
Facilities: Disabled, meditation room, conferences, garden, library, guest
    lounges, payphone.
Spiritual Help: Personal talks, meditation, directed study, spiritual direction,
    personal retreat direction.
Guests Admitted to: Unrestricted access.
Meals: Meals taken together. Whole food, vegetarian, organic when possible.
    Special diets, vegan. Self-catering sometimes available.
Special Activities: Planned programme – send for brochure. Regular medi-
    tation, aqua and hatha yoga, healing and counselling.
Situation: Very quiet, in the village. Within easy reach of Glastonbury, Wells,
    Bath, Bristol, Yeovil.
Maximum Stay: By arrangement.
Bookings: Letter, fax, e-mail, online, telephone 9.30a.m.–5.30p.m. best time.
Charges: £34.50 per day full board in shared room. Therapy courses charges
    are extra – see brochure.
Access: Collecting service from the nearest train stations. Car: via A303.

Taunton

Amitabha Buddhist Centre
St Audries House
West Quantoxhead
Taunton
Somerset TA4 4DS

Tel: 01984 633200
Fax: 01984 633807
e-mail: buddha@amitabha.net

Buddhist – New Kadampa tradition
Meditation retreats in beautiful Somerset sums this place up. The setting is lovely, the surrounding woods glorious in the autumn, and the programme includes various meditation courses including those for beginners. There are also courses on relationship building and introductions to Buddhist thought. The centre is home to a large community of ordained and lay Buddhist practitioners, families and others wanting this way of life.

Open: Most of year. Receives men, women.
Rooms: Both singles and doubles are available.
Facilities: Camping, garden, park, library, guest lounge, guest telephone.
Spiritual Help: Spiritual direction, meditation, directed study.
Guests Admitted to: Unrestricted access.
Meals: Everyone eats together. Vegetarian food. Special diets.
Special Activities: Programme of courses – brochure available.
Situation: Quiet, in countryside.
Maximum Stay: 1 month.
Bookings: Letter, fax, e-mail, telephone.
Charges: Single £24 per night, twin £20 per person per night, dormitory £15 per night. Prices include three meals.
Access: Train: Taunton. Bus: No. 28 from Taunton. Car: A39.

Yatton

Claverham Meeting House
Near Yatton
Somerset

Contact:
1 Verlands
Congresbury
Bristol BS49 5BL

Tel: 01934 834663

Quaker
An eighteenth-century Quaker meeting house with two adjoining cottages that can be used for retreats, simple holidays and residential workshops. The accomodation for twelve people is basic and self-catering. There is also the possibility of camping in the gardens.

> Women's participation in the process of rural development is essential.
> SATISH KUMAR

WILTSHIRE

Heddington

International Meditation Centre
Splatts House
Heddington
Calne
Wilts SN11 OPE

Tel: 01380 850238
Fax: 01380 850833
e-mail: mail@imc-uk.org
Website: www.imc-uk.org

Buddhist – Theravada
The International Meditation Centre, founded by the Sayagyi U Ba Khin Memorial Trust, provides for the instruction and practice of Theravada Buddhist Vipassana meditation, guided by teachers who have practised and taught meditation for fifty years. Ten-day residential courses are held each month. The meditation practice is based on the Eightfold Noble Path as taught by the Buddha, which divides into three parts: morality, concentration and wisdom. To practise morality the students abstain from killing, stealing, sexual misconduct, lying and intoxicants for the ten days. To attain a calm mind, mindfulness of the breath is practiced for five days. Insight (Vipassana) is practised for the second five days. The daily timetable for the retreats begins at 4.30a.m. and runs through to 9p.m., with alternating periods of meditation in the hall, rest periods, meals and lectures. Splatts House is a handsome Queen Anne red-brick building. The beautiful and inspiring Light of the Dhamma Pagoda is the focal point of the Centre. Many people have come here for the ten-day courses with good results.

Open: All year for 10-day retreats. Receives men, women, young people.
Rooms: Dormitories and some doubles.
Facilities: Disabled access, Light of the Dhamma Pagoda, garden, library.
Spiritual Help: Meditation. Students observe *noble silence* but may speak with their teacher and the staff at any time.
Guests Admitted to: Most areas. Light of the Dhamma Pagoda, meditation hall, residential areas.
Meals: Everyone eats together. Vegetarian food. Special diets accommodated as far as possible.
Special Activities: Daily schedule of meditation practice. Planned schedule for the courses – send for course information.
Situation: Quiet, on edge of a village and standing in its own 4 acres of grounds.
Maximum Stay: 10 days.
Bookings: Letter, fax, e-mail, online, telephone.
Charges: £200 for 10 day retreat. No charges for the teaching.
Access: Train (from Paddington to Chippenham), bus, and car all possible. See brochure with map.

The Holy Spirit was present in the act of Creation.
BASIL THE GREAT

Salisbury

Alabaré House of Prayer
15 Tollgate Road
Salisbury
Wilts SP1 2JA   Tel/Fax: 01722 501586/340206
                                     e-mail: leeproctor@hotmail.com
Christian
Accommodation here includes a lift and ground-floor rooms. There is a six-week course on *Praying the New Testament* and a short but good year's programme of events and courses, including some on subjects such as sacred dancing and creative arts spirituality. There are also special day retreats for mothers with young children.

Sarum College
19 The Close   Tel: 01722 424800
Salisbury   Fax: 01722 338508
Wilts SP1 2EE   e-mail: admin@sarum.ac.uk
                                    Website: www.sarum.ac.uk
Inter-denominational
Sarum College is an ecumenical institution being developed as an innovative resource for all the churches in England and Wales. It occupies historic buildings, directly opposite the great Salisbury Cathedral. There are extensive facilities, ranging from an excellent theological library to a book shop. A flourishing Institute for Christian Spirituality, which offers courses in spiritual direction, retreats and workshops here and around the country, is operating from the College and there is also an Institute for Liturgy and Mission. The programme offers a good range of retreats and courses, including events organised among others by the Marian Study Centre and the Centre for Creation Spirituality (see London section).

Open: All year. Receives everyone. Families not easily accommodated but worth enquiring. Children welcome.
Rooms: 30 singles, 10 doubles. No smoking.
Facilities: Conferences, library, guest lounge, TV, direct dialing (01722 327846).
Spiritual Help: Personal talks, spiritual direction, group sharing, meditation, personal retreat direction, directed study.
Guests Admitted to: Unrestricted.
Meals: Everyone eats together. Traditional food. Vegetarian and special diets.
Special Activities: Planned programme – send for brochure.
Situation: Rather busy, in a cathedral close.
Maximum Stay: By arrangement.
Bookings: Letter, fax, e-mail, telephone.
Charges: Single room from £32.90, double from £51 (per room). Meals not included (breakfast £4.70, lunch/supper £8.81).
Access: Train, bus, car. In centre of Salisbury.

Warminster

St Denys Retreat Centre
2 Church Street
Warminster
Wilts BA12 8PG

Tel: 01985 214824
Fax: 01985 219688
e-mail: stdenys.ivyhouse@btopenworld.com

Anglican

This is a big brick and stone house set right on the street. The community offers individual retreats as well as *Walk Into Quietness* days, on which a team of sisters welcomes you to a quiet and peaceful day-retreat in the centre. The Centre is well organised and friendly, with the aim of helping people to *be* rather than *do*.

Open: All year except Christmas and first 2 weeks of January. Receives men, women, young people, groups.
Rooms: 17 singles, 4 twins.
Facilities: Small conferences, chapel, garden, guest lounges, dining room, payphone.
Spiritual Help: Personal talks, spiritual direction, personal retreat direction.
Guests Admitted to: Unlimited access.
Meals: Everyone eats together. Traditional and simple food. Vegetarian available. Special diets with advance notification.
Special Activities: Planned programme – send for brochure.
Situation: Quiet, in the town. Old-fashioned garden with stream. Listed building.
Maximum Stay: Varies, so enquire.
Bookings: Letter, telephone 9a.m.–5p.m.
Charges: Varies greatly, so check out current charge list, but 1 full day with overnight stay about £35 and a weekend about £70.
Access: Train: Portsmouth–Cardiff line. Bus: from Salisbury, Bath or Trowbridge. Car: via B3414, off A36. Good maps in brochure and leaflet.

> " Why not listen a little? Why not slow down some, hush up a bit, sit still a moment, turn on your dreams and listen to the wind, to the woods, to the water? Bend over and look down into the dark pool of your own depths and do not be afraid. "
> MATTHEW KELTY

South &
South East

Ascot

Ascot Priory
Ascot, Berks SL5 8RT   Tel: 01344 885685

Anglican
Open: All year. Receives men, women, young people, groups.
Rooms: 22 singles, 2 doubles.
Facilities: Conferences, camping, park, guest lounge, TV, payphone.
Spiritual Help: Group sharing.
Guests Admitted to: Chapel.
Meals: Self-catering.
Special Activities: None.
Situation: Very quiet, in the countryside.
Maximum Stay: By arrangement.
Bookings: Letter.
Charges: Ask for current rates.
Access: Rail and bus both possible – send for detailed instructions.

Kintbury

St Cassian's Centre
Kintbury, Berks RG17 9SR   Tel: 01488 658267

Roman Catholic
The De La Salle Brothers run this centre for young people. Thousands come here to participate in the various group events. The retreats are almost entirely offered to groups from schools, and individual retreats are not possible. However, most years there are family weekends in summer and there is a self-catering cottage which sleeps eight and is sometimes available for quiet breaks or private retreats.

Open: Most of year. Receives young people in school years 10, 11 and sixth form. There are family weekends.
Rooms: 5 singles, 29 doubles, self-catering cottage.
Facilities: Conferences, garden, guest lounges, payphone.
Spiritual Help: Personal talks, group sharing.
Guests Admitted to: Unrestricted access.
Meals: Everyone eats together.
Special Activities: Planned programme of group events for young people, mainly schools.
Situation: Very quiet, in the countryside.

Maximum Stay: According to programme.
Bookings: Letter.
Charges: Ask for rates.
Access: Train: Kinbury. Car: via A4.

Reading

Douai Abbey
Upper Woolhampton   Tel: 01189 715399
Reading   Fax: 01189 715303
Berks RG7 5TQ   e-mail: guestmaster@douaiabbey.org.uk
                            Website: www.douaiabbey.org.uk

Roman Catholic
This is one of the most famous monasteries in Europe. The retreat house is
open to all, while men may make a private retreat in the monastery itself with
its atmosphere of religious community life and prayer. Organised retreats are
offered by the Abbey's Pastoral Programme, which also runs conferences and
events (see below). This is a traditional monastery in the countryside and yet
not far from London, Reading and Oxford.

Open: All year except Christmas and mid-August to mid-September.
  Receives men, women, young people, families, groups.
Rooms: 15 singles, 5 doubles, dormitories, hostel.
Facilities: Chapel, choir, conferences, park, library, guest lounge, payphone.
Spiritual Help: Personal talks.
Guests Admitted to: Chapel, choir, gardens.
Meals: Everyone eats together. Traditional food. Vegetarian available. Self-
  catering facilities.
Special Activities: Planned retreats (see below).
Situation: Quiet, in the countryside.
Maximum Stay: A few days usually. Otherwise by arrangement with guest
  master.
Bookings: Letter, fax, e-mail, telephone.
Charges: By arrangement – currently about £25–£40 per person per night.
Access: Train: Midgham (about 11 miles). Bus: No. 102. Car: via M4, Exit
  1. Good map in brochure.

Douai Abbey – Guest Accommodation and Pastoral Programme
Upper Woolhampton
Reading   Guest Accommodation: Tel: 01189 715342
Berks RG7 5TH   Pastoral Programme Enquiries: Tel: 01189 715333
                            Fax: 01189 715203
                            e-mail: douaiabbey@aol.com
                   Website: http://members.aol.com/douaiweb

Roman Catholic
Guest accommodation is available at the monastery (see above) and you may
join the monks in the chapel and for the daily schedule of prayers. The
Pastoral Programme offers a variety of spiritual and educational opportunities
in the areas of theology, ministry and spirituality. For example, one series of
lectures is on the English saints from St Bede to St Hugh of Lincoln. The

arrangements for guests on a private visit and those attending a Pastoral Programme event are different, so do ask for details when you contact.

Open: Most of year except Christmas, Easter, and mid-July to mid-August. Receives men, women, young people, groups, non-retreatants. Children welcome.

Rooms: 17 singles, 5 doubles, hostel. Various combinations of accommodation depending on whether you are attending programme events or are on a private visit. It is informal, self-catering and small rooms – even camping is possible. Ask what is on offer when you contact the guest master or programme director.

Facilities: Conferences, chapel, garden, library, guest lounge, payphone.

Spiritual Help: Meditation, directed study, sharing in the daily round of prayer in a planned event stay. Organised retreats.

Guests Admitted to: Chapel, choir.

Meals: Everyone eats together on programme events in the guest house. Traditional food. Vegetarian and special diets. Otherwise self-catering.

Special Activities: Planned programme – send for brochure.

Situation: Quiet, in the countryside.

Maximum Stay: 2 weeks.

Bookings: Letter, telephone, fax, e-mail best.

Charges: Suggested fee of £35 per day.

Access: Train: Midgham (about 11 miles). Bus: No. 102. Car: via M4, Exit 1. Good map in brochure.

Spleen

**Elmore Abbey
Church Lane
Spleen, Newbury
Berks RG13 1SA**   Tel: 01635 33080

Anglican

This is a distinguished Anglican abbey with a new and beautiful church whose oak columns seem like trees in woodland. The little cloister courtyard at the entrance could not be prettier or more charming. All the refurbishment, rebuilding and designing have been done with obvious care and considerable talent. Everywhere is elegant and peaceful and so too seems the community of monks that lives here. There is a large oblate membership who come often, and they have first priority on the guest accommodation.

Open: All year except Christmas. Receives men, women, day retreatants.

Rooms: 6 singles.

Facilities: Chapel, garden, library with permission.

Spiritual Help: Personal talks, individual guidance if on a private retreat but not on guided retreats.

Guests Admitted to: Chapel, some work of community.

Meals: Everyone eats together. Traditional food. Vegetarians catered for.

Special Activities: None.

Situation: Quiet, in the countryside.

Maximum Stay: By arrangement.

Bookings: Letter.
Charges: On application.
Access: By train to Newbury or by car.

Thatcham

Cold Ash Centre
The Ridge, Cold Ash, Thatcham
Berks RG18 9HU

Tel: 01635 865353
Fax: 01635 866621
e-mail: fmmcac@aol.com

Roman Catholic – Inter-denominational
The planned programme of retreats here, run by the Franciscan Missionaries of Mary, is small but good, offering both preached and directed retreats. There are pleasant warm rooms and fine views in this very large building, and the welcome is friendly. This is a popular place so you may need to book well in advance.

Open: All year except August. Receives men, women, young people, groups.
Rooms: 28 singles, 3 doubles.
Facilities: Conferences, garden, small library, coffee rooms, guest lounges, TV, payphone, direct dialing. Take towel, soap and soft shoes for indoor use.
Spiritual Help: Spiritual direction, personal retreat direction.
Guests Admitted to: Chapel, church, oratory.
Meals: Taken in the guest house. Traditional and vegetarian food. Special diets.
Special Activities: Planned programme of events, preached retreats, bio-spiritual focusing retreats and workshops, massage retreats – send for brochure.
Situation: Quiet, in the countryside.
Maximum Stay: 1 month.
Bookings: Letter.
Charges: Currently about £27 full board per person per night.
Access: Train: Thatcham. Bus: Newbury or Reading. Car: 4 miles from Newbury. Map available on request.

HAMPSHIRE

Alton

Alton Abbey
Kings Hill, Beech, Alton
Hants GU34 4AP

Tel: 01420 562145
Fax: 01420 561691

Anglican
The Abbey is a place where you may find stillness and, hopefully, that reflection which may lead to worship and prayer with the community. On offer are Benedictine hospitality and a very wide range of retreats tailored to a guest's needs.

Open: Most of the year except Christmas period. Receives everyone. Children welcome.

Rooms: 12 singles, 6 doubles. No radios, tape/CD players. Silence from 8.30p.m–9.30a.m.

Facilities: Garden, guest lounge.

Spiritual Help: Personal talks, meditation, directed study, spiritual counsel, personal guided retreats.

Guests Admitted to: Chapel.

Meals: Everyone eats together in refectory. Simple traditional food. Vegetarian and special diets.

Special Activities: Planned programme.

Situation: Quiet, in the countryside, village setting.

Maximum Stay: 8 days.

Bookings: Letter.

Charges: £15 per day if less than 24 hours. £25 for 24 hours.

Access: Train: Alton, then No. 208 bus. Car: off A339.

Ampfield

Hebron Christian Retreat
Broadgate House
Hook Road, Ampfield, Romsey
Hants SO51 9BY   Tel: 02380 252673

Christian – Ecumenical
This is a new Ecumenical retreat centre open to both individuals and groups, with accommodation of single, double and triple rooms – all ensuite. Four more rooms are being added later. A chapel, garden, sun lounge and home cooking are on offer too.

Basingstoke

Malshanger Estate
Newfound, Basingstoke, Hants

Anglican – Ecumenical
Do not call or write to the estate, as it is used by several church groups in London (such as Holy Trinity, Brompton, and All Souls, Langham Place) for group events and for *Land-Mark Retreats*, and you must apply through them. **Contact St Mark's Church, Battersea Rise, London SW11 1EJ in first instance.** Malshanger itself is a large country house in a private estate of over 3,000 acres. Retreats are usually concerned with renewal and inspiration.

Bordon

Acorn Christian Foundation   Tel: 01420 478121
Whitehill Chase   Fax: 01420 478122
High Street, Bordon   e-mail: info@acornchristian.org
Hants GU35 OAP   Webstite: www.acornchristian.org

Inter-denominational – Anglican tradition
A Christian retreat and healing centre set in a large nineteenth-century hunting lodge with six acres of gardens and woodlands. The Acorn Christian

Foundation exists as a retreat centre with a programme for individuals and groups and as a teaching resource on Christian healing and medicine for churches and society at large. There is an extensive programme of teaching, training and retreats. Typical themes are *Deeper Healing Day, Renewing the Church, Body and Soul, Christ, Stress and Glory, Family Dynamics, Beginning a Healing Ministry in the Church, Bible Retreat, Myers Briggs Weekend, Ignatian Weekend* and *Angels and Miracles*. The chapel is especially attractive, with much light and seating arrangements around the altar. There is an open day every Tuesday and a healing service every day at 12 noon. Quiet days take place every month. A retreats and courses programme available. Also see the website.

Open: For the programme. Receives men, women, young people, groups, religious.

Rooms: Singles, doubles, twins.

Facilities: Disabled, chapel, conferences, garden, library, large lounge, TV, book shop, payphone.

Spiritual Help: Personal talks, spiritual direction (with chaplain if available), healing services, chapel for prayer and contemplation.

Guests Admitted to: Unrestricted access.

Meals: Everyone eats together in refectory. Traditional food. Vegetarian and special diets.

Special Activities: Planned programme – send for brochure.

Situation: In a small town but rural area.

Maximum Stay: 1 week.

Bookings: Letter, fax, e-mail, telephone 10a.m.–3p.m.

Charges: Various rates ranging from £16 to about £210, but the usual range is about £110–£160.

Access: Train possible as there is a rail-bus link. Car route easy. Good map in brochure.

Bramdean

The Krishnamurti Centre
Brockwood Park
Bramdean
Hants SO24 OLQ

Tel: 01962 771748
Fax: 01962 771755
e-mail: kcentre@brockwood.org.uk
Website: www.brockwood.org.uk/centre

Non-religious – Universal spirituality
J. Krishnamurti, who was born in India and died in the United States in 1986, was a universal man whose major contribution to twentieth-century thought, many say, was in questioning the basis upon which we make our judgements. According to Krishnamurti, misinterpretation of our reality causes us much unhappiness. He believed truth to be a pathless land. The Centre is intended for the serious study of his teachings. It is for people who would like to spend a few days in a quiet environment where they can devote their full attention to his teachings and their implications for their own lives. There is an excellent library on Krishnamurti's work, with video and audio tapes and other records. The Centre offers themed weekends and study retreats, the subjects of which may include the following, based on

Krishnamurti's writing: *Does Life have a Meaning? What is Meditation? Conflict and Co-operation, What is the Self? Transformation of Man, What is Freedom?* and *What is a Religious Mind?* Here is an example of his thought: 'What is it that binds us together? It is not our needs. Neither is it commerce and great industries, nor the banks and the churches; these are just ideas and the result of ideas. Ideas do not bind us together. We may come together out of convenience, or through necessity, danger, hate, or worship, but none of these things holds us together. They must all fall away from us, so that we are alone. In this aloneness there is love, and it is love that holds us together.' (From *Commentaries on Living*, Second Series.) **Highly Recommended.**

Open: All year except January. Receives men, women. No children. Day guests by arrangement.
Rooms: 19 singles. No smoking, alcohol or drugs. Mobile phones may be used only outside buildings.
Facilities: Garden, park, library, specialist library, quiet room, payphone.
Spiritual Help: None. The Centre does not provide spiritual guidance or therapeutic help.
Guests Admitted to: Unrestricted access except to kitchen and office areas.
Meals: Taken in dining room. Vegetarian food only.
Special Activities: Themed weekends and study retreats – brochure available on Centre and programme.
Situation: An oasis of quiet in the countryside.
Maximum Stay: 2 weeks.
Bookings: Letter, fax, e-mail, online, telephone.
Charges: £38–£55 per day, including full board and use of study facilities.
Access: Detailed information sheet available on request.

Lyndhurst

Furzey House
Minstead, Lyndhurst
Hampshire SO43 7GL   Tel: 023 8081 2015
                                          e-mail: daveandjill@ic24.net
Christian
With a chapel, lounge, reading room and two bedrooms, this quiet place is available for a private retreat or a day group. Its aim is to provide a small retreat house centred on the healing spirit of Christ where the atmosphere of peace will bring rest and renewal. Those in Christian ministry are particularly welcome for a break away.

Lymington

St Dominic's Priory
Shirley Holms Road
Lymington, Hants SD41 8NM   Tel: 01590 681874

Christian
This is a women's religious community which receives guests. Please contact them about what may be on offer for guests making a private retreat.

Southampton

**The Cenacle
48 Victoria Road
Netley Abbey
Southampton SO31 5DQ**

Tel/Fax: 02380 453718
e-mail: cenacle.netley@ntlworld.com

Roman Catholic
The aim at the Cenacle retreat house is to offer silent retreats for those wanting daily spiritual direction; hence, there is no programme of activities. The guest house is a silent one.

Open: All year except Christmas and New Year. Receives men, women.
Rooms: 6 singles. Silence in house.
Facilities: Garden, library, guest lounge.
Spiritual Help: Personal talks, spiritual direction, personal retreat direction.
Guests Admitted to: Chapel.
Meals: Taken in guest house. Traditional food. Vegetarian and special diets.
Special Activities: None.
Situation: Quiet, in a village.
Maximum Stay: 30 days.
Bookings: Letter, fax, e-mail, telephone.
Charges: £32 per person per 24 hours.
Access: Train and car possible. Ask for directions.

Southsea

**House of Bethany
7 Nelson Road
Southsea
Hants PO5 2AR**

Tel: 02392 833498

Anglican
An Anglican community runs this facility for non-residential groups plus guest accommodation of three singles and one twin. The programme is mostly quiet days, which run from 10a.m. to 4p.m., with guidance from a leader from the community or a member of the clergy.

Stroud

**The High House
Stroud
Petersfield
Hants GU32 3PN**

Tel: 01730 262520

Christian
Here is a big spacious house with its own indoor swimming pool, oratory, library and beautiful gardens in which to sit and meditate. There is also a small two-bedroom flat. A maximum of twenty-five people can come here at the same time, and quiet days, workshops, themed retreats and Ignatian spirituality are all possible.

Wickham

Park Place Pastoral Centre
Winchester Road
Wickham
Fareham
Hants PO17 5HA

Tel: 01329 833043
Fax: 01329 832226
e-mail: parkplacecentre@aol.com
Website: www.parkplacepastoralcentre.co.uk

Roman Catholic – Inter-denominational
This is a conference and retreat centre where people of all faiths and none are welcomed. There is lots of room here, including a youth wing with self-catering. All of it is situated in some 18 acres of grounds, overlooking open countryside. The Centre is fairly booked up by parish groups because it is geared to group bookings – but it is a good place for a family to go on retreat. Individuals of any denomination are welcome to spend time on a retreat here with or without guidance.

Open: All year except August. Receives men, women, young people in self-catering youth wing, families, groups, religious, and non-retreatants for study purposes. **Mainly receives group bookings.**
Rooms: 40 singles, 2 dormitories in youth wing, self-catering house for 10 people.
Facilities: Conferences, garden, guest lounge, TV, book shop, payphone.
Spiritual Help: Personal talks, group sharing, personal retreat direction, meditation, Indian Christian Spirituality. Handiwork such as painting and calligraphy are used with prayer and can be very helpful in opening the heart to God.
Guests Admitted to: Chapel, church, choir.
Meals: Everyone eats together. Traditional food. Vegetarian, special diets. Indian meal on request. The guest house is available on a self-catering basis for retreat groups and non-retreatants.
Special Activities: Planned programme of events – send for brochure.
Situation: Very quiet, in a village and countryside.
Maximum Stay: 7 days.
Bookings: Letter, fax, e-mail, telephone 9a.m.–4p.m.
Charges: From £45 per person per day full board. Charges are negotiable according to circumstances (such as unwaged or student).
Access: Train: Fareham. Buses from Southampton, Winchester to Fareham. Car: via M3 and A333 – see brochure.

Old Alresford

Old Alresford Place
Winchester Diocesan Retreat and Conference Centre
Old Alresford
Hants SO24 9DH

Tel/Fax: 01962 732518
e-mail: old.alresford.place@dail.pipex.com

Anglican – Inter-denominational
This is a Georgian complex set in extensive grounds in Old Alresford (the birthplace of the Mothers' Union). Run as a diocesan retreat, conference and training centre, the buildings are tastefully decorated and furnished, the library and meeting rooms light and airy. The team who run the house

provide good food and are happy to help with any queries. All the bedrooms are warm and each has a wash-basin.

Open: All year except Christmas. Receives men, women, young people, families, groups, non-retreatants. Children welcome.
Rooms: 25 bedrooms accommodating 47 people, hermitage, barn, camping, hostel, caravans possible.
Facilities: Chapel, conferences, small area for camping, 5-acre garden, car parking, library, guest lounge, payphone.
Spiritual Help: Discuss what your needs are when you book.
Guests Admitted to: Unrestricted access.
Meals: Taken in dining room. Traditional food. Vegetarian and special diets.
Special Activities: Planned programme of events – send for brochure.
Situation: Quiet, in village and countryside.
Maximum Stay: 2 weeks.
Bookings: Letter or telephone 9a.m.–5p.m. weekdays.
Charges: £44 per person per 24 hrs.
Access: Train: Alton or Winchester. Bus: from Alton. Car: via A31, then B3046.

KENT

Addington

The Seekers Trust
Centre for Prayer and Healing
The Close   Tel: 01732 843589
Addington   Fax: 01732 842867
West Malling   e-mail: theseekerstrust@supanet.com
Kent ME19 5BL   Website: www.theseekerstrust.org.uk

Inter-denominational – Christian tradition
Addington Park is a large place set in 39 acres of woodlands and gardens. Here, the Seekers Trust operates a centre of prayer for healing and spiritual guidance, with prayer chapels, a healing sanctuary and prayer help for anyone, regardless of their beliefs, for which there is no charge. **Contact healing** and **absent healing** are practised. Regular open contact healing days are held, and absent healing is done through prayer in harmony prayer circles, which are held regularly. Otherwise healing is by request. (Such healing is considered not as an alternative to traditional Western medicine but as a complementary therapy.) A programme of events is also run. Brochures on the Seekers Trust, their work, and the annual events programme are all available on request.

Open: All year. Receives men, women. Open to the public but children must be supervised.
Rooms: 5 singles, 3 doubles. These are in the form of guest flats. No smoking.
Facilities: Conferences, garden, park, library, payphone.
Spiritual Help: Healing ministry in the form of contact healing and absent healing.
Guests Admitted to: Unrestricted access in grounds. Quiet is requested.

Meals: Self-catering only.
Special Activities: Prayer and healing. Groups for other activities such as yoga, meditation, tai chi, feng shui, circle dancing. Send for events diary.
Situation: Quiet.
Maximum Stay: 2 weeks.
Bookings: Letter, fax, e-mail, online, telephone in office hours.
Charges: Single flats £98–£110 per week, double flats £167 per week. Different rates for 1–3-night stays – see price list in accommodation brochure.
Access: Train: London Victoria to Borough Green, taxi to Addington. Local map on request if coming by car.

Canterbury

Centre Space
3 Alcroft Grange,
Tyler Hill
Canterbury CT2 9NN   Tel: 01227 462038
                          e-mail: podger@centrespace.freeserve.co.uk

Inter-faith – Christian based
Silent and shared retreats are available here, with meals alone or in company. Music, painting, calligraphy, healing therapies, inner growth courses, sacred dancing and day conferences are all possible, as well as private personal retreats. There is a quiet room, woodland and that special place – a hermit's hut.

Open: All year. Receives everyone.
Rooms: 4 singles, 2 doubles, camping, caravans, hermit's hut.
Facilities: Conferences, camping, garden, library, guest lounge, TV, guest telephone, woodland nearby.
Spiritual Help: Personal talks, group sharing, spiritual direction, personal retreat direction, meditation, yoga, spinal touch therapy.
Guests Admitted to: Almost everywhere.
Meals: Everyone eats together. Organic whole food. Vegetarian and special diets. Self-catering facilities.
Special Activities: Planned events – send for information.
Situation: Very quiet, in the countryside.
Maximum Stay: Open.
Bookings: Letter, fax, telephone – best time mornings.
Charges: £15–£20 B&B, half board £25–£30, non-residential day rate £10.
Access: Train: easy – taxi from station. Coach and bus also possible. Car: easy.

Edenbridge

Sisters of St Andrew
Eden Hall
Stick Hill   Tel: 01342 850388
Edenbridge   Fax: 01342 851383
Kent TN8 5NN   e-mail: dianereynolds@standrews1.freeserve.co.uk

Roman Catholic – Ecumenical
Quiet days and facilities are available for groups. Individuals come here for a silent or individually guided retreat, which is also much in silence, and live in a

part of the house reserved for that purpose. Otherwise there are retreats and event days on the programme. Topics such as *Kindle the Flame – Spirit of Pentecost, What's the Spirit saying to the Churches?* and *Grounding the Word* gives a feel of what is on offer here. Eden Hall is an area of outstanding natural beauty and the facilities are comfortable. The Sisters of St Andrew say, 'Come ... relax, read, pray, walk, reflect, create, listen, share ... and just be yourself.'

Open: All year. Receives men, women, young people, families, groups for the day, non-retreatants. No groups in August.

Rooms: 25 singles, 3 doubles. Mobile phones discouraged. No radios or tapes.

Facilities: Disabled, chapel, conferences, camping, garden, National Trust walk in the grounds, guest lounge, TV, library, resource room.

Spiritual Help: Personal talks, group sharing, spiritual direction, personal retreat direction, meditation. Ecumenical team members available to spiritually journey with retreatants.

Guests Admitted to: Chapel, oratory, reflection oasis, work in garden.

Meals: Everyone eats together. Self-catering possible or meals can be taken in room. Traditional food. Vegetarian and special diets.

Special Activities: Mainly Bible and contemporary spirituality issues, plus quiet day retreats.

Situation: Quiet, in countryside.

Maximum Stay: Usually 8 days.

Bookings: Letter, fax, e-mail, telephone in evening.

Charges: By donation, suggestion being £5–£75 depending on what is being provided.

Access: Train: Edenbridge or Edenbridge Town. Car is easiest.

Hythe

Cautley House
Christian Centre for Healing and Wholeness
95 Seabrook Road
Seabrook   Tel: 01303 230762
Hythe   e-mail: cautleyhouse@compuserve.com
Kent CT21 5QY   Website : www.cautleyhouse.org.uk

Christian – Anglican – Healing ministry
Here is a Christian centre open to everyone, with daily services and staff available for prayer ministry and confidential and private spiritual talks. Most of the fifteen rooms have sea views and all are ensuite.

Maidstone

The Friars
Aylesford Priory   Tel: 01622 717272
Aylesford   Fax: 01622 715575
Kent ME20 7BX   e-mail: friarsevents@hotmail.com
                         Website: www.thefriars.org.uk

Roman Catholic – Inter-denominational
The Carmelite Friars say that hope is a source of joy and that joy is a source of strength. At Aylesford they offer an open door to everyone seeking spiri-

tual renewal. The Marian Shrine is a special feature. The retreat programme is a solid one, including such events as an inner child retreat, a singles weekend for those who live their baptismal calling as a single person, looking at different Carmelite themes for modern people, Holy Week and Lenten retreats, looking at women in the Bible, and an introduction to the spirituality of St John of the Cross. Pilgrimages, retreats, a guest house, a conference centre, an excellent bookshop, craft workshops, and a tearoom and shop all serve to make Aylesford an interesting retreat centre.

Open: All year except Christmas. Receives everyone. Children welcome.
Rooms: 24 singles, 24 twins.
Facilities: Conferences, guest lounge, garden, library, TV, payphone.
Spiritual Help: Personal talks, spiritual direction, personal retreat direction.
Guests Admitted to: Chapel.
Meals: Guests eat together. Traditional food. Vegetarian and special diets.
Special Activities: Planned programme of events – send for brochure.
Situation: Can be busy, but situation is quiet, in a village.
Maximum Stay: 2 weeks.
Bookings: Letter, fax, e-mail, telephone 9a.m.–5p.m.
Charges: £34 full board per person per night, B&B £19 per person per night.
Access: Train, coach and car all possible. Map and directions in brochure.

Ramsgate

St Augustine's Abbey
Ramsgate   Tel: 01843 593045
Kent CT11 9PA   Fax: 01843 582732
                                         e-mail: ablauvence@aol.com

Roman Catholic
The guest house was once the home of Augustus Pugin, leader of the Gothic Revival, and he built the Abbey church. Men are welcomed into the monastic ambience and to share the life of quiet and prayer here – but the community does do parochial work and runs a school which is not on site. You will be expected at Mass and the Evening Office of Vespers at least. **Religious vocation discernment and advice is available.** There is silence in the cloisters. Leave mobile phones and radios at home – after all you are getting away from it all. If guests learn about living in harmony with others and find peace and time to explore their journey with God, then the community's hospitality will have been fruitful indeed.

Open: All year except Christmas period. Receives men.
Rooms: 8 singles.
Facilities: Garden, library.
Spiritual Help: Personal talks, spiritual direction.
Guests Admitted to: Chapel, most parts of the Abbey, some work of community (usually manual chores).
Meals: Everyone eats together. Traditional simple food. Vegetarians catered for.
Special Activities: None.
Situation: Near a busy road but also next to the sea and quiet.
Maximum Stay: 1 month.

Bookings: Letter, telephone 10a.m.–noon, 3–6p.m.
Charges: By donation of what can be afforded but between £10 and £20 per day full board.
Access: Train: Ramsgate, then taxi. Bus: from Ramsgate. Car: M2, A299, A253.

St Mildred's Abbey
Minster
Ramsgate
Kent CT12 4HF

Tel: 01843 821254

Roman Catholic
A graceful place built mainly of stone, with some remains visible of the first monastery. It is very comfortable and peaceful, with a beautiful and reverent liturgy. The gardens are spacious and attractive. The Crypt is Norman and a prayerful place. Guests are received as individuals or in groups. There is room for some forty people, and families may come in the summer. Those on private retreat are welcome from January until October. There is a programme, which includes such retreats as a Quaker Retreat, an Alcoholics Anonymous retreat, a yoga retreat and a retreat for parents of disabled children.

Speldhurst

Centre of New Directions
White Lodge
Stockland Green Road
Speldhurst
Kent TN3 OPA

Tel: 01892 863166
Fax: 01892 861330
e-mail: info@lightcoloursound.com
Website: www.centreofnewdirections.com

Mind Body Spirit
This is an inter-denominational spiritual centre which has a chapel. It provides meals for groups and a range of spiritually based courses. Light, colour and sound are used for healing. This is the home of spiritual psychotherapeutics – see the website for details.

Open: All year. Receives everyone.
Rooms: 2 singles, 3 doubles.
Facilities: Conferences, camping, garden, library, guest lounge, payphone.
Spiritual Help: Personal talks, spiritual direction, meditation, directed study.
Guests Admitted to: Chapel and garden.
Meals: Only B&B for individual stays. Meals provided for groups.
Special Activities: Workshop programme – see website.
Situation: Quiet, in countryside.
Maximum Stay: By arrangement.
Bookings: Letter, fax, e-mail, telephone 10a.m.–3p.m.
Charges: £20 per person per night B&B.
Access: Train: Tonbridge, then taxi. Details of car route supplied when you book.

Tunbridge Wells

Burrswood Chapel House
Groombridge
Tunbridge Wells
Kent TN3 9BR

Tel: 01892 863637
Fax: 01892 863632
e-mail: admin@burrswood.org.uk

Inter-denominational Christian with the Anglican Church
The retreat house is Chapel House and it is part of a large Christian centre for health care and ministry that includes a medical centre, a hospital, guest accommodation and a resident community. The facilities here are modern and very pleasant. The house was recently refurbished and it is very comfortable, with a welcoming and homely atmosphere. All rooms have ensuite bath or shower, telephone and TV. A private chapel is at hand for private prayer and there is a full-time guest hostess to enable guests to make the most of their stay. There is a country house feel to the centre and you are invited to explore the beautiful surrounding area, where you will find such places as Chartwell and Sissinghurst Gardens. A pool and tennis court are also available, as well as (for a small extra charge) the services of a physiotherapist and the use of the hydrotherapy pool. This is a good place to come for both tranquility and healthy activity. The church is impressive. Burrswood, founded in 1948 as a healing centre for Christian health care and ministry, is a unique partnership between medicine and Christianity – a place of healing. **Highly Recommended.**

Open: All year. Receives everyone.
Rooms: 10 singles, 3 doubles.
Facilities: Conferences, garden, park, library, guest lounge, hydrotherapy pool, book shop, TV, guest telephones in each bedroom.
Spiritual Help: Spiritual direction, personal retreat direction, personal talks with Chaplain by request, healing service with laying on of hands, daily Eucharist, evening prayers.
Guests Admitted to: Unrestricted access except for hospital wing.
Meals: Taken in dining room. Traditional food. Vegetarian and special diets.
Special Activities: None, but brochures available about the guest house and Burrswood.
Situation: Quiet, in the countryside.
Maximum Stay: As arranged.
Bookings: Letter, fax, telephone.
Charges: Single from £36 per night, double £54. B&B, half-board and full board available.
Access: Train: Tunbridge Wells, then bus 290 or taxi. Car: access from A264, then B2110.

West Kingsdown

Stacklands Retreat House
School Lane, West Kingsdown
Kent TN15 6AN

Tel: 01474 852247

Anglican – Ecumenical
The first purpose-built retreat house in England, Stacklands is an Anglican centre for the study and giving of retreats according to the spiritual exercises

of St Ignatius Loyola. It is also concerned with training retreat conductors, and there is, in addition, a programme of preached, open, and other retreats on offer. It is a quiet place, its solitude and silence enhanced by the many acres of grounds in which to wander.

Open: All year except Christmas and New Year. Receives men, women, young people, groups.
Rooms: 21 singles.
Facilities: Conferences, garden, library, guest lounge, direct dial telephone.
Spiritual Help: Spiritual direction, personal retreat direction.
Guests Admitted to: Chapel.
Meals: Everyone eats together. Traditional food. Vegetarian and special diets. Optional self-catering for day visitors only.
Special Activities: Planned programme of events – brochure available.
Situation: Quiet, in the countryside.
Maximum Stay: 10 days.
Bookings: By letter or telephone.
Charges: £30 per 24 hours full board.
Access: Train: London Victoria to Swanley. Car: via A20.

West Wickham

Emmaus Centre
Layhams Road, West Wickham
Kent BR4 9QJ

Tel: 020 8777 2000
Fax: 020 8776 2022

Roman Catholic – Ecumenical
Run by a religious community and a lay team, this rather large centre manages to be very homely and offers good-sized, well-equipped rooms. There are two chapels – one grand and one more modest. Good walks can be taken in the nearby woods. There is a small flat for silent private retreats. The Centre is a popular place for both organisations holding annual retreats and meetings and for individuals wishing to come for a quiet time. There are a number of art-related retreats on offer, with themes including patchwork, painting and pottery. All denominations are welcome.

Open: All year except Christmas. Receives men, women, groups, religious, non-retreatants.
Rooms: 9 singles, 32 doubles, 3 flats.
Facilities: Conferences, 2 chapels, garden, 2 libraries, guest lounge, book shop, internet connect station, simultaneous translation equipment available, payphone.
Spiritual Help: Spiritual direction, individually guided retreats, preached retreats, spirituality workshops, personal counselling by arrangement.
Guests Admitted to: Chapel and all retreat house facilities.
Meals: Everyone eats together. Traditional/vegetarian food. Special diets. Silent meals on request.
Special Activities: Planned programme of events – send for brochure and annual programme of activities.
Situation: Quiet, on the edge of the countryside – good walks. Also good access to public transport.

Maximum Stay: Unlimited.
Bookings: Letter, fax e-mail, telephone.
Charges: Proposed offerings are shown on the booking form when informa-
tion is sent.
Access: Train: Hayes, Bromley South or East Croydon. Bus: No. 119, 138.
Car: Centre is near A232.

Whitstable

Convent of Our Lady of Mercy
Northwood Road
Tankerton
Whitstable
Kent CT5 2EY   Tel: 01227 272649

Roman Catholic
Open: Most of year except August and December. Receives women.
Rooms: 4 singles.
Facilities: Garden, library.
Spiritual Help: Individually guided retreats only.
Guests Admitted to: Chapel.
Meals: Taken in guest house. Traditional food.
Special Activities: None.
Situation: Quiet, near the sea.
Maximum Stay: As arranged.
Bookings: Letter.
Charges: About £20 per night.
Access: Train or car.

MIDDLESEX

Edgware

St Mary at the Cross Convent
Priory Field Drive
Edgware   Tel: 020 8958 7868
Middlesex HA8 9PZ   Fax: 020 8958 1920
                                       e-mail: nuns.osb.edgware@btclick.com

Anglican
The Anglican Benedictine Community of St Mary at the Cross Convent has
an atmosphere of peace which enfolds the visitor and comes as a surprise in
the otherwise rushed and busy suburb of Edgware. The provision of care has
long been the mission of this community, and today they welcome guests
who want a retreat in tranquility, not far from the heart of London.

Open: All year except Holy Week and Christmas. Receives men, women,
young people. Children welcome.
Rooms: 6 singles, hermitage.
Facilities: Conferences, garden, library, guest lounge, TV, payphone, bookshop.
Spiritual Help: Personal talks, sharing in the Divine Office.

Guests Admitted to: Church, chapel. Some work for the community may be possible if you ask.
Meals: Everyone eats together. All meals taken in silence. Simple food. Vegetarian and special diets.
Special Activities: None.
Situation: Quiet, in a town.
Maximum Stay: 7 days.
Bookings: Letter, fax, e-mail, telephone 9a.m.–4p.m. Monday to Friday.
Charges: Suggested donation from about £4–£15 per person per night. (These are among the most modest suggested charges in the guide, and we suggest you up this amount to a more realistic figure.)
Access: Underground, bus, car.

Harrow on the Hill

St Mary's Church House
Church Hill, Harrow
Middlesex HA1 3HL   Tel: 020 8422 8409

Anglican
St Mary's Church House, a Victorian annexe, has been renovated and made into a small conference centre providing self-catering accommodation for up to 12 people. It has a quiet atmosphere away from busy life, yet it is within easy reach of central London. **It is for groups of six to twelve only** and stands adjacent to St Mary's Church and the vicarage.

Open: All year except August. Receives men, women, young people, groups.
Rooms: 1 room for 4 and another for 2.
Facilities: Small conferences, guest lounge, library, TV, payphone.
Spiritual Help: None.
Guests Admitted to: Unrestricted access.
Meals: Self-catering only. Well-equipped kitchen.
Special Activities: None.
Situation: In an area of character amidst the vast suburban sprawl of West London. Next door is the 900-year-old Church of St Mary and beyond the churchyard are woods.
Maximum Stay: By arrangement.
Bookings: Letter, fax, telephone.
Charges: Ask what is expected when you book. Usually very reasonable.
Access: Underground, bus, car.

Isleworth

Relaxing the Mind
Administration Office
8 St John's Court   Tel: (Local rate) 0845 456 1051
Isleworth   e-mail: info@relaxingthemind.com
Middlesex TW7 6PA   Website: www.relaxingthemind.com

All the courses, workshops and retreats share a common aim, which is to promote well-bring and develop skills that support confidence and creativity.

The programme includes tai chi and meditation retreats on Holy Island (see Scotland section) and in Dorset. The costs for the Holy Island retreat, for example, are £150 plus accommodation for 7 nights full board. Rooms run from about £140 to £280 for the week. Send for a programme and information on the work of this organisation led by Sue Weston.

Osterley

Osterley Retreats
Campion House
112 Thornbury Road   Tel: 020 8568 3821
Osterley   Fax: 020 8847 6227
Middlesex TW7 4NN   e-mail: Osterley.Retreats@btinternet.com
                          Website: www.campionhouse.org.uk
Roman Catholic
Campion House is situated in very spacious grounds just outside London. It is best known for the number of priests who started here. Now it combines this training with the work of a full-time centre of Ignatian spirituality. There are Ignatian four-, eight- and thirty-day retreats, and various other retreats and workshops on offer, including art-themed ones.

Open: All year except Christmas. Receives men, women, groups, religious.
Rooms: 75 bed spaces altogether. No smoking.
Facilities: Garden, park, guest lounge, payphone.
Spiritual Help: Personal talks, group sharing, meditation.
Guests Admitted to: Chapel.
Meals: Everyone eats together. Traditional food. Vegetarian and special diets.
Special Activities: Varied programme of retreats and workshops – send for brochure.
Situation: Close to Central London and Heathrow Airport, with a large park and nearby banks and shops.
Maximum Stay: 1 month.
Bookings: Letter, telephone.
Charges: About £30 per night full board. Ask for current year's charges.
Access: Underground, bus, car.

Pinner

The Grail Centre
125 Waxwell Lane
Pinner   Tel: 020 8866 2195/0505
Middlesex HA5 3ER   Fax: 020 8866 1408
                          e-mail: waxwell@compuserve.com
Roman Catholic
Just 25 minutes from Baker Street underground station, the Grail Centre stands in some 10 acres of grounds. It offers small cedar-wood chalets set in the woods where you can experience *poustinia*, which in Russian means 'a place apart'. Here you can live in silence, reflection and prayer like a hermit. Everyone of whatever faith, or of none, is welcomed. At the time of writing, The Grail is undergoing an extensive rebuilding and renovation programme and so retreat accommodation and programmes have stopped except for the

hermitages. The chapel is also closed during this time. It is hoped that the Centre will reopen in 2005 with its new facilities and programme for retreats. Meanwhile, if you want to have a solitary private retreat and experience the hermit life for a little, then contact The Grail.

Open: Most of the year. Receives men, women.
Rooms: Hermitage chalets – 1 in winter, 6 in summer.
Situation: Quiet, on edge of London, in a town.
Maximum Stay: By arrangement.
Bookings: Letter, telephone.
Charges: Send for details as there are various charges.
Access: Underground: Baker Street to Pinner. Bus: from Harrow.

Teddington

The Eden Centre
252 Kingston Road
Teddington   Tel: 020 8977 4034
Middlesex TW11 9JQ   Fax: 020 8977 7747
e-mail: teddington@welcome100.freeserve.co.uk
Roman Catholic
The Eden Centre is about a mile from Kingston-on-Thames with its beautiful riverside walks. There is easy access to Bushy Park and its lakes and nature, as well as Hampton Court in its extensive grounds. The team here at the Eden Centre offer preached, directed and private retreats, with quiet days, spiritual accompaniment, and counselling if wished.

Open: All year except August. Receives men, women, groups, non-retreatants.
Rooms: 16 singles, 1 double. No Smoking.
Facilities: Disabled access – limited. Conferences, garden, park, library, guest lounge, TV, guest phone (020 9943 9731).
Spiritual Help: Personal talks, group sharing, meditation, spiritual direction, personal retreat direction.
Guests Admitted to: Unrestricted access except private office and sitting room.
Meals: Guest dining room. Whole food. Vegetarian and special diets.
Special Activities: Planned programme of events – send for brochure.
Situation: Rather busy – just beside Bushy Park and Hampton Court Palace.
Maximum Stay: By arrangement.
Bookings: Letter, fax, e-mail, telephone 9a.m.–5p.m.
Charges: £32 per person per 24 hours, £18 B&B.
Access: Train, bus, car all possible. Details in brochure.

Shallow brooks murmur most, deep silent slide away.
SIR PHILIP SIDNEY

Camberley

Tekels Park Guest House
The Guest House
Tekels Park, Camberley
Surrey GU15 2LF   Tel: 01276 23159
                                    e-mail: Ghouse.tekels@btclick.com

Mind Body Spirit
The Park is owned by the Theosophical Society in England and the
programme on offer may include events such as: *Mayan Mysteries, The Sacred
Circle, New Aspects of Space and Time, The Rebirthing Experience* and
Dancing the Sevenfold Energies of Life. Tekels is a wooded estate set in over
50 acres of secluded woods and fields which form a wildlife sanctuary, yet is
within 35 miles of London. The Guest House has earned a reputation for
serving excellent vegetarian food.

Open: All year. Receives men, women, young people, groups, religious, non-
    retreatants.
Rooms: Both singles and doubles are available.
Facilities: Camping, garden, park, library, guest lounge, TV, payphone.
Spiritual Help: Personal talks, groups sharing, meditation, directed study.
    Healing courses available.
Guests Admitted to: Unrestricted access.
Meals: Guests eat together. Vegetarian and whole food. Special diets catered for.
Special Activities: Some events – send for brochure.
Situation: Very quiet, in the countryside, with spacious grounds.
Maximum Stay: By arrangement.
Bookings: Letter, telephone.
Charges: Enquire when sending for information.
Access: Rail or car.

Cheam

Ruth White Yoga Centre
Church Farm House
Springclose Lane   Tel: 020 8641 7770
Cheam   Fax: 020 8287 5318
Surrey SM3 8PU   e-mail: info@ruthwhiteyoga.com
                                          Website: www.ruthwhiteyoga.com

Yoga – Mind Body Spirit
Retreats are usually on the weekends but there are also four-day breaks and a
summer holiday. Workshops are held throughout Britain and all are in peaceful country residences with pretty surroundings conducive to yoga spirituality and practice. Both John and Ruth White are exceptionally able teachers
well-known in Britain and have several yoga centres operating. See the
website for details of places, courses, and charges. **Highly Recommended.**

Open: For individual retreats. Receives everyone.
Rooms: Depends on venue. Otherwise Church Farm House has 30 bed
    spaces. Full Board for groups.

Facilities: Ask what is available.
Spiritual Help: Meditation, yoga breathing and postures, karuna yoga.
Guests Admitted to: Whatever are the guest areas.
Meals: Guests eat together. Vegetarian whole food.
Special Activities: Planned programme of events – send for brochure. Guest groups received.
Situation: Quiet, in a town.
Maximum Stay: Per programme event.
Bookings: Letter, fax, e-mail, telephone.
Charges: Specific for each event and venue.
Access: Will provide a map.

Chobham

Brook Place Ecumenical Centre
Bagshot Road
Chobham, Woking   Tel: 01276 857561
Surrey GU24 8SJ   Fax: 01276 858273
                          e-mail: retreats@brookplace.org.uk
Ecumenical
A Christian centre for hospitality, prayer and recreation. There is a tithe barn here for large groups, and a garden cottage for two to four people. The Centre is set in its own grounds, with a lake and a hermitage hut. There are daily ecumenical prayers. On offer is a week of guided prayer, open door retreats, and quiet day retreats. Silence is not observed but it is a quiet house.

Open: All year except August. Receives men and women in groups and religious only. Individuals may come for quiet days.
Rooms: 7 doubles.
Facilities: Conferences, garden, guest lounge.
Spiritual Help: None.
Guests Admitted to: Chapel.
Meals: Guests eat together. Traditional food. Vegetarian and special diets.
Special Activities: None.
Situation: Quiet, in the countryside.
Maximum Stay: According to group stay, or by day.
Bookings: Letter, telephone, fax, e-mail.
Charges: Rates vary, so send for leaflet of current charges.
Access: Train then taxi. Car.

Dormansland

Claridge House
Dormans Road
Dormansland   Tel: 01342 832150
Near Lingfield   Fax: 01342 836730
Surrey RH7 6QH   e-mail: welcome@claridgehouse.freeserve.co.uk
                 Website: www.claridgehouse.freeserve.co.uk
Quaker – Ecumenical
This is a Quaker centre of healing, rest and renewal, run by the Society of Friends Fellowship of Healing and open to everyone. The centre is an old

Victorian house in a small village, standing in its own two acres of lovely gardens. There are facilities for group conferences, retreats and private visits, and a programme of courses on offer. These may include such events as a *Walkers Week*, self-healing, exploring fine arts, massage, silent retreats, *Healing Power of Sound*, an *Easter Break, Stress Management and Relaxation, You Are What You Write* and a *Music and Dance Weekend*. There is a warm and peaceful Quaker atmosphere, with delicious vegetarian food. You will find peace and the time to recover yourself in this place. **Highly Recommended.**

Open: All year except first week of January. Receives men, women, young people, families, groups, non-retreatants.
Rooms: 4 singles, 7 doubles.
Facilities: Disabled, quiet room, conferences, garden, library, guest lounge, guest phone (01342 832920).
Spiritual Help: Personal talks, personal retreat direction.
Guests Admitted to: Unrestricted access.
Meals: Everyone eats together. Vegetarian, special diets.
Special Activities: Planned programme of events – send for brochure.
Situation: Quiet, in a village, in the countryside.
Maximum Stay: 4 weeks.
Bookings: Letter, fax, e-mail, telephone – best time 9a.m.-6p.m.
Charges: Ask for tariff leaflet – currently Monday to Friday Break £98–£150, weekend workshop from £130, mid-week workshop from £200. B&B is available at about £40 per person.
Access: Rail from London Victoria. Car: M25, A22, B2028

East Molesey

House of Prayer
35 Seymour Road
East Molesey
Surrey KT8 0PA

Tel: 020 8941 2313
Fax: 020 8941 2313
e-mail: houseofprayerem@aol.com

Roman Catholic – Ecumenical
Many people appreciate the space and freedom available here – and at only 17 miles from London, it is convenient to get to. This is a spacious and comfortable house for rest and relaxation with a community who offer a daily rhythm of prayer. Self-organised groups are often going on here but overnight stays and individual retreats can be arranged. Hermitages are available for silence and solitude. There is a modest but good programme of events on offer, which largely centre on prayer and include celebrations for Advent and Lent and study of the Enneagram system. The community especially welcomes those who may need a retreat during an important transitional stage in their lives.

Open: All year except July and Christmas. Receives men, women, young people, groups.
Rooms: 5 singles, 3 doubles. (Ensuite in 5 rooms.) No smoking. No tape recorders.
Facilities: Disabled, conferences, garden, library, guest lounge, TV, prayer room.

> What thou liv'st, live well, how long or short permit to Heaven.
> MILTON

Spiritual Help: Spiritual direction, meditation, personal retreat direction, personal talks.
Guests Admitted to: Oratory, garden, work of community.
Meals: Eat together or in room. Mostly organic food. Vegetarian, special diets.
Special Activities: Planned programme of events – send for brochure. Counselling.
Situation: Quiet, in village.
Maximum Stay: 30-day retreat.
Bookings: Letter, telephone.
Charges: £30 full board per day, including spiritual direction. Day rates. B&B £15 excluding spiritual direction – fees for spiritual direction/counselling negotiable.
Access: Train: Hampton Court. Car: A3, M25

Goldalming

Ladywell Retreat Centre
Ladywell Convent
Ashstead Lane
Godalming
Surrey GU7 1ST   Tel: 01483 428083

Roman Catholic
Near to Ladywell is an ancient shrine on one of the main old pilgrim routes to Canterbury. Guests who only want a holiday and are not prepared to make an effort to use the contemplative environment to seek peace through prayer should try another place. Individually directed retreats and on-going spiritual direction are available to help each person along this path, combined with the community's notable spirit of hospitality. The retreat centre itself is in a wing of the main building, with a small oratory and prayer room.

Open: Most of year. Receives men, women, young people, groups.
Rooms: 29 singles, 5 doubles.
Facilities: Conferences, garden, library, guest lounge, TV, payphone.
Spiritual Help: Personal talks, meditation.
Guests Admitted to: Chapel, choir.
Meals: Guests eat together. Traditional food. Vegetarian and special diets.
Special Activities: Planned programme of events – send for brochure.
Situation: Quiet, in the countryside, with spacious grounds and gardens.
Maximum Stay: 8 days.
Bookings: Letter, telephone.
Charges: From about £25 per day full board.
Access: Rail or car.

Tuesley Retreat
Tuesley Manor
Goldalming
Surrey GU7 1UD   Tel: 01483 417281
                                                     Fax: 01483 420415

Roman Catholic – Ecumenical
Tuesley Retreat is based around a large restored barn with a dining and
sitting area, a group room, a kitchen for self-catering, a garden, a covered and
heated swimming pool, a chapel and a choice of rural walks. The manor
estate itself is set in 13 acres of countryside. This is a non-residential retreat
place and charges are negotiable for both individuals and groups – but in a
range of £60–£100 per day. As to accommodation, they can provide you with
some recommended local B&B places.

New Malden

Inigo's Place
Inigo Enterprises New International Centre
Links View
Traps Lane   Tel: 020 8949 1670
New Malden   Fax: 020 8942 8202
Surrey KT3 4RY   e-mail: inigonewmalden@cs.com
                                        Website: www.inigonet.org

Roman Catholic – Ecumenical
A Jesuit priest, Father Billy Hewett, SJ, founded and runs Inigo Enterprises
as an organisation for communicating Ignatian spirituality. There are workshops, retreats of various durations at different venues, introductory days and
talks. Subjects may include the life and spiritual exercises of St Ignatius
reflected in the light of the French writer René Girard, the centring techniques of Anthony De Mello, journaling, focusing using Eugene T. Gendlin's
bio-spiritual work as a basis, praying with poetry, and integration using Celtic
spirituality approaches. Courses take place at Inigo's Place and at various
other venues. For example, there have been residential retreats at Campion
House, Osterley, Ushaw College Durham and in Ireland. Inigo Enterprises is
for experiencing Ignatian inspired ways of praying, journaling, centring and
focusing, and for sharing stories and being in relationship in daily living.
Tapes, books and course materials are also available. Write for the current
programme or visit their website.

Open: All year. Receives everyone.
Rooms: None – non-residental.
Facilities: Disabled, conferences, garden, library, 2 meeting rooms for a
maximum of 16.
Spiritual Help: Personal talks, group sharing, spiritual direction, personal
retreat direction, meditation, directed study, journaling and other spiritual
exercises.
Guests Admitted to: Meeting rooms, garden.
Meals: Self-catering facilities. A simple lunch can sometimes be provided if
pre-arranged.
Special Activities: Planned programme of events – send for brochure.
Situation: Quiet, in suburbs, with lovely garden.

Maximum Stay: Daytime only, for the duration of the course or retreat.
Bookings: Letter, fax, e-mail, telephone 9a.m.–9p.m.
Charges: By negotiation/donation. £20 per day suggested, but no one is excluded because they can only give a smaller amount.
Access: Rail, bus, car. Map provided on request.

Richmond

St Michael's Convent
56 Ham Common
Richmond
Surrey TW10 7JH

Tel: 020 8940 8711/8948 2502
Fax: 020 8332 2927
e-mail: sisters.csc.ham@fish.co.uk
Website: www.tap.net/csc

Anglican
St Michael's Convent, where the Community of the Sisters of the Church live, is a smart place on Ham Common in Richmond, with the park nearby for walks and a large garden in which to sit. Founded in 1870, the Community of the Sisters of the Church is an international body of women within the Anglican Communion. Here the sisters are committed to a life of prayer, worship and community service, and their outreach work includes hospitality, informal education, and leading retreats and workshops, for which they have earned a deserved reputation. The Community has a special interest in the idea of prayer and the clown, and runs **clown workshops** as part of its extensive and interesting retreat and workshop programme. This may also include circle dancing, Enneagram work, Taize and Iona music, prayer through dance, Myers-Briggs work, and a look at Mary of Nazareth as a model for contemporary women and men. There are opportunities for women aged eighteen to thirty to live with the community and experience a life of prayer and fellowship.

Open: Almost all year, closed early January and early August. Receives men, women, young people, groups.
Rooms: 11 singles, 3 doubles.
Facilities: Conferences, garden, library, guest lounge, guest phone (outgoing calls only). No B&B.
Spiritual Help: Personal talks, spiritual direction, personal retreat direction all by prior arrangement. Eucharist most days.
Guests Admitted to: All areas except sisters' private quarters. Help in the garden usually welcomed.
Meals: Everyone eats together, mainly in silence. Traditional/whole food. Vegetarian, vegan and special diets. Self-catering facilities.
Special Activities: Planned programme of events – send for brochure.
Situation: Quiet, but only 8 miles from Heathrow. In a suburban area near Richmond Park, with access to the Thames.
Maximum Stay: 1 week or by arrangement.
Bookings: Letter, telephone.
Charges: Suggested donation £30 per person per day including meals, £8 for quiet day with one meal, conference area £70 per day, smaller room £5 per bed per day.
Access: Rail, bus and car all easy.

Woking

St Columba's House
Maybury Hill
Woking
Surrey GU22 8AB

Tel: 01483 766498
Fax: 01483 740441
e-mail: retreats@st.columba.org.uk
Website: www.stcolumbashouse.org.uk

Anglican – Ecumenical

St Columba's welcomes men and women of all faiths or none and provides a common ground for ecumenical discussion and prayer. Refurbished about five years ago, this is a pleasant and comfortable place in pleasant surroundings, with home-style meals. There is a garden prayer walk and a collection of contemporary paintings. The chapel is modern, light, and impressive in its simplicity. The annexe to the retreat house was a convent guesthouse and the accommodation afforded there is going to available from late 2004 onwards. The lower convent rooms will be turned into budget silent retreat space, and these will also be ready in late 2004. The retreat programme includes preached weekend retreats centring on the Desert fathers, full-week retreats devoted to prayer (in which alternative healing and relaxation therapies such as aromatherapy and reflexology are introduced) and basic Zen retreats.

> *The human body, at peace with itself, is more precious than the rarest gem. Cherish your body, it is yours this one time only.*
> TSONGKAPA

Open: All year except Christmas and New Year. Receives men, women, young people, families, groups, non-retreatants.

Rooms: 22 singles, 3 twins (about 45-bed accommodation in total). No smoking.

Facilities: Disabled, conferences, chapel, garden, library, guest lounge, TV, guest telephone (01483 766499).

Spiritual Help: Personal talks, groups sharing, spiritual direction, personal retreat direction, meditation, spiritual healing.

Guests Admitted to: Everywhere.

Meals: Everyone eats together. Traditional simple food. Vegetarian, special diets. Self-catering suite.

Special Activities: Planned programme of events – send for brochure. Weekly quiet day each Monday. Open to all. £5 and bring your own lunch, 10a.m.–4p.m. Liturgical education. Specialist facilities for business and corporate quiet days. Aromatherapy.

Situation: Very quiet, in a town. Retreat house is within the grounds of the convent.

Maximum Stay: 2 weeks.

Bookings: Letter, fax, e-mail, telephone.

Charges: £40.70 + VAT per day full board. Cost of the retreats from about £89 to over £200.

Access: Train: London Waterloo to Woking then taxi (station 1 mile from house). Car: via Maybury Hill, off the B382 – avoid entering Woking town.

SUSSEX EAST

Battle

Crowhurst Christian Healing Centre
The Old Rectory
Crowhurst
Battle
E Sussex TN33 9AD

Tel: 01424 830204
Fax: 01424 830053
e-mail: divine@theway.co.uk

Christian – Healing ministry
Ministry of the Word, Holy Communion healing services, prayer and a Listening Ministry are available here for guests. There are 16 singles, 3 twins and 5 twins ensuite. The programme of events is short but very good, including *Christian Healing*, *Painting and Craft Week* and a *Pentecost House Party*.

Penhurst Retreat Centre
The Manor House
Penhurst
Battle
E Sussex TN33 9QP

Tel: 0845 458 0602
e-mail: penhurst@fish.co.uk

Ecumenical
Next to the parish church, Penhurst is a Jacobean manor house with a programme of guided retreats. It is a new centre so the programme is still developing. There are a number of single and double rooms, and one triple family-size room. Private retreats and groups are welcomed.

Brighton

St Benedict's
1 Manor Road
Kemp Town
Brighton
E Sussex BN2 5EA

Tel: 01273 674140
Fax: 01273 680527
e-mail: generalate@graceandcompassion.co.uk
Website: www.dabnet.org/gcb.htm

Roman Catholic
A retreat establishment at the edge of the city, near the sea and run by the Grace and Compassion sisters – so you know all will be comfortable and the welcome warm. Here you can relax and step out of your ordinary daily life for some reflection on your values and lifestyle in a friendly and pleasant environment.

Open: All year. Receives everyone. Children welcome. Pets by permission.
Rooms: 8 singles, 8 doubles, hermitage. Ask about self-catering accommodation.
Facilities: Conference room, garden, park, library, guest lounges, TV, guest phone (01273 674140), direct dialing (01273 878201).
Spiritual Help: Private retreats.
Guests Admitted to: Chapel, choir.
Meals: Taken in dining room of guest house. Whole food/vegetarian food. Special diets.

Special Activities: None.
Situation: Quiet, on edge of town, near the seashore.
Maximum Stay: By arrangement.
Bookings: Letter, fax, e-mail, telephone 9.30a.m.–12.30p.m. and 7–8p.m.
Charges: Apply for current rates.
Access: Train: Brighton, then No.7 bus. Coach from Victoria Coach Station. Car via A23.

Robertsbridge

Darvell Bruderhof Community   Tel: 01580 883300
Robertsbridge   Fax: 01580 881171
E Sussex TN32 5DR   e-mail: info@bruderhof.com
          Website: www.bruderhof.org
Christian
There are eight Bruderhof communities in Britain and the States. The two in England are this one in Robertsbridge and Beech Grove Bruderhof, Nonington, Kent. Bruderhof is a Christian movement of over 2,500 single people, families and older people living together in a life-style based on the teachings of Jesus to love one another, not judge our enemies, make peace and not worry about tomorrow. Issues of justice, community life, value for all life, and peace are major concerns of Bruderhof. They publish a magazine, *The Plough*, which is free, and run a publishing house, Plough Publishing, which you can find on the net. They welcome visitors, but you need to contact them so details of your stay can be worked out.

Waldron

Monastery of the Visitation
Waldron
Heathfield   Tel: 01435 812619
E Sussex TN21 ORX   Fax: 01435 813088
          e-mail: Vis1610@uk2.net
Roman Catholic
The sisters here, who are an enclosed contemplative monastic community, are called to be a praying presence in the world. At the Monastery of the Visitation they offer an environment of stillness, prayer and spiritual renewal to those women who wish to share their lives for a time. Retreatants are asked to stay within the enclosure throughout their stay. The Order of the Visitation was founded in 1610 by St Jeanne de Chantal and St Francis de Sales, whose book *Introduction to the Devout Life* continues to be one of the most famous and widely read Christian spiritual works. This is a place for silence, contemplation and the regaining of inner peace.

Open: From March until end November. Receives women only.
Rooms: 3 singles – at top of house, so there are stairs to climb.
Facilities: Garden, small number of books, direct dialing (01435 812619).
Spiritual Help: Personal talks, spiritual direction.
Guests Admitted to: Chapel, choir, work in the garden if they wish.
Meals: Everyone eats together. Simple food. Vegetarians catered for.
Special Activities: None.

Situation: Very quiet, in the countryside in 50 acres of parkland with beautiful views over South Downs.
Maximum Stay: 1 week.
Bookings: Letter addressed to Retreat Mistress.
Charges: Cost is by donation. As a guideline £20 per day is currently suggested, and there is a £5 fee for booking.
Access: Rail then taxi (8 miles). Car route easiest.

SUSSEX (WEST)

Arundel

Convent of Poor Clares
Crossbush
Arundel
W Sussex BN18 9PJ

Tel: 01903 882536
Fax: 01903 885131

Roman Catholic
Here is a traditional convent with all the gentleness and space to pray that one could want. The dove of peace is one of the little signs of this praying community. The surrounding countryside is beautiful, with the South Downs at hand and the sea but four miles away. The Community has a small guest house where people are welcome to stay for a private retreat or just to rest and be quiet. While there is no garden for guests, there are a small patios and places to sit outside, and walks in the country are easily accessible. A comfortable sitting room with television is also available. The accommodation is modest but the welcome very warm. Guests are always invited to join the community for Mass and Divine Office if they wish to do so. There is no charge for food and accommodation, only donations. However, these donations provide one of the few sources of income for the community, so if you are employed, why not be generous? **Highly Recommended.**

Open: All year except 1 November to 8 December. Receives women, families in the caravans on site, groups up to eight. Men are received here but only with a reference.
Rooms: 5 singles, 3 doubles, 2 large pleasant large caravans.
Facilities: Guest lounge, TV, payphone, craft shop, 2 patios.
Spiritual Help: Spiritual direction, personal retreat direction.
Guests Admitted to: Chapel.
Meals: Taken in guest house, usually in your room. Traditional, simple, and vegetarian food. Caravan guests self-catering.
Special Activities: None.
Situation: Quiet but on a busy road. Lovely countryside with good walks nearby. A few miles from the coast.
Maximum Stay: 2 weeks.
Bookings: Letter, fax, telephone 9.30a.m.–5p.m.
Charges: By donation, suggested rate £15–£20 per day, which is very modest indeed (see above).
Access: Train: Arundel (5 minutes away). No easy buses. Car via A27.

Chichester

Catholic Bible School
Nutbourne House
Farm Lane
Nutbourne
Chichester
W Sussex PO18 8SD

Tel: 01243 371766
Fax: 01243 371459
e-mail: info@catholic-bible-school.org
Website: www.catholic-bible-school.org

Roman Catholic
This is a non-residential place which accommodates groups of up to 35 people. The aim of the Catholic Bible School Trust is to make the Word of God a living experience for all who come here. All denominations and those of none are welcome. Christian counselling training, spiritual direction training and scripture courses are all available, plus Saturday workshops every month, which are lead by internationally known speakers. The house itself is a sixteenth-century and Georgian one, only a few minutes walk from the coast.

Coolham

Blue Idol Guest House
Coolham
W Sussex RH13 8QP

Tel: 01403 741241
e-mail: jspencer@nationwideisp.net

Quaker
Lawned gardens surround this house, which offers accommodation with bed and breakfast. The timber-framed house dates back to 1850, but a Friends Meeting House has been offering hospitality on the site since 1691. If you want to get away from it all, Blue Idol offers a good base for quiet walking, beautiful surroundings and a meditative atmosphere. The house is very rural, so you need to have a car. Sometimes single day retreats are held, so enquire what is available.

Crawley

Grace and Compassion Convent
Paddockhurst Road
Turners Hill
Crawley
W Sussex RH10 4GZ

Tel: 01342 715672

Roman Catholic
Open: All year. Receives men, women, young people, non-retreatants. Children by special arrangement.
Rooms: 1 double (or single).
Facilities: Small garden, library, guest lounge, TV, guest telephone.
Spiritual Help: None.
Guests Admitted to: Chapel, choir.
Meals: Everyone eats together, or can eat alone if this is preferred. Traditional/whole food. Vegetarian catered for.
Special Activities: None.
Situation: In the countryside but rather busy.

Maximum Stay: By arrangement.
Bookings: Letter or telephone – best time 10a.m.–12.30p.m.
Charges: £25 per person full board.
Access: Rail: Three Bridges. No bus. Car route from Crawley.

Monastery of the Holy Trinity
Crawley Down
Crawley
W Sussex RH10 4LH

Tel: 01342 712074

Anglican – Contemplative community
This is an enclosed contemplative order for men, and another of our favourite retreat places. Guests are asked to respect the timetable and silence of the monks' daily life. Within the Christian vision of life, the community here offers traditional liturgy and prayer from a perspective common to both the Christian East and the Christian West. For all guests, both the committed and uncommitted, the community offers a place of natural beauty, silence and peace to facilitate openness and stillness. This is not a suitable retreat place for those who are under psychological stress or feel that they could not handle silence and lack of conversation. Having said that, this is a fine place to share in the liturgical and contemplative life of a monastic community. **Highly Recommended.**

Open: All year except for certain days or weeks around holy days, so you need to ask during the current year (usually 1 week in spring and 1 week in December). Receives men, women. Groups only for the day.
Rooms: Up to 11 singles. Silence is observed.
Facilities: Garden, library, guest telephone.
Spiritual Help: Personal talks, personal retreat direction, spiritual direction, participation in the Divine Office and group prayers, which usually include the Jesus Prayer.
Guests Admitted to: Chapel, grounds of monastery except monastic enclosure, work of the community, refectory.
Meals: Everyone eats together. Whole food and simple cooking with provision for vegetarians and special diets within reason.
Special Activities: None.
Situation: Very quiet, in the midst of 60 acres of woodland.
Maximum Stay: 1 week.
Bookings: Letter or telephone – best times 9.45–11.45a.m., 2–5p.m.
Charges: Donation guide: £15 per day, but this is a very modest donation, so if you are employed perhaps you will be more realistic.
Access: Ask for travel instructions when booking.

Prayer is the the queen of virtues.
JOHN CLIMACUS

Worth Abbey
Centre for Spirituality
Paddockhurst Road
Turners Hill
Crawley
W Sussex RH10 4SB

Tel: 01342 710318
Fax: 01324 710311
e-mail: spirituality@worth.org.uk
Website: www.worth.org.uk

Roman Catholic

This community of monks places its main emphasis on the experience of Benedictine hospitality and spirituality. They are committed to a collaborative ministry in the service of the Church and the community in the south-east of England. The community also places a strong emphasis on ecumenism. The setting is beautiful, and quiet can be found. Guest accommodation has been updated and there is a good programme on offer. Individuals are not received unless coming for one of the organised retreats – although men may apply for a private retreat with the monastic community.

Open: All year except Christmas and New Year. Receives everyone except non-retreatants. Children welcome.
Rooms: 10 twins, 2 family rooms, singles in monastery for men, camp site, huts.
Facilities: Disabled, conferences, camping, garden, guest lounge, library, payphone.
Spiritual Help: Communal Prayer, monastic liturgy, personal talks, group sharing, spiritual direction, personal retreat direction, directed study, meditation, tai chi, yoga.
Guests Admitted to: Chapel, church, choir, gardens.
Meals: Guest house. Traditional, simple food. Vegetarian and special diets.
Special Activities: Planned programme – ask for information about what may be on offer. Guests are welcome to attend Divine Office as well as Mass.
Situation: In the countryside, with beautiful grounds.
Maximum Stay: 7 days.
Bookings: Letter, fax, e-mail.
Charges: Rates upon request. Weekend residential retreats run at about £85.
Access: Train from London Victoria to Three Bridges. Car via M23, Exit 10 to East Grinstead.

Copthorne

Franciscan Convent
Borers Arms Road
Copthorne
W Sussex RH10 3LN

Tel: 01342 712088

Christian – Franciscan spirituality

With 7 singles and 2 twins, all ensuite, the Convent offers a short programme based on topics such as *The Sacrament of Creation* and *Rejoicing in Hope*. There is a Chapel, Oratory and conference room available to guests.

East Grinstead

Neale House Conference Centre
Moat Road
East Grinstead
W Sussex RH19 3LB   Tel: 01342 312552

Anglican
Neale House offers a centre from which to explore the Sussex countryside, and there are plenty of things to do locally. It is usual for guests to be groups who have arranged their own retreat programme, but special help on spiritual matters can be arranged for individuals who wish to stay.

Open: Weekends (from Friday supper to Sunday tea-time). Closed August and Christmas. Receives men, women, young people, families, groups, non-retreatants. Children welcome.
Rooms: 5 singles, 9 doubles, 6 dormitories.
Facilities: Conferences, newly designed garden, park nearby, books to read, guest lounge, TV, payphone.
Spiritual Help: Personal talks.
Guests Admitted to: Unrestricted access.
Meals: Everyone eats together. Traditional food. Vegetarian and special diets.
Special Activities: None.
Situation: In a town, close to Sussex countryside.
Maximum Stay: 4 days.
Bookings: Letter, telephone.
Charges: On application.
Access: Rail: East Grinstead, then a 10-minute walk. Car: A22.

St Margaret's Convent
St John's Road
East Grinstead
W Sussex RH19 3LE

Anglican
The community will be moving to a new location in the future, so for now they are able to welcome day-retreat guests only as there is no guest accommodation available. Please write in the first instance.

Horsham

St Cuthman's
Coolham
Horsham   Tel: 01403 741220
W Sussex RH13 8QL   Fax: 01403 741026
                                    e-mail: stcuthmans@dabnet.org
Roman Catholic
A tranquil environment in a beautiful rural setting with comfortable ensuite rooms, central heating and log fires in the winter. The house, owned by the Diocese of Arundel and Brighton, operates as a quiet house, with some rooms being silent and others not. It is set in five acres of land, with a lake

and a site of special nature conservation. There is a new garden room, set well away from the main house, with separate access and parking, which provides a space for small day-groups for courses and non-residential days of prayer. The chapel is a simple and lovely one. The food is professionally prepared with fresh ingredients. St Cuthman's is a good place for a silent private contemplative retreat. It is open to guests of all denominations and faiths.

Open: All year except Christmas and Easter weeks. Receives men, women.
Rooms: 8 singles, 8 doubles, 2 hermitages.
Facilities: Disabled, chapel, garden, library, guest lounge, payphone.
Spiritual Help: Spiritual direction, personal retreat direction. A simple time of prayer takes place morning and evening, and there is a Mass celebrated regularly as well.
Guests Admitted to: Unrestricted access.
Meals: There are two dining rooms, one silent. Traditional food. Vegetarian and special diets. Hermitages self-catering.
Special Activities: Programme of conservation crafts and other activities on offer and some non-residential sessions of prayer, scripture and other spirituality-related topics. Occasionally there are concerts.
Situation: Quiet, in countryside.
Maximum Stay: By arrangement but a 2-night stay is minimum booking.
Bookings: Letter, fax, e-mail, telephone 9a.m.–9p.m.
Charges: £49 per day full board. Hermitages: Chapel Hut residential £20, day use £15; Cricket Field Hut residential £15, day use £12.
Access: Rail. Car: on the A272, south of Horsham.

Hassocks

Priory of Our Lady
Sayers Common
Hassocks
W Sussex BN6 9HT

Tel: 01273 832901
Fax: 01273 835501

Roman Catholic – Inter-faith
'One heart and one soul in God' sums up the way of life of this flourishing Augustinian monastic community. All men and women of good faith, whether Christian, Buddhist, Hindu or Jew, are welcomed by the sisters at their delightful modern priory set at the end of a drive that is edged with daffodils in the spring. The Roman Catholic community here has strong links with the Church of England. The retreat centre is in a separate house, and there is a simple but good programme ranging from a weekend on awareness of the invisible and the meaning of prayer, to an adventure in painting and prayer, to redemption made meaningful in the twenty-first century, to praying with the psalms. **Highly Recommended.**

Open: All year except closed season, which is usually mid-August to mid-September. Receives men, women, young people, families, groups, non-retreatants. Facilities are not really suitable for young children.
Rooms: 3 singles, 14 doubles, 1 room with 4 beds. Sometimes it is possible to camp. No smoking inside buildings. No pets. Silence of individuals and groups on retreat must be respected.

Facilities: Conferences, garden, library, guest lounge, TV, payphone.
Spiritual Help: Personal talks, spiritual direction, personal retreat direction. Guests are welcome at Divine Office and Mass with the community.
Guests Admitted to: Church, choir, oratory, occasionally work of community.
Meals: Taken in guest house. Traditional food. Vegetarians catered for.
Special Activities: Planned programme of events – send for brochure.
Situation: Increased motorway traffic has lessened the former quiet, but it is still peaceful in the countryside.
Maximum Stay: 8 days.
Bookings: Letter, fax, telephone 9a.m.–noon, 3.30–5p.m.
Charges: £30 per person per day. Donations accepted.
Access: Rail: Hassocks then taxi. Car: A23, then B2118 to Sayers Common. Bus: stops at Sayers Common.

ISLE OF WIGHT

Ryde

Abbey of Our Lady of Quarr
Ryde
Isle of Wight PO33 4RS

Tel: 01983 882420
Fax: 01983 884402
Website: www.quarrabbey.co.uk

Roman Catholic
Here you may share for a few days in the life of a contemplative Benedictine men's monastic community, following their daily life of prayer and work. The purpose of your visit should be to enter fully into this place of silence and recollection in order to dedicate time to the things of God. The daily Mass is at the heart of the monastic day.

Open: All year except during period of annual community retreat and other occasional periods. Receives men.
Rooms: 9 singles. No radios/tape recorders.
Facilities: Chapel, garden, park, guest lounge.
Spiritual Help: Personal talks, spiritual direction. Opportunities for spiritual advice. All services in the Abbey Church are open to guests, including daily Mass. All Divine Offices are sung, much of them in Gregorian chant.
Guests Admitted to: Church, monastery grounds, work of community.
Meals: Usually in refectory. Traditional food. Vegetarians catered for.
Special Activities: None.
Situation: Near sea, farm, countryside, woodlands. A quiet place.
Maximum Stay: 2 weeks.
Bookings: Letter, fax, telephone.
Charges: Donation.
Access: Ferry: Portsmouth to Ryde.

The Garth Retreat
St Cecilia's Abbey
Ryde
Isle of Wight PO33 1LH

Tel/Fax: 01983 562602
e-mail: sca@stceciliasabbey.org.uk
Website: www.stceciliasabbey.org.uk

Roman Catholic
Divine Office is sung in Gregorian chant by this Benedictine community of nuns. Many people find great serenity and rest in this peaceful, modal music and in the tranquil rhythm of the liturgy and psalmody. Moreover, the Abbey itself is a very quiet place near the sea. The Garth, adjacent to the monastery, offers guest accommodation to those wishing to spend some days in an atmosphere of prayer and recollection. The Garth is entirely self-catering. There is a small hermitage also.

Open: Most of the year except Christmas week. Receives women, families, small groups, young people.
Rooms: 2 singles, 3 twins.
Facilities: Small garden, library, guest lounge.
Spiritual Help: Personal talks possible. Spiritual direction.
Guests Admitted to: Extern chapel of the Abbey church.
Meals: Self-catering only.
Special Activities: None.
Situation: Quiet, on the outskirts of a seaside town.
Maximum Stay: 1 week.
Bookings: Letter (with SAE if possible), fax, telephone 10.30a.m.–6.30p.m.
Charges: No fixed charge – donations accepted.
Access: By ferry. Taxi from landing stage if required.

> Christianity is not to find the city of love, but to build it. It is in the building of it that we discover it.
> MATTHEW KELTY

East &
East Anglia

BEDFORDSHIRE

Biggleswade

Yoga for Health Foundation
Ickwell Bury
Biggleswade
Beds SG18 9EF

Tel: 01767 627271
Fax: 01767 627266
e-mail: admin@yogaforhealthfoundation.co.uk
Website: www.yogaforhealthfoundation.co.uk

Mind Body Spirit – Non-religious
This is a special place for caring retreats for those who have health problems and disabilities of various kinds as well as the fit and healthy – no division is made between the fit and the severely disabled; everyone is given the same loving attention by the staff. The Foundation, a charity operating in many parts of the world, is situated in what must be the last unspoiled bit of this commuter-belt county. A seventeenth-century grand manor and farm, the site is surrounded by parkland, and you drive up a sweeping entrance road. There are fine gardens, and a fishing lake left over from the Middle Ages, when an abbey occupied the site. Inside the house all is given over to creating an atmosphere of care and helpfulness with a family feel. The food is excellent, and much is home-produced. There are nursing staff and the place is well equipped for the disabled. Yoga training and other healing treatments are available. This is a place where people share and grow in strength together. The health benefits of regular yoga practice, particularly for those suffering from stress, are well established. On any visit here you are likely to encounter people who will praise the improvements in their lives that stays here have brought them. **Highly Recommended.**

Open: All year except Christmas. Receives men, women, young people, families, groups, non-retreatants. Children welcome. Pets by prior arrangement.
Rooms: 10 doubles – supplement for a single. 3 singles, 3 dormitories. Caravans and camping by prior arrangement only.
Facilities: Disabled. Meditation room, small conferences, camping by arrangement, garden, library, guest lounge, payphone (01767 627335).
Spiritual Help: Personal talks, group sharing, meditation, directed study. Full range of yoga activities for both able-bodied and disabled guests.
Guests Admitted to: Unrestricted access. Work of resident community by arrangement.
Meals: Everyone eats together. Vegetarian whole food only. Special diets possible.
Special Activities: Send for programme of events, which include a 10-day Family Festival of Yoga.

Situation: Peaceful, in countryside and village.
Maximum Stay: Open.
Bookings: Letter, e-mail, telephone 9a.m.–4p.m.
Charges: £275 per person per week all in. Rates for shorter stays.
Access: Train: Biggleswade then taxi. Buses: coach to Bedford; local bus runs twice a day. Car: via A1 to Biggleswade.

Turvey

Monastery of Christ Our Saviour
Abbey Mews
Turvey
Beds MK43 8DH

Tel: 01234 881211
e-mail: turveymews@aol.com

Roman Catholic
This is one of two Benedictine communities at Turvey who worship in common and work in close co-operation. The monks' guest house has been converted from a stone barn. The rooms are spacious and comfortable, with lots of books to read, an easy chair in every room and a guest kitchen. This can be a busy place but it is one where personal silence is very much respected. If you are on a private retreat, you will be left in peace to get on with it. As it is a small community, help in the garden is usually welcome. The life here is deliberately kept simple – organic gardening, tomato growing and pottery are some of the specialities of the monks. Guests are expected to respect the silence of others. Attached to the monastery is the Turvey Centre for Group Therapy. Its main activity is to provide courses, both for beginners and professionals. These are run in conjunction with Brookes Oxford University. The courses take place over weekends, with the students being resident at the monastery or nearby. For a private retreat go when the course is not meeting. Although the community is small in number, it is big in talent, and if you want to experience what monastic life is about, this is one of the best places to do it. Nothing is grand, everything is real. This is a peaceful place of prayer and seeking God. **Highly Recommended.**

Open: All year except Christmas and Easter. Receives men, women if not alone, young people, families. Extra accommodation can be arranged for groups if there are not enough rooms available within the guest house.
Rooms: 6 singles, 1 double. A silent, peaceful guest house. Radios and other noise discouraged.
Facilities: Conferences, garden, library, guest lounge, kitchen, payphone, nearby fields in which to walk.
Spiritual Help: Personal talks.
Guests Admitted to: Chapel, work of community.
Meals: Taken in the guest house. Self-catering for lunch; breakfast and evening meal provided. Full catering for groups if required. Provision for vegetarians if requested.
Special Activities: None.
Situation: The village has a lot of traffic, but the guest house and gardens are quiet – and the walled vegetable garden is not just for food; it is also has wild places and hidden sanctuaries for all manner of natural wildlife. Beautiful countryside with well marked footpaths.

Maximum Stay: By agreement.
Bookings: Letter, e-mail, telephone 9–11.30a.m., 3–5p.m.
Charges: Suggested donation £20 per person per night with breakfast and supper, £25 full board.
Access: Train: Bedford or Northampton, then local bus – not frequent however. Taxi from train station easy. Car: via M1, Exit 14 to Olney.

Priory of Our Lady of Peace
Turvey Abbey
Turvey
Beds MK43 8DE

Tel: 01234 881432
Fax: 01234 881538
e-mail: sisterlucy@turveyabbey.freeserve.co.uk

Roman Catholic
Although the Abbey is next to a busy road, the sisters have created an oasis of peace and prayer in this picturesque stone village by the River Ouse. The nuns are a lively and hard-working community who warmly welcome their guests and put them immediately at ease. If you have never been in a chapel when the monastic prayers are sung, then here is something not to be missed – there may be organ or zither music, or the Prioress herself (who is American) strumming melodies on her guitar to accompany the nuns and monks lifting up their voices in the ancient songs of praise to God. There are books to help you join them, so give it a go! Guests do not have to join these daily offices of prayer, of course, but the beautifully sung liturgy helps immeasurably in the calming of the mind and body and the opening of the heart. The modern guest house is warm, and the bedrooms are well appointed, with very good beds with immaculate linen. The adjoining guest house of the monks is also sometimes utilised (see above), which is also very comfortable and private. There is a garden in which to sit, while the grounds offer good walks through Abbey Park and beyond to open fields. The chapel is modern, full of light and simply decorated by the Community, who are famous for the quality of the design and execution of their projects. Religious symbols and objects are kept to a minimum at Turvey and what there is makes a simple direct statement of the faith of the community in Christ Jesus. Their series of posters based on scripture is justly popular across Europe, as is the embroidery work on the church vestments they make, led by Sister Paula. The meals are excellent and served either in the small guest dining room or in a beautiful stone carriage house attached to the chapel. The programme of events is very popular and run with efficiency and much good humour, so book well in advance. The *Icon Painting and Prayer* retreats and workshops run by Sister Esther are among the best available anywhere. There is an annual summer event for men and women under forty to join both communities for a week of living the Benedictine monastic life. If you are at all interested in how the religious contemplative life in community can be successfully lived today, here is a good place to visit. You do not need to be a Catholic to come here. The communities at Turvey Abbey are here for all those seeking God – that is, seeking to find meaning for their life and spiritual journey. People of any faith or none are welcomed. **Highly Recommended.**

Open: All year except 1–15 July, Christmas and Easter. Receives men, women, young people, groups, religious.

Rooms: 6 singles, 3 doubles. No mobile phones. Silence expected from 9p.m.–9a.m.

Facilities: Small conferences of up to about 40 people, garden, park, nearby woodlands and fields, library, guest lounge, payphone. Day retreats scheduled from time to time, including some for mothers with young children.

Spiritual Help: Guests are welcome to join in the Divine Office and are provided with books, which are easy to follow even if you never have attended such a service before. From time to time introductory talks are given to help people participate more deeply. Daily Mass, personal talks, meditation, spiritual direction, personal retreat direction, group sharing.

Guests Admitted to: Chapel, Divine Office, library, occasionally work of the community.

Meals: Meals are taken in a guest house. Food is more or less traditional, with some whole food dishes. Vegetarian and special diets (that are not too complicated) with advance notice.

Special Activities: Planned programme of events – examples include *Calligraphy and Prayer, Hearing the Word Within, Monastic Experience Week, Icon Painting* – send for brochure.

Situation: In the village, near countryside, with fields to the rear and side.

Maximum Stay: 3 nights or by arrangement.

Bookings: Preferably by letter.

Charges: Private retreats suggested donation £28 per 24 hours, retreat weekends £80–£85 inclusive – the programme gives prices for organised retreats, otherwise ask Sister Lucy for details.

Access: Train: Bedford or Northampton, then local bus – not frequent however. Taxi from train station easy. Car: via M1, Exit 14 to Olney.

CAMBRIDGESHIRE

Buckden

St Claret Centre
The Towers
Buckden
Cambs PE18 9TA

Tel: 01480 810344
Fax: 01480 811918
e-mail: Claret_centre@claret.org.uk
Website: www.claretcentre.fsnet.co.uk

Roman Catholic

Buckden Towers is a famous historic place. Today, the owners are the Claretian Missionaries, a religious community. They run a large rural parish, welcoming visitors from all over the world. There is a church and two chapels. The accommodation is currently arranged in self-contained apartments.

Open: Open all year. Receives everyone. Children welcome.

Rooms: Various accommodation so ask when contacting them. Refurbishments are going on and additional accommodation will become available.

Facilities: Disabled, conferences, camping, garden, park, TV in some accommodation.

Spiritual Help: Personal talks, group sharing, spiritual direction, personal retreat direction, meditation.

Guests Admitted to: Unrestricted access.

Meals: Self-catering.
Special Activities: None at this time.
Situation: Quiet, in the countryside.
Maximum Stay: 3 weeks.
Bookings: Letter, fax, e-mail, telephone.
Charges: Vary according to type of booking and individual circumstances of
guest. Sometimes it is a matter of a donation, so ask when booking what
rate you will be paying or not, as the case may be.
Access: Good map and details in the brochure.

Cambridge

The Institute for Orthodox Christian Studies	Tel: 01223 741037
Wesley House	Fax: 01223 741370
Jesus Lane	e-mail: info@iocs.cam.ac.uk
Cambs CB5 8BJ	Website: www.iocs.cam.ac.uk

Christian – Orthodox
Although the Institute is non-residential, it is able to provide a list of local
B&B guest houses. A programme is run with lectures, courses, and weekends
on Orthodox Christianity and choir practice as well.

Ely

Bishop Woodford House	
Barton Road	
Ely	Tel: 01353 663039
Cambs CB7 4DX	Fax: 01353 665305
	E-mail: bpwoodford@e-l-y.freeserve.co.uk

Anglican
This is a 1973 purpose-built modern place with lawns, in the grounds of an
old theological college. The chapel is large and traditional and there are plans
to update the whole place in time – this is needed as many of the beds could
do with replacing. There is a book shop and a bar, and the staff here are
welcoming and helpful. The centre is five minutes walk from the cathedral,
the river and the town.

Open: All year. Receives all. Children welcome.
Rooms: 32 singles.
Facilities: Conferences, chapel, garden, library, guest lounge, TV, payphone.
Spiritual Help: None.
Guests Admitted to: Unrestricted access.
Meals: Everyone eats together. Traditional food. Vegetarian and special diets.
Special Activities: Some planned events – send for brochure.
Situation: In a town and next to a school – quiet in the school holidays and
at night.
Maximum Stay: 7 nights.
Bookings: Letter, fax, telephone.
Charges: From £35 for full board per 24 hours.
Access: Rail or bus to Ely. Car: A10.

Horseheath

Mill Green House
Mill Green
Horseheath
Cambs CB1 6QZ

Tel: 01799 584937
Fax: 01799 584390
e-mail: walkermgh@nascr.net

Inter-denominational

Sixteenth-century Mill Green House is available for all who wish to have time and quiet in which to pray, read and wait upon God. It is a family house, but with the children mostly away. Individual counselling, day retreats and opportunities for individuals to be alone and for groups to follow their own programme are on offer. All are welcome to share in this informal, comfortable and pleasant home.

Open: All year except August. Receives men, women, young people, non-retreatants, religious, groups on a day basis.
Rooms: 2 doubles, camping.
Facilities: Conferences, garden, chapel/library, guest lounge, guest phone.
Spiritual Help: Personal talks, group sharing, spiritual direction, personal retreat direction, counselling, meditation, directed study.
Guests Admitted to: Everywhere.
Meals: Everyone eats together. Traditional simple food. Vegetarians. No special diets.
Special Activities: Planned programme – send for brochure.
Situation: Quiet, in the countryside.
Maximum Stay: 2 weeks.
Bookings: Letter, fax, e-mail, telephone 9a.m.–5p.m.
Charges: £17.50 B&B, £3.50 simple lunch, £7 supper, £60 per day hire for groups. Donations for spiritual direction/retreat direction £15–£50.
Access: Train possible. Car route easy. Good map in brochure.

Rumwood
Cardinal's Green
Horseheath
Cambs CB1 6QX

Tel: 01223 891729
Fax: 01223 892596
e-mail: maryrobinellis@rumwood.demon.co.uk
Websites: www.reikiteaching.co.uk & www.thoughtfield.co.uk

Mind Body Spirit

Rumwood is a large, specially designed and generous wooden house, very warm and nicely furnished, with various extensions made over the last few years – for example, a summerhouse and sauna. The sitting room has a wonderful fire and there is an amazingly designed open stone fire as well. Carpeted throughout, this is a place where much thoughtfulness has gone into making people feel comfortable and relaxed. People come here to rest and to release tension and stress. On offer are several healing therapies, including Thai healing massage, Bach Flower Remedies, lifestyle analysis, Reiki, and herbal nutrition. **Thought Healing Therapy** is a major interest of the owners and one is a Reiki Master. Information is available on both these healing approaches. One speciality course sometimes available is on peace-making between men and women.

Open: All year, mainly at weekends. Closed for Christmas. Receives men, women, couples.

Rooms: 2 singles, 2 doubles.

Facilities: Garden, guest telephone, library. Bring soft shoes for indoors and a beach towel if you want to use the sauna.

Spiritual Help: Personal talks, spiritual direction.

Guests Admitted to: Unrestricted access.

Meals: Everyone eats together. Simple whole food, organic if possible. Vegetarian and vegan.

Special Activities: Special programme – send for brochure.

Situation: Quiet, in a small village.

Maximum Stay: 3 days.

Bookings: Letter, fax, e-mail, telephone.

Charges: £80 weekends, £100 Monday to Friday.

Access: Train, bus, coach and car all possible.

Huntingdon

Houghton Chapel Centre (URC)
Chapel Lane
Houghton
Huntingdon
Cambs PE28 2AY   Tel: 01480 469376
                              e-mail: Gerry.feakes@one-name.org

Christian

Group retreats here, with sleeping accommodation for 30 guests. Weekday bookings are also possible.

St Francis House
Community of the Resurrection
29 High Street
Hemingford Grey
Huntingdon
Cambs PE28 9BJ   Tel: 01480 462185
                              e-mail: hemingford@mirfield.org.uk

Anglican

Renovated a few years ago, St Francis House is designed for retreatants and the aim is to maintain a peaceful atmosphere at all times. Although the house is in the village, there is a large garden and you can walk beside the nearby river and through the meadows. Central to the life of the house is the simple but elegant chapel on the upper floor. Rooms are quiet and comfortable. The beautifully kept garden, with roses and chestnut trees, can be seen from the bedrooms. Every effort is made by the warden here to ensure your peace and comfort. There are open retreats, closed group retreats and quiet days. The programme is a full one, with many closed group retreats and almost every month retreats open to all, which are well lead by established and experienced facilitators. **Highly Recommended.**

Open: All year except August. Receives men, women, young people, groups.

Rooms: 20 singles, 3 doubles.

Facilities: Chapel, garden, large cheerful sitting room, pleasant dining room, library, payphone.
Spiritual Help: Retreatants may talk personally with the retreat conductor.
Guests Admitted to: Unrestricted access.
Meals: Everyone eats together. Traditional food. Vegetarian and special diets.
Special Activities: Planned retreats – send for brochure.
Situation: Quiet, in a village.
Maximum Stay: 5 days.
Bookings: Letter, e-mail, telephone 9a.m.–6p.m.
Charges: Depends on length of stay and the retreat so ask for special leaflet giving details, but around £100 Monday to Friday, £80 weekend.
Access: Car: via A604.

ESSEX

Boreham

The Barn
Diocesan Pastoral Centre
New Hall
Boreham
Chelmsford
Essex CM3 3HT

Tel: 01245 451760
Fax: 01245 462961
e-mail: THEBARNNH@aol.com
Website: www.newhall.org.uk

Roman Catholic – Ecumenical
Do not have second thoughts when you come up the drive to New Hall and think with all the big buildings it will lack warmth and peace – nothing could be further from the truth. The centre itself is a 250-year-old converted barn, adjoining New Hall. It is alongside a small lake, surrounded by lawns, trees and shrubs, and beyond is a big field. Although you are not far from busy roads, country walks abound. The hospitality is excellent here, and the conversion with its own chapel offers small sitting rooms, comfortable and modern bedrooms and plenty of space for prayer and silence. It is very well equipped, fresh, neat, and warm. The programme of retreats includes such topics as *Clowning and Prayer, Prayer and Clay, Music for Advent,* a day of reflection – *The Spirit of the Lord is upon me, Myers-Briggs Shadow Workshop, Augustine – a Fellow Pilgrim, The Icon in Sacred Space* and *Guided Prayer.*

Open: All year except for Christmas and August. Receives men, women, young people, groups, non-retreatants.
Rooms: 9 singles, 4 twins. No smoking.
Facilities: Disabled – limited. Conferences, garden, park, library, guest lounge, TV.
Spiritual Help: Personal talks, spiritual direction, personal retreat direction, meditation, group leaderships for days of prayer and recollection. The centre is attached to a religious community whose regular prayer services all are welcome to attend.
Guests Admitted to: Chapel, choir oratory.
Meals: Cafeteria or in guest house – it varies. Self-catering facilities available. Traditional food – good choice. Vegetarian and special diets.

Special Activities: Planned programme – send for information.
Situation: Quiet, in the countryside, with garden and in a lake setting.
Maximum Stay: 7 days.
Bookings: Letter, fax, e-mail, telephone office hours.
Charges: Donations – suggested rate £30 full board per person per day, £18 per person self-catering.
Access: Train or coach to Chelmsford. Local buses.

Bradwell-on-Sea

Othona Community
East Hall Farm
East End Road, Bradwell-on-Sea   Tel: 01621 776564
Essex CMO 7PN   e-mail: centre@othona-bos.org.uk
Website: www.othona.org

Ecumenical – Open spirituality
This place is in the far reaches of the Essex estuary, which stretches right out into the North Sea. You drive and drive, and the lanes get narrower and you find a farm and then – surprise! Here in the middle of nowhere is the Othona Community. A new building, purpose-built, centrally heated, and opened only a few years ago, provides lots of space for visitors. The new dormitories and rooms in the new building are not quite completed as far as decoration goes but they are comfortable enough. There is provision for school groups and families. Hidden here and there are tiny hermitages without toilets or electricity for those who want a real desert spirituality experience. There is a special site of scientific interest nearby, on account of the abundant birds (this is a well-known spot for bird-watchers). All in all, the atmosphere is one of birds, busy people, silence, peace and wilderness. This is one of two Othona Communities; the other is in Dorset (see Dorset section). Founded by Canon Norman Motley in 1946, the Othona Community is a deeply British concept and aims to explore and experience the meaning of fellowship of the Holy Spirit and to promote unity among all Christians. There is an excellent brochure available about the movement. Up to 100 people for a conference or 28 guests staying overnight can be accommodated here. The setting, close to a nature reserve and the sea, makes this a very special retreat place for those who are keen on wildlife. The Community has use of the seventh-century chapel of St Ceed, which dates from 645 AD. It sits on a windswept and grassy rise on the edge of the sea. Empty of all furnishings and built of deeply weathered stone, it is one of Britain's oldest places of prayer.

Open: All year. Receives everyone.
Rooms: Lots of rooms – singles, doubles, dormitories, tents, barn, hermitages – and everything slowly being rebuilt or upgraded.
Facilities: Conferences, camping, garden, park, guest lounge, guest telephone.
Spiritual Help: Depends on programme. The Community works closely with the local churches.
Guests Admitted to: Everywhere except Community private rooms.
Meals: Everyone eats together. Simple, whole food. Vegetarian and special diets. Self-catering facilities available.
Special Activities: Planned programme – send for brochure.

Situation: Quiet and remote with its own beach, fields, orchards, woodlands and ancient chapel.
Maximum Stay: By arrangement.
Bookings: Letter, e-mail, telephone.
Charges: Programme events about £15 per person per day. Children's and concessionary rates available.
Access: Bus, train and car are possible – **you need to ask for specific instructions.**

Brentwood

Abbotswick
Diocesan House of Prayer
Navestock Side
Brentwood
Essex CM14 5SH

Tel: 01277 373959
Fax: 01277 375327

Christian – Franciscan
Abbotswick is open every day except Mondays for guests who want time to pray and reflect. Day retreats are held but otherwise the events spring from Diocesan needs. 15 singles ensuite. Private guided retreats are available on request.

Frinton-on-Sea

Great Holland Retreat Centre
Rectory Road
Great Holland
Frinton-on-Sea
Essex CO13 0JN

Tel: 01255 676389/675336

Christian – Methodist
A non-residential quiet place with a conference room, chapel and self-catering facilities. Inter-denominational and welcoming all Christian groups.

Pleshey

Chelmsford Diocesan Retreat House
The Street
Pleshey
Chelmsford
Essex CM3 1HA

Tel: 01245 237251
Fax: 01245 237594
e-mail: retreathouse.pleshey@virgin.net
Website: www.retreathousepleshey.com

Anglican – Inter-denominational
Parish groups mostly use the House of Retreat; individuals are welcome when there is room. A good range of weekend retreats are available, ranging from an introduction to the John Main method of meditation to instruction on how to breathe and use the body most effectively when you have embarked on the journey of prayer. There are courses such as *Praying with Evelyn Underhill* and *The Creation Gospel*. The House of Retreat has been called 'the New Jerusalem just off the M25'.

Open: Most of the year except Christmas, New Year, Easter. Receives men, women, young people, groups, non-retreatants.
Rooms: 23 singles, 3 doubles.
Facilities: Disabled, garden, library, day conferences, guest lounge.
Spiritual Help: Personal talks, personal retreat direction, directed study, spiritual direction.
Guests Admitted to: Everywhere.
Meals: Everyone eats together. Traditional simple food. Vegetarian. Special diets – on limited basis. Self-catering facilities.
Special Activities: Myers Briggs retreats, open retreats, quiet days, course for spiritual directors – send for the brochure.
Situation: Quiet, in historic Essex village, in countryside.
Maximum Stay: 7 days.
Bookings: Letter, fax, e-mail, telephone 9a.m.–1p.m.
Charges: £42 per day full board, groups special rates.
Access: Train or bus to Chelmsford. Car: via M11.

Stansted

The Arthur Findlay College	Tel: 01279 813636
Stansted Hall, Stansted	Fax: 01279 816025
Essex CM24 8UD	e-mail: afc@snu.org.uk
	Website: www.snu.org.uk

Spiritualist
The Arthur Findlay College for the Advancement of Psychic and Spiritual Science has been going since 1964. The seven principles of Spiritualism are: the fatherhood of God, the brotherhood of man, the communion of spirits and the ministry of angels, the continuous existence of the human soul, personal responsibility, compensation and retribution hereafter for all good and evil deeds done on earth, and the eternal progress open to every human soul. The College runs an extensive series of courses and programmes, and you need to send for their brochure to get any real idea of the range available and the various costs involved. Some examples might be as follows: *Crystal Enlightenment, Dance of the Spirits, Psychic Art Weekend* and *Investigating the Paranormal.*

Open: All year according to programme.
Rooms: 14 singles, 2 doubles, plus other rooms available. No smoking.
Facilities: Conferences, garden, library, guest lounge, TV, payphone.
Spiritual Help: Personal talks, group sharing, spiritual direction, personal retreat direction, meditation, directed study. Many other ways available such as acupuncture, aromatherapy, massage, aura soma, spiritual healing, private spiritual sittings/readings.
Guests Admitted to: Unrestricted access.
Meals: Everyone eats together. Traditional/vegetarian food. Special diets.
Special Activities: Planned programme – brochure available each year.
Situation: Set in 15 acres of parkland and woods.
Maximum Stay: No limit.
Bookings: Letter, fax, telephone.
Charges: Day visits from £30, residential £106–£350, therapies from £8, spiritualist sittings £25. No charge for healing.
Access: Easy from airport and motorways.

HERTFORDSHIRE

Buntingford

Country Churches Day Retreats
The Rectory
Warren Lane
Cottered
Buntingford
Herts SG9 9QA   Tel: 01763 281218

Anglican
On offer here are day retreats only. These are organised by an Anglican vicar trained in the Ignatian exercises and take place in the quiet villages that she serves. Both individuals and groups are welcome. In the main church there is a Lady Chapel, while for those who want to be active or want a meditative personal retreat with nature, there are specially designed faith and nature trails between the churches – a clever idea that will appeal to many people. The fees for the day are from £5 to £20 – or an hour's gardening. You can be picked up at the train station. The venues are easy to get to by car and impossible by bus. This is a very pleasant, gentle and appealing kind of retreat, and rather English in style.

Hemel Hempstead

Amaravati Buddhist Monastery
Great Gaddesden
Hemel Hempstead
Herts HP1 3BZ

Buddhist – Theravadan Buddhist tradition
This is a Community of Buddhist monks and nuns of the Theravada tradition, but people of any or of no formal religious affiliation are welcome here. In fact, from time to time, you may well meet nuns and monks from other faiths visiting, and certainly people who are new to Buddhism. The temple, opened only a few years ago, is very grand and beautiful, with a large enclosed courtyard. Retreats are held in separate facilities away from the often busy life of the Amaravati religious community itself. There are three possibilities for staying at Amaravati. First, you may stay with the monks or nuns as a monastic guest. Such a stay is by arrangement and at the discretion of the community. You must participate fully in the monks or nuns daily routine of meditation, meals and work. Second, you may undertake one of the retreats on the retreat programme led by a monk or nun from the monastic community. Guests on these retreats are asked to take part in the regular meditation routine and to help in the kitchens in the morning or to join in the morning work period with others. Accommodation is basic in domitories, so enquire as to what you need to bring – for example a warm sleeping bag, a blanket for use during meditation, and a towel and soap. Pack heavy socks or slippers too, as no shoes are worn indoors. Third, you may come to attend an event or course offered by the lay association of Amarvati, the Amaravati Upasaka/Upasika Association (AUA). These retreats are led by experienced lay teachers and provide a balance of silent practice with occasional small group work. Guidance is

offered to beginners. Whether led by monks and nuns or lay people, there is a full calendar of events, talks and long and short retreats on the programme. The following sets out what is on offer on each of these three types of visits, all of which are recommended. **Highly Recommended.**

Monastic Community
Amaravati Buddhist Monastery
Great Gaddesden
Hemel Hempstead
Herts HP1 3BZ

Tel: 01442 842455
Fax: 01442 843721
Website: www.amaravati.org

Men stay with the monks, women with the nuns. Write to either the Guest Monk or the Guest Nun, depending on your gender. If received as a monastic guest you will be expected to follow fully the regular monastic programme of the monks or nuns, including all meditations and work.

Retreat Centre
Amaravati Buddhist Monastery
Great Gaddesden
Hemel Hempstead
Herts HP1 3BZ

Tel: 01442 843239
Fax: 01442 843721
e-mail: retreats@amaravati.org
Website: www.amaravati.org
Related websites:
Amaravati Newsletter: www.forestsangha.org
Amaravati dhamma talks: www.dhammatalks.org.uk
Amaravati Lay Events: www.buddhacommunity.org
Amaravati Family Eevents: www.amaravati.org

Group retreats are mostly held in silence, with a routine that emphasises formal meditation practice and instruction. Guests have access to the monastery meditation rooms. Retreats are may be for a weekend or for up to ten days. Retreatants are expected to respect the retreat schedule. Mobile phone use and beeping watches are discouraged. The programme and information brochure tell you in detail what to bring and what happens during the retreat day. **Highly Recommended.**

Open: April to December. Receives men and women of all creeds.
Rooms: Mainly large dormitories, limited number of single and twin rooms. Men and women are separated in accommodation and certain other areas.
Facilities: Disabled, lounge, guest payphone, library, garden, shrine room, temple.
Spiritual Help: Meditation, time for refuge from the stresses of the world, encouragement for peaceful reflection, guided meditation, walking meditations possible in nearby woodlands.
Guests Admitted to: Temple, work of the community, all daily work routines.
Meals: Everyone eats together. Simple vegetarian food. No special diets or vegan possible.
Special Activities: Festivals, retreats, workshops, courses, long retreats – send for programme. Morning and evening chanting and meditation. A

quiet contemplative atmosphere is maintained.

Situation: Quiet, in countryside.

Maximum Stay: 10 days.

Bookings: Letter, website. Please note that bookings can not be made via telephone or e-mail.

Charges: Donations towards running costs welcome. These are calculated at about £15 per person per day. Retreatants are invited to give whatever they are able to offer.

Access: See website for travel details.

Amaravati Upasaka/Upasika Association (AUA)
Great Gaddesden   Tel: 020 8740 9748 / 01442 890034
Hemel Hempstead   e-mail: upasika@btinternet.com
Herts HP1 3BZ   Website: www.buddhacommunity.org

Open: All year. Receives men, women, groups.

Rooms: Mostly dormitories, a limited number of singles and twins (see entry above).

Facilties: Disabled, garden, lounge, library, payphone.

Spiritual Help: Personal talks, optional group sharing, sitting and walking meditation. Yoga and/or chi kung are offered on most retreats.

Guests admitted to: Shrine room, retreat centre complex, monastery temple, non-restricted areas of the monastery.

Meals: Everyone eats together. Vegetarian food. Special diets possible.

Special activities: Programme of events and retreats available from website. Saturday Days of Practice throughout year.

Situation: Very quiet, in countryside.

Maximum stay: 5 days.

Bookings: Letter, website.

> Men speak of perfection but they do precious little about it.
> Abba Alonius, Desert Father

Charges: On a donation basis. Suggested donations to cover costs are: weekend retreat £45, long weekend £55. Donations for longer retreats should be discussed. Days of Practice: bring food to share for mid-day meal and make a voluntary contribution towards the Retreat Centre operational costs.

Access: See website.

St Albans

All Saints Pastoral Centre
Shenley Lane
London Colney
St Albans   Tel: 01727 822010
Herts AL2 1AF   Fax: 01727 822880
                          e-mail: Conf.office@allsaintspc.org.uk

Christian

This is a big place which was once a convent. It sits in some 70 acres of grounds and has its own chapel. While private retreats can be organised for you here, the place is best suited for group retreats, conferences and meetings.

SPEC Centre for Young Adults
Fall Saints Pastoral Centre
London Colney
St Albans
Herts AL2 1AF

Tel: 01727 828888
Fax: 01727 822927
e-mail: spec@compuserve.com
Website: www.spec-centre.org.uk

Christian
Here is another good facility for young people from the age of 16 to 30 years. It is run by a team, headed up by a married couple, and there is accommodation for some seventy young guests. In addition, the Centre runs The Loft, a residential facility for 36 that accommodates children from 7 to 15 years of age. This latter facility is run by a team of volunteers. This is altogether a great place for retreats for youth groups.

Watford

Bhaktivedanta Manor
Hilfield Lane
Aldenham
Watford
Hertfordshire WD25 8EZ

Tel: 01923 854270
Fax: 01923 852896

In a lovely spot in the countryside, this Buddhist centre provides an ideal setting for a retreat. Weekend retreats are on offer, which teach Indian practices of mantra meditation and Bhakti yoga in ways that are attuned to the modern world.

> The spiritual life has nothing unconscious or passive about it.
> PAUL EVDOKIMOV

LINCOLNSHIRE

Bourne

Edenham Regional House
Church Lane
Edenham
Bourne
Lincs PE10 0LS

Tel/Fax: 01778 591358
e-mail: athawes@tsicali.co.uk

Christian – Ecumenical
This is a Georgian rectory, set in a lovely garden, which welcomes both individuals and small groups. There is a programme of quiet days and study courses, and Ignatian retreats are possible too. Two single and two twin bedrooms, as well as self-catering accommodation are on offer for guests. In addition there is a guest lounge, a large drawing room for meetings, a chapel and the parish church at hand.

Lincoln

Edward King House
The Old Palace
Lincoln
Lincs LN2 1PU

Tel: 01522 528778
Fax: 01522 527308
e-mail: enjoy@ekhs.org.uk
Website: www.ekhs.org.uk

Anglican
Once the residence of the Bishops of Lincoln, this beautiful and historic house is set in the area of the cathedral and next to the Old Palace. A programme of open events is on offer, which may include such retreats as *Journey of the Senses, Path of Holiness* (a pilgrimage around the cathedral), *Holocaust Theology, Individually Guided Prayer* and *Cursillo Spirituality.*

Open: All year except Christmas and New Year. Receives everyone. Children welcome.
Rooms: 5 singles, 11 twins.
Facilities: Conferences, garden, library, guest lounge, TV, payphone. No smoking.
Spiritual Help: Personal talks, spiritual direction.
Guests Admitted to: Unrestricted access.
Meals: Everyone eats together. Traditional food. Vegetarian and special diets.
Special Activities: Planned events – send for brochure.
Situation: In the city.
Maximum Stay: By arrangement.
Bookings: Letter, fax, e-mail, telephone.
Charges: B&B £21.50 per person per day, full board about £38.
Access: Train, coach, car to Lincoln.

Market Rasen

The Calyx Trust
Redhurst, Holton-cum-Beckering
Market Rasen
Lincs LN8 5NG

Tel/Fax: 01673 857927

Non-religious
This is a self-supporting trust, which is non-religious and aims to offer people a space in which to reflect, recuperate and find some stress-free time. The house, Redhurst, is set in a garden with an orchard, a heated pool and a little wood, on the edge of a village in farmlands. We have received mixed reactions from guests who have stayed here. Some have found it acceptable and others have complained about building works going on and food not up to scratch. We think it is best to write or telephone prior to any booking and tell them exactly what your expectations are as to standards of quiet and food.

Open: All year. Receives everyone. No pets.
Rooms: 1 single with private facilities, 2-twins with ensuite shower room. No smoking.
Facilities: Disabled – ground-floor accommodation in one of the twin rooms. Garden, small library, TV on request for room.
Spiritual Help: None.

Guests Admitted to: Unrestricted access.
Meals: Served in dining room or taken in room. Traditional food, some organic and garden produce. Vegetarian and special diets.
Special Activities: None.
Situation: Very quiet, in a village in the countryside.
Maximum Stay: By arrangement.
Bookings: Letter, fax, telephone 7a.m.–10p.m.
Charges: B&B £22–£25 per person, lunch £5.50, dinner £8.50, quiet day with lunch and refreshments £17.50.
Access: Train: Lincoln to Market Rasen – pick-up from station can be arranged. Bus and coach possible – ask for details. Car: Map provided with brochures.

Woodhall Spa

Time Away
Station House
Stixwold
Woodhall Spa
Lincs LN10 5HW   Tel: 01526 352548
                         e-mail: timeaway@stixwold.surfaid.org

Anglican – Non-religious
There is no chapel, daily offices or programme of retreats here, and many guests come for non-religious reasons. Having said that, Time Away, does offer itself for individuals to come on a private retreat, and the house is sufficiently rural to enable quiet to be enjoyed. The village church is at hand for prayer and worship. Groups of up to twelve may come for quiet days.

Open: All year. Receives everyone. Children welcome. Pets by arrangement.
Rooms: 4 rooms adaptable to single or twin occupancy.
Facilities: Garden, library, guest lounge that is very light, TV, direct dial phone, conferences for a maximum of 12 people.
Spiritual Help: Personal talks, village church nearby – no chapel on site.
Guests Admitted to: Unrestricted access.
Meals: Everyone eats together or taken in room. Traditional food. Vegetarian and special diets.
Special Activities: None.
Situation: Very quiet, in the countryside, overlooking river.
Maximum Stay: By arrangement but normally 2 weeks maximum.
Bookings: Letter, e-mail, telephone.
Charges: Quiet day with lunch and refreshments £14.50, full board £35 per person per day, £20 B&B.
Access: Train and bus possible – see brochure. Pick up from stations can be arranged. Car route.

The only reason for love is love.
BR LUC WHITEAKER

NORFOLK

Bowthorpe

Bowthorpe Community Trust
1 St Michael's Cottages
Bowthorpe Hall Road
Bowthorpe
Norwich
Norfolk NR5 9AA   Tel: 01603 746380

Ecumenical
The Trust offers short-stay accommodation set up through the combined sponsorship of Anglican, Baptist, Methodist, Quaker, Roman Catholic and United Reform churches. Nearby is a woodcraft workshop for the disadvantaged. A small sitting room, a selection of devotional books, and a prayer and study room, plus all meals provided, make this one of the more cosy places to stay. The Walsingham shrines are only an hour's drive away.

Open: All year. Receives men, women, non-retreatants.
Rooms: 1 single, 1 double.
Facilities: Garden, guest lounge, TV, phone, direct dialing.
Spiritual Help: Personal talks.
Guests Admitted to: Most areas.
Meals: Everyone eats together. Traditional food with provision possible for vegetarians. No special diets.
Special Activities: None.
Situation: Quiet, in town.
Maximum Stay: 2 weeks.
Bookings: Letter.
Charges: Day and weekly rate – ask for leaflet.
Access: Train: from Norwich to Thorpe. Car: via A47.

Bungay

The Community of All Hallows
Ditchingham
Bungay (Suffolk)
Norfolk NR35 2DZ   Tel: 01986 892840

Anglican
The Anglican Community of All Hallows runs a number of establishments from here. The list of their retreat places is as follows: All Hallows House (which comprises two places), The Gatehouse, Holy Cross House, St Gabriel's Conference Centre, St Mary's Lodge, and St Michael's House. The Gate House is a small self-catering house that provides lots of silence and solitude but is also ideal for a family holiday or retreat. Holy Cross House is the guest wing of the convent for those seeking to share in the worship of the Community. St Gabriel's is a huge complex with all modern facilities and to the very highest standards (details of St Gabriel's are given below). St Michael's House has its own chapel (for details of St Michael's, see below). There is a happy atmosphere here and group retreatants often return on an

individual basis. Open retreats of various kinds are held, bearing such titles as *An Introduction to Hildegard of Bingen, Circle Dancing and Quiet Spaces* and *Journey with the Saints*, while Advent and summer courses are available for residential groups. As to All Hallows House itself, it can hardly be faulted for hospitality, comfort, nice food, and its pleasant sitting room. Do not be confused about where this place is situated. It is in Norfolk (about 12 miles from Norwich) but the postal address puts it in Suffolk because of the Bungay address. The community here really work hard to make going on retreat a comfortable and spiritual event. The choice of accommodation is wide and the church and domestic arrangements among the best. **Highly Recommended.**

St Gabriel's Centre
All Hallows Convent
Ditchingham
Bungay (Suffolk)   Tel: 01986 892133
Norfolk NR35 2DT   Fax: 01986 895838
Website: www.All-Hallows.org.uk

Anglican
Open: Most of the year except Christmas and Easter. Receives men, women, young people, families, groups, non-retreatants.
Rooms: 40 singles, 40 doubles.
Facilities: Disabled, conferences, payphone.
Spiritual Help: None.
Guests Admitted to: Chapel and gardens.
Meals: Everyone eats together. Traditional food. Vegetarian and special diets.
Special Activities: None.
Situation: Quiet.
Maximum Stay: 2 weeks.
Bookings: Letter, telephone.
Charges: £28.50 per person per night mid-week, £35–£40 inclusive weekends.
Access: Car is easiest, but coach from Victoria Station to Bungay, train to Norwich both possible. Discuss when you book if not coming by car.

St Michael's House
All Hallows Convent
Ditchingham
Bungay (Suffolk)
Norfolk NR35 2DT   Tel: 01986 895636
Website: www.Allhallows-retreats.co.uk

Anglican
Open: Most of year. Receives everyone.
Rooms: 17 singles, 3 doubles.
Facilities: Disabled, conferences, chapel, garden, library, guest lounge, payphone (01986 894607).
Spiritual Help: None.
Guests Admitted to: Convent chapel and gardens.
Meals: Everyone eats together. Traditional whole food. Vegetarian and special diets.
Special Activities: Planned programme of events – send for brochure.

Situation: Quiet.
Maximum Stay: 2 weeks.
Bookings: Letter, telephone.
Charges: £28 per person per night mid-week, £33.50–£40 inclusive weekends.
Access: Car is easiest, but coach from Victoria Station to Bungay, train to Norwich both possible. Discuss when you book if not coming by car.

Norwich

Community of the Sacred Passion
All Hallows
Rouen Road, Norwich
Norfolk NR1 1QT   Tel: 01603 624738
e-mail: Sister.pamela@talk21.com

Church of England – High Anglican
Though it is on a busy street, All Hallows House has a peaceful atmosphere inside. St Julian's Church is next door and contains a chapel that is built on the site of the cell of the fourteenth-century mystic Julian of Norwich. Her *Revelations of Divine Love* is a classic English Christian mystical work and can be obtained at all good book shops. Reading her book and then coming here for a retreat built around some of her writings might prove a worthwhile spiritual journey.

Open: All year. Receives men, women, groups, young people.
Rooms: 3 singles, 4 twins.
Facilities: Church, chapel, garden, small library, Julian Library next door, guest lounge, TV. No smoking. Silence observed after night prayers of Compline.
Spiritual Help: Personal talks, spiritual direction, personal retreat direction.
Guests Admitted to: Chapel.
Meals: Everyone eats together. Traditional food. Vegetarian and special diets on request.
Special Activities: None.
Situation: In the town, a busy location, next to St. Julian's Shrine and Church.
Maximum Stay: 2 weeks.
Bookings: Letter, e-mail, telephone before 8.30p.m. please.
Charges: By donation – usually £10–£15 per night.
Access: Rail, bus or car to Norwich.

Surlingham

Padmaloka Buddhist Retreat Centre for Men
Lesingham House
Surlingham   Tel: 01508 538112
Norwich   Fax: 01508 538076
Norfolk NR14 7AL   e-mail: padmaloka@padmaloka.org.uk
Website: www.padmaloka.org.uk

Buddhist – Friends of the Western Buddhist Order
This is a Buddhist retreat centre for men only, run by the Friends of the Western Buddhist Order. Here, no time is wasted in getting you into stillness,

simplicity and the study of what may be the fastest growing spiritual tradition in the West. In addition to meditation and other related classes, you can discover how to make spiritual practice work in your career through talks by men who have achieved it. They may be managing directors of successful companies or even medical school lecturers, but all have developed what Buddhists term 'right livelihood'. Bring a sleeping bag, towel, soap, and old clothes and shoes for the work periods that everyone does during the day. For meditation wear loose clothes. There is much here that will prove meaningful to modern men who are burdened with career and personal responsibilities and are searching for balance and spiritual nourishment in their lives. The teaching is soundly based on the Buddhist way of life and principles. Padmaloka is a centre for the ordination of men; others may join but must first go to some introductory meditation courses at one of the FWBO centres. All this is explained in the various brochures available. The main purpose of open retreats is to introduce men to meditation and Buddhist rituals, and to discuss central Buddhist themes including the life story of the Buddha, Buddhist insight and what spiritual friendship really means. Fellowship, friendship and harmony among men are the aim. Many men are seriously challenged to look again at their present lifestyle and values when they have made a Buddhist commitment at Padmaloka. Facilities are modern and handsome with comfortable rooms, and there is a garden and a small delightful courtyard. This is a happy, peaceful and justly famous place with a gracious atmosphere. **Highly Recommended.**

> It is not so much the organism or the species that evolves, but the entire system, species and environment. The two are inseparable.
>
> ALFRED LOTKA

Open: All year. Receives men only to spend a set period of time up to two weeks on retreat.

Rooms: Dormitories – bring your own towel and sleeping bag. The term 'dormitories' needs a bit of unpacking here; these are like a double room but with bunks, and they are modern and not at all prep-school-style.

Facilities: Disabled, camping, garden, park, library, guest lounge, guest telephone, book shop.

Spiritual Help: Personal talks, spiritual direction, group sharing, meditation, directed study, yoga, tai chi, Buddhist devotional practice.

Guests Admitted to: Unrestricted access except to Ordination Team and Support Team areas. Work of the community.

Meals: Everyone eats together. Vegan food.

Special Activities: Planned programme – send for brochure.

Situation: Quiet, in a village, in countryside.

Maximum Stay: 2 weeks.

Bookings: Letter.

Charges: £25 per person per night – concession £22.

Access: Rail to Norwich then taxi or bus. Bus to Surlingham village drops you at the gate.

Sutton

St Fursey's Orthodox Christian Study Centre
St Fursey's House
111 Neville Road
Sutton, Norwich
Norfolk NR12 9RR   Tel: 01692 580552

Orthodox Christian in the Patriarchate of Antioch
St Fursey's House is a small Orthodox Christian home and study centre made
from a modern house, set in the Norfolk Broads. It exists to help nurture the
Orthodox Christian faith in an English context through regular quiet days
and talks on Orthodox spirituality, weekly ecumenical Bible studies and
evenings of discussion. There are facilities for overnight stays and individual
retreats. The chapel has a remarkable atmosphere of peace and there is a
wealth of icons. **Highly Recommended.**

Open: Most of the year. Receives men, women, young people, non-retreatants.
Rooms: 1 single, 1 double.
Facilities: Garden, library, guest lounge, TV.
Spiritual Help: Personal talks, spiritual direction, personal retreat direction,
    directed study, Orthodox spirituality, daily services, monthly liturgy.
Guests Admitted to: Chapel and work of community.
Meals: Everyone eats together. Simple traditional food. Vegetarian and
    special diets. Discuss meals when you ask for information.
Special Activities: Daily services, visits to other Orthodox churches, pilgrim-
    ages and other visits, weekly Bible study.
Situation: Village.
Maximum Stay: 5 days.
Bookings: Letter.
Charges: By donations.
Access: Rail is possible, but car is best. Ask for details of route.

Walsingham

Shrine of Our Lady of Walsingham
Knight Street   Tel: 01328 820239
Walsingham   Fax: 01328 820990
Norfolk NR22 6BW   e-mail: accom@olw-shrine.org.uk
                                     Website: www.walsingham.org.uk

Anglican
Walsingham Shrine is an ancient place of Christian pilgrimage and this is a
famous, busy pilgrimage centre. This means that you will not find facilities for
silence or for spiritual guidance. To go on a pilgrimage to a holy place is a long-
established religious practice of most major world faiths. It can, and ought to
be, regarded as a kind of retreat, especially as the pilgrim hopes for a deepening of personal spirituality. Before starting out, read about the history of
Walsingham so that you may understand what has drawn Christians there over
the centuries. This should put meaning into what might otherwise simply be a
visit to another monument. The Centre is a pleasant place to stay and from
which to visit either this Anglican shrine or the Roman Catholic one situated a
mile away. Both continue to attract many thousands of people every year.

Open: 1 February to 8 December. Receives everyone. Children welcome.

Rooms: 59 singles, 56 doubles, 13 triples (accommodation office at 6 Common Place).

Facilities: Disabled, conferences, garden, library, guest lounge, TV, payphone.

Spiritual Help: No facilities for silence, and spiritual direction only on request. Personal talks, group sharing on retreat. There is a Shrine priest who can help with spiritual programmes.

Guests Admitted to: Church, chapel, shrine room, work of community.

Meals: Everyone eats together. Traditional simple food. Vegetarian and special diets. Self-catering facilities.

Special Activities: Each weekend there is a programme organised by the parish groups attending. This usually includes Stations of the Cross, Procession and Benediction.

Situation: Rather busy, in the village.

Maximum Stay: 1 month.

Bookings: Letter, fax, e-mail, telephone 9a.m.–7p.m. Monday to Friday.

Charges: £22 per person per night.

Access: By car is best, but public transportation is possible. Ask for best routes.

Sue Ryder Retreat House
Walsingham
Norfolk NR22 6AA

Tel: 01328 820622
Fax: 01328 820505

Inter-denominational

Facilities are offered here for groups and individuals to make private retreats. There are no spiritual programmes or direction available. Groups usually have their own facilitator. The staff concentrate on providing for the practical needs of visitors.

Open: All year. Receives all. Children welcome.

Rooms: 8 singles, 9 doubles, dormitories, hermitage.

Facilities: Conferences, small garden, guest lounge, TV, payphone.

Spiritual Help: None.

Guests Admitted to: Chapel.

Meals: Taken in guest house. Traditional food. Vegetarian and special diets.

Special Activities: None.

Situation: Quiet, in the countryside.

Maximum Stay: None.

Bookings: Letter, fax, telephone.

Charges: Ask for rates.

Access: Car route best.

The Friars' Quire
Order of Malta Volunteers
5 High Street
Walsingham, Norfolk

Contact details: Write to or telephone Peter Cole, 10 Radnor Walk, London SW3 4BN. Tel: 07788 584300. Do not write directly to The Friars' Quire.

The Friars' Quire is a converted Victorian school house next door to a Methodist Chapel and within walking distance of both the Anglican and Catholic Walsingham shrines. It has accommodation for ten self-catering guests. There is wheelchair access.

SUFFOLK

Beccles

Ringsfield Eco-Study Centre
Ringsfield Hall
Ringsfield
Beccles
Suffolk NR34 8JR

Tel: 01502 713020
e-mail: info@ringsfield-hall.freeserve.co.uk
Website: www.ringsfield-hall.freeserve.co.uk

Educational Christian foundation – Eco-spirituality
This is a large brick house set in 14 acres of grounds offering an amazing variety of amenities, including woodlands, meadows, ponds, and gardens. In addition there is a playing field with football pitch, adventure play equipment, campfire circle and barbecue, small chapel, and a renovated hermitage set in a new woodland. This is a great place for a retreat, particularly for the young or for someone who wants a few days of solitude alone in the woodlands in the hermitage. The programme includes a number of workshops on topics such as emotional and social literacy, conflict resolution, earth education and biblical themes. There are earth walks and story-telling as well.

> *Be strong, let your heart take courage, all who hope in the Lord.*
> PSALM 30

Open: All year for self-catering, otherwise for programme. Receives all. Children welcome.
Rooms: Dormitories, hermitage, cottage with 9 beds.
Facilities: Conferences, garden, park, library, guest lounge, games facilities, tennis court, nature trails, playing fields.
Spiritual Help: Group sharing, personal retreat direction.
Guests Admitted to: Unrestricted access.
Meals: Everyone eats together. Traditional food. Vegetarian and special diets. Self-catering facilities.
Special Activities: Plannned programme relating to faith and environment – brochure available. Quiet day retreats.
Situation: Quiet, in the countryside, in 14 acres of grounds.
Maximum Stay: 1 week.
Bookings: Letter, fax, e-mail, telephone.
Charges: Full board £18–£85.50 depending on how many nights you stay and the number of people in your group. Self-catering groups £10.50 per person per night. There is a youth weekends tariff as well. Hermitage donation £5.10 daily to The Ringsfield Hall Trust.
Access: Car route best. 3 miles from Beccles.

Broadwater

Niggles House
Broadwater, Near Framlingham
Suffolk IP13 9LS   Tel: 01728 723800

Christian – Russian Orthodox
People of all spiritual traditions are invited to stay here for short periods to enjoy some peace and to renew their sense of God's love for them. The two foundation stones of the residents are the biblical way of contemplation as taught by the Fellowship of Contemplative Prayer (see Helpful Address section) and the Russian Orthodox Church. Throughout the year there is a series of quiet days and various events of a religious nature. For those seeking solitude, there is a hermitage in the garden. A weekly timetable gives structure to your stay here.

Open: All year except Christmas. Receives men, women, young people, groups. Non-retreatants for the day only.
Rooms: 2 singles, 1 double, hermitage.
Facilities: Chapel, garden, library, guest lounge.
Spiritual Help: Personal talks, meditation through contemplative prayer.
Guests Admitted to: Chapel, garden.
Meals: Everyone eats together. Whole food. Vegetarian and special diets.
Special Activities: Planned programme – send for brochure.
Situation: Quiet, in the countryside, open views.
Maximum Stay: 1 week.
Bookings: Letter.
Charges: About £20 full board per day. Otherwise see brochure for rates.
Access: Train: Wickham Market, pick-up can be arranged. Car: via A12 or A14, signed to Framlingham.

Bury St Edmunds

Hengrave Hall Centre   Tel: 01284 701561/2
Bury St Edmunds   Fax: 01284 702950
Suffolk 1P28 6LZ   e-mail: co-ordinator@hengravehallcentre.org.uk
                                   Website: www.hengravehallcentre.org.uk
Christian – Ecumenical
Hengrave Hall is a Tudor mansion set in its own grounds of some 45 acres and is the home today of an ecumenical community of Christians living, working and worshipping together. Membership is drawn from any of the Christian churches. It is a community devoted to reconciliation. The programme, available on their website, offers a range of retreats, including quiet days.

Open: All year except Christmas, Easter. Receives everyone. Children welcome. No pets.
Rooms: 10 singles, 4 doubles, 2 dormitories, barn, hermitage, campsite, 6 caravan spaces. Mobile phones and radios/tapes permitted.
Facilities: Disabled, conferences, camping, garden with Prayer Walk, library, group TV, guest phone (01284 754801).
Spiritual Help: Personal talks, group sharing, spiritual direction, personal retreat direction, meditation.

Guests Admitted to: Church, chapel, grounds, work of community.
Meals: Everyone eats in guest house. Food is simple and traditional.
Vegetarian and special diets. Self-catering.
Special Activities: Planned programme of events – send for information.
Situation: Quiet, in a village, near countryside.
Maximum Stay: 14 days.
Bookings: Letter, fax, e-mail, online, telephone 9a.m.–5p.m. week days.
Charges: Full board £39–£50 per 24 hours, B&B £25.
Access: Train or bus to Bury St Edmunds, then taxi. Car route easy.

Hengrave Hall Youth Centre   Tel: 01284 754537
Bury St Edmunds   Fax: 01284 702950
Suffolk IP28 6LZ e-mail: administrator@hengravehallcentre.org.uk
         Website: www.hengravehallcentre.org.uk

Christian – Ecumenical
The Centre is self-catering, with use of the grounds of Hengrave Hall and beds
for 41 guests and group leaders. There are also meeting rooms, a kitchen, a
dining room and a wheelchair accessible gymnasium. In addition there is a barn
dormitory which can take another 28 in bunk beds. Camping is also possible.

Clare

Clare Priory
Clare, Sudbury   Tel: 01787 277326
Suffolk CO10 8NX   Fax: 01787 278688
        e-mail: clare.priory@virgin.net

Roman Catholic
Set in eight acres of secluded gardens beside a river, Clare Priory remains behind
its walls in the same solitude and quiet that it has enjoyed for centuries. Now it
is a place to share the daily routine of the Augustian friars and the lay community. Private or guided retreats for individuals and groups are available, as well as
a regular programme of retreats, events, quiet days, away days and theme weekends. Spiritual guidance is also available by arrangement. There is a chapel and
a library. Telephone the Secretary Monday to Friday 9.30a.m.–1p.m. and find
out what is currently on offer at this lovely monastic retreat in Suffolk.

Great Ashfield

Water Hall Retreat Centre
Great Ashfield, Bury St Edmunds
Suffolk IP31 3HP   Tel: 020 8981 1225 (all enquiries)

Buddhist
Water Hall, a simple farmhouse with dormitories, is run by the London
Buddhist Centre specifically for retreats. These are usually in the form of
introductory weekend retreats for adults wishing to learn meditation as well
as attending more advanced classes. Classes are taken by practising Buddhists
who are members of the Friends of the Western Buddhist Order. There are
also courses about Buddhism where you can learn who the Buddha was, what
he taught and what relevance his teaching has for us in the West today. There

are short courses, summer retreats and gay men's retreats. You book through the London Buddhist Centre (see London section).

Open: During organised group retreats. Receives everyone – depending on kind of retreat.
Rooms: Dormitories.
Facilities: Please enquire.
Spiritual Help: Meditation, directed study.
Guests Admitted to: Unrestricted access.
Meals: Everyone eats together. Vegetarian.
Special Activities: Special programme of planned events – send for brochure.
Situation: Very quiet, in the village, in countryside. No passing traffic.
Maximum Stay: 10 days.
Bookings: Letter, telephone.
Charges: See brochure as charges depend on course.
Access: Rail: Bury St Edmunds. Car.

Newmarket

**The Old Stable House Centre
3 Sussex Lodge
Fordham Road, Newmarket
Suffolk CB8 7AF**
Tel/Fax: 01638 667190
e-mail: louis@bautain.fsnet.co.uk

Roman Catholic
Very close to Newmarket Heath, this former stable offers a warm, comfortable environment with as much freedom as possible for individuals and groups to work on their personal and spiritual development. The atmosphere is informal and home-like. The idea has been to create an environment that supports your inner journey, encourages growth toward wholeness, and challenges you to be open and aware.

Open: Most of the year. Receives men, women, young people, families, groups, non-retreatants. **Children welcome over 14 years of age.**
Rooms: 4 singles, 4 twins, 1 family room. No smoking.
Facilities: Disabled, conferences, library, garden, park, guest lounge, TV, guest phone. Use of school hall for yoga, dance and other activities.
Spiritual Help: Retreats and workshops designed to meet the needs of individual groups. Group sharing, directed study, meditation, spiritual guidance, acupuncture, Reiki.
Guests Admitted to: Unrestricted access.
Meals: The Centre is a self-catering one.
Special Activities: Planned programme of events – send for brochure.
Situation: Quiet, with a small woodland area and paddock. 5 minutes walk from the local town and supermarkets. National Racing Stud nearby. 12 miles from Cambridge.
Maximum Stay: 1 week.
Bookings: Letter, fax, telephone 9a.m.–6p.m.
Charges: About £15 per 24 hours. Rates in leaflet.
Access: Rail: Newmarket (5 minutes away). Local buses. Car: via A45. Excellent map available when you book.

Central England

BIRMINGHAM AND WEST MIDLANDS

Birmingham

Woodbrooke Quaker Study Centre　　　Tel: 0121 472 5171
1046 Bristol Road　　　　　　　　　　Fax: 0121 472 5173
Birmingham B29 6LJ　　e-mail: enquiries@woodbrooke.org.uk
　　　　　　　　　　　　　Website: www.woodbrooke.org.uk

Quaker

Woodbrooke welcomes all of any faith or none and runs a programme of courses in addition to retreat facilities, with twice-daily meetings for worship. It is set in ten acres of organically managed grounds – an oasis in the city. It is one of the Selly Oak Colleges and therefore part of a unique campus, a centre for ecumenical and international relationships. The library is excellent. Guided individual and group retreats are available, as well as accredited courses.

Open: All year. Receives everyone.
Rooms: Up to 70 singles and doubles.
Facilities: Conferences, gardens, park, library, guest lounge, TV, guest telephone.
Spiritual Help: Spiritual direction, meditation, directed study.
Guests Admitted to: Public rooms, meeting room, silent room.
Meals: Everyone eats together. Vegetarian and special diets.
Special Activities: Planned programme – send for information.
Situation: Quiet in city.
Maximum Stay: By arrangement.
Bookings: Letter, telephone.
Charges: See programme or ask for charges when you telephone.
Access: Train: Birmingham New Street. Bus: Nos. 61, 62. Car: A38, six miles from M42.

Solihull

Fellowship of Contemplative Prayer
202 Ralph Road
Solihull
West Midlands B90 3LE　　　　　　Tel/Fax: 0121 745 6522

Inter-denominational

The Fellowship of Contemplative Prayer is a loose-knit association of individuals and groups who follow the way of prayer taught by the founder, Robert Coulson, which is called 'The Prayer of Stillness'. Central administration is minimal and groups and retreats are largely self-run. There are various publications available and various retreats offered around the country. An annual newsletter gives details of Fellowship contacts and retreats held in the UK and Ireland. Membership and details are available on request.

Wolverhampton

The Parkdale Yoga Centre
10 Park Dale West
Wolverhampton WV1

Tel: 01902 424048
e-mail: info@heartyoga.org.uk
Website: www.heartyoga.org.uk

Yoga spirituality
Located in the southern part of Wolverhampton, the Parkdale Yoga Centre is in a Victorian house and has been going now for some years. It is run by a small urban commune which focuses on yoga practice and teaching, organic growing and holistic living. There is a host of yoga classes held here so you need to call to find out what is available when and discuss your level and requirements. Beginners, intermediate and advanced classes are available. There are both summer and weekend yoga retreats on offer, as well as a special beginners weekend yoga retreat.

BUCKINGHAMSHIRE

Buckingham

The Courtyard Centre at Barton Manor
Barton Hartshorne Manor
Barton Hartshorne
Buckingham MK18 4JU

Open spirituality
Guided individual retreats are on offer here, as well as private retreats. Health and healing, meditation, counselling, and body and breath work are all of particular interest. This is an old manor set in peaceful Buckinghamshire surroundings with easy access from Milton Keynes and only an hour from London. It is a busy place that is involved in business retreats and workshops, weddings and baby naming ceremonies and other activities. There is accommodation for some 19 people, plus spaces for workshops and group retreats.

Chalfont St Peter

Mount Carmel Prayer House
Holy Cross Convent
Chalfont St Peter
Buckinghamshire SL9 9DW

Tel: 020 8997 2858

Christian – Ecumenical
The House has self-catering accommodation with 6 singles. There is a chapel, lounge and conference room. All rooms are on ground level.

---

66 Tread softly! All earth is holy ground. 99
CHRISTINA ROSSETTI

Chesham

Little Grove
Grove Lane
Chesham Tel: 01494 782720
Bucks HP5 3QQ e-mail: bookings@cortijo-romero.co.uk
Website: www.Cortijo-Romero.co.uk

Mind Body Spirit
Little Grove is close to London but quiet in the Bucks countryside and situated in two acres of fields. Courses at Little Grove include topics such as holistic massage, psycho-drama, sacred dancing and African drumming. There is also *Moving with the Landscape, Finding Your Voice*, and *Hidden Talents*. The aim of all the courses and events is personal growth.

Open: All year. Receives men, women, young people, families, groups, non-retreatants. Children welcome at certain events – check first if it is suitable.
Rooms: Single and double rooms available.
Facilities: Conferences, camping, garden, guest lounge, payphone, direct dialing.
Spiritual Help: Varies according to what course you attend.
Guests Admitted to: Almost everywhere.
Meals: Taken in guest house. Self-catering facilities. Whole food. Vegetarian and special diets.
Special Activities: Planned programme of events – send for brochure.
Situation: Quiet.
Maximum Stay: None.
Bookings: Letter, telephone
Charges: See brochure, or for individuals please telephone.
Access: Train, bus and car all possible.

Henley on Thames

St Katharine's
Parmoor
Henley-on-Thames RG9 6NN Tel: 01494 881037
e-mail: srpf@fish.co.uk

Christian – Ecumenical
This is a retreat house run by the Community of Sue Ryder Prayer Fellowship. It is set in lovely and generous grounds. The facilities include day groups, conferences and residential retreats for individuals and groups. Everyone is welcome.

Milton Keynes

Society of the Sacred Mission Priory
1 Linford Lane
Willen, Milton Keynes
Bucks MK15 9DC Tel: 01908 663749

Anglican
This is a small Community of older women who want guests to enjoy their community home, so you will get a warm welcome. Other members of the

> *Let all guests that come be received like Christ.*
> Rule of Saint Benedict

community and different associates live nearby, and the whole community joins forces in the two local churches for services and worship. There is Morning Prayer, Midday Office and Evensong in the parish church, and Compline in the house chapel.

Open: All year. Receives men, women.
Rooms: 1 single, 1 double. Silence from 9p.m.–9a.m. No mobile phones, radios, tapes.
Facilities: Garden, library, TV.
Spiritual Help: None.
Guests Admitted to: Unrestricted access.
Meals: Everyone eats together or meals can be taken in room. Traditional food. Vegetarians.
Special Activities: None.
Situation: Quiet.
Maximum Stay: 10 days in first instance.
Bookings: Letter.
Charges: Donations usually, but ask please when booking.
Access: Best by car.

Stoke Poges

The Quiet Garden Movement
Stoke Park Farm
Park Road
Stoke Poges
Bucks SL2 4PG

Tel: 01753 643050
Fax: 01753 643081
e-mail: quiet.garden@ukonline.co.uk
Website: www.quietgarden.co.uk

Ecumenical
Here is your opportunity to have some quiet sanctuary time somewhere near at hand without going away on a retreat. The Quiet Garden Trust movement begun in 1992 and was the vision of Rev Philip D. Roderick. The trust encourages the provision of local venues where there is an opportunity to spend time in rest and prayer. A quiet garden comes into being when someone opens their home and garden for occasional days of stillness and reflection. Another development has been to offer quiet spaces in cities to give opportunities for prayer, learning about Christian life, hospitality and healing. Quiet gardens and quiet spaces have taken root also in retreat houses, churches, schools and hospitals. The mission statement of this ministry of hospitality and prayer sums it up: 'The primary vision of the Quiet Garden Movement is to initiate and resource a network of local opportunities for prayer, silence, reflection and the appreciation of beauty; for learning about Christian life and spirituality; and for experiencing creativity and healing in the context of God's love.' Send for information and a list of quiet gardens across the world. **Highly Recommended.**

DERBYSHIRE

Alfreton

**Community of the Prince of Peace
Baptist Monastery
4 Church Street
Riddings, Alfreton
Derbys DE55 4BW**

Tel: 01773 603533
e-mail: commpp@ukonline.co.uk

Baptist
The Community of the Prince of Peace is a new Baptist religious community serving the church, which was founded in 1997. The Community is listed as a Baptist organisation in the Baptist Union Directory and it is a member of the ecumenical Conference of Religious. The monastery itself is an attractive Victorian house in two acres of grounds in a quiet location with nice views over parkland. Close to the M1, it is easily accessible.

Open: All year. Closed Sunday and Monday afternoons. Receives men, women, small groups.
Rooms: 1 single, 3 doubles, self-contained flat with 2 bedrooms. No smoking. Bring own soap and towel.
Facilities: Sitting room, dining room, library, garden, chapel.
Spiritual Help: Personal talks, personal retreat direction, spiritual direction if requested.
Guests Admitted to: Almost everywhere.
Meals: Taken with Community in silence. Self-catering for breakfast and refreshments. Plain food. Vegetarian and special diets if notice given.
Special Activities: None as such, but all are welcome to share in community prayers.
Situation: Quiet, in a small town.
Maximum Stay: By arrangement.
Bookings: Letter, telephone.
Charges: No fixed charge but donation guidelines of £25 per person per night full board, £10 for a Quiet Day with lunch and a room.
Access: Car: M1/J26 and J28

Bakewell

**Bradford Dale Retreat
Bankside
Youlgrave, Bakewell
Derbys DE45 1WD**

Tel: 01629 636550

Quaker
Here there are five major retreat options: *Just Relax and Enjoy Retreat, Focus and Reflect* (as an individual guided retreat), *Life Decision Retreat* (during a time of change in your life), *Working Retreat* and *Regular Support Retreat* (on which you partake of personal spiritual direction on a regular basis, say once a month). Bradford Dale Retreat offers quiet space designed for those who need time out from a stressful or overly busy lifestyle.

Open: All year. Receives men, women.

Rooms: 1 single, 1 double. There is a cottage called Honey Pot and a Listening Hut, which is a small summerhouse for contemplation, rest and just quiet sitting.

Facilities: Guest lounge, garden.

Spiritual Help: Personal talks, spiritual direction, personal retreat direction, meditation, directed study. Alternative healing therapies available locally.

Guests Admitted to: Unrestricted access.

Meals: Self-catering.

Special Activities: Themed retreats.

Situation: Very quiet, in a village, in the countryside.

Maximum Stay: 1 week.

Bookings: Letter, telephone 6–7p.m.

Charges: Charges run at about £48 for an Away Day Retreat, £92 for a 22-hour retreat, £156 for a 46-hour retreat over three days.

Access: Train, bus and car all possible. Directions given on booking.

Belper

Community of St Lawrence
Field Lane, Belper
Derbys DE5 1DD   Tel: 01773 822585

Anglican

Open: All year. Receives everyone.

Rooms: 24 singles, 7 doubles.

Facilities: Conferences for small groups, guest lounge, library, garden, TV, payphone.

Spiritual Help: Personal talks if requested.

Guests Admitted to: Chapel.

Meals: Everyone eats together. Plain food. Vegetarian and special diets.

Special Activities: No planned programme of events, as most groups bring their own spiritual director.

Situation: Quiet, in a small town.

Maximum Stay: By arrangement.

Bookings: Letter, telephone.

Charges: About £25 per 24 hours.

Access: Train: Belper, then short walk. Bus: Derby to Belper. Car: A6.

Horsley Woodhouse

Sozein Trust
The Old Vicarage
Church Lane
Horsley Woodhouse
Derbys DE7 6BB   Tel: 01332 780598

Ecumenical – Anglican sacraments

Sozein is a New Testament verb signifying the setting free, making safe and healing of the individual or the community. It refers to God's work on behalf of us all. This defines the purpose and the work carried out at the Old

Vicarage by the Rev Neil Broadbent and his wife. Healing services, group prayer, the offering of a quiet healing environment and the laying on of hands are some of the activities here. Special activities include courses on *Christian Spirituality, Christian Mystics, The Fruits of Silence, Julian of Norwich,* and *Prayer and Contemplative Practice,* among other subjects.

Open: Open by arrangement – but closed for Christmas, Holy Week. Receives men, women, groups. Non-retreatants for Quiet Days or counselling.
Rooms: 1 single, 1 double.
Facilities: Disabled welcome on a day visit – but toilet facilities are not suitable for wheelchairs. Chapel, garden, library, TV, guest telephone, direct dialing.
Spiritual Help: Personal talks, spiritual direction, personal retreat direction, prayer, Anglican sacraments.
Guests Admitted to: This is a family house. Prayer room, library, kitchen access.
Meals: Taken together as part of family or may be taken privately in your room if you wish. Traditional/organic food. Vegetarian and special diets by prior arrangement.
Special Activities: Retreats are individually tailored, so discussion is necessary beforehand.
Situation: Quiet, in the countryside, with hills in background.
Maximum Stay. Usually 4 days.
Bookings: Letter, telephone 9–10a.m., 6–7p.m. Monday to Friday.
Charges: By donation – realistically £20 to £40 per day suggested, depending on individual spiritual talks and direction.
Access: Bus, car routes possible. Train plus bus from Derby. See leaflet.

Morley

Morley Retreat and Conference House
Church Lane
Morley   Tel: 01332 831293
Ilkeston   Fax: 01332 834944
Derbys DE7 6DE   e-mail: wardens@morleyretreat.co.uk
Website: www.morleyretreat.co.uk

Anglican
Modern accommodation has been built for guests next to the old Morley Rectory. There is a good programme of retreat and house events, ranging from Quiet Days to a weekend devoted to silent prayer called, appropriately, *Listening to God* and such retreats as *Painting and Photography Holiday, Looking at Trees – in the Bible and in the Garden, Nothing Impossible with God, Enneagram Workshop.* The house is a former Georgian rectory set in its own five acres of grounds amid rich farmlands. There is a large meeting room with a log fire in winter, two smaller sitting rooms, a chapel and even a bar. Accommodation is both in the main house and in an annexe.

Open: Most of the year on request except first week of New Year. Receives men, women, young people, non-retreatants, groups.
Rooms: 24 singles, 5 twins. **Ask what you need to bring.**
Facilities: Chapel, conferences, garden, 5-acre park, guest lounge, TV, payphone (01332 832383).

Spiritual Help: None.

Guests Admitted to: Unrestricted access.

Meals: Everyone eats together. Traditional food. Vegetarian and special diets.

Special Activities: Planned events, which include walking and other craft holidays – send for brochure.

Situation: Very quiet, in the countryside, with a walled garden and 14th-century parish church, set in the midst of 5 acres of grounds.

Maximum Stay: By arrangement.

Bookings: Letter, fax, e-mail, telephone 7.30a.m.–10.30p.m.

Charges: £38 full board per 24 hrs, £20 B&B.

Access: Rail: Derby, but there are no local bus services. Car: via M1, Exit 25, followed by A52, A61 and A608.

Community of the Holy Name
Convent of the Holy Name
Morley Road
Oakwood
Derbys DE21 4QZ

Tel: 01332 670483
Fax: 01332 669712
Website: www.chnderby.org

This is a small cottage offering room for about eight guests. It is a place for silence and space. You can join the community for Mass and any of the prayer offices said during the day.

Unstone

Unstone Grange
Crow Lane
Unstone, Dronfield
Derbys S18 4AL

Tel: 01246 412344
Fax: 01246 412344
e-mail: admin@unstonegrange.co.uk
Website: www.unstonegrange.co.uk

Open spirituality – Mind Body Spirit

With over two acres of organic gardens and orchards, Unstone offers guided retreats, private retreats and working holidays. Meditation, prayer and group process are among the events that this centre focuses on, plus a lot more too. There are 35 bed spaces. Group B&B is possible, as well as self-catering and camping. Special diets can be catered for. The atmosphere is attractive and pleasant. From about £11 per person per night self-catering.

Whaley Bridge

Community of the King of Love
Whaley Hall
Reservoir Road
Whaley Bridge
High Peak
Derbys SK23 7BL

Tel: 01663 732495
e-mail: the guardiansckl@compuserve.com
Website: www.whaleyhallckl.org.uk

Christian Ecumenical

This is an 1853 grit-stone house built for a mill-owner which has now run for many years as a retreat centre. The community is ecumenical and composed of both men and women. This is a warmly welcoming house, run on peaceful and unhurried lines, where you are made to feel at home. The lounge is full of comfortable chairs and the dining room a cheerful and lively place during meals. Many Anglican clergy and others come here for meetings and a few days retreat as a group. Close by are good walks. We liked it especially as a place for a private retreat. There is a programme of Quiet Days and various events. **Highly Recommended.**

Open: All year. Receives everyone.
Rooms: 4 singles, 13 twins.
Facilities: Conferences, guest lounge, library, garden, TV, guest phone, chapel.
Spiritual Help: Personal talks, spiritual direction, personal retreat direction.
Guests Admitted to: Unrestricted access.
Meals: Everyone eats together. Traditional food. Vegetarians and special diets.
Special Activities: Planned programme of events.
Situation: Quiet, in a small town.
Maximum Stay: By arrangement – usually only short stays.
Bookings: Letter, telephone.
Charges: £42 for 24 hours, £80 for 48 hours. Longer stays negotiable.
Access: Train: Whaley Bridge. Car: A6.

GLOUCESTERSHIRE

Cheltenham

Glenfall House
Mill Lane
Charlton Kings
Cheltenham
Glos GL54 4EP

Tel: 01242 583654
Fax: 01242 251314
e-mail: glenfall@surfaid.org
Website: www.glenfall-house.co.uk

Christian
This is a country house, refurbished and neat as a pin. Accommodation includes singles (some ensuite), 3 doubles ensuite and a self-catering cottage. There is a programme of events including Quiet Days.

Cranham

Prinknash Abbey and St Peter's Grange
Cranham
Gloucester GL4 8EX

Tel: 01452 813592
Fax: 01452 814187
e-mail: spgprinknash@freeuk.com
Website: www.stpetersgrange-prinknash.com

Roman Catholic
The monastery sits on a hill looking rather stark and modern, but inside all is warm, comfortable, and purpose-built. Male retreatants are received here in separate guest accommodation. Men, women, young people, families and groups can all come and stay at St Peter's Grange, the monks' main guest house, which is very comfortable. The chapel is at the side of the monastery and gives the impression of going downstairs, but the liturgy is inspiring and there is a reassuring modesty in the simplicity of the place. You may attend the

daily round of services and there is usually some work to do if you feel you want to contribute in that way. St Peter's Grange is a distinguished place of mainly Tudor buildings and was originally a monastic property connected with Gloucester Cathedral. The present community of monks used it as the monastery until they built the new Abbey in the 1970s. St. Peter's Grange is about a mile away but within the estate and connected by a long drive, which is a pleasant walk to the chapel. The Grange is a mellow pile of stone set against a hill with a small quiet garden entrance. Inside, most of the paneling and other antique features have been retained. This includes a remarkably beautiful decorated chapel and choir. At the time of writing, St Peter's Grange is under threat as a great deal of money must be raised to meet new fire regulations and it has launched an appeal for funds. Meanwhile St Peter's is continuing to receive guests who, like those before them, will find peace and renewal at this Abbey. The following information applies to St Peter's Grange.

Open: All year except Christmas and two weeks in summer. Receives men, women, families, groups.
Rooms: 13 singles, 5 doubles. Some 3–4-bedded rooms as well.
Facilities: Estate grounds, library, garden, guest lounge, TV, payphone, visitors centre, gift shop.
Guests Admitted to: Grounds, church, chapel.
Spiritual Help: Personal talks.
Meals: Everyone eats together in guest house. Traditional food. Vegetarian and special diets with notice.
Special Activities: Days of recollection and prayer. Ask for dates.
Situation: On a great hill with sweeping views across the Cotswold countryside and the Malvern Hills.
Maximum Stay: 6 days.
Bookings: Letter, fax, e-mail. Telephoning is all down to luck but there is an answer phone.
Charges: Donations around £23 B&B, £35 full board.
Access: Train: Stroud from London, or if coming from the North, then take train to Cheltenham. Bus: usually a service – ask for details. Car: M5 then A46.

Longhope

May Hill Methodist Church
May Hill
Longhope
Glos   Tel: 01452 830729

Christian – Methodist
This is a non-residential centre for Quiet Days, retreats and conferences. Facilities include a comfortable chapel, kitchen and several meeting rooms. It is in a small village near beautiful countryside. **Enquiries: 27 Lambourne Avenue, Huntley, Glos GL19 3HW or on above telephone number.**

Newnham

**The Old Vicarage
Newnham
Gloucester GL14 1EL**

Tel: 01594 510282
e-mail: nickandmay@fsnet.com

Inter-Denominational – Christian
This is a retreat in a home, offering sensitivity and understanding to people
with eating disorders, crafts through which you may seek God, and acceptance of people exploring who they are.

Open: All year. Receives everyone.
Rooms: 1 single, 3 doubles.
Facilities: Garden, library, guest lounge, guest telephone.
Spiritual Help: Group sharing, spiritual direction. Counselling by appointment.
Guests Admitted to: Public rooms, garden.
Meals: Everyone eats together. Traditional, whole food, vegetarian. Special diets.
Special Activities: None.
Situation: Very quiet, walking distance to river.
Maximum Stay: 5 days.
Bookings: Letter, fax, telephone.
Charges: £25 B&B, £10 dinner, £5 lunch, £5 craft sessions, £50 per day for
any courses held.
Access: Ask for details – train and bus possible.

Nympsfield

**Nympsfield in the Cotswolds
Marist Convent
Nympsfield
Stonehouse
Glos GL10 3TY**

Tel: 01453 860228
Fax: 01453 861331
e-mail: Marist_sisters@lineone.net

Roman Catholic
Nympsfield is a village of great antiquity – a real village with a tangible sense
of community that has the convent very much at its heart. Back in the 1800s
the house was given to the Marist Community to become a family home for
children in care. Within the grounds of the convent are a small school and a
church, and there is still a strong sense of cohesiveness within this charming
complex. The convent itself ceased to be a children's home in the 1980s and
became a very successful retreat house. Groups and individuals are welcome,
although spiritual direction is only offered to individuals coming on personal
retreat. Guided retreats around Easter and other Christian festivals are offered
to religious sisters but anyone is invited to participate. There is a chapel and
prayer room within the convent. Rooms are simply but nicely furnished and,
while these are not en-suite, there is no shortage of bathrooms. There is a very
kind and warm welcome from the community, who are flexible and accommodating. Gentleness is indeed a key word here. **Highly Recommended.**

Open: All year. Receives everyone.
Rooms: 4 singles, 13 doubles. More can be accommodated if necessary.
Facilities: Disabled, conferences, garden, park, library, guest lounge, TV.

Spiritual Help: Spiritual direction, personal retreat direction. Groups usually bring their own spiritual director.

Guests Admitted to: Chapel and all areas not private to the Community.

Meals: Taken in guest house together. Self-catering kitchens. Meals can be provided if needed. Vegetarian and special diets.

Special Activities: None – but there is a brochure about the centre.

Situation: Quiet, in a village.

Maximum Stay: 1 week.

Bookings: Letter, fax, e-mail, telephone during day.

Charges: £15 a day self-catering, £27 a day full board, 6-day retreats £170.

Access: Train and car routes. Ask for travel directions if taking train.

Randwick

More Hall Convent
Benedictine Sisters of Our Lady of Grace and Compassion
Randwick
Stroud
Glos GL6 6EP   Tel: 01453 764486
                          e-mail: sisterjenita@morehallconvent.fsnet.co.uk

Roman Catholic

Located at the foot of one of the Cotswold's charming villages, More Hall Convent is an old stone building with its own delightful small chapel within the grounds. The Convent is chiefly run as a residential home for the elderly and disabled, but retreatants are welcome. This is a retreat for someone seeking solitude and self-direction. The facilities in the self-contained small flat are superb and guests are encouraged to choose their own level of independence. Meals can be taken with the community, alone or fully self-catered. The Sisters live by the Rule of St Benedict and follow the Divine Office with additional sessions of meditation within the daily rhythm of prayer. No one is expected to participate but everyone is welcome. There is a daily Eucharist. For those seeking greater emphasis on a private retreat, the Sisters suggest staying at the community's retreat house in Malmesbury in Wiltshire. The Guest Sister can tell you about this accommodation.

Open: All year. Receives men, women, young people, non-retreatants.

Rooms: 3 singles.

Facilities: Garden, library, guest phone (01453 762203).

Spiritual Help: Personal talks. Silence from 8p.m.–9a.m. Join Community in prayers. There is a resident chaplain to whom guests may talk of spiritual concerns.

Guests Admitted to: Chapel and sometimes help with the work of the community, which is care of the elderly.

Meals: Everyone eats together. Traditional food.

Special Activities: None.

Situation: Quiet, in the countryside.

Maximum Stay: 2 weeks.

Bookings: Letter.

Charges: From £20 per night.

Access: Train: Stroud, then bus or taxi (2 miles). Car route easy.

Stroud

Hawkwood College Tel: 01453 759034
Painswick Old Road Fax: 01453 764607
Stroud e-mail: info@hawkwoodcollege.co.uk
Gloucester GL6 7LE Website: www.hawkwoodcollege.co.uk

Anthroposophical – Rudolf Steiner tradition
Situated at the head of a small Cotswold valley, Hawkwood provides a beautiful setting for retreats, adult education courses and conferences. The facilities are centred on a nineteenth-century manor house with fields and woodlands. Music, Celtic studies, alternative lifestyle exploration, arts and crafts, bodywork, meditation, prayer, eco-spirituality and educational training are all subjects you can find at Hawkwood. They have their own programme, so check it out on their website.

Open: All year. Receives everyone.
Rooms: 14 singles, 17 doubles.
Facilities: Conferences, garden, library, guest lounge, TV, guest telephone.
Spiritual Help: Spiritual direction, meditation, courses in Ayurveda, kinesiology, yoga.
Guests Admitted to: Public areas.
Meals: Everyone eats together. Traditional, whole food. Vegetarian and special diets.
Special Activities: Planned events – send for brochure.
Situation: 42-acre estate with Cotswold valley views.
Maximum Stay: Open.
Bookings: Letter, fax, telephone.
Charges: Around £100 per person per weekend. Prices can vary.
Access: Train possible – enquire. Car easy.

HEREFORDSHIRE

Harewood End

Vipassana Trust ★
Dhamma Dipa
Harewood End Tel: 01989 730234
Hereford HR2 8NG Fax: 01989 730450
e-mail: dhammadipa@compuserve.com

Non-religious
Vipassana means 'to see things as they really are'. It is a way of self-purification by self-observation and is one of India's most ancient meditation techniques. It is grounded in reality of self and there is no visualisation, verbalisation or mantras involved, just careful observation of the body and self. Today in India over 600 Roman Catholic nuns, for example, use the Vipassana techniques, and there is an increasing demand for it around the world, East and West. The Trust offers courses in the tradition of Sayagyi U Ba Khin, as taught by S.N. Goenka. You need to give all your effort on these courses, observing the rules of the house and taking your study seriously. The daily timetable that all are urged to follow starts at 4a.m. and goes on until 9.30p.m. Noble silence

reigns here and there is complete segregation of men and women – and this includes married couples and partners. The silence is important, so if you are a chatterbox, self-adjustment will be necessary. One of the reasons for silence between students is to keep yourself focused and not be distracted. You can talk to your teacher on a one-to-one basis, however, and there may be group discussions. People come here to meditate, serve on courses or help with improvement of the property, which is set in 22 acres of gentle rolling countryside near the cathedral city of Hereford. There are local practising Vipassana groups in London, Bedfordshire, Bristol, Liverpool, Suffolk, Sussex, Devon and Wales. A newsletter is published three times a year giving details of short and long courses throughout Europe with address of Vipassana centres around the world. This is a serious retreat centre with established programmes and basic accommodation in a peaceful setting for those looking for increased self-awareness and development. **Highly Recommended.**

Open: All year. Receives men, women. Young people for specific courses.

Rooms: A few singles, 15 doubles, 3 dormitories. **Men and women are segregated and restricted to their own areas.** Rooms for men are basic, but beds and central heating are good. Toilet/shower block is modern and clean. Women's quarters are slightly more comfortable.

Facilities: All facilities are basic and segregated. Garden, new meditation hall to accommodate 120 guests. A new building plan looks to establish an ideal and modern facility for Vipassana practice and retreats.

Spiritual Help: Meditation. Teachers are available to guide students and answer questions about technique.

Guests Admitted to: Almost everywhere, but male and female guests have designated and separate areas.

Meals: Men and women eat separately. Vegetarian. Special diet arrangements only for specific medical reason. **There is a morning and mid-day meal, and that is it, with only fruit consumed until the next morning – most people find this no problem. It keeps you alert and attentive.**

Special Activities: Very specific courses on offer – send for information, which fully explains what is on offer and how the courses are run.

Situation: Quiet, in the countryside.

Maximum Stay: None but there is an 11-day minimum (unless for a 3-day course).

Bookings: Letter, fax, e-mail, telephone, requesting **application form, which must be completed.**

Charges: Donations only, according to what people wish to give.

Access: Details with booking information. Train, bus and car all possible – but the centre is located up a long lane.

Hereford

Belmont Abbey Retreat Centre
Belmont Abbey
Hereford HR2 9RZ

Tel: 01432 374712
Website: www.belmontabbey.org.uk

Roman Catholic
The community at Belmont Abbey offers very modern and comfortable guest facilities in Hedley Lodge guest house and a full programme of

courses with such titles as *Plainsong and Prayer*, *Jesus as a Man of Prayer* and *Not Angles but Angels*, and workshops on human development and spiritual growth, Christian architecture and music, and calligraphy and prayer. Some of the course leaders are very well known. Retreats at Belmont centre on the Divine Office of prayer with the monks, but this leaves ample time for private prayer, spiritual guidance and rest. The facility is an unusual mixture of monastic and modern living environments. It mostly works, but some people on retreat may find the ordinary activities taking place here (for example wedding parties) not quite in keeping with their expectations. Perhaps such things serve to remind us that our spiritual life is not a thing apart from us and that it goes on in the midst of our ordinary living, which should be joyous – just like a wedding feast. The garden fronting the abbey is splendid and there are places to walk and sit in perfect solitude. **Highly Recommended.**

Open: All year. Receives men, women, young people, families, groups, non-retreatants. Children welcome.

Rooms: 3 singles, 17 doubles – many with ensuite facilities. All rather luxurious and up-market.

Facilities: Disabled – limited to day visitors because there is no lift to the accommodation at this time. Conferences, park, library, TV, payphone, direct dialing, Abbey bookshop, small oratory that is warm and always open. There is an extended choir for guests to take part.

Spiritual Help: Personal talks, sharing in Divine Office, group sharing, spiritual direction, personal retreat direction, meditation, directed study.

Guests Admitted to: Church, chapel, choir, oratory.

Meals: Eaten in guest house. Buffet lunch and a good solid supper are served. Traditional food. Vegetarian, special diets.

Special Activities: Planned programme of events – send for information.

Situation: Close to beautiful countryside, River Wye, Welsh mountains.

Maximum Stay: 1 week.

Bookings: Letter, e-mail.

Charges: Varied scale – apply for details but about £40 per person per day for organised full-board retreats. From £30 B&B.

Access: Hereford is easily reached by rail, bus or car.

Poulstone Court	Tel: 01432 840251
Kings Caple	Fax: 01432 840860
Hereford HR1 4UA	e-mail: poulstone@btinternet.com
	Website: www.poulstone.com

Mind Body Spirit

The Court is regularly used for courses in meditation, healing, counselling, and yoga. There is a self-contained flat available, plus thirty-six bed spaces in various types of room. All food is vegetarian and special diets can be catered for. There is a large indoor space for yoga and other activities. Inner process as well as yoga and ritual shamanic practice are interests here. The centre is non-smoking.

Ross-on-Wye

Courtfield Retreat Centre
Mill Hill Missionaries
Courtfield
Ross-on-Wye
Herefordshire HR9 6JJ
Tel: 01594 860215
Fax: 01594 860221

Roman Catholic
This location in the beautiful Wye Valley seems ideal for relaxation, rest and reflection for the day, weekend or longer. There is a lovely church dating from 1875 attached to Courtfield and a priest available, if needed, for spiritual direction and retreats. A rather famous house in its day, Courtfield is now owned by the Mill Hill Missionaries.

Open: All year. Receives everyone, but limited room for those not on retreat.
Rooms: 22 singles, 9 doubles.
Facilities: Conferences, garden, park, guest lounge, guest telephone.
Spiritual Help: Personal talks, group sharing, spiritual direction, personal retreat direction, meditation.
Guests Admitted to: Unrestricted access.
Meals: Everyone eats together. Traditional whole food. Vegetarian and special diets.
Special Activities: None.
Situation: In an area of outstanding natural beauty.
Maximum Stay: Indefinite.
Bookings: Letter, fax, telephone during office hours.
Charges: Donation £30 a day full board.
Access: Train: Hereford or Gloucester. Bus: from Ross-on-Wye. Car: M50/A40.

LEICESTERSHIRE

Coalville

Mount St Bernard Abbey
Coalville
Leicester LE67 5UL
Tel: 01530 832298
Fax: 01530 814608
e-mail: guest house@abbeymsb.fsnet.co.uk

Roman Catholic
Built of local stone, the Abbey buildings are simple, not over-ornate, and in keeping with the Cistercian tradition. In the fine and very large granite church, Latin Mass is sung once a month and the vernacular Mass daily. Rooms are clean, comfortable and have good new beds. The Abbey has a large working pottery, as well as carpentry and printing shops. Meals are very traditional. Located in the middle of the famous Quorn Hunt country, the Abbey offers good walking over hill, pasture and moor. Create your own retreat here, using a Bible and a devotional book, as the monks are not available for guided retreats. This monastery is a very popular place and you may find it hard to get accommodation unless you book well in advance. The monks here are welcoming but overstretched, so you are encouraged to look

after yourself. This is, after all, a place for prayer and seeking God. So if you go to Mount St Bernard Abbey, just get on with it!

Open: All year except one month from mid-January and Christmas. Receives men, women, young people, families, groups, non-retreatants.

Rooms: The Guest House accommodation is reserved for relatives and friends of the monks and for retreatant guests. The main guest house provides rooms for 2 married couples and up to 9 male guests in single rooms. The Lodge provides single and double rooms for 7–10 women. Small leaflet available about the Abbey guest arrangements.

Facilities: Disabled, well stocked library, guest lounge, garden, payphone, direct dialing. **No chapel in guest house.** 'Great Silence' from 8p.m. until after Mass the next morning. This should be observed by guests.

Spiritual Help: Group sharing, meditation.

Guests Admitted to: Chapel.

Meals: Taken in guest house. Plain food with provision for vegetarians and special diets if required. You can talk during the meals if you want.

Special Activities: None.

Situation: 150-acre estate in hills of Charnwood Forest, with commanding views of Soar river valley. Very quiet.

Maximum Stay: 5 days (4 nights)

Bookings: Letter, telephone 9a.m.–noon, 2.30–5.15p.m.

Charges: Donation average about £15 per day.

Access: Train: Loughborough, then taxi. Car: M1, Exit 23.

East Norton

Launde Abbey
East Norton
Leics LE7 9XB

Tel: 01572 717254
Fax: 01572 717454
e-mail: Launde@leicester.anglican.org
Website: www.launde.org.uk

Anglican – Ecumenical

This is a huge redbrick house built by Thomas Cromwell in 1540 on the site of an early Augustinian priory. It retains today the old-fashioned comfort and charm of a distinguished private country mansion, with a cheerful drawing room fire, and a panelled dining room and games room. A beautiful chapel, still intact from the fifteenth century, is the jewel of Launde Abbey. You may be given a room in either the house, a small annexe or the refurbished Georgian stable-block, which overlooks a large pond. All this is set in 350 acres of parkland. *Calligraphy and prayer* and *Praying through Playing* are some of the retreat topics offered here. Everyone is welcome. **Highly Recommended.**

Open: All year. Receives men, women, young people, families, groups, non-retreatants – including charities, and cultural and educational groups for conferences. Children welcome.

Rooms: 10 singles, 10 doubles, 21 twins, camping, caravans, self-contained cottage, hermitage.

Facilities: Disabled, conferences, chapel, good-sized garden, park, library, guest lounge, TV, payphone.

Spiritual Help: Personal talks, spiritual direction, personal retreat direction, opportunity to join in regular worship with resident community, meditation, group sharing, directed study.

Guests Admitted to: Unrestricted access.

Meals: Everyone eats together in an oak-panelled room. Traditional food. Vegetarian and special diets. Vegan organic. **Sticky toffee pudding is sometimes a speciality here.** Some self-catering. You can eat alone in your room if you like.

Special Activities: Planned programme of events. 8- and 5-day retreats. Send for brochure.

Situation: Very quiet, in the countryside.

Maximum Stay: By arrangement.

Bookings: Letter, fax, e-mail, telephone – 9a.m.–5p.m. weekdays.

Charges: £50 per person per 24 hours. Course prices vary from a Quiet Day at £10 to a 5-day retreat with spiritual directors at £200. For groups the rate is £45 per 24 hours per individual.

Access: Very close to Leicester. Train: Oakham (6 miles away). Bus: No. 147 to Leicester. Car: via A47 from Leicester.

Stathern

Stathern Retreat Centre
Chapel Lane
Stathern
Leicester

Tel: 01949 20179
e-mail: jbhunter@fish.co.uk
Website: www.members.aol.com/stathern

Methodist – Ecumenical

This is a non-residential centre with wheelchair access, set in a small village. It is used as a day retreat centre. There is a chapel, kitchen, and gardens. To contact the Centre by letter, write to: 33 Kneeton Road, East Bridgford, Nottingham NG13 8PG.

Theddingworth

Hothorpe Hall Christian Conference Centre
Theddingworth
Leics LEA 6QX

Tel: 01858 880257
e-mail: office@hothorpe.co.uk
Website: www.hothorpe.co.uk

Inter-denominational

This is a big grand house looking out over grass and fields and specialising in offering a wide range of conference facilities to Christian, charitable and disability organisations. Most of the guests are Christian groups or individuals. Hothorpe Hall is not a retreat centre as such but many people come here for Quiet Days.

Open: All year except Christmas week. Receives everyone. Children welcome.

Rooms: 3 singles, 48 doubles, 6 family rooms.

Facilities: Conferences, garden, library, guest lounge, TV, payphone.

Spiritual Help: None.

Guests Admitted to: Chapel, guest areas.

Meals: Everyone eats together. Wide selection of food with provision for vegetarians. Special diets possible.

Special Activities: None.
Situation: In the countryside.
Maximum Stay: No restriction.
Bookings: Letter, telephone.
Charges: Ask for rates.
Access: Train: Market Harborough. Car route easy.

NORTHAMPTONSHIRE

Daventry

Our Lady of the Passion
The Monastery
Badby Road West, Daventry
Northants NN11 4NH

Tel: 01327 702569
Fax: 01327 702965
e-mail: info@cpnuns.org
Website: www.cpnuns.org

Roman Catholic
This is a very small retreat house for women, religious and priests. It is self-catering and quiet.

Ecton

Ecton House
Church Way, Ecton
Northants NN6 OQE

Tel: 01604 406442
Fax: 01604 787052

Anglican
The spiritual heart of Ecton House is the chapel, which is used for corporate worship and private prayer. This old house has welcomed many guests over the years, not least William Hogarth, who came to sketch and relax, and Benjamin Franklin, who came to seek out his ancestors. It is a good setting for a retreat and a rest. The programme on offer includes Franciscan and Holy Week retreats and sometimes retreats for widowed, separated or divorced people.

Open: All year. Receives men, women, young people, families, groups, non-retreatants.
Rooms: 25 singles, 1 double.
Facilities: Chapel, conferences, garden, library, guest lounge, TV, payphone.
Spiritual Help: Chapel, personal talks by prior arrangement.
Guests Admitted to: Chapel, guest areas.
Meals: Everyone eats together. Traditional food. Vegetarian and special diets.
Special Activities: Planned retreats – send for brochure.
Situation: Quiet, in a village.
Maximum Stay: By arrangement.
Bookings: Letter, fax, telephone.
Charges: About £30 full board for 24 hours.
Access: Train: Northampton or Wellingborough. Bus: Ecton from either Northampton or Wellingborough. Car route: M1 Junction 15.

Kettering

Thrapston Baptist Church
33 Huntingdon Road
Thrapston, Kettering
Northants NN14 4NF　　　　　　　　Tel/Fax: 01832 734880
　　　　　　　　　　　　　　　　e-mail: thrappyhappy@hotmail.com

Baptist – Christian
Thrapston Baptist Church is used for non-residential Quiet Days and work-shops, and it has good facilities for groups. Other congregations use it for training days, Holy Spirit days and for the popular Alpha courses. There is spiritual direction by arrangement available throughout the year from quali-fied associates of the Church.

Northampton

The Neighbours Community
140–148 Ardington Road
Northampton NN1 5LT　　　　　　　　Tel: 01604 633918
　　　　　　　　　　　　　　　　e-mail: neighbours@totalise.co.uk

Christian
This is an unusual community of adults and families living in adjacent house-holds and sharing gardens and events. It is an Ecumenical Christian commu-nity, which holds various events, including Quiet Days, creativity days, Taizé prayers, children's events and sometimes two-day workshops. Members belong to various church congregations. They meet for prayers each morn-ing and have meals together several times during each week. Send for their programme of the current year's events.

OXFORDSHIRE

Aston Tirrold

Centre for Reflection
Spring Lane
Aston Tirrold　　　　　　　　　　Tel: 01235 850423
Oxfordshire OX11 9EJ　　　　　Website: www.reflect.freeuk.com

This centre is non-residential but nearby B&B can be arranged. It has excel-lent facilities and is set near a pretty country church. It is affiliated to the Quiet Garden Trust. There is a Quiet Day with led meditations on the third Thursday of each month from 10a.m. until 4p.m. A leaflet is available from Becky Fisher on: 01235 847270.

True love grows through acts.
A CARTHUSIAN MONK

Boars Hill

Carmelite Priory
Boars Hill
Oxford OX1 5HB

Tel: 01865 730183

Roman Catholic
Boars Hill is an ideal location for this centre run by the Teresian Discalced
Carmel Friars. The Centre, where a lot of new building has been done to
offer even better facilities, stands in its own 17 acres of woodland. It aims to
provide courses on prayer and spirituality, special attention being given to the
teaching on prayer of the great Carmelite writers such as St Teresa of Avila,
St John of the Cross and St Teresa of Lisieux. There is an annual vocation
weekend open to all young men interested in the religious life and the
Carmelites in particular. The programme of planned retreats and events is an
exciting, intelligent and full one. **Highly Recommended.**
Open: All year except Christmas and New Year. Receives men, women,
    young people, families, groups.
Rooms: 15 singles, 14 doubles.
Facilities: Chapel, garden, park, payphone.
Spiritual Help: Personal talks, group sharing, meditation, directed study.
Guests Admitted to: Unrestricted access.
Meals: Everyone eats together. Traditional food. Vegetarian and special diets.
Special Activities: Planned programme – send for brochure.
Situation: Very quiet, in the countryside.
Maximum Stay: 1 week.
Bookings: By telephone but confirm by letter with a deposit.
Charges: Voluntary offering.
Access: Train: Oxford, then taxi (5 miles). Car via A34 – send for a map, as
    route is a little complicated.

Burford

Priory of Our Lady
Burford
Oxon OX18 4SQ

Tel: 01993 823605
e-mail: bookings@burfordosb.org.uk

Anglican
Pretty Burford, with its stone houses, antique shops, tourists and air of new
money and material success, is also the home of Burford Prior, a small
community of Anglican Benedictine monks and nuns. They have a special
concern for the fulfillment of Christ's prayer 'that all may be one'. The
community seeks to offer a place of reconciliation and prayerful encounter. It
enjoys a vitality, and a growing number of both men and women come to try
the contemplative life here. The guest house is a late-sixteenth-century house
in its own gardens within the Priory grounds. The bedrooms are well
equipped and there is an oratory. The Priory is not so easy to get to by public
transportation, but once you are there, you will find a warm Benedictine
welcome and an atmosphere in which you may pray, study and reflect. Try
not to be tempted out into Burford with its many little shops, entertaining as
it all may seem. This may be a test of your desire to withdraw from the world
for a little while, but the monastery and its prevailing atmosphere of spiritual

calm will help you. Most people who come here want space, silence and a place just to be quiet. The Priory atmosphere is conducive to this. Guests are cared for in a non-intrusive manner. Many moments of profound spiritual sharing between complete strangers occur because they have met here at the deep level of their common humanity. **Highly Recommended.**

Open: All year except Christmas, Easter and other short periods. Receives men, women, young people, groups. Children welcome in the retreat house.

Rooms: 5 singles, 3 doubles. No pets, radios. No smoking. Silence between 9p.m. and 9a.m.

Facilities: Chapel, gardens, park, woods, library, guest lounge. **Not suitable for wheelchairs**.

Spiritual Help: Personal talks.

Guests Admitted to: Chapel, choir, work of the community.

Meals: Everyone eats together. Simple whole food. Vegetarian and special diets. Mobile phones must be switched off during meals and when attending services.

Special Activities: None.

Situation: Quiet, on the village edge, but Burford is a busy place, especially in summer. Splendid views of Windrush Valley.

Maximum Stay: 6 nights.

Bookings: Letter, e-mail, telephone 10–11.30a.m.

Charges: No formal charge but donation invited. Guideline is £30 per day and £10 for a pastoral session.

Access: Buses from Oxford or Cheltenham. Best by car from A40.

Charney Bassett

Charney Manor
Charney Bassett
Nr Wantage
Oxon OX12 OEJ

Tel: 01235 868206
e-mail: charneymanor@quaker.org.uk
Website: www.charneymanor.demon.co.uk

Quaker

The Manor is a Grade I listed building and one of the oldest inhabited buildings in the Vale of the White Horse. It is well maintained, very clean, with an old-fashioned sitting room, and has a country home feeling. The rooms are neat, modern and reasonably up-to-date, and meals are professionally prepared. There are Quakers living here, so a warm welcome awaits all guests. Quakers say: 'Each person is unique, precious, a child of God.' Short courses and retreats on offer include an exploration of radical faithfulness and Quaker marriage, spiritual music, calligraphy and meditation and an exploration of masculine spirituality from a Quaker-Christian perspective. Others may be *The Way of the Mystic* and *The Contemplative Call in an Active Society*. Many of those who have come here say they came away feeling uplifted at sharing troubles and with renewed hope for the future. **Highly Recommended.**

Open: All year. Receives men, women, young people, families, groups. Children welcome.

Rooms: 14 singles, 11 doubles. Self-catering cottage, The Gilletts, in the grounds – 2 ensuite rooms. Camping possible.

Facilities: Conferences, garden to walk in with places to sit, library, guest lounge, TV, payphone (01235 868 531), crafts and workshops, small Anglican Church almost in the garden – Sunday services.
Spiritual Help: None.
Guests Admitted to: Unrestricted access.
Meals: Everyone eats together. Traditional food. Vegetarian and special diets.
Special Activities: Planned programme of retreats and events – send for brochure.
Situation: Very quiet, in village, in countryside.
Maximum Stay: 2 weeks self-catering.
Bookings: Letter, fax, e-mail, telephone.
Charges: About £59.50 per person per 24 hours. Extra days pro rata. See room and conference rate sheet, which details various other rates and combinations of prices.
Access: Rail: Didcot Parkway, then taxi. Bus: South Moor. Car route easy.

Nuneham Courtney

Global Retreat Centre
Nuneham Park
Nuneham Courtney
Oxon OX44 9PG

Tel: 01865 343551
Fax:01865 343576
e-mail: info@globalretreatcentre.com
Website: www.globalretreatcentre.com

Non-religious
The Brahma Kumaris World Spiritual University (See London section) run this international centre in a magnificent Palladian Villa built by the Earl of Harcourt in 1796. George II called it 'The most enjoyable place I know,' and Queen Victoria wrote after one of her many visits 'This is a most lovely place, with pleasure grounds in the style of Claremont.' About fifteen minutes' drive from Oxford, the house is situated by the River Thames in 55 acres of land and gardens. The Brahma Kumaris live together as a spiritual family and take part in a daily routine of meditation, study and work. They advocate the highest spiritual values and seek to live and teach those values. Together they run the Centre with a level of care and efficiency that comes from a true commitment to and understanding of service. As well as regular retreats lasting from one day to one week, there are a variety of seminars, workshops and courses offering a range of opportunities to learn meditation, develop personal skills and explore the common values essential to world harmony. Regular courses include *Stress-free Living*, *Positive Thinking*, and *Meditation Insights*. **Highly Recommended.**

Open: All year. Receives men, women, young people, families, groups. The building is open to the public during certain weekends of the year.
Rooms: 12 singles, 20 doubles.
Facilities: Conferences, garden, park, guest lounge, payphone.
Spiritual Help: Group sharing, meditation, personal talks, spiritual direction.
Guests Admitted to: Unrestricted access.
Meals: Everyone eats together. Vegetarian and special diets. **No alcohol is allowed.**
Special Activities: Planned programme of events. Guests are expected to attend the scheduled programme. Ask for information.

Situation: Very quiet, in its own parkland, surrounded by countryside.
Maximum Stay: 2 day/nights.
Bookings: Fax, e-mail.
Charges: No charges are made but donations are welcome.
Access: Train: Oxford. Car: M40 or from Oxford.

Oxford

Convent of the Incarnation
The Community of the Sisters of the Love of God
Fairacres
Oxford OX4 1TB   Tel: 01865 721301
                                        e-mail: prioress.slg@amserve.net

Anglican
Tucked into one of the busy residential parts of east Oxford, the Convent of
the Incarnation offers a haven of peace where silence and solitude are hallmarks
of the contemplative life. Founded in 1906, The Community of the Sisters of
the Love of God was the first contemplative community for women in the
Church of England. The simple, dedicated life of witness and prayer spanning
nearly 100 years contributes to a stability and depth of peace that makes this a
very special place. There is very comfortable accommodation for a limited
number of guests, who stay either in the guest house or in self-contained
bungalows. The emphasis is on solitude and self-directed retreats, so anyone
coming on retreat for the first time would probably be offered a room in the
guest house. There is a beautiful chapel within the grounds, where silent participation in the Eucharist and Divine Office is encouraged. There is a small guest
garden and shared use of some of the community's grounds.

Stanton St John

Stanton House   Tel: 01865 358807
Stanton St John   Fax: 01865 358474
Oxford OX33 1HQ   e-mail: office@stantonhouse.fsnet.co.uk

Christian – Evangelical – Inter-denominational
This is a handsome Victorian house in beautiful, spacious grounds overlooking the rolling hills of west Oxfordshire and within five minutes' walk of the
attractive village of Stanton St John. Stanton House began as a Christian
retreat centre in 1978 and offers very comfortable accommodation in an
informal family atmosphere – where home cooking is definitely a speciality!
The emphasis is on peace and quiet, and guests, whether individuals or
groups, are encouraged to relax and rest as much as they need to. There is no
formal structure to the day, but everyone is invited to gather after dinner in
one of the lounges for prayer, songs and Bible reflection. At other times,
guests are welcome to use the prayer room in the house or the prayer cabin
in the grounds – and the village church is a short and secluded walk through
the grounds and over a stream that cascades down a series of gentle waterfalls
into the nearby river. All guests are encouraged to take the time and space
offered to find and experience God for themselves.

Open: All year except Christmas. Receives, men, women. Groups by arrangement.

Rooms: 4 singles, 4 twins, 2 doubles.

Facilities: 2 sitting rooms, prayer room. Space for up to 18 for day groups and 12 for residential groups.

Spiritual help: Team members available for prayer on request.

Guests admitted to: Unrestricted access except community members' rooms.

Meals: Home cooking. Vegetarian and special diets.

Special activities: Evening devotions.

Situation: In 5 acres of grounds, not far from Oxford.

Maximum Stay: 3 weeks.

Bookings: Telephone for more information and bookings.

Charges: Donation to cover costs – enquire as to appropriate amount.

Access: Train: to Oxford. Bus: to Stanton St John.

Sutton Courtenay   ★

The Abbey   Tel: 01235 847401
Sutton Courtenay   Fax: 01235 847608
Oxon OX14 4AF   e-mail: Admin@theabbeysc.demon.co.uk
                              Website: www.theabbey.uk.com

Multi-faith – Christian traditions

This remains a *very* special place. The Abbey seeks to offer space, peace and support for individuals and groups who want to be still and find closer connection with the sacred dimension of life and with God. The Abbey, with its charming inner courtyard, flowers and surrounding meadow-like areas, has been going for a number of years and the community here is engaged in projects ranging from the dynamics of unemployment to the complementary relationship of men and women working in the ministry. The current community is small but dynamic, full of cheer and thoughtfulness. The programme of events is designed to encourage personal, social and ecological transformation, as well as the nourishment of our inner lives. There are many courses on offer at the Abbey. They may include Qi *Gong* and the *Tree of Life*, Tibetan healing exercises, the mysteries that lead us to Easter, music as the bridge of the soul, prayer retreats and *Sacred Economics: Spirit, Money, and Peace*. The Abbey community is willing to discuss with you the possibility of joining them to experience their life and work. **Highly Recommended.**

> "We all need to become conscious cells in the body of Gaia, assisting the healing process."
> ALAN WATSON FEATHERSTONE.

Open: All year by arrangement but sometimes closed for community needs. Receives men, women, young people. Groups by arrangement.

Rooms: 10 singles, 1 twin in Abbey. Camping possible.

Facilities: Conferences, 4-acre garden, library with Gandhi archive, guest lounge, payphone.

Spiritual Help: Meditation.

Guests Admitted to: Unrestricted access except Community members' rooms. Work of the community.

Meals: Vegetarian food. Can be taken alone or with the community. Self-catering in guest house.

Special Activities: Planned programme – send for brochure. Courses on crafts and sculpture. Green ecology lectures. Gandhi School of Non-violence programme has been offered for a number of years.

Situation: Surrounded by 4 acres of wooded grounds. The Abbey is of archaeological importance because of the underlying Roman and Saxon remains. Quiet, in a village.

Maximum Stay: 1 week.

Bookings: Letter, telephone 9.30a.m.–1p.m. weekdays.

Charges: About £40 full board per 24 hours. Other rates available for different stays, so enquire.

Access: Train: Didcot Parkway (3 miles away). Bus: No. 32 from Oxford runs every half an hour. Car: via A34.

Wallingford

Braziers Park
Ipsden
Wallingford   Tel/fax: 01491 680221
Oxon OX10 6AN   e-mail: admin@braziers.org.uk
                                            Website: www.braziers.org.uk

Non-religious

Braziers Park is a non-religious residential adult college deep in the south Oxfordshire countryside and is not a retreat house as such. But it is receptive to other organisations running retreats here, and individual guests making their own retreat time and space are welcomed. It does not at first glance appear to have much spiritual slant in its courses and events; however, the programme actually takes you into areas of concern and learning that are broadly spiritual, especially where personal creativity and the environment are concerned. For example, there are permaculture events and courses, yoga, a *Living Water Workshop*, a healing vibrations course and a painting course. It is not necessary to attend a course to stay here. The informal, relaxed and very supportive environment at Braziers encourages many people to come here for a break or to find some peace and quiet in which to think through their personal problems or situations.

Open: All year except Christmas. Receives men, women.

Rooms: 3 singles, 11 doubles, camping, caravans.

Facilities: Conferences, garden, park, library, guest lounge, guest telephone (01491 680481).

Spiritual Help: None.

Guests Admitted to: Unrestricted access.

Meals: Everyone eats together. Traditional plus vegetarian, vegan, special diets.

Special Activities: Planned programme – send for brochure.

Situation: Countryside.

Maximum Stay: 2 weeks.

Bookings: Letter, fax, e-mail, telephone mornings.

Charges: £54 per 24-hour stay. Courses in range £108–£210.

Access: Car: M40.

Wantage

St Mary's Convent
Community of St Mary the Virgin
Wantage
Oxon OX12 9DJ

Tel: 01235 760170
e-mail: guestwing@csmv.co.uk

Anglican
Within walking distance of the town centre, St Mary's is a large, rather institutional but open-spirited convent that dates from 1848. The Community of St Mary the Virgin, numbering about sixty sisters, live and work here, balancing their time between prayer and ministry in the outside community. There are two chapels – the larger of which is used for the Divine Office and Eucharist. The original chapel is reserved for private prayer and special celebrations – and here there is evidence of the artistic strength of the community, with Stations of the Cross beautifully carved in wood by a former Mother at the Convent and a modern metallic cross replicating the configuration of particles observed by an atomic physicist. The guest wing is very spacious, with plenty of communal sitting space and rooms reserved for private interviews. A sister is usually available for spiritual direction or as a listening ear, but it is best to request this well in advance. Guests are free to use the time and space as they wish, and are asked to observe silence in accordance with the life of the community. Creative expression is encouraged in a recently converted art room.

Open: Most of the year. Receives men, women, young people, groups.
Rooms: 10 singles, 1 double. Silence is maintained in the guest area.
Facilities: Disabled, garden, library, guest lounge, payphone, small art room, bookstall.
Spiritual Help: Personal talks, spiritual direction, personal retreat direction.
Guests Admitted to: Chapel.
Meals: Taken in guest house in silence. Traditional food. Vegetarian possible – ask when booking.
Special Activities: None.
Situation: Quiet, in a town.
Maximum Stay: 8 days.
Bookings: Letter, telephone.
Charges: Suggested contribution £25 per person per night full board.
Access: Information provided when you book.

SHROPSHIRE

Clunbury

The Llan Retreat House
Twitchen
Clunbury, Craven Arms
Shrops SY7 0HN

Tel: 01588 660417
e-mail: LlanT-P@beeb.net

Anglican
This may well be the dream retreat place of most people. It is set in a magnificent part of England, just on the edge of Wales; the views are stunning; the

gardens are lovely and well-designed; the facilities are up-to-the-minute, comfortable, tastefully furnished, and quiet; and the chapel is an inspiring place of prayer and holy celebration. If this makes you want to say, 'Wow!', then go ahead, because this is an idyllic retreat house. For this reason it is very popular – and is particularly well used by local folk. This is great, but the result is that if you want to be a guest you must book well in advance. Just 8 miles west of Craven Arms and not far from the attractive Georgian town of Ludlow, Llan Retreat House is a converted seventeenth-century range of barns. The building includes a Great Hall with seating for about twenty people, a library, quiet rooms, a dining room and a chapel, where worship is offered daily. The accommodation offers room for up to fourteen people and is suitable for individuals, groups, and parish conferences and retreats. There is a self-contained wing for individuals, clergy couples and small families. All facilities are self-catering but full board is also available. The costs have been kept as low as possible. The retreat house is run by a married couple, both of whom are active Anglican priests and who continue through this retreat house to serve God, the Church and people with enthusiasm, intelligence and kindness. The home of the owners is adjacent but separate from the retreat house, so everyone has plenty of privacy. **Highly Recommended.**

Open: All year except Christmas and Easter.
Rooms: 2 singles, 6 doubles.
Facilities: Small conferences, gardens, library, guest lounge, TV.
Spiritual Help: Personal talks, spiritual direction, daily Divine Office and Eucharist in the chapel, 2 priests available.
Guests Admitted to: Mostly unrestricted access. Chapel.
Meals: Everyone eats together. Traditional, simple food – organic where possible. Vegetarian and special diets by prior arrangement.
Special Activities: None.
Situation: On a working farm, high on a hill in the Welsh Mountains – quiet and beautiful.
Maximum Stay: 1 week.
Bookings: Letter, telephone.
Charges: On application – brochure available.
Access: By car is best. Map on request.

Ellesmere

The Grange	Tel: 01691 623495
Ellesmere	Fax: 01691 623227
Shrops SY12 9DE	e-mail: rosie@thegrange.uk.com
	Website: www.thegrange.uk.com

Interfaith
A lovely short drive hedged with cherry trees and magnolias and spring daffodils brings you to this mellow, comfortable and welcoming old country house. Rooted in Christianity but open to all faiths, the Grange has been continually updating itself with bright and light new decorations and landscaping more of the gardens. Retreat here is offered with the slogan: 'Here is the house, let's use it for peace and quiet!' There is traditional B&B accommodation as well as a programme of courses. For older women there are weekends and courses to reflect, reassess and search for new personal potential

within the security of a small group. Indeed one of the main concerns here has long been to explore and celebrate the second half of life for women. These sessions have grown in strength over the years. Craft courses are being developed, with the idea that these can be spiritual adventures for personal development and not just past-times. These include painting and writing workshops. There is also a Natural Therapy Centre with various therapeutics on offer, such as counselling, aromatherapy, reflexology and reiki. Yoga sessions and courses have increased in number as a result of growing demand. The garden has a labyrinth based on the one in Chartres Cathedral. The garden together with woodland and pasture gives the guest over 10 acres in which to wander. Peace, harmony and kindness are to be found here.

Open: March to November. Receives men, women, young people, groups, non-retreatants.
Rooms: 4 singles, 11 doubles. Most rooms are ensuite and have tea/coffee facilities.
Facilities: Conferences, meditation, garden, fields and woodland, small library, guest lounge, TV, guest telephone, direct dialing.
Spiritual Help: None.
Guests Admitted to: Everywhere except private family rooms.
Meals: Everyone eats together. Lots of vegetarian food. Innovative cooking with interesting menus, making the most of the organic produce from the garden. Special diets possible.
Special Activities: Courses that aim to promote inner understanding and spirituality. Non-retreatants are offered a place for stillness and enjoyment. Send for information.
Situation: Quiet, about 10 minutes walk from a small town.
Maximum Stay: 5 days.
Bookings: Letter, telephone.
Charges: £165 for courses, with a £15 supplement for single occupancy. B&B £30 per person per night.
Access: Train: Shrewsbury (17 miles away). Infrequent buses. Car: via A528 from Ellesmere.

Ludlow

Bishop Mascall Centre
Lower Galdeford
Ludlow   Tel: 01584 813882
Shrops SY8 1R2   Fax: 01584 877945
                      e-mail: housemanger@bmcresources.org.uk

Anglican – Inter-denominational
About five minutes walk from Ludlow railway station, this centre has been going for some years and caters for groups and others who arrange their own retreats or programmes. The staff will help in such arrangements if you need. Ludlow, a pretty and busy Georgian town, has been revived by tourism. It is now a very popular destination and often crowded in the centre. There are all manner of smart and interesting shops and cafés, including a specialist art bookshop with a national reputation, run by a knowledgeable and helpful American woman. Just across the street from her shop is an art gallery featuring many local artists who also exhibit nationally. Ludlow also boasts

Michelin star restaurants, an annual Food Festival and a long-established Arts and Music Festival centred around its famous Castle.

Open: All year. Receives everyone.
Rooms: 16 singles, 4 doubles, 2 dormitories.
Facilities: Conferences, library, guest lounge, TV, guest telephone.
Spiritual Help: None.
Guests Admitted to: Unrestricted access.
Meals: Everyone eats together. Traditional food. Vegetarian and special diets.
Special Activities: None.
Situation: Former church school, in town.
Maximum Stay: By arrangement.
Bookings: Letter, telephone.
Charges: 3 rates available, up to £30 per person per day in a single, full board.
Access: Train and car easy.

Pontesbury

Monastery of St Antony and St Cuthbert
Gatten
Pontesbury
Shrops SY5 OSJ   Tel: 01588 650571

Orthodox Christian
In the south Shropshire hills, just by the famous Stiperstones, a little Orthodox Christian monastery welcomes guests to cells where they may spend a few days on a quiet retreat. The community of monks and nuns live in hermitages around the place and have a central church and refectory. There are Orthodox liturgies four times a week.

Rowley

Retreat Cottage
Charles and Sylvia Ruxton
New Place
Rowley
Near Westbury
Shrops SY8 9RY   Tel: 01743 891636
                         e-mail: sylviaruxton@btinternet.com
Christian
A simple old retreat cottage is on offer here that guests may use to find rest and peace. It is attached to the main house. The owners are especially interested in guests who may not have been on retreat before, and they are willing to be helpful and offer guidance if it is wanted. There is a Quiet Room for morning prayer each day. Children, including babies, are welcome here – and even well-behaved dogs downstairs in the cottage. Guests are welcome to join the family for morning prayers. There is no smoking, and mobile phones are not allowed.

Open: Most of year. Receives everyone except groups. Babies and children welcome. Pets by arrangement.

Rooms: 1 single, 2 doubles.
Facilities: Garden, guest lounge.
Spiritual Help: Personal talks, personal retreat direction, spiritual direction, therapeutic massage.
Guests Admitted to: Guest areas, Quiet Room.
Meals: Self-catering facilities. The Retreat Cottage has its own kitchen but a single guest is welcome to join the family for the evening meal. Whole food.
Special Activities: None.
Situation: Very quiet, on hillside, with lovely views.
Maximum Stay: 7 nights.
Bookings: Letter, telephone.
Charges: Donation of £20 minimum suggested for self-catering per night, plus £5 if evening meal with the family included. Back massage £10 a session.
Access: Train and bus possible – ask for information. Car easiest.

Shrewsbury

Hawkstone Hall
International Pastoral Centre   Tel: 01630 685242
Marchamley   Fax: 01630 685171
Shrewsbury   e-mail: hawkstone@aol.com
Shrops SY4 5LG   Website: www.hawkstone-hall.com

This is a huge place set in extensive parks and gardens and run by the Redemptorists as a centre for both lay and religious. There are short and three-month courses, plus a retreat programme running through most of the year. Accommodation for over sixty guests.

Whitchurch

Taraloka Buddhist Retreat Centre for Women
Bettisfield, Whitchurch
Shrops SY12 2LD   Tel: 01948 710646
                                e-mail: taraloka@compuserve.com

Buddhist
This is one of our favourite places, where we would happily send our sisters, mother, aunts and any woman we know for a retreat whether she was Buddhist or not. Situated on the plains of the Welsh borderlands, this Buddhist women's community acts as a focal point for women throughout the world from various walks of life. It provides inspiration and affords a glimpse of new spiritual and personal vistas for all who come. Taraloka is one of the few retreat centres specifically run by women for women and it has developed a kind and gentle space in which all women may find relaxation and support in their spiritual journey. Over the last fifteen years the Centre has established clear and simple methods of teaching meditation and Buddhism through its yearly programme. The retreats run from complete beginners to committed practising Buddhists. **To stay here, you have to come on one of the retreats or events in the programme**, which teaches Buddhist meditation and study within the context of the Friends of the Western Buddhist Order. All teachers are well qualified, having been practicing meditation and Buddhism for many years. Those with no experience of

meditation and Buddhism can come for an introductory weekend course including a first exploration of various meditation practices and Buddhist principles and eithics. Other features are yoga weekends, courses on spiritual life and motherhood, and retreats. The retreat centre is separate from the community house. The facilities are modern, light and airy. The accommodation has been converted from farm buildings, most of the work being done by women. It includes a solitary suite for a private retreat, with a bedroom, small kitchen and conservatory, all of which is so delightful that you may want to stay in it forever. There is a garden, views, a pond and flowers – in the early spring white magnolias are in bloom. Everywhere shines out with cleanliness and there is an art room for those who want to paint and make. On your stay you will meet a wide range of other women you might not ordinarily meet, and this too can be a very spiritual experience. There is a strong emphasis here on ethical practice, aiming for more kindness, generosity, contentment, truthful speech and clarity of mind. Taraloka is place of peace, self-discovery and transformation. **Highly Recommended.**

Open: Specific programme of retreats for women – no other guests received.
Rooms: Singles, dormitories.
Facilities: Shrine room, guest lounge, camping, garden.
Spiritual Help: Personal talks, group sharing, meditation, directed study, personal retreat direction, spiritual direction.
Guests Admitted to: Shrine room.
Meals: Taken in guest house. Vegetarian and vegan food. Special diets.
Special Activities: Planned events only available – send for brochure.
Situation: Very quiet, in the countryside, with beautiful country walks – near the Shropshire Union Canal. Nearby is a peat reserve of special scientific interest.
Maximum Stay: For the duration of the retreat.
Bookings: Letter, e-mail, telephone.
Charges: £85 per person for weekend, £50 per person concessionary rate.
Access: Map and details are provided with booking confirmation.

STAFFORDSHIRE

Leek

**Croft Meadows Farm
Horton
Leek
Staffs ST13 8QE**   Tel: 01782 513039

Non-denominational
A spacious self-contained cottage with three single bedrooms, one twin double and one double on the ground floor. It is set in countryside on a farm, and there is a chapel and garden. The cottage offers a quiet retreat place for up to sixteen people, either for the day or residential self-catering.

Stone

Shallowford House Retreat and Conference Centre
Norton Bridge
Stone   Tel: 01785 760233
Staffs ST16 0NZ   Fax: 01785 760390
e-mail: warden@shallowfordhouse.freeserve.co.uk

Anglican
A big old house which is the centre of the Lichfield diocese. The aim of Shallowford is to offer Christian hospitality to all that visit. There is a small programme run during the year, which includes topics such as *The Enneagram and Spirituality, Painting and Prayer* and *Healing in the Church*. This is a place of warm welcome, nice food and pleasant surroundings.

Open: All year. Receives men, women, young people, families, groups.
Rooms: 15 singles, 12 twins.
Facilities: Disabled, conferences, garden, bookstall, guest lounge, TV and guest phone (01785 760589).
Spiritual Help: None.
Guests Admitted to: Unrestricted.
Meals: Everyone eats together. Vegetarian and special diets.
Special Activities: Planned programme of events – send for brochure.
Situation: Quiet, in the countryside.
Maximum Stay: By arrangement.
Bookings: Letter, fax, e-mail, telephone 9a.m.–5p.m.
Charges: £37.50 per person per 24 hours full board. £12 to £20 per person for a day visit, including meals.
Access: Train: Norton Bridge. No buses.

WARWICKSHIRE

Leamington Spa

Offa House
Offchurch   Tel: 01926 423309
Leamington Spa   Fax: 01926 330350
Warwicks CV33 9AS   e-mail: offahouse@btconnect.com
Website: www.offahouseretreat.co.uk

Church of England
The Coventry Diocesan Retreat House and Conference Centre are situated in an old Georgian vicarage with a large garden. The house has been organised in such a way that all visitors are helped to feel that this is their own special place, and the staff try to be as non-intrusive as possible. The programme usually offers both Julian and Cursillo retreats, as well as other retreats and courses such as *Searching for God through Imaging Clay, Celtic Insights into Prayer, The Power of the Inner Critic and Self-esteem* and *Creation and Recreation*. The Quiet Days have themes reflecting Christian spirituality and are intended to focus your day's retreat away from ordinary living.

Open: All year. Receives men, women, young people, families, groups, non-retreatants. Children welcome.

Rooms: 16 singles, 8 doubles. Self-contained cottage sleeping 5.

Facilities: Disabled, church, conferences, chapel, garden, library, guest lounge, TV, payphone.

Spiritual Help: Personal talks, personal retreat direction, spiritual direction.

Guests Admitted to: Everywhere.

Meals: Everyone eats together. Traditional food. Vegetarian and special diets.

Special Activities: Planned programme of events – send for brochure. Massage and aromatherapy.

Situation: Quiet, in the village, in countryside.

Maximum Stay: 30 days for guided retreats.

Bookings: Letter, fax, e-mail telephone.

Charges: £37 per 24 hours full board, weekend £69, Quiet Days £10. Self-contained cottage £250 per week in July/August, £190 per week outside these months.

Access: Rail, bus, car and airport links are all excellent.

Stratford upon Avon

Red Hill Christian Centre
Snitterfield
Stratford upon Avon
Warwicks CV37 OPQ
Tel/Fax: 01789 731427
e-mail: office@redhillcentre.fsnet.co.uk

Christian

This centre is set in some 50 acres of land and offers singles and doubles plus a self-catering cottage sleeping two or three people. Meals can be provided for booked retreats including day retreats, but otherwise you get a French breakfast – no eggs, sausage and beans – and then you fix your own lunch and dinner. There is a converted barn for conferences. A programme of events is also available.

WORCESTERSHIRE

Chadwick

Community for Reconciliation
Barnes Close
Chadwick
Bromsgrove
Worcs B61 ORA

Tel: 01562 710231
e-mail: cfrenquiry@aol.com

Ecumenical

Enjoying close links with the United Reform Church through founder members, prayer and financial support, the community here has developed ecumenically in its team, membership and patterns of work. Barnes Close is a group of buildings situated on the southern slopes of Waseley Hill with 5 acres of grounds and near a country park. There are fine view of the Malvern Hills and beyond towards the Cotswolds. Accommodation is comfortable in a homely way and some rooms are ensuite. There is a common room with a real fire, a chapel, a library, a coffee bar, seminar rooms, two conservatories, a craft stall, a bookshop and even a sweet shop for those who love their chocolate. The programme has a number of retreats based on prayer, reflection, peace and rest. If you want a private silent retreat then you should discuss this first when you contact the community. Otherwise the programme has a group silent retreat based on Bible passages concerning peace and justice. The community has a network of friends who help with the work of reconciliation and justice, and charitable projects are going in Romania, Africa and other places. The centre is close to Bromsgrove and Birmingham. **Highly Recommended.**

Open: All year. Receives everyone. Children welcome. Guide dogs only.
Rooms: 3 singles, 8 doubles, 1 triple, 2 family rooms.
Facilities: Disabled, conferences, garden, library, guest lounge, TV, conservatory, payphone (01562 710682). There is usually a smoking room – otherwise no smoking.
Spiritual Help: Personal retreat direction.
Guests Admitted to: Almost everywhere in public rooms.
Meals: Everyone eats together. Traditional home-cooked food. Vegetarian and special diets.
Special Activities: Planned programme – send for details.
Situation: Quiet, in the countryside.
Maximum Stay: 2 weeks or by arrangement.
Bookings: Letter, e-mail, telephone 9.30a.m.–4.30p.m.
Charges: From £35 to £115 and up depending on the retreat. Reflection Day of Prayer £12 (including lunch). There are rates for the unwaged and reductions for under-16s.
Access: Close to Bromsgrove and Birmingham. Train: Longbridge, then taxi (6 miles). Bus: Rubery, then taxi. Car: 1 mile from Junction 4 of M5 (easy route).

Cropthorne

Holland House
Retreat, Conference and Laity Centre
Cropthorne
Pershore
Worcs WR10 3NB

Tel: 01386 860330
Fax: 01386 861208
e-mail: laycentre@hollandhouse.org
Website: www.hollandhouse.org.uk

Inter-denominational
Holland House was set up to help people who are trying to relate their prayer life more closely to the world around them. It is a big seventeenth-century place, with lots of thatch and gardens laid out by Lutyens. There is a chapel and a modern conference and bedroom wing. The house is close to the village church, and although not far from busy roads, it is quiet. In addition to retreat courses, there are non-residential and quiet days. Titles of some of the events offered include: *Painting and Prayer, Millennium Men, Myers-Briggs, Retreat on the Streets, Modern Theological Approaches, Icon Painting Workshop, Women at the Well Network – Women Saints, Judas and the Coptic Church, Creative Writing Day* and *Circle Dancing. Come let us Play,* an introduction to playfulness and prayer, sounds like serious spiritual fun. This is a good place for a retreat, with a wide-ranging and interesting programme, coupled with comfortable accommodation. **Highlly Recommended.**

Open: All year except Christmas and the week after Easter. Receives men, women, young people, families, groups, non-retreatants. Children welcome.
Rooms: 18 singles, 6 doubles.
Facilities: Chapel, garden, library, payphone (01386 860071), TV.
Spiritual Help: Group sharing on certain courses, personal talks.
Guests Admitted to: Unrestricted access.
Meals: Everyone eats together. Traditional food. Vegetarian and special diets.
Special Activities: Planned programme of events – send for brochure.
Situation: Quiet, in the village, in countryside.
Maximum Stay: 1 month.
Bookings: Letter, e-mail, telephone during office hours.
Charges: £45–£55 per 24 hours.
Access: Train: Evesham (3½ miles away). Buses: from Evesham. Car: via M5, Exit 7, then A44.

Kidderminster

Harvington Hall   Tel: 01562 777846
Near Kidderminster   Fax: 01562 777190
Worcs DY10 4LR   e-mail: thehall@harvington.fsbusiness.co.uk
                          Website: www.harvingtonhall.org.uk

Christian – Inter-denominational
This is a moated Tudor manor house, owned by the Archdiocese of Birmingham and featuring, among other things, three chapels, gardens and a restaurant. Everyone is welcome for Quiet Days and parish group away-days. The hall is non-residential.

Shrawley

Society of St Francis
Glasshampton Monastery
Shrawley   Tel: 01299 896345
Worcs WR6 6TQ   Fax: 01299 896083
                e-mail: glasshampton@franciscans.org.uk

Anglican
Up a road beyond cultivated fields and other houses, Glasshampton sits waiting for you. If you take the bus you will have a good long walk to get here, and this may well be a perfect meditation time before commencing your retreat. The monastery is well established and was built from the stable blocks of a once very grand house that burned down years ago. It is a simple place with a certain elegance about it – homely and silent, yet charming and welcoming. Services in chapel are open to guests. The guest rooms are modern and pleasant, and there is a library. The Guest Master will welcome you warmly and make certain you are comfortable. The books of Br Ramon, famous for his writings on spirituality, are available to read. This Franciscan friary has a lifestyle based on ideals of simplicity, hospitality and prayer. This is a serious place for a private retreat.

Open: All year Tuesday to Sunday except for Christmas and Easter. Receives men, women.
Rooms: 5 singles.

Facilities: Garden, library, guest area, guest telephone, direct dialing.
Spiritual Help: Personal talks, spiritual direction.
Guests Admitted to: Chapel, library.
Meals: Everyone eats together. Very plain traditional food. Vegetarians. Special diets only within reason, so always discuss before you go.
Special Activities: None.
Situation: Very quiet and peaceful, in the countryside.
Maximum Stay: 6 days.
Bookings: Letter, fax, telephone.
Charges: Suggest donation of £20 per day.
Access: Train, bus, car.

West Malvern

**Runnings Park
Croft Bank
West Malvern
Worcs WR14 4DU**

Tel: 01684 573868
Fax: 01684 892047
e-mail: info@runningspark.co.uk

Mind Body Spirit
Built about one hundred years ago by Lady Howard de Walden as a model dairy farm, Runnings Park has been converted to a hotel and rest centre with an emphasis on health, relaxation and self-development. The place has all the sort of modern comforts and the programme is a continuous one. Meditation, channeling, healing and Celtic spirituality, and taking control of your destiny are regular topics that give a good idea of what to expect. Some group courses have titles such as *Planetary Alignment, Exploring the Chakras of the Hills, Crop Circle Phenomenon* and *Power of Myths.* Massage, aromatherapy, reflexology, floatation, counselling, hypnotherapy, nutritional therapy and healing are all on offer. Facilities are many, and the centre is comfortable, large and airy. There are spectacular views, and a sauna and pool are available to all. Food is moving towards the organic and the rooms are what you would expect in a hotel. The atmosphere is quietly busy, and even with larger groups in residence there is space and peace to be found here.

Open: All year except Christmas. Receives men, women, groups.
Rooms: 18 singles, 8 doubles. No family rooms.
Facilities: Conferences, park, TV, telephones in all bedrooms, direct dialing.
Spiritual Help: Personal talks, self-development courses. Some counselling. Health and relaxation centre on site. Various therapies available.
Guests Admitted to: Unrestricted access.
Meals: Dining room/restaurant. Vegetarian available with prior notice.
Special Activities: Send for brochure.
Situation: Very quiet, in countryside.
Maximum Stay: Open.
Bookings: Letter, fax, telephone.
Charges: These vary considerably, so check it out when you ask for information. Current examples: £29 B&B per person per night, therapies from £12.50 a session.
Access: Train and car both possible.

Worcester

St Mary's House
Stanbrook Abbey
Callow End
Worcester
Worcs WR2 4TD

Tel: 01905 830307
e-mail: warden@stmarysstanbrook.org.uk
Website: www.stanbrookabbey.org.uk

Roman Catholic

St Mary's is the guest house of Stanbrook Abbey, one of the best-known Benedictine women's religious communities in Britain, with an international reputation for literary, musical and artistic work. Its influence can be seen and heard in the liturgical arrangements of many other monastic communities. The sisters are enclosed, which means you do not meet many of them, but the welcome is very warm and friendly. This is a grand monastery with an enclosed walled area for the community that is one of the largest remaining in Europe. The church is on the same scale too, and the Divine Office is sung in Latin and English with some handsome voices to be heard. Rooms at St Mary's are modern, comfortable and pleasant. There is a simple, elegant oratory in the house and a big library open to all. The guest kitchen and dining room are excellent and just outside a little garden full of flowers. There are retreats run by the community nuns and others run by those outside the community. The programme is mostly day retreats and day group retreats. This is a classic Christian place for making a private retreat, where the rich monastic choir provides a good framework for your stay. **Highly Recommended.**

Open: All year except 2 weeks at Christmas and in August. Receives men, women, young people, groups.

Rooms: 10 singles, 4 doubles.

Facilities: Garden, library, guest lounge, guest phone (01905 831770), bookshop in monastery.

Spiritual Help: Personal talks. Guests are welcome to attend Divine Office in the church.

Guests Admitted to: Church, extern chapel and guest house facilities.

Meals: Eaten in the guest house. Traditional food. Vegetarian, vegan and special diets.

Special Activities: None.

Situation: Quiet, in village.

Maximum Stay: 2 weeks usually, or by arrangement.

Bookings: Letter.

Charges: £30 full board per 24 hours. £28 per day for Monday to Friday 5-day stays. Concessions for unwaged and students.

Access: Train: Worcester Shrub Hill or Foregate Street, then taxi. Buses are very infrequent. Car: via M5, Exit 8, then take Malvern Road.

> Fools enjoy their careless pleasure, but their way is dark and leads to danger.
> Qu Yuan

Northern England

CHESHIRE

Chester

**Chester Retreat House
11 Abbey Square
Chester
Cheshire CH1 2HU**

Tel: 01244 321801
e-mail: Chester.retreat@tiscali.co.uk
Website: www.chester-retreathouse.org

Inter-denominational

A lay canon of Chester Cathedral manages this retreat centre which consists of two elegant Georgian houses, now joined, situated in a quiet corner near the Cathedral. There are sitting rooms, a good library and a large and well maintained garden. Both dining room and meeting rooms (plus disabled lavatory) are on the ground floor, and plans are being made for a lift and ensuite rooms for better disabled access. While groups use this centre, individuals are also welcomed, and last-minute bookings are very often possible, so it is worth a try if you suddenly decide that a few days away for some interior meditation and time alone are what you need. Parking is difficult because of the situation of the house, but public transport is available, so discuss which travel method will be best for you with the warden of the centre.

Open: All year except during part of August. Receives men, women, young people, groups, families.
Rooms: 27 singles, 4 doubles.
Facilities: Disabled, chapel, conferences, garden, library, guest lounge, guest phone.
Spiritual Help: Morning and evening prayer, spiritual direction, quiet days or part of a day, group sharing, directed study.
Guests Admitted to: Unrestricted access.
Meals: Everyone eats together. Generous traditional food with fresh ingredients. Vegetarian and special diets. Meals can be taken in room.
Special Activities: Planned programme of events – send for brochure.
Situation: In the city square, by the cathedral.
Maximum Stay: By arrangement.
Bookings: Letter, e-mail, telephone during office hours.
Charges: £34 for 24 hours, £64 per weekend, £18 for day use of facilities.
Access: Rail, bus or car to Chester.

Crewe

Oblate Retreat and Spirituality Centre
Wistaston Hall
89 Broughton Lane   Tel: 01270 568653
Crewe   Fax: 01270 650776
Cheshire CW2 8JS   e-mail: oblate@wistaston-hall
                                     Website: www.oblate.fsworld.co.uk

Roman Catholic
This is a 200-year-old cheerful-looking country house, set in 6 acres of garden and peaceful countryside. The Centre is staffed by Oblate Fathers and some forty guests can be accommodated. The aim is to enable those who come here to wind down from the stresses and strains of modern living and to enter into a deeper experience of prayer and reflection in the presence of Christ. Much effort goes into making guests feel comfortable, with professional catering and log fires in the winter months. The retreats and courses on offer are wide-ranging and include *Autumn Venture, Advent Retreat, The Effects of Colour on our Well-being, Touched by God* and *Massage: The Art of Anointing.* Private retreats with spiritual accompaniment can be arranged.

Open: All year except first half of August. Receives all. Children welcome.
Rooms: 2 singles, 18 doubles. Some ensuite.
Facilities: Disabled – some ground-floor rooms. Conferences, chapel, large garden, library, guest lounge, TV, guest phone.
Spiritual Help: Spiritual direction, personal retreat direction.
Guests Admitted to: Unrestricted access.
Meals: Everyone eats together. Traditional whole food. Vegetarian, vegan and special diets.
Special Activities: Planned programme of events.
Situation: Very quiet, in the village.
Maximum Stay: Usually 1 week or length of course.
Bookings: Letter, fax, e-mail, telephone 9a.m.–5p.m.
Charges: Non-residential day rate £20, residential day rate £30, weekend full board £60, B&B £20. Directed retreat £30 per day. Reduced prices for students, unwaged and senior citizens.
Access: Rail: Crewe, then taxi (5 minutes to Centre). Car: via M6.

Frodsham

Foxhill
Chester Diocesan Conference Centre
Tarvin Road
Frodsham   Tel: 01270 568653
Cheshire WA6 6XB   Fax: 01270 650776
                          e-mail: Oblate@wistaston-hall.fsworld.co.uk

Anglican
The Centre welcomes all. It offers sixteen single rooms, twelve twins and two family rooms. It is excellent for group retreats.

Malpas

St Joseph's Retreat and Conference Centre
Tilston Road   Tel: 01948 860416
Malpas   Fax: 01948 860055
Cheshire SY14 7DD   e-mail: scj@malpas2000.freeserve.co.uk
                              Website: www.malpas2000.freeserve.co.uk

Roman Catholic – Ecumenical
St Joseph's mission is to help people find the God of love and compassion, and
in particular to bring about reconciliation and integration in life. Run by the
Sacred Heart Fathers, this former seminary is a welcoming and homely place.
The modern wing is perhaps rather institutional, but the original house has
some wonderful rooms – a good library, a reading room, a chapel and a delightful Victorian conservatory. The grounds are extensive and have wonderful
views across the border into Wales. Private retreatants are welcome at any time
and may receive spiritual guidance if they wish. There is also a programme that
includes Reconciliation Days, retreats around Lent and Advent, and walking
and relaxation retreats. St Joseph's is also happy to provide tailor-made retreats
or workshops or to accommodate groups running their own programme. For
those seeking real solitude, there is a Poustinia, and for those wishing to self-
cater, The Beeches Lodge House is self-contained and comfortable.

Open: All year except Christmas and 2 weeks in August. Receives all.
Rooms: 32 singles, 2 doubles, hermitages, some camping, 3-bed self-
contained gate lodge.
Facilities: Disabled, conferences, garden, park, library, guest lounge, TV,
payphone.
Spiritual Help: Personal talks, group sharing, meditation, directed study,
personal retreat direction, spiritual direction, Sacrament of Reconciliation,
Eucharist.
Guests Admitted to: Chapel and church.
Meals: Taken in dining room. Traditional food. Vegetarian and special diets.
Special Activities: Planned programme – send for brochure.
Situation: Quiet, in a small village.
Maximum Stay: Up to 2 weeks.
Bookings: Letter, fax, e-mail, telephone 9.30a.m.–4.30p.m. Monday to
Friday.
Charges: Varies according to retreat – contact Centre for rates.
Access: Train: Whitchurch. Bus: National coach to Chester. Car: A41
between Chester and Whitchurch.

Warrington

Tumble Trust
7 Grammar School Road
Warrington   Tel: 01925 635662
Cheshire WA4 1JN   e-mail: Tumble-trust@yahoo.co.uk
                              Website: www.tumbletrust.co.uk

Interfaith
Tumble Trust, now ten years old, runs organised relaxation courses at some
of the most hospitable retreat centres in the UK. Tumble's aim is to relax,
enlighten, encourage and sustain you – laughter is part of the deal here.

Taking its main inspiration from the Christian contemplative tradition, Tumble puts an emphasis on community and shared spiritual journeys. Some of the titles of their courses are very inviting – *Enneagram* – *Way of Transformation, Relaxation and the Art of Foolishness* and *For God's Sake Relax!* Remember please, just in case you forgot, that being relaxed and enjoying life can be combined with contemplative prayer – indeed relaxing and being filled with joy is a great way to greet God. The psalm tells us God does not want sacrifice but thanksgiving, so what better way to say 'Thanks for life!' than through your happiness? All-inclusive prices for a weekend currently range from £65 to £80. The summer week that Tumble has held at Ilkley for some years costs about £195. Send for brochure. A new perspective about yourself is highly likely.

CUMBRIA

Ambleside

Rydal Hall
Carlisle Diocesan Retreat and Conference Centre
Ambleside   Tel: 01539 432050
Cumbria LA22 9LX   Fax: 01539 434887
                                          e-mail: Bookings@rydalhall.org
                                          Website: www.rydalhall.org

Anglican – Ecumenical
There is a relaxed atmosphere in this big Georgian house set in the heart of the Lake District, in a 30-acre estate with waterfalls and formal gardens. It is mainly used by groups, but individuals are welcomed and there is no pressure to join in any activities that may be taking place. There is a good family and youth emphasis here.

Open: All year except 2nd week December. Receives everyone. Children welcome.
Rooms: 10 single, 15 twins, 3 triples, 5 family rooms, camping, 36-bed hostel for young people in groups.
Facilities: Disabled, conferences, camping, garden, library, guest lounge, TV, guest phone (01539 433431), book shop.
Spiritual Help: None except by prior arrangement.
Guests Admitted to: Unrestricted access.
Meals: Everyone eats together. Traditional food. Vegetarian and special diets. Self-catering in hostel.
Special Activities: Planned programme of events – send for brochure.
Situation: Quiet.
Maximum Stay: No limit.
Bookings: Letter, fax, telephone 9a.m.–5p.m.
Charges: From £30 B&B to £47.50 weekend full board.
Access: Train: Windermere. Bus: Ambleside. Car: via M6, Exit 40 from north, Exit 36 from south, then A591.

Grasmere

**Glenthorne Quaker Centre
Easedale Road
Grasmere
Cumbria LA22 9QP**   Tel: 01539 435389

Quaker
Glenthorne is a fairly large country house that is both a holiday centre and a
retreat centre for those desiring an atmoshere of peace and friendship. A
brochure is available. Glenthorne is a few minutes walk from the village
centre and there are open views to the fells. It stands in its own 1½ acres of
gardens. Glenthorne accommodates up to 50 people in a variety of rooms,
some ensuite, and including family rooms and singles. There are two self-
catering flats.

Greystoke

**Friends Fellowship of Healing
Lattendales
Berrier Road
Greystoke**
Penrith   Tel: 01768 483229
Cumbria CA11 OUE   Fax: 01768 483058
                     Website: www.lattendales/info.com

Society of Friends – Quaker – Interfaith
This is a lovely old stone house with gardens and a peaceful atmosphere.
Worship in the manner of the Religious Society of Friends is held most mornings. The Fellowship is run in accordance with the principles of the Society
of Friends but is open to all, irrespective of religious beliefs. The house is situated on the edge of Lakeland National Park, with easy access to the Lake
District, Scotland and the North Pennines, and set in its own 17 acres. The
accommodation is comfortable, clean and pleasant. The function of
Lattendales is to provide a sanctuary for all who feel in need of rest, whether
it is spiritual, mental or physical. There is a good if small range of retreats on
offer here. Self-catering is possible. **Highly Recommended.**

Open: March to October. Receives men, women, young people, families,
     groups, non-retreatants. Children welcome.
Rooms: 8 doubles, 5 singles, all with hot and cold water. One on ground
     floor. 2 separate flats.
Facilities: Disabled facilities limited – check out if what is available is OK for
     you. Quiet room, garden, library, guest lounge, payphone (01768 483450).
Spiritual Help: Personal talks.
Guests Admitted to: Unrestricted access.
Meals: Taken in the guest house. Traditional simple food, with provision for
     vegetarian, vegan and special diets. Self-catered meals taken in room.
Special Activities: Planned programme of events – send for brochure.
Situation: Quiet, in village, in countryside just outside Lakeland National
     Park. Grade II listed building.
Maximum Stay: By arrangement.
Bookings: Letter, telephone.

Charges: £43 full board per person per night.
Access: Train: Penrith. Car: M6/A66 Junction 40, A592 to Penrith, sign-posted after Penrith railway station.

Ulverston

Manjushri Buddhist Centre	Tel: 01229 584029
Conishead Priory	Fax: 01229 580080
Ulverston	e-mail: info@manjushri.org.uk
Cumbria LA12 9QQ	Website: www.manjushri.org.uk

Buddhist – New Kadampa Mahayana tradition
Manjushri is located in the beautiful wooded surroundings of Coniston Priory and a gentle ten-minute stroll from the coast. The now largely restored Priory (home to over fifty resident monks) stands alongside the recently erected modern temple, which is large enough to accommodate 2,000 people (who come for the two-week summer festival). Its interior is dominated by a magnificent display case containing countless representations of the Buddha. This is an ideal setting for the courses, which are teachings and meditation led by Gen-la Samden Gyatso, the principal teacher here. The spiritual guide is the Venerable Geshe Kelsang Gyatso, a Tibetan-born internationally known teacher of Buddhism. Here is what one guest had to say of his experience at Manjushri during the summer festival: 'I found the summer festival to be a really rewarding experience. During the festival the Centre had a welcoming, friendly and family atmosphere with a mix of people of all ages from around the world. There was even a crèche and a clown to keep children and some adults entertained. I was extremely impressed with the teachings that I received. Geshe Kelsang Gyatso delivered them with a great humour and humility, and as he spoke I certainly felt as though I was receiving some hidden esoteric knowledge.' There is a general programme, a foundation programme and teacher training courses. Manjushri has a large community of some 100 lay and ordained Buddhists. The New Kadampa Tradition (NKT) is a sect founded by Geshe Kelsang Gyatso. The Geshe (a title equivalent to a doctorate in Tibetan Buddhism) came to England in 1977 from India and, after having earned a name as a writer and teacher of Buddhism, established the NKT in 1991. The NKT centres are conspicuously devoid of any portrait of the H.H. The Dalai Lama, with whom Geshe Kelsang Gyatso, a former friend, had a theological and political dispute some years ago. This seems to have done nothing to halt the growth of NKT, which is now the fastest-growing Buddhist sect in England.

Open: All year. Receives men, women – residential and non-residential possible. Young people, families, groups, non-retreatants.
Rooms: 15 singles, 10 doubles, dormitories.
Facilities: Disabled limited, so check it out with them first. Temple, meditation/teaching rooms.
Spiritual Help: Spiritual direction, meditation.
Guests Admitted to: Unrestricted access.
Meals: Taken together. **Vegetarian food only.**
Special Activities: Planned programme of events – send for brochure.
Situation: Quiet, in countryside.

Maximum Stay: 4 weeks.
Bookings: Letter, website.
Charges: £140 single full board for weekend course. Double, dormitory and other rates available, so enquire.
Access: The brochure gives details for train and car and includes a small map.

Rookhow Centre
Rusland
Ulverston
Cumbria LA12 8LA

Tel: 01229 860231
Fax: 01229 860231
e-mail: rookhow@britishlibrary.net

In 14 acres of woodland, Rookhow provides accommodation in a set of former stables for individual self-directed and guided group retreats. It specialises in arts and crafts, conservation, body and breathwork, and meditation.

Swarthmoor Hall
Ulverston
Cumbria LA12 OJQ

Tel: 01229 583204
Fax: 01229 583283
e-mail: swarthmrhall@gn.apc.org
Website: www.swarthmoorhall.co.uk

Renovated and refurbished not long ago, Swarthmoor Hall offers sixteen bed spaces in two flats, as well as group full board and self-catering facilities. Children are welcome and there is wheelchair access. There are several good spaces for activities. Special interests here are group process, inner process and prayer.

DURHAM

Claypath

St Antony's Priory Durham
St Antony's Priory
Ecumenical Spirituality Centre
Claypath
Durham DH1 1QT

Tel: 0191 384 3747
Fax: 0191 384 4939
e-mail: Ssm.durham@whih.net

Christian – Ecumenical
St Antony's offers accommodation in a guest cottage for anyone needing peace and space. There are daily offices, as well as Ecumenical spiritual direction and Ignatian retreats by request. The programme is a large one with a number of quiet days, courses and retreats.

> The Resurrection is to life, not to death.
> D.H. LAWRENCE

LANCASHIRE

Blackburn

Whalley Abbey
Blackburn Diocesan Retreat House and Conference Centre
Whalley
Clitheroe
Lancs BB7 9SS

Tel: 01254 828400
Fax: 01254 828401
e-mail: office@whalleyabbey.org

Anglican – Ecumenical
Here is a comfortable and gracefully furnished house within the historic ruins of an ancient Cistercian abbey. Whalley Abbey was once the ecclesiastical power centre for northern England, but like so many others it was destroyed during the Reformation. An elegant manor house was built in the sixteenth century and it is this building that is used today for retreats and conferences. The accommodation has recently been refurbished to include self-contained apartments as well as single, twin and family rooms – many of which have wonderful views over the ruins and gardens. Meals, which are delicious, are served in a Jacobean-style dining room with all the refinement of a first-class restaurant. Whalley Abbey is not a place for the austerities of some spiritual retreats but offers a warm and gentle Christian hospitality that is conducive to deep rest and relaxation. You will be very well looked after! There are guided retreats, quiet days, a weekly meditation meeting, musical appreciation retreats, Ignation reflections, painting courses, senior citizen holidays and Whalley Abbey dinners. It is also possible to come on private retreat, but ask about accommodation if you are seeking quiet and solitude – particularly if the Abbey is busy.

Open: All year except Christmas and New Year. Receives everyone. Children welcome.
Rooms: 10 singles, 9 twins – two of these have 3 beds with cot. No radios/tape recorders in rooms.
Facilities: Disabled, conferences, garden, guest lounge, TV, payphone, gift shop, coffee shop.
Spiritual Help: Spiritual direction.
Guests Admitted to: Unrestricted access.
Meals: Everyone eats together. Traditional food. Vegetarian and special diets.
Special Activities: Planned programme – send for brochure.
Situation: Quiet and peaceful environment, with beautiful tranquil gardens and the ruins of a 14th-century Cistercian abbey.
Maximum Stay: Usually 7 days.
Bookings: Letter, fax, e-mail, telephone 8a.m.–6p.m. Monday to Saturday.
Charges: £16 per day non-residential, £102 for 5-day full board stay.
Access: Train or bus to Whalley. Car via A59 to Whalley.

Carnforth

Capernwray Holidays
Carnforth
Lancs LA6 1AG

Tel: 01524 733908
Fax: 01524 736681
e-mail: holidays@capernwray.org.uk
Website: www.capernwray.org.uk

Christian
'Where God changes lives ...' is the slogan of Capernwray, where the Capernwray Missionary Fellowship of Torchbearers plan and run scripture-based courses, including those with internationally famous speakers on the Word of God. Send for the current year's programme, which is a good one, full of interesting courses and conferences which will help to move you ahead in your Christian commitment and bring you inspiration in and group sharing of your faith.

Monastery of Our Lady of Hyning
Warton
Carnforth
Lancs LA5 9SE   Tel: 01524 732684

Roman Catholic
Particularly suitable for private retreats and day retreats, the Monastery is set in private grounds. In some rooms cheerful fires greet you in winter, while there is a peaceful and welcoming atmosphere everywhere. A barn has been converted into a church, where guests may join the sisters in their daily schedule of prayer.

Open: All year except mid-July to late August. Receives everyone.
Rooms: 8 singles, 1 double, 14 twins.
Facilities: Conference room, garden, library, guest telephone.
Spiritual Help: Personal talks, one-to-one retreats by arrangement.
Guests Admitted to: Chapel, choir.
Meals: Large and small dining rooms serving mainly traditional food. Vegetarian and special diets.
Special Activities: Programme of events – send for information.
Situation: Quiet, in the countryside.
Maximum Stay: By arrangement.
Bookings: Letter, telephone.
Charges: Ask for the tariff.
Access: Train: Carnforth. Some local buses pass the gate. Car: M6, Exit 35, and A6.

Old School
Yealand Conyers
Carnforth
Lancashire LA5 9SH   Tel: 01524 732336

Quaker
The Old School is adjacent to the Meeting House and offers simple self-catering accommodation at very reasonable prices. Bring a sleeping bag, as there are no beds in the dorm-like rooms. Groups of up to thirty can be accommodated. There are lots of local attractions, such as the RSPB bird reserve at Leighton Moss.

Preston

Tabor Carmelite Retreat House
169 Sharoe Green Lane
Fulwood, Preston
Lancs PR2 8HE

Tel: 01772 717122
Fax: 01772 787674
e-mail: ocdpreston@hotmail.com
Website: www.carmelite.org.uk

Christian
Here a small community of friars offers five single self-catering rooms with a
kitchen and lounge for their guests. There is also a conference room for
about fifty people. This is a quiet place where spiritual accompaniment and
guidance are available. You can also arrange for reflexology and counselling.
A liturgy room, prayer room and reconciliation room are also available for
use. There is always a warm welcome from the community here.

MANCHESTER

Ananda Marga Centre
42 Keppel Road
Chorlton
Manchester M21 0BW

Tel: 0161 282 9224
e-mail: anandamarga.mcr@gmx.net
Website: www.anandamarga.org

Yoga
The Ananda Marga movement was founded by the Indian philosopher, teacher
and poet P.R. Sarkar. Yoga and meditation are taught and practised as methods
for self-development and self-realisation, whilst social service is emphasised as
an outward expression of developing the human potential. The centre is in a
Victorian terraced house in south Manchester. Quiet, informal and friendly, the
Centre offers yoga classes and regular meetings for meditation. Creative writing and painting workshops are also on offer, and regular evenings of inspirational song, music and poetry draw the local community together.

Manchester Buddhist Centre
16–20 Turner St
Northern Quarter
Manchester M4 1DZ

Tel: 0161 834 9232
e-mail: info@manchesterbuddhistcentre.org.uk
Website: www.manchesterbuddhistcentre.org.uk

Buddhist – FWBO
This is an old Victorian warehouse right in the heart of Manchester city
centre, sensitively restored and now a Buddhist centre offering classes in
meditation and Buddhism. Exposed brick and natural wood contribute to an
atmosphere of calm, whilst the integrity of architecture, building materials
and voluntary human effort are an inspiration. There are two shrine halls, a
larger one for groups and a smaller one for private meditation or prayer.
Introductory classes are offered in meditation and Buddhism. Upstairs the
natural health centre, Bodywise, offers a spacious yoga studio; a wide range
of yoga classes; qi gong classes; and treatment rooms for massage, reflexology, pain management, acupuncture and shiatsu. There is a book shop and a
reference library, and the award-winning vegan Earth café is a haven of

healthy eating and drinking. The Centre is non-residential but weekend retreats are sometimes organised in venues in surrounding areas.

MERSEYSIDE

Freshfield

St Joseph's Prayer Centre
Blundell Avenue, Freshfield
Merseyside L37 1PH

Tel: 01704 875850/01704 870114
e-mail: Prayer.Centre@btintenet.com

Christian
Only half a mile from the sea and set near National Trust land, the Centre offers Ignatian retreats, quiet days, Alpha groups and retreats for reflection and prayer or just for relaxation. There are sixteen single rooms plus one double ensuite. Contact the Guest sister.

Liverpool

Cenacle Retreat Centre
Lance Lane, Wavertree
Liverpool L15 6TW

Tel: 0151 722 2271
Fax: 0151 722 6485
e-mail: Cenale.liverpool@virgin.net

Roman Catholic
A retreat team runs courses here. The Centre is non-residential and open for quiet days, courses and one-to-one retreats.

Sandymont House of Prayer
16 Burbo Bank Road
Blundellsands
Liverpool L23 6TH

Tel: 0151 924 4850
Fax: 0151 924 4439

Christian – Ecumenical
Just by the seashore, this centre is available for both residential and non-residential visits. Sandymont has a programme of retreats. It sleeps up to fifteen guests.

Prescot

⭐

Loyola Hall Spirituality Centre
Warrington Road
Rainhill, Prescot
Merseyside L35 6NZ

Tel: 0151 426 4137
Fax: 0151 431 0115
e-mail: loyola@clara.net
Website: www.loyolahall.co.uk

Roman Catholic – Ecumenical
This is a Jesuit retreat centre, and that usually means some hard work on prayer, personal introspection and spiritual growth if you want to undertake an individually guided retreat. In addition to this form of spiritually concentrated retreat, there are preached ones, days of prayer and reflection, guided prayer weeks, theme retreats on icons and the Enneagram, women's retreats and special

courses for those who work with young adults. **Particular attention is drawn to the workshops for women, including those for women of all sexual orientations and the retreats for gay and bisexual men. Same-sex partnership couples also attend these retreats.** While these retreats are ones of reflection, sharing and prayer, they are firmly placed within Christian teaching, and more specifically Roman Catholic dogma, by the facilitators. This having been said, many men and women coming to these retreats return for further ones on an annual programme basis. Among the many compliments on the accommodation and retreat programmes at Loyola Hall have been these: 'The greatest asset they have are the little basement prayer spaces and oratories – very contemplative', 'Rates are reasonable', 'Many places outside the gardens for walks, especially Pex Hill', 'Friendly and efficient and very welcoming'. The Centre itself is set in a park and consists of a combination of older buildings and functional new ones. The facilities are modern and excellent, the rooms comfortable with ensuite facilities and the food, while traditional, is good. The Centre has special programmes aimed at the eighteen-to-thirty age groups. The colour brochures available are exceptionally well designed and informative. **Highly Recommended.**

Open: All year except Christmas week. Receives men, women, young people, groups.
Rooms: 43 singles, 2 doubles. Most rooms ensuite.
Facilities: Conferences, garden, library, guest lounge, payphone, prayer rooms, exercise equipment, sauna.
Spiritual Help: Personal talks, group sharing on some retreats, individually guided retreats in the tradition of St Ignatius Loyola, courses on spiritual direction, prayer guidance. Massage and art room used on some retreats.
Guests Admitted to: Unrestricted access.
Meals: Eaten in the guest dining rooms. Traditional food. Vegetarian and special diets.
Special Activities: Planned programme of events, including conferences, courses on spiritual direction, lecture programme, parish retreats. Send for brochure.
Situation: Quiet, in a village, large private grounds.
Maximum Stay: Depends on course undertaken (longest is 3 months).
Bookings: Letter, fax, e-mail, website, telephone.
Charges: See brochure. Concessions usually available for students and unemployed. As a guide, £37 per night (£23 concessions). Retreat courses about £120–£270. 11-week training course up to £2,300.
Access: Train: Rainhill. Bus: Nos. 106, 10A, 61. Car: via M62, Exit 7 to Prescot.

NORTHUMBERLAND

Alnmouth

The Friary of St Francis
Alnmouth, Alnwick
Northumberland NE66 3NJ

Tel: 01665 830213
Fax: 01665 830580
e-mail: ssf@almouthfriary.fsnet.co.uk

Anglican
The Friary is situated on the mouth of an estuary, on the coastline of Northumberland, with the wild and beautiful Scottish Borders nearby. This

is a popular place. The community of Franciscan brothers offers support and accommodation for those wanting a retreat of a religious nature and for those seeking a more informal and relaxed break. There is a deep sense of peace and spirituality here, which is palpable in the chapel and in particular in the small oratory where the Blessed Sacrament is exposed. Truly a Holy of Holies. The gardens are charming, with small areas cultivated individually, enabling reflection on different aspects of the Christian story.

Open: Most of the year. No guests on Sunday evenings. Receives men, women, young people, groups, non-retreatants.
Rooms: 12 singles. No smoking.
Facilities: Garden, library, guest lounge, TV, payphone.
Spiritual Help: Spiritual direction, day events, Quiet Days, rest and break for carers. Personal talks if needed, but this is a small community with a full and busy schedule, so such talks cannot always be arranged immediately.
Guests Admitted to: Chapel, work of the community.
Meals: Everyone eats together unless on silent retreat. Simple, traditional food. Vegetarian available. Breakfast is a silent meal.
Special Activities: Planned programme of events – send for leaflet.
Situation: Edge of village, beside the sea, with great views.
Maximum Stay: Monday to Sunday afternoon.
Bookings: Letter addressed to Guest Brother.
Charges: By donation, which is expected to be realistic – about £18–£22 per person per 24 hours.
Access: Train: Alnmouth (1 mile away). Bus from Alnmouth to the Friary.

Belsay

Aruna Ratanagiri Buddhist Monastery
Wat Nong Pah Pong
2 Harnham Hall Cottage
Harnham, Belsay
Nothumberland NE20 OHF   Tel: 01661 881019

Buddhist

Berwick Upon Tweed

Marygate House
Holy Island of Lindisfarne
Berwick Upon Tweed   Tel: 01289 389246
Northumberland TD15 2SD   e-mail: ian@marygateho.freeserve.co.uk
                        Website: www.lindisfarne.org.uk/marygate
Christian – Inter-denominational
This is a very special place, not least because it's situated on an island teeming with natural life, protected by the tides that ensure peace and quiet for long periods of each day. Holy Island is the cradle of Christianity in northern England and is a popular place for pilgrims and tourists. The Marygate House Holy Island Trust has two houses, Marygate House and Cambridge House. Marygate House is the home of a small community and residential centre for groups of up to twenty-two people who come for religious, educational or

cultural reasons. Cambridge House is for private retreats, study time or for individuals wanting a few days' rest and reflection. Marygate is attractive and spacious, if a little cold in winter, and set in its own gardens, which create a mini-haven in this otherwise busy end of the island. The community meets for simple prayers twice a day in the crypt, and there are daily services in the various churches on the island. It's easy to see why the saints fell in love with this place! **Highly Recommended.**

Open: All year. Receives everyone except children. Pets are welcome but must not come into the kitchen.

Rooms: 6 twin rooms, 3 doubles, dormitories. Altogether about 30 beds. Bring your own towels. Warm windproof clothes are suggested. Radios discouraged. Mobile phones allowed. A quiet house is maintained. No smoking.

Facilities: Conferences, garden, library, guest lounge, guest telephone.

Spiritual Help: Disabled if aided – but ask exactly what is available. Personal talks, personal retreat direction, quiet place set aside for prayer and regular prayer times, local RC and Anglican churches.

Guests Admitted to: Unrestricted access.

Meals: Everyone eats together. Traditional, simple whole food. Vegetarian and special diets.

Special Activities: None.

Situation: An island, accessed by car when tide is low.

Maximum Stay: 2 weeks.

Bookings: Letter, fax, e-mail, telephone 10a.m.–12.30p.m. and 6.30–7p.m.

Charges: Rates vary but about £23 per person per night B&B as the baseline.

Access: Train: Berwick upon Tweed. Bus: Beal. Car: A1, 7 miles south of Berwick upon Tweed

---

The Open Gate
Community of Aidan and Hilda
Holy Island
Berwick upon Tweed
Northumberland TD15 2JZ

Tel: 01289 389222
e-mail: theopengate@theopengate.ndo.co.uk
Website: www.aidan.org.uk

Inter-denominational

The Open Gate is an old farmhouse on the island of Lindisfarne, a place of ancient spiritual history. The Guardian of the Community of Aidan and Hilda, Ray Simpson, is a leading figure in the Celtic tradition and facilitates workshops here as well as in other centres. Themes such as *Walking in the Steps of the Saints, Prayer Walking with St Cuthbert* and *St Hilda's Weekend* exemplify the way in which prayer, the saints, pilgrimage and nature are woven together by this community. There are also opportunities for individuals to undertake private retreats or Anamchara Retreats, on which a retreat schedule is discussed on arrival and then reviewed before departure, with additional reflection time given during the course of the stay if requested. The Open Gate has a few very comfortable, ensuite rooms where non-retreatants are also welcome. Simple home cooking is offered to those staying on retreat. **Highly Recomended.**

Open: All year. Receives everyone.

Rooms: 2 twins, 2 doubles. No smoking. A quiet house is maintained.

Facilities: Garden, library, guest lounge.

Spiritual Help: Personal talks, group sharing, spiritual direction, personal retreat direction, directed study, chapel, local church services on island.

Guests Admitted to: Unrestricted access.

Meals: Meals are provided only on organised retreats, otherwise just B&B, but there are 4 hotels within 250 yards of The Open Gate and pubs that serve food.

Special Activities: Send for leaflet detailing special events.

Situation: Quiet.

Maximum Stay: Unlimited.

Bookings: Letter, fax, e-mail, telephone.

Charges: £27 B&B per person per night.

Access: Train: Berwick upon Tweed. Car route best.

St Cuthbert's Centre
Fiddlers Green
Holy Island
Berwick-upon-Tweed   Tel: 01289 389254
Northumberland TD15 2JF   e-mail: revhutch@supanet.com
Website: www.holyislandproject.org

United Reform Church – Christian

A fresh, bright and modern Christian centre for church and group hire. Everyone is welcome here for a day visit, and private and guided retreats can be arranged. There are prayer walks and public worship. The programme is short but nice, with topics such as *Christian Skills for Peaceful Living* – something we can all have more of in our lives.

Carrshield

Throssel Hole Buddhist Abbey   Tel: 01434 345204
Carrshield   Fax: 01434 345216
Hexham   e-mail: gd@throssel.org.uk
Northumberland, NE47 8AL   Website: www.throssel.org.uk

Buddhist – Order of Buddhist Contemplatives (Soto Zen lineage)

Throssel Hole is a monastery and retreat centre in the Order of Buddhist Contemplatives. The Serene Reflection Meditation tradition (Soto Zen) emphasises the practice of meditation, living by the Buddhist precepts, expressing compassion in daily life and training to realise one's spiritual potential. Originating in Japan, the Soto Zen tradition came to Britain in the 1970s, when the Abbey's founder, Rev Master Jiyu-Kennett, returned to England after several years of study and training in the Orient. Throssel Hole Buddhist Abbey was founded in the remote and beautiful West Allen valley, in 39 acres of field and woodland. Here men and women have equal status and are both eligible for training for priesthood. There is a clear and strict structure to daily life here, which guests are expected to take part in. This ensures the continuity of monastic life for the community but also offers an invaluable opportunity to let worldly distractions fall away and to experience the benefits of mindfulness for oneself. Whether eating, working or resting, attention is given to integrating the openness, awareness and compassion of meditation into every aspect of daily life. Newcomers to the Abbey are invited to attend one of the many weekend introductory retreats. Longer, private or more advanced retreats are only open to those who have attended the introductory retreat. For those who want to take their study and practice further, lay ordination is possible. There is a quarterly journal and mail-order service offering books, taped lectures, meditation benches and cushions. A variety of other services are offered: teachings and public talks, spiritual counselling over the telephone, naming ceremonies for children, a cemetery plot and memorial services. Smaller centres are situated throughout Britain. These include sub-priories in Reading and Telford, staffed by monks and associated groups of lay people meeting together in twenty-one cities in Britain plus four in Europe.

Reading Buddhist Priory	Tel: 0118 986 0750
Telford Buddhist Priory	Tel: 01952 615574
Portobello Buddhist Priory	Tel: 0131 669 9622
Great Ocean Dharma Refuge	Tel: 01239 891 360
Place of Peace Dharma House	Tel: 01970 626805
Rochdale Zen Retreat	Tel: 01706 525 951

There is a sister monastery, Shasta Abbey, in California.

Open: Most of the year. Closed for certain pre-published periods, sometimes May and December. Receives men and women over 18 years. Families received only on specific weekends. Group educational visits from schools and colleges by arrangement. Non-retreatants taken for tours of the monastery by appointment. Children welcomed for specific events only – discuss this with the guest master.

Rooms: 6 singles, dormitories (men and women are housed separately), 1 caravan.

Facilities: Disabled – limited. Garden, park, library, common room, payphone.

Spiritual Help: Spiritual direction, meditation, classes led by senior monk, private spiritual guidance on request. Full instruction given in meditation. Guidance is also given for private study and reflection.

Guests Admitted to: The ceremony hall, lay common room, ceremonies with monks, work of community.

Meals: Taken together whenever possible. Vegetarian food. Non-dairy diet can be catered for.

Special Activities: Special programme, public talks, group evenings, day retreats, long retreats – send for brochure.

Situation: Remote. Very quiet, in the countryside. Designated area of outstanding natural beauty.

Maximum Stay: By arrangement with guest master.

Bookings: Letter, fax, e-mail, telephone 9.30–11.30a.m., 2.30–4.30p.m.

Charges: For a stay of a month or longer £12 per person per night. Suggested donations: weekend retreats £50, other retreats £20 per night.

Access: Train: from Newcastle or Carlisle to Hexham, then taxi. Bus: from Newcastle to Hexham and Allendale. Car: via M6 or A1 to Bishop Auckland.

Consett

Minsteracres Retreat Centre
Minsteracres Monastery
Nr Consett DH8 9RT

Tel: 01434 673248
Fax: 01434 673540
e-mail: minsteracres@lineone.net
Website: www.minsteracres.com

Roman Catholic – Ecumenical

Giant Wellingtonia sequoia trees line the drive to this former mansion, set in 60 acres of grounds and once the home of the Silvertop family. In 1949 it became a monastery for the Passionists, a Catholic congregation founded in the 1700s in Italy. The Passionists were joined in 1976 by a group of Catholic sisters, and today Minsteracres is run by a mixed community of monks, nuns and lay volunteers – and two rather special cats. It's all very informal and relaxed here, with an emphasis on providing a service to the local parish and dioceses, which means it can be a busy place. There are guided weekend retreats in such topics as *Celtic Spirituality* and *Exploring Liturgy*, but individuals are welcome any time, and if you really want to be alone, a charming Poustinia is available – with its own tiny chapel. The main church is beautiful and is used on Sundays and Holy Days. Community services are held in a chapel adjoining the main house, with wonderful views across the Cheviot Hills. There is a self-contained retreat house for larger groups, a youth centre and an old walled garden restored and worked by Northumbria Day Break, a charity working with adults with learning difficulties.

Open: All year except mid-December to end of January and latter part of July. Receives everyone. Children welcome.
Rooms: 35 singles, 12 doubles, hermitage, self-contained and self-catering youth hostel accommodating 36.
Facilities: Conferences, camping, garden, park, library, guest lounge, TV, payphone (01434 673303).
Spiritual Help: Personal retreat direction, spiritual direction, meditation, group sharing, personal talks.
Guests Admitted to: Church, chapel, oratory, work of community.
Meals: Everyone eats together. Traditional food. Vegetarian and special diets.
Special Activities: Planned retreats and events – send for brochure.
Situation: A little busy but in the countryside, in 60 acres of grounds, with lots of walks and super views.
Maximum Stay: 1 week.
Bookings: Letter, fax, telephone 9a.m.–5p.m.
Charges: Average rate about £25 per person per night full board.
Access: Car route best. Enquire as to train and local bus.

Riding Mill

Shepherds Dene Retreat House
Riding Mill
Northumberland NE44 6AF

Tel: 01434 682212
Fax: 01434 682311
e-mail: shepherds_dene@newcastle.anglican.org
Website: www.shepherdsdene.co.uk

Anglican – Inter-denominational

An old Victorian house tucked away behind this pretty Northumbrian village, Shepherds Dene nestles in extensive grounds – with its own medieval labyrinth in the style of Chartres Cathedral. It offers a variety of Quiet Days and creative spirituality retreats, as well as space for non-guided personal retreats. Warm and homely, with its own chapel, this is a centre that caters strongly for groups. Individuals are welcome, however, when there is space, and there may be room in the self-contained lodge, especially if you are seeking greater independence.

Open: All year except Christmas, Easter and first week of August. Receives everyone. Children welcome. Pets only by arrangement.
Rooms: 8 singles, 8 twins.
Facilities: Disabled, conferences, garden, TV, payphone (01434 682582).
Spiritual Help: Therapies, alternative healing practices, counselling.
Guests Admitted to: Everywhere.
Meals: Everyone eats together. Traditional and whole food. Vegetarian and special diets. Self-catering in summer and for a week after Easter.
Special Activities: A few open events, otherwise independent group retreats. Indiduals can stay alongside groups.
Situation: Quiet, in the countryside.
Maximum Stay: By arrangement.
Bookings: Letter, telephone.
Charges: About £48 per person per 24 hours.
Access: Train: station 1¼ miles away. Bus: stop ¾ miles away. Car route best, but ask for details of other travel arrangements.

Whitfield

Burnlaw Healing and Retreat Centre
Burnlaw
Whitfield
Northumberland NE47 8HF   Tel: 01434 345391

Baha'I
Burnlaw is a small North Pennines upland farm in a designated area of outstanding natural beauty. Here a community of Baha'I live and work together, specialising in sustainable lifestyle and holistic living. The Healing and Retreat Centre was established to provide a space where people could realise 'the sacredness of all existence'. Hill walking, painting, dancing, singing, horticulture and conservation work are all part of the life here. Whether you are visiting for a short break, or taking part in a working holiday, there is plenty to nourish and sustain.

> Sex is the allegory of Love in the physical world. It is from this fact that it derives its power.
> EDWARD CARPENTER

YORKSHIRE (SOUTH)

Doncaster

Hexthorpe Manor
Old Hexthorpe
Doncaster
South Yorkshire DN4 OHY

Tel: 01302 818184
e-mail: office@hexthorpemanor.sagehost.co.uk

Christian – Quiet Garden Trust
Hexthorpe is a peaceful manor house set in a walled garden and is a member of The Quiet Garden Trust. On offer are quiet days, led retreats and residential accommodation. There is a small but nice programme of events, including a Healing Service.

Sheffield

The Listen Centre
Glen Mount, Rivelin Glen
Sheffield S6 5SE

Tel: 0114 251 7679
e-mail: thelistencentre@aol.com

Christian Tradition
The Listen Centre is secluded and peaceful yet only twenty minutes or so from the centre of the city. It is set in an acre of land, with terraced garden and various sacred spaces, in the Rivelin Valley, which offers many good walks. This is also a family home, so the atmosphere is warm but with some boundaries. There is a well stocked spirituality and theology library open to guests. The food is good, simple and home-cooked. Retreat space is available for individuals to make a silent and/or guided retreat. Facilities comprise single rooms ensuite and a private chapel with a small seminar room for small group quiet days and workshops. A hermitage is available for those who wish to make a more rugged retreat. In addition to this, the Listen Centre has available a four-bedroom cottage in the Peak District village of Castleton (30 minutes from the Listen Centre) for small group retreats and gatherings. The cottage has a sunny courtyard and small chapel. All these facilities can be booked for private use or as a group for a guided retreat with the Listen Centre. The initial and developing programme includes the Listen Course, for those with little experience of Christianity and faith, to help them have an experience of the living God and to learn to listen to themselves, to the world and to God. There are two internships, which are five-day immersions in the prophetic spirit, combining teaching and experience of contemplative prayer, and encounters with the underside of our society and projects where prophetic action is being taken. There are also contemplative living workshops, teaching the art and practice of silence and listening; workshops about living in a celebratory way and not from a place of guilt; personal transformation workshops based on the Enneagram as a tool for self-knowledge and opening up to God's grace; **male and female spirituality days**, looking at men's and women's journeys using the latest work on these key issues, especially the teaching of Father Richard Rohr; bereavement and grief work drawing on the work of the sacred art of living centre in Bend Oregon and the contribution of Richard and Mary Groves; and contemplative Bible Study – taking Luke's Gospel as a text for 2004. For more information regarding forthcoming programmes, dates and costs contact the Centre.

Whirlow Grange Diocesan Conference Centre   Tel: 0114 236 3173
Eccleshall Road South   Fax: 0114 262 0717
Sheffield S11 9RE   e-mail: manager@whirlowgrange.co.uk
                                       Website: www.whirlowgrange.co.uk

Anglican
The Centre occupies a grey-stone house on a rise on the outskirts of
Sheffield, near Peak District beauty spots. The place is a little institutional,
but it has comfortable rooms and nice facilities. There have been healing
seminars, sacred dance group weekends and Franciscan directed retreats in
the past, and the Centre is trying to develop its work in retreats and spirituality with many flexible ways to take time for retreat, prayer and reflection.
Plans are in the making to renovate and rebuild the Centre with more accomodation and facilities.

Open: All year. Receives men, women, young people, families, groups, non-
   retreatants. Children welcome.
Rooms: 20 singles, 10 twins.
Facilities: Conferences, garden, bookstall, library, guest lounge, TV, payphone.
Spiritual Help: Personal talks, group sharing, personal retreat direction,
   meditation, directed study, creative aproaches to prayer.
Guests Admitted to: Chapel.
Meals: Everyone eats together. Traditional food. Vegetarian and special diets.
Special Activities: Planned programme of events – send for brochure.
Situation: Quiet, on the outskirts of the city. Peak District National Park
   within easy reach.
Maximum Stay: None.
Bookings: Letter, fax, telephone.
Charges: £42 per person per 24 hours. Bursaries available.
Access: By rail, bus or car (via A625).

YORKSHIRE (NORTH)

Ampleforth

Ampleforth Abbey   ⭐
Ampleforth   Tel: 01439 766889
N Yorks YO62 4EN   e-mail: pastoral@ampleforth.org.uk
                                        Web: www.ampleforth.org.uk

Roman Catholic
A very well known and popular place to go on retreat, Ampleforth is situated
north of the historic city of York and just below the rolling North Yorkshire
Moors. Ampleforth Abbey dates from 1925 and is home to a monastic
community whose life of prayer is central to the many activities going on in
this busy place. Guests are welcome for private retreats, but there is also a lively
programme of retreats and workshops led by members of the community. As
well as the more traditional Christian retreats, you can turn your hand to
woodworking or candlemaking, or find out about winetasting the Biblical
way! Here is just one example of a retreat available on the Ampleforth
programme: Pilgrimage of Faith – Spiritual Walks. On this retreat you have
time and quiet for reflection and exercise, a chance to share in the monastic
prayer of the community, and walks to beautiful places in fellowship with other

pilgrims on the spiritual path. The daily schedule looks like this: Late Monday arrival with tea and then Vespers, followed by three days of walks, and depart on the Friday after breakfast. The cost of such a retreat is about £150 residential and £80 non-residential. Accommodation at Ampleforth is wide-ranging and very comfortable: The Archway, The Park, The Guesthouse and The Grange all offer something a bit different. This is a big, rambling and beautiful place with grounds that extend as far as the eye can see over some two and a half thousand acres. Ampleforth School adds to the liveliness of the place, but it is surprisingly peaceful and quiet. Guests are welcome to attend and participate in the Divine Office, and anyone interested in living the monastic life and seeking God through prayer and apostolic work should contact Fr Bede at bede@ampleforth.org.uk. **Highly Recommended.**

Open: All year except Christmas and a few other weeks. Receives everyone.
Rooms: 26 singles, 10 twins, domitories, barn, camping, hostel. Mobile phones do not work here. Personal stereos discouraged.
Facilities: Disabled, church, choir, chapel, conferences, guest lounge, guest phone, plenty of places to walk, book shop.
Spiritual Help: Personal talks, group sharing, spiritual direction, personal retreat direction.
Guests Admitted to: Church, choir.
Meals: Everyone eats together. Good traditional food. Vegetarian and special diets.
Special Activities: Full programme – ask for details.
Situation: Quiet, in the countryside.
Maximum Stay: 4 days.
Bookings: Letter, fax, e-mail, telephone 9a.m.–2p.m.
Charges: Various – see programme brochure. As an idea, £12 non-resident day, £21.50 per person per night B&B, £77 weekend. Monastic living stays usually involve a donation rather than charges, but you will need to discuss this with Fr Bede (see above).
Access: Train or coach: York (23 miles away). Bus: ask about local public transport when you book. Car: via B1363 from York. Ask for travel directions leaflet.

Harrogate

Dowgill Farm
Summerbridge
Harrogate   Tel/Fax: 01423 780467
N Yorks. HG3 4JR   e-mail: Info@dowgillfarm.co.uk
                                        Website: www.dowgillfarm.co.uk
Mind Body Spirit
Set in the North Yorkshire Dales, Dowgill has developed as a venue for personal fulfillment workshops and courses, which include reiki, *Flower of Life* and other Mind Body Spirit subjects. There is accommodation for six people in the farm, plus camping on the land. The centre is no smoking. Children are welcomed if over five years old. Guided individual retreats are possible.

Kettlewell

Scargill House
Kettlewell
Skipton
N Yorks BD23 5HU

⭐

Tel: 01756 760234
Fax: 01756 760499
e-mail: bookings@scargillhouse.co.uk
Website: www.scargillhouse.co.uk

Ecumenical

In the heart of the Yorkshire Dales, Scargill House is home to a community of Christian men, women, families and young people who come from all walks of life and many parts of the world. Together they live and work within a broad-based and open-hearted spirituality, and there is a strong sense of Christian regeneration here. The present warden has introduced radical changes, which have refocused the vision of the centre. There is now greater emphasis on youth work, ecology, and ecumenical and interfaith dialogue. This often makes Scargill House a lively, busy place to stay – with accommodation for up to ninety people – so if you're looking for a more contemplative atmosphere, you might be disappointed. However, the grounds offer something for everyone, from a children's play area to an old walled garden, a Tarzan Trail assault course, a sanctuary within a woodland walk. The 100-acre estate is sensitively managed for all types of visitor. If you're looking for a quiet retreat, good timing is probably all that is necessary. The chapel is particularly special, a modern building with a high sweeping roof and clear glass windows that look out onto the lovely Wharfedale countryside. The daily rhythm of prayer brings the community and guests together, but it is all very informal and often spontaneous. Whoever is moved to lead the prayers is welcome to do so. The community organises and runs a rich and varied programme including a *Youth Worker's Retreat*, a *Parenting Retreat, Ancient Highways and Byways of the Dales, Flashes of Colour, Spirituality and Film, The Spirituality of The Simpsons, Community and Growth, Dry Stone Walling* and *Whose Forest is it anyway*. The one we found most exciting was *The Bread Makers*, in which you learn about bread-making and the shared pleasure of preparing and sharing this food of life, and consider the symbolic elements of bread as Sacrament. This is not just a place in the heart of the Dales, it is a place to open your heart. **Highly Recommended.**

Open: All year, except for a few weeks in January, July and September, and Christmas week. Receives everyone. Children welcome.

Rooms: 15 singles, 20 doubles, 12 cabins accommodating guests in bunk beds, 2 family rooms.

Facilities: Disabled – limited. Chapel, conferences, garden, park, library, guest lounges, payphone (01756 760261/250). Mobile phones are unlikely to work in this geographical area.

Spiritual Help: Preached retreats with individual talks.

Guests Admitted to: Chapel, house and grounds.

Meals: Everyone eats together. Traditional simple food. Vegetarian and special diets.

Special Activities: Planned programme – send for information.

Situation: Quiet, in the countryside, in the Yorkshire Dales National Park.

Maximum Stay: By arrangement.

Bookings: Letter, fax, e-mail, telephone 8.30a.m.–4.30p.m.

Charges: See programme.

Access: Train: nearest station is 15 miles away but there are arrangements with a local taxi company, so ask for details when you book. Car route easy.

Kirkby Fleetham

Kirkby Fleetham Hall
Kirkby Fleetham
Northallerton
N Yorks DL7 OSU   Tel/Fax: 01609 748747

Mind Body Spirit
A big and rather elegantly English house as you approach, but inside all is devoted to the art of living in peace and well-being. The range of courses on offer covers yoga, regression therapy (or soul drama, as it is now called), the art of loving in peace, shiatsu and neuro-linguistic programming.

Open: March to October. Receives men, women, groups, non-retreatants.
Rooms: Doubles but singles available for a supplementary charge.
Facilities: Garden, guest lounge, TV, payphone.
Spiritual Help: None, but a therapy centre is being planned.
Guests Admitted to: Guest areas.
Meals: Everyone eats together. Vegetarian whole food. Special diets catered for.
Special Activities: Planned events – send for brochure.
Situation: Very quiet, in the countryside.
Maximum Stay: By arrangement.
Bookings: Letter.
Charges: See programme brochure.
Access: Train: Northallerton (8 miles away). Bus service limited. Car route easiest.

Pickering

The Orange Tree   Tel: 01751 417219
Rosedale East   Fax: 01751 417219
Pickering   e-mail: relax@theorangetree.com
N Yorks YO18 8RH   Website: www.theorangetree.com

Open spirituality
The Orange Tree is a family run place where the emphasis is on *relaxation!* Situated in a peaceful and rather beautiful location deep in the North Yorkshire Moors, it offers residential *Relaxation Workshop Weekends.* The centre accommodates up to fifteen people and serves quality vegetarian food. Aromatherapy, massage, saunas and lovely walks are all on the agenda to help you get relaxed. Comfortable rooms and an informal atmosphere all assist guests to unwind. Charges are about £148 per person, which includes two nights accommodation, all meals and relaxation demonstrations. This charge is based on sharing a twin room. The Orange Tree has won a lot of awards in a short time and worked hard to achieve its aim.

Scarborough

**Highbank Wholistic Hotel
5 Givendale Road
Scarborough
N Yorks YO12 GLE**   Tel: 01723 365265

Mind Body Spirit

Open: All year. Receives all.
Rooms: 1 single, 4 doubles, 1 dormitory.
Facilities: Garden, library, guest lounge, TV, guest telephone.
Spiritual Help: Personal talks, meditation, aromatherapy, creative visualisation, bereavement counselling.
Guests Admitted to: Unrestricted access.
Meals: Taken in guest house. Traditional/vegetarian/organic food. Vegetarian and special diets.
Special Activities: None.
Situation: Quiet, in town, close to sea and parks.
Maximum Stay: None
Bookings: Letter, fax, telephone.
Charges: From £19 per person per night B&B. Therapies from £20. Ask for other rates.
Access: Train, bus and car all possible. Ask for directions.

**Wydale Hall and Emmaus Centre
Brompton by Sawdon
Scarborough
N Yorks YO13 9DG**

Tel: 01723 859270
Fax: 01723 859702
e-mail: retreat@wydale.co.uk
Website: www.wydale.co.uk

Anglican – Inter-denominational
This is an old house set in 14 acres with formal gardens with good views to the Yorkshire Wolds. Quiet Christian hospitality is on offer here, with the purpose of creating a place where people can unwind, rest and perhaps draw nearer to God. The retreats and one-day workshops cover a wide range from assertiveness skills and stress management to a Creative Arts Retreat Movement painting and prayer retreat.

Open: All year except New Year. Receives men, women, young people, families, groups, non-retreatants. Children welcome. Guide dogs only.
Rooms: 6 singles, 21 doubles (7 rooms ensuite).
Facilities: Disabled, chapel, conferences, garden, library, guest lounge, bookstall, TV, payphone, direct dialing (01723 859331).
Spiritual Help: Personal talks.
Guests Admitted to: Unrestricted access except staff areas.
Meals: Everyone eats together. Traditional food. Vegetarian and special diets. Self-catering in the Emmaus Centre.
Special Activities: Programme of events – send for brochure.
Situation: Quiet, in the countryside. 14 acres of grounds.
Maximum Stay: By arrangement.
Bookings: Letter, fax, e-mail, telephone during office hours.

Charges: Send for details – but example is £43 per person per 24 hours full board.
Access: Train: Scarborough. Buses: from Scarborough. Car: Wydale Hall is 1 mile north of A170.

Skipton

Parcevall Hall
Appletreewick, Skipton
N Yorks BD23 6DG
Tel: 01756 720213
Fax: 01756 720656
e-mail: parcevall@bradfordanglican.org

Anglican – Ecumenical
This is an Elizabethan manor house with grand views in a super setting. The interior is filled with oak and atmosphere. Legends and history abound, and the nine acres of garden are said to have been admired by the late Queen Mary. This is a traditional place for either a private retreat or participation in the programme of events, which includes many parish group retreats but also retreats such as *Spirituality of Julian of Norwich*, *Painting and Prayer* and *Spring Walkers Weekend Retreat*. **Highly Recommended.**

Open: All year. Receives everyone.
Rooms: 7 singles, 10 doubles.
Facilities: Disabled, conferences, garden, guest lounge, TV, payphone.
Spiritual Help: Directed study, group sharing.
Guests Admitted to: Unrestricted access.
Meals: Everyone eats together. Traditional food. Vegetarian and special diets by prior arrangement only.
Special Activities: Programme of events – send for brochure.
Situation: Very quiet, in the countryside.
Maximum Stay: By arrangement.
Bookings: Letter, fax, telephone during office hours.
Charges: £25–£45 per person per 24 hours full board.
Access: Train: Skipton, then taxi. Car possible.

Thirsk

Holy Rood House and Community
Centre for Health and Pastoral Care
10 Sowerby Road
Sowerby
Thirsk
N Yorks YO7 1HX
Tel: 01845 522580
Fax: 01845 527300
e-mail: holyroodhouse@centrethirsk.fsnet.co.uk
Website: www.holyroodhouse.freeuk.com

Open Spirituality – Inter-denominational – Ecumenical
Here is an unusual and rather special place to go on retreat. Holy Rood House is a warm and welcoming centre, where you are so well looked after that you will be hard pushed to make yourself a cuppa! Founded by Stanley and Elizabeth Baxter, both of whom are Anglican ministers and therapists, Holy Rood is strongly recommended to those seeking therapeutic support within the context of a retreat. Here is a safe place where guests can feel

> The two places where people don't smile are in churches and health food shops.
>
> BROTHER JAMES FAHEY

empowered to work towards their own healing. A team of volunteers trained in counselling, psychotherapy, art therapy, drama therapy, massage, weaving and pottery offer short- and long-term support, and the centre has become a place of healing for many people, some of who travel long distances to stay. Whilst rooted in the Christian faith, Holy Rood is open to people from all faiths or none – there is a deep and genuine kindness shown here that has nothing to do with religion or spiritual conviction, and guests are free to choose how much they participate in the spiritual life of the community. The gardens are lovely – there are many places to sit quietly: around the pond, in the secret garden, on the lawns. A labyrinth and scented garden for the sense-impaired are planned, and a small field for the resident pony, goat and chickens provides a sanctuary for animals and guests alike. Next door is Thorpe House, now a Centre for the Study of Theology and Health. This is a new and exciting enterprise that seeks to take a serious look at the relationship between spirituality and healing. Conferences, seminars, research days and courses provide an atmosphere of openness and learning, and are bringing together many people from the disciplines of theology, psychiatry, science and holistic health. Holy Rood House is an organisational member of the British Association for Counselling and Psychotherapy. **Highly Recommended.**

Open: All year except August. Receives everyone. Children and pets welcome.

Rooms: 8 singles, 8 doubles.

Facilities: Disabled – ground-floor room and chair lift to first floor. Chapel, conferences, garden, library, guest lounge, TV, guest phone (01845 525843), aromatherapy, massage, art therapy, professional counselling.

Spiritual Help: Personal talks, group sharing, meditation, directed study, counselling, psychotherapy, ministry of healing, personal retreat direction, spiritual direction, directed study, stress management, massage, shiatsu, reflexology, aromatherapy, art therapy, yoga relaxation, theology courses, women's spirituality courses.

Guests Admitted to: Unrestricted access.

Meals: Everyone eats together. Good whole-food cooking. Vegetarian, special diets.

Special Activities: Planned programme of events and courses – send for brochure. Counselling, psychotherapy, creative arts, massage, body therapies. There is no nursing here and no treatment offered to those with mental health problems who may create unsafe environments for others.

Situation: Quiet, in the village.

Maximum Stay: 3 weeks.

Bookings: Letter, fax, e-mail, website, telephone 9a.m.–4p.m. Monday to Friday.

Charges: Enquire when booking, but £37 per person per 24 hours full board is the suggested donation. Suggested donation for therapy £10–£30 per session. Suggested donation for courses depends on the nature of the course.

Access: Train: Thirsk (1½ miles away). Bus: Thirsk, then 10-minute walk. Car: A61 to B1448, or A19 and A168. Coach also possible.

Sneaton Castle Centre
Whitby
N Yorks YO21 3QN

Tel: 01947 600051
Fax: 01947 603490
e-mail: sneaton@globalnet.co.uk
Website: www.sneatoncastle.co.uk

Anglican
This is a peaceful and picturesque location providing a Christian venue for conferences, B&B, music workshops, and retreats. It is a big place with room for many guests.

Open: All year except Christmas. Receives everyone.
Rooms: 17 singles, 44 doubles, 6 family rooms. No smoking.
Facilities: Disabled, conferences, garden, library, guest lounge, TV, payphone, book shop.
Spiritual Help: Personal talks, spiritual direction, personal retreat direction.
Guests Admitted to: Chapel, work of community by arrangement.
Meals: Everyone eats together. Traditional food. Vegetarian and special diets.
Special Activities: Currently none but ask, as a programme is being considered.
Situation: Quiet, on the edge of a fishing town and near moors and National Park.
Maximum Stay: By arrangement or for duration of event, course, retreat.
Bookings: Letter, fax, e-mail, website, telephone 8a.m.–6p.m. weekdays.
Charges: £21.50–£41.
Access: Train: Middlesborough. Bus: Whitby. Car: motorway.

St Hilda's Priory
Sneaton Castle
Whitby
N Yorks YO21 3QN

Tel: 01947 602079
Fax: 01947 820854
e-mail: ohppriorywhitby@btinternet.com

Anglican
The Priory itself is not a retreat house as such. Guests come for a quiet retreat on an individual basis and there is no structured programme other than the daily pattern of worship.

Open: Open all year except 3 weeks in August. Recieves men, women.
Rooms: 6 singles, 2 doubles.
Facilities: Garden, library, guest lounge, use of telephone if needed.
Spiritual Help: Personal talks, personal retreat direction.
Guests Admitted to: Chapel, refectory.
Meals: Main meals taken together. Self-catering facilities. Vegetarian and special diets.
Special Activities: None.
Situation: In the countryside, on edge of town and near National Park.
Maximum Stay: 1 week.
Bookings: Letter.
Charges: Suggested donation £25 per person per day full board, £10–£15 per person per day self-catering.
Access: Train: Sacrborough via York. Bus: Whitby. Coach: Coastliner. Car: From Teeside A171. From York A169.

St Oswald's Pastoral Centre
Woodlands Drive
Sleights
Whitby
N Yorks YO21 1RY

Tel: 01947 810496
Fax: 01947 810750
e-mail: ohpstos@globalnet.co.uk
Website: www.ohpwhitby.org

Anglican

St Oswald's is a small complex of buildings set in wonderful surroundings between the villages of Sleights and Aislaby, near Whitby. It is run by the Order of the Holy Paraclete, and several of the sisters live at the centre. The sisters welcome guests to conducted retreats and individually guided retreats, and for private quiet time for rest and study. The views here are lovely and the large gardens and natural woodland offer a great setting for walking, painting, meditating or just relaxing. Peace and beauty abound with the warmest of welcome. This is a happy place to be. **Highly Recommended.**

Open: All year. Receives men, women, groups, non-retreatants.
Rooms: 10 singles, 3 doubles.
Facilities: Garden, library, guest lounge, TV, payphone.
Spiritual Help: Personal talks, spiritual direction, personal retreat direction.
Guests Admitted to: Unrestricted access except to community quarters.
Meals: Everyone eats together. Traditional simple food. Some meals are taken in silence. Vegetarian and special diets within reason.
Special Activities: Planned programme – send for brochure.
Situation: Very quiet, in the countryside, near to the moors.
Maximum Stay: 1 week.
Bookings: Letter, fax, e-mail, telephone.
Charges: By donation. Guideline available in a separate leaflet but examples are £32 per 24 hours, £58 weekend retreat.
Access: Leaflet available giving full information.

York

St Bede's Pastoral Centre
21 Blossom Street
York YO24 1AQ

Tel: 01904 464900
Fax: 01904 464967
e-mail: stbedes@freenetname.co.uk
Website: www.stbedes.org.uk

Roman Catholic

St Bede's was founded in 1987 as a joint venture by the Middlesborough Diocese and the Ampleforth monks. It is a base for ecumenical work right in the heart of York and next door to the historic Bar Convent. St Bede's is a lovely place, with a museum, café, shop, and gallery around a central court-yard. There is a small pretty garden at the rear. There are events, exhibitions and talks throughout the year, often including Julian meetings, bible study, and prayer and reflection courses. Worship, prayer and courses in creative prayer and bible study are also held here – send for leaflets. This is a friendly and welcoming place in the heart of a great and hospitable city.

Open: All year except Christmas. Receives everyone.
Rooms: Non-residential.
Facilities: Disabled, conferences, chapel.

Spiritual Help: Spiritual direction, personal retreat direction, meditation and personal retreat direction are all part of the retreat events.
Guests Admitted to: Chapel and areas open to the public.
Meals: Nearby.
Special Activities: Programme of events and courses – send for brochure.
Situation: Busy, in the city, but once inside quite peaceful.
Maximum Stay: For course or event, during the day or evening.
Bookings: Letter, fax, e-mail, website, telephone weekdays office hours.
Charges: Ask for current charges for B&B at Bar Convent.
Access: By rail, bus or car to York, then walk.

YORKSHIRE (WEST)

Halifax

Stod Fold Barn
Ogden
Halifax HX2 8XL
Tel: 01422 244854
Website: www.stodfod.co.uk

Christian
This is a lovely old place right on the edge of the moors. There is a small chapel and a studio for creative activities. It is a good place for small groups wanting to run their own retreat or have a Quiet Day together. It sleeps up to eleven people, and there are extra rooms available nextdoor to the Barn.

Hebden

Hebden House
The Birchcliffe Centre
Birchcliffe Road
Hebden Bridge
W Yorks HX7 8DG
Tel: 01422 843 626
Fax: 01422 843648
e-mail: enqs@hebden-house.co.uk
Website: www.hebden-house.co.uk

Open spirituality
This residential wing of the centre is a peaceful and secluded place running courses, workshops, seminars and retreats. There are almost sixty bed spaces, of which fifteen are ensuite rooms. A little courtyard offers a pleasant place to sit in good weather. Meals are vegetarian, and vegan food is considered one of their specialities. Special diets are catered for. The centre is no smoking. Full board is about £35 to £43.

> If only people could realise what an enrichment it means to find one's own guilt, what a sense of honour and new spiritual dignity.
> CARL JUNG

Ilkley

Briery Retreat Centre
38 Victoria Avenue
Ilkley
W Yorks LS29 9BW

Tel: 01943 607287
Fax: 01943 604449
e-mail: srscp@aol.com
Website: www.members.aol.com/srscp

Roman Catholic
The Briery retreat team are Sisters of the Cross and Passion, and their programme is firmly spiritually based in such traditions as the Rosary, preached retreats and transformation retreats. Even for those who do not attend church on a regular basis or may not feel committed to a particular spiritual path, there can be great spiritual strength to be gained from a retreat that is strongly focused on a deeply held faith and within an established religious tradition. Individuals and small groups may make a retreat by joining some of the parish groups for a weekend if they want. Directed and private retreats are also available.

Open: All year except Christmas and New Year. Receives men, women, young people over 18, groups, non-retreatants.
Rooms: 23 singles, 3 twins.
Facilities: Conferences, garden, guest lounge, library, TV, payphone.
Spiritual Help: Personal talks, spiritual direction, group sharing, personal retreat direction.
Guests Admitted to: Church, chapel oratory, public rooms.
Meals: Everyone eats together. Traditional food. Vegetarian and special diets.
Special Activities: Planned programme of events – send for brochure.
Situation: 10 minutes walk from Ilkley town, but in countryside and surrounded by Ilkley Moor.
Maximum Stay: 14 days.
Bookings: Letter, fax, e-mail, telephone during normal business hours.
Charges: Suggested offerings about £37 per person per day full board.
Access: Train, bus, car all possible.

Pocklington

Madhyamaka Buddhist Centre
Kilnwick Percy Hall
Kilnwick Percy
Near Pocklington
York YO42 1UF

Tel: 01759 304832
Fax: 01759 305962
e-mail: Info@madhyamaka.org
Website: www.madhyamaka.org

Buddhist
The centre is located in a very large and beautiful country mansion built in 1784. Its aim is to preserve and promote the teachings and traditions of Buddhism. There is a large community here, ranging in age from twenty to seventy years, who regard this as their home. Some are ordained and all of them work and study together. Many are Buddhist teachers. There are group discussions, weekend and day courses throughout the year, and a summer school. Other centres are in Bath, Buxton, and Ulverston. Some of the retreat courses have great titles – such as *The Hitch-hikers Guide to the Mind* and *Stop the Week* – and others are more the kind of thing one expects in such a place, for exam-

ple *Meditation for Beginners, Path to Inner Peace* and *Prayers for World Peace.*
Madhyamaka Buddhist Centre is a place for spiritual work. Courses are offered
for beginners and for those ready to undertake a more in-depth exploration of
Buddhist teachings and meditation. **Highly Recommended.**

Open: Most of the year except August. Receives men, women, groups.
Families, children and non-retreatants depending on purpose of visit.
Rooms: 6 singles, 3 twins, dormitories, camping.
Facilities: Disabled, shrine room, camping, garden, park, library, guest
lounge, guest phone (01759 304863). No loud music, alcohol or smok-
ing on the property.
Spiritual Help: Spiritual direction, meditation, directed study, group teachings.
Guests Admitted to: Unrestricted access. Sometimes work of Community.
Meals: Everyone eats together. **Vegetarian food. No special diets that
include meat.**
Special Activities: Special programme, including working holidays – send for
brochure. Ask about their other centres in Bath, Buxton and Ulverston.
Situation: Quiet, in the countryside. Grade II listed house.
Maximum Stay: Usually one week, although they are flexible.
Bookings: Letter, fax, e-mail, website, telephone 2–5p.m. Monday to Friday.
Charges: Various. Evening classes £4, day courses £15 including lunch.
Other courses, single full board £45, twin full board £40 per person,
dormitories full board £28. Enquire about charges for camping.
Access: Train, bus, car all possible. York is 10 miles away. Ask for directions
when you book – a small but excellent map is in the contact information.

Leeds

Hinsley Hall
Diocese of Leeds Pastoral Centre
62 Headingley Lane
Leeds LS6 2BX

Tel: 0113 261 8000
Fax: 0113 224 2406
e-mail: info@hinsley-hall.co.uk

Roman Catholic
This is a rather grand place with any number of very comfortable, bright,
modern, high-standard rooms and facilities. There is a lovely chapel with new
furnishings, a library and a book shop. The chapel has continuous circle seating around the altar for praying and celebrating together, which we liked.
The Yorkshire Dales are within easy reach. Hinsley has evolve into a conference centre rather than a retreat centre as such, so there can be lots of people
and the place noisy and busy. If you want a silent place, then Hinsley Hall is
not for you – but the facilities are excellent and the chapel and grounds are
available for prayer and meditative walking. You can always try going inside
yourself, into your own inner silence, and practise being in the world but not
of it. Not silent, not monastic, but you may just find that this centre suits.

Open: All year. Receives men, women, groups.
Rooms: 36 singles, 16 doubles. Mainly ensuite.
Facilities: Disabled, conferences, garden, library, chapel, guest sitting areas –
all you would expect in a modern place.
Spiritual Help: None.

Guests Admitted to: Public rooms, chapel.
Meals: Dining room. Traditional food. Vegetarian and special diets.
Special Activities: None.
Situation: Rather busy.
Maximum Stay: None.
Bookings: Letter, fax, telephone 8a.m.–4p.m. Monday to Friday.
Charges: £70 per person per day full board.
Access: Train: 2 miles from main station. Bus: On main bus route. Car: A660 from Leeds.

Mirfield

Community of the Resurrection
House of the Resurrection
Stocksbank Road
Mirfield
W Yorks WF14 0BN

Tel: 01924 494318
e-mail: cr@mirfield.org.uk
Website: www.mirfield.org.uk

Anglican
Here is a famous monastery and community which finds its roots in the monastic tradition of the Christian Church. It follows a tradition concerned with the quest for God in prayer and worship in the common life and in work and service. The church, the chapel and the buildings are splendid, and there are lots of them. There is a programme of retreats and events.

Open: All year except July. Receives men, women, young people over 16, groups.
Rooms: 24 singles, 2 doubles. Guest accommodation is in guest house, where silence is the norm.
Facilities: Disabled, conferences, garden, park, library, guest lounge, payphone.
Spiritual Help: Personal talks, group sharing, spiritual direction, personal retreat direction, directed study. Guests are expected but not required to attend services.
Guest Admitted to: Church, chapel, oratory.
Meals: Everyone eats together. Simple food. Vegetarian and special diets within reason.
Special Activities: Planned programme and details of other houses – send for brochure.
Situation: In Green Belt but on edge of built-up area.
Maximum Stay: 2 weeks.
Bookings: Letter.
Charges: See brochures.
Access: Train: Wakefield Westgate. Bus: from Leeds or Huddersfield. Coach: Dewsbury. Car: M1 Exit 40, M62 Exit 25.

Queensbury

Mountain Hall
Queensbury
W Yorks BD13 1LH

Tel: 01274 816258

Mind Body Spirit – Wicca – Non-traditional

Mountain Hall is perched 1,200 feet up, affording magnificent views over the city of Bradford, the Dale, and to the distant mountains. Built by a local mill owner in the last century as a social institution for his workers, it now functions as a residential centre for rest and theme holidays. There is an annual programme – a mixed choice of offerings here, but the direction is toward occult spirituality with emphasis on elements of Wicca and Tarot.

Open: All year. Receives men, women, groups, non-retreatants.
Rooms: 4 singles, 7 doubles, some twins, 1 self-catering apartment.
Facilities: Conferences, guest lounge, TV, payphone, car parking.
Spiritual Help: Various relaxation techniques and methods, aromatherapy massage, reiki.
Guests Admitted to: All public rooms.
Meals: Everyone eats together in guest dining room. Traditional food. Vegetarian. Special diets (supplementary charge).
Special Activities: Planned programme of events – send for the brochure.
Situation: Quiet.
Maximum Stay: By arrangement.
Bookings: Letter, telephone 6–7p.m.
Charges: Currently £20–£25 B&B per night, double B&B £30–£35 per night. Courses about £40 per day, including lunch, plus accommodation costs.
Access: Train possible. Bus: No. 526 from Halifax to Bradford. Car: via A644.

Todmorden

Losang Dragpa Buddhist Centre
Dobroyd Castle
Pexwood Road
Todmorden
W Yorks OL14 7JJ

Tel: 01706 812247
Fax: 01706 818901
e-mail: LosangD@aol.com
Website: www.losangdragpa.co.uk

Buddhist

A growing community of over twenty-five live in this old castle, and they offer a very wide range of courses and retreats, some with intriguing titles such as *Free Your Mind, Patience* and *Dancing in the Play of Impermanence*. There are also beginner's classes. Many projects are in hand here to transform this beautiful place and its 24 acres of grounds, plus a walled Victorian garden. To help in all this, there are working holidays available involving thirty-five hours work a week in exchange for food, accommodation and teachings. A leaflet is available with all the details. It sounds a good deal. Losang Dragpa Centre is part of the New Kadampa tradition of Buddhism, a tradition founded in the West by the Venerable Geshe Kelsang Gyatso, a respected scholar and mediation master from Tibet who has written extensively on Buddhism and founded other centres around the world. **Highly Recommended.**

Open: Most of year except January retreat period, but guests can stay over it. Receives men, women, young people.

Rooms: 12 singles, 2 doubles, dormitories.

Facilities: Garden, park, library, guest lounge, payphone. No smoking. Silence in public rooms.

Spiritual Help: Meditation, directed study.

Guests Admitted to: Unrestricted. Work of Community.

Meals: Everyone eats together. Vegetarian, organic.

Special Activities: Planned programme of events – weekend retreats, residential courses, meditation classes and workshops, day courses, working holidays. Send for brochure.

Situation: Very quiet, near a village, in countryside.

Maximum Stay: By arrangement.

Bookings: Letter, fax, e-mail, telephone 2–4p.m.

Charges: Weekend retreat from about £45 per person in a dormitory (bring a sleeping bag), £63 per person in a double and £70 in a single. Programme details charges for the various types of retreats and stays here.

Access: Train or car both good. By train only a 15-minute walk from station – but it is uphill all the way.

> India will teach the West the tolerance and gentleness of the mature mind, the quiet content of the unacquisitive soul, the calm of the understanding spirit and a unifying, pacifying love for all living things.
> WILL DURRANT

Wales

Anglesey

Sue Rowlands Centre for Psychic and Spiritual Studies

Tre-ysgawen Hall Tel: 01248 750750
Capel Coch Fax: 01248 750035
Llangefni e-mail: enquiries@sue-rowlands-centre.org.uk
Isle of Anglesey LL77 7UR Website: www.sue-rowlands-centre.org.uk

Mind Body Spirit – Psychic spiritualism
This is a country house hotel in the heartland of Anglesey with all the facilities you would expect of such a place – from the 1882 drawing room and library to an American type bar, four-poster beds and jacuzzis. However, do not let the top-class luxury put you off, for the Sue Rowlands Centre runs a serious programme of events designed to deepen spiritual awareness and enable self-revelation. The range of courses is wide, with themes including meditation practices, healing, mediumship and awareness.

Open: All year except Christmas. Receives everyone.
Rooms: 8 singles, 19 twins.
Facilities: Disabled, conferences, garden, park, guest lounge, TV in each room, direct dialing.
Spiritual Help: Personal talks, spiritual direction, meditation.
Guests Admitted to: Unrestricted access except for staff rooms.
Meals: Restaurant type catering with set menus and buffets.
Special Activities: Planned programme of courses – send for brochure.
Situation: Very quiet and tranquil, in countryside.
Maximum Stay: Usually for duration of course.
Bookings: Letter, fax, e-mail, telephone.
Charges: £305–£355 per course, everything included. £140 B&B double as hotel guests only. £90 B&B single. Ask about other rates – all are outlined in well produced course programme.
Access: Ask for brochure, which details routes by car.

Bangor

Life Foundation International Course Centre
Nant Ffrancon
Bethesda Tel: 01248 602900
Bangor Fax: 01248 602004
Gwynedd LL57 2EG e-mail: enquiries@lifefoundation.org.uk
Website: www.lifefoundation.org.uk

Mind Body Spirit – Yoga
Situated in the beautiful Welsh mountains of Snowdonia National Park, this centre is the home base of the World Peace Flame, a peace initiative by peacemakers around the world. The team at the centre is from a wide range

of backgrounds that have come together to provide spiritual awareness, self-empowerment, and self-development courses. Specialities include Dru Yoga, meditation retreats and spiritual development courses. 'Tools for transformation' sums it up best.

Open: For retreat and course programme. Receives men, women, groups.
Rooms: 3 singles, 3 doubles. No smoking. No alcohol.
Facilities: See brochure.
Spiritual Help: Inner self-development, self-help tools, yoga, meditation.
Guests Admitted to: Unrestricted access.
Meals: Everyone eats together. All meals are vegetarian.
Special Activities: Programme of events – brochure available.
Situation: Welsh mountains of Snowdonia National Park.
Maximum Stay: Duration of retreat.
Bookings: Letter, telephone 10a.m.–5p.m.
Charges: 2-day retreats from £130, 6-day retreats £340.
Access: Bus, coach and car all possible. Ask for travel directions.

Brecon

The Beacon
4 The Watton
Brecon
Powys LD3 7ED   Tel: 01874 625862
                                        e-mail: dafyddjohn@supanet.com

Ecumenical Holiday Retreat
The centre is situated within a National Park, and there are beautiful walks literally from the doorstep.

Open: All year. Receives men, women, young people, families, non-retreatants.
  No pets.
Rooms: 1 single, 1 double. No smoking.
Facilities: Garden, guest lounge, TV.
Spiritual Help: Personal talks if requested. Ask whether spiritual direction
  and aromatherapy are available, as these were being planned at the time of
  going to press.
Guests Admitted to: Guest areas.
Meals: Everyone eats together in guest house. Traditional food. Vegetarian
  and special diets by prior arrangement.
Special Activities: Planned programme.
 Situation: Quiet, in an area of outstanding natural beauty.
Maximum Stay: By arrangement.
Bookings: Letter, e-mail, telephone.
Charges: B&B £22 per person per night, half board £28, full board £32.
Access: Train: Abergavenny. Bus: Brecon. Car via motorways M4, M50; A
  Roads A470/A40.

Buckland Hall

Buckland Hall
Bwlch
Brecon
Powys LD3 7JJ

Tel: 01874 730276
Fax: 01874 730740
e-mail: info@buklandhall.co.uk
Website: www.bucklandhall.co.uk

Open spirituality

Meditation, group and inner process, earth mysteries, body and breath work, alternative lifestyles and technology, arts and crafts, and ritual and shamanism are just a few subjects that are of special interest here. Buckland Hall is a place dedicated to celebrations, courses and retreats of all kinds. It is a big old place offering some sixty-eight bed spaces arranged in various types of rooms. Food is exclusively vegetarian. Children are welcome. The centre is no smoking. Full board runs from about £48 to £60.

Coleg Trefeca
College Lane
Trefeca
Brecon
Powys LD3 OPP

Tel: 01874 711423
Fax: 01874 712212
e-mail: post@trefeca.org.uk
Website: www.trefeca.org.uk

Presbyterian Church of Wales

The centre, open to all, consists of a group of eighteenth-century buildings and a modern block, standing in five acres of grounds set in the Brecon Beacons National Park. It was once the home of Howell Harris (1714–1773), one of those who led the evangelical revival in Wales. Short retreats, guided group retreats, prayer, arts and crafts, ecumenical activities, and holiday weeks for older folk and young people are usually on offer. There are healing retreats and sometimes a children's weekend. The brochure and retreats are often in both Welsh and English. This is a good place for a stimulating retreat, mixing with other like-minded people. See the website for the current programme. The centre takes groups principally, but can take individuals on a B&B basis at any time and on a full-board basis when a group is in residence.

Open: All year. Receives men, women, young people, families, groups. Children welcome. Pets by arrangement.
Rooms: 39 bed spaces including singles and a family room. No smoking. Children welcome.
Facilities: Disabled – wheelchair access. Conferences, garden, library, guest lounge, TV, guest phone.
Spiritual Help: Personal talks, group sharing, spiritual direction, personal retreat direction, meditation.
Guests Admitted to: Unrestricted access.
Meals: Everyone eats together. Traditional home cooking. Vegetarian and special diets by prior arrangement.
Special Activities: Planned programme, though groups, churches and secular organisations may follow their own programme. See website.
Situation: Very quiet, in an area of outstanding natural beauty, 10 miles from Brecon. An ideal centre for those who wish to walk, climb, pony-trek or simply admire the views.

Maximum Stay: By arrangement.
Bookings: Letter or telephone but must confirm in writing.
Charges: Reasonable. See website for current prices, but about £14–£17 per person B&B, £30–£40 per person full board, depending on group.
Access: Train: Abergavenny (18 miles away, but transport can be arranged). Bus: Brecon, then pickup by prior arrangement. Car: via B4560.

Llangasty Retreat House
Llangasty
Brecon   Tel/Fax: 01874 658250
Powys LD3 7PJ   e-mail: llangasty.rh@btconnect.com
                                              Website: www.llangasty.co.uk

Church in Wales (Anglican) – Ecumenical
This large isolated stone house, hidden away from roads and the busy world, is comfortable and cheerful and overlooks a marvellous lake. There are magnificent views to the Black Mountains and superb walking. The guest lounge is large and comfortable, the library small but good, and the dining room offers home cooked meals with the fellowship of the other guests. The new Chapel of the Transfiguration has daily prayer and weekly worship. There is a small but rather nicely considered programme with such courses as a creative arts, music and prayer retreat, an Ash Wednesday retreat, and a walking and talking retreat.

Open: All year except Christmas and New Year. Receives men, women, young people, families, groups. Children welcome.
Rooms: 6 singles, 11 doubles.
Facilities: Disabled, conferences, garden, library, guest lounge, payphone, direct dialing.
Spiritual Help: Personal talks, group sharing, meditation, spiritual direction.
Guests Admitted to: Unrestricted access except for the kitchen.
Meals: Everyone eats together. Traditional food. Vegetarian and special diets by arrangement.
Special Activities: Programme of events – send for brochure.
Situation: Very quiet, in the countryside, in a lovely situation.
Maximum Stay: By arrangement.
Bookings: Letter, fax, e-mail, telephone.
Charges: Ask for current rates.
Access: By car via Brecon.

Caernafon

Lon Batus
Carmel
Near Caernarfon LL54 7RL   Tel/Fax: 01286 881970

Christian – Orthodox
From May until September you can come here for a two-day break. There is a daily Orthodox Office of prayer during most weekdays. Lon Batus is set in an open landscape, with accommodation for three people.

Cardigan

St David's Monastery
Rhydgarnwen
Cardigan
Dyfed SA43 NW1

Tel/Fax: 0239 615265
The following links are in French:
Website: www.beatitudes.fr
Website: www.institut.beatitudes.free.fr

Roman Catholic
This is the first house opened in Britain by the Communauté des Béatitudes
(Community of the Beatitudes). It now has houses in some thirty dioceses in
France (See France section) and thirty-five houses abroad, including this one.
Adoration and intercession prayers, hospitality and the witness of brotherly
life are important elements in the mission of the Community at St David's.
Their first venture was a book shop intended to reach out to Christians of all
denominations.

Corwen

Coleg Y Groes
Corwen
Denbighshire LL21 OAU

Tel/fax: 01490 412169
e-mail: colegygroes@btopenworld.com
Website: www.colegygroes.co.uk

The Church in Wales – Anglican
Two women deacons of the Church of Wales and a pastoral counsellor run
this small retreat house with six bedrooms in a big, comfortable house. It
nestles in a quiet spot between church and mountainside near the River Dee.
There is counselling and prayer for healing, and individual needs are catered
for in an environment that aims to convey the peace of Christ. The centre is
open to all.

Open: All year except Christmas. Receives men, women, young people, fami-
lies, small groups, non-retreatants. Children welcome. No pets.
Rooms: 6 rooms available for use as singles or doubles.
Facilities: Garden, quiet room, books to read, guest lounge, TV. Local
computer bureau available with fax, computers, e-mail. Parish church
adjoining.
Spiritual Help: Personal talks, individually guided retreats, Ignatian spiritual
exercises, directed study, spiritual direction.
Guests Admitted to: Garden, retreat house.
Meals: Taken in the guest house or in room. Good varied home cooking.
Vegetarian and special diets.
Special Activities: None, but the retreat team is available to help you. It is possi-
ble to arrange a 30-day Ignatian Retreat or an individually guided retreat.
Situation: Quiet, in a small town with countryside around it.
Maximum Stay: By arrangement.
Bookings: Letter, fax, e-mail, telephone.
Charges: £22 B&B per person per night, £8.50 evening meal, £4.50 packed
lunch.
Access: Train or bus from Wrexham.

Vajraloka Buddhist Meditation Retreat Centre for Men
Tyn-y-ddol, Treddol
Corwen   Tel: 01490 460406
Clwyd LL21 OEN   e-mail: info@vajraloka.com
                                    Website: www.vajraloka.com

Buddhist – Friends of the Western Buddhist Order
Vajraloka is the longest established meditation centre of the Friends of the Western Buddhist Order (FWBO). It is a men's Buddhist centre with retreats open to those who have attended a basic meditation course run by FWBO (see London section, The London Buddhist Centre). **Only guests who have attended FWBO meditation classes in public centres are accepted.** Men from other Buddhist traditions may be received for short retreats of one week if they have about six months experience of Samatha meditation – Mindfulness of Breathing/Metta. The centre's purpose is to provide facilities for the practice of meditation, and there are meditation retreats for various levels of experience, as well as visualisation retreats. The programme brochure, issued annually, is detailed and interesting, and shows the depth and variety of the retreats and courses on offer. The Centre is set in the beautiful countryside of North Wales and is a very peaceful place. There is a facility for solitary retreats. Silence is maintained during a retreat, and there is abstention from sexual activity and from reading books. No alcohol or other intoxicating substances are permitted. Mobile phones are left off throughout the retreat. This is one of the very few single-sex Buddhist meditation centres in Europe where meditation continues throughout the year. **Highly Recommended.**

> "Happiness is a matter of changing troubles."
> COLETTE

Open: All year. Receives men (see above conditions of booking and requirements during the retreat), male religious who have completed an FWBO meditation course at a public centre.

Rooms: 6 singles, 2 doubles, dormitories, solitary facility.

Facilities: Shrine room, garden, library, direct dialing phone.

Spiritual Help: Meditation – on all retreats the community teaches a creative approach in meditation workshops. Personal talks, group sharing, spiritual direction, personal retreat direction.

Guests Admitted to: Shrine room, gardens, all public and guest designated areas.

Meals: Guests eat together. **Vegetarian/ vegan food only is served.**

Special Activities: Planned programme of events – send for the brochure. Some events may be restricted depending on a person's experience.

Situation: Very quiet, at the end of a country lane, in rolling hills. Remote.

Maximum Stay: 3 months.

Bookings: Letter, fax, e-mail, telephone.

Charges: £25 per person per night, £22 concessions. **You must book for the entire period of the retreat.**

Access: By car, but ask when you book as the route is a little complicated. Taxi and bus possible.

The Vajrakuta Buddhist Study Centre for Men
Blae-y-ddol
Corwen
Clwyd LL21 OEN   Tel: 01490 460648

Buddhist – Friends of the Western Buddhist Order
The Vajrakuta Buddhist Study Centre for Men is a Dharma study centre of
the Friends of the Western Buddhist Order with a community team dedicated
to the study of this spiritual practice. It is linked to Vajraloka centre, which is
about half a mile down the road. Some eight- to ten-week study seminars are
offered each year. This is primarily a study centre for members of the Friends
of the Western Buddhist Order, and there are general study courses for men
with some basic Buddhist knowledge. The retreat programme is a short but
excellent one, including such topics as *White Lotus Sutra*, *Nature of Existence*
(based on the text of Sangharakshita) and the *Bodhisattva's Way of Life*. The
daily programme includes meditation, group study and ritual. Some retreats
are suitable for beginners and you do not have to be a Buddhist to come here
– **but it is best to have had some contact with another FWBO centre
before coming here.**

Open: All year. Receives men.
Rooms: Mostly in shared quarters, but sometimes a single is available.
  Hermitages, a caravan with all facilities in grounds, and a cottage several
  miles away are available for solitary retreats.
Facilities: Shrine room, garden, library, 2 solitary retreat facilities.
Spiritual Help: Meditation practice, directed study.
Guests Admitted to: Shrine room.
Meals: Everyone eats together. **All meals are vegetarian or vegan.**
Special Activities: Programme of events – send for details.
Situation: In green hills with ample grounds and beautiful surrounding
  countryside.
Maximum Stay: By arrangement.
Bookings: Letter, telephone.
Charges: See brochure for current rates.
Access: Most people come by train and bus – ask for specific directions.

Cowbridge

Ty Teilo
The Rectory
Llandow
Cowbridge
Glamorgan CF71 7NT   Tel: 01656 890205
                    e-mail: peter@theleonards.org.uk
Anglican
This is a day retreat house belonging to the Diocese of Llandaff. It is for
groups, and there is a chapel, a meeting room and a kitchen for self-catering.
The place is converted from a stable block, and there are gardens and nearby
country walks.

> *Try to spread your loving mind and heart to all that they may have peace and happiness in their lives.*
> VEN. DHAMMAVIJITHA THERA

Dolgellau

**Carmelite Monastery
Cader Road
Dolgellau
Gwynedd LL40 1SH**   Tel: 01341 422546

Roman Catholic
This monastery of stone buildings with modern additions is home to a traditional Carmelite community and offers private retreats only, in a guest bungalow near the chapel.

Open: All year. Receives women, men, young people, religious, non-retreatants.
Rooms: 1 double. Facility available to women considering the Carmelite religious life.
Facilities: Garden, TV, books to read, payphone.
Spiritual Help: Personal talks.
Guests Admitted to: Chapel.
Meals: Self-catering – facilities available.
Special Activities: None.
Situation: Quiet, in the countryside, with opportunities for walks in the mountains.
Maximum Stay: 1 week.
Bookings: Letter.
Charges: Donation by agreement.
Access: Bus to nearest town or by car.

Fishguard

**Fflad-y-Brenin Christian Retreat Centre
Pontfaen
Fishguard   Tel: 01348 881382
Pembrokeshire SA65 9UA**   e-mail: info@ffald-y-Brenin.co.uk
                                Website: www.Ffald-y-Brenin.co.uk

Christian
Fflad-y-Brenin Christian Retreat Centre is set high up in the Pembrokeshire Coast National Park and has wonderful views. The sea is only about five miles away, so the situation is ideal. Individuals are self-catering, but meals can be arranged for groups. There are any number of combinations of rooms, from singles to family and self-contained. There is a craft room, a chapel, and a meeting room. Guests may join in with the chapel services if they want. There is a regular event programme, which often includes Celtic Christianity retreats.

Hawarden

St Deiniol's Library
Hawarden
Flintshire CH5 3DF

Tel: 01244 532350
Fax: 01244 520643
e-mail: deiniol.visitors@btinternet.com
Website: www.st-deiniols.chester.ac.uk

Christian

Claimed to be Britain's finest residential library, St Deiniol's is unique, attracting scholars and others from around the world. As well as the outstanding library, it offers bed and board in beautiful surroundings and peace and quiet. It seems a dream but it really is there, with a programme of courses, seminars and day conferences on a variety of theological and Victorian themes, led by eminent scholars. The library, founded in 1889 by William Ewart Gladstone, has a collection of over half a million journals and books, with its main strengths being in theology and the Victorian period. It also contains Britain's largest private collection of material on St Francis and the early Franciscans. **If you wish to use the library, a reference is usually required in advance, as with all specialist libraries.** This is a relaxed place to study and to have a good rest. It is amazing that in this modern age such traditional civility still exists. This is a particular place, but if it seems right for you, then it could be the ideal retreat. **Highly Recommended.**

Open: Open all year except Christmas. Receives everyone.
Rooms: 12 singles, 8 doubles, 3 twins.
Facilities: Conferences, garden, park, guest library, guest lounge, TV, guest telephones in all bedrooms, direct dialing. No mobile phones in Reading Rooms.
Spiritual Help: None.
Guests Admitted to: Chapel, library and other facilities such as common room.
Meals: Everyone eats together. Traditional food. Vegetarian and special diets.
Special Activities: Planned programme – send for information sheet.
Situation: Friendly, quiet and historic village setting. Own grounds.
Maximum Stay: None.
Bookings: Letter, telephone 9a.m.–4.30p.m. Monday to Friday.
Charges: £37 per person per night with dinner (£27.50 clergy rate), £22.50 B&B. Ensuite supplement £10 per room per night.
Access: Train: Hawarden or Shotton. Bus: from Chester. Car: A55 and A550.

Knighton

The Bleddfa Trust
Centre for Caring and the Arts
The Old School
Knighton
Powys LD7 1PA

Tel: 01547 550349

Non-religious

Bleddfa does not offer accommodation but is a well worth a day visit or attendance at one of the workshops. The wide range of workshops at the centre covers many aspects of spirituality, poetry and meditation, all in a tran-

quil setting which is perfect for walking, sitting, painting, thinking and growing in peacefulness. The Bleddfa Art Gallery, which is part of the operation
here, has gained a national reputation for the quality of its exhibitions. There
is a small book and gift shop, and you may take tea inside or in a charming
herb garden.

Open: April to November. Receives everyone.
Rooms: Non-residential (local B&B accommodation).
Facilities: Various meeting rooms, Old School gallery, book shop, a barn
    centre for groups and workshops.
Spiritual Help: Quiet days, personal talks by arrangement.
Guests Admitted to: Everywhere.
Meals: Teas. Food arranged for some events, other times bring your own.
Special Activities: Send for brochure.
Situation: In wonderful countryside with distant views.
Maximum Stay: For duration of event.
Bookings: Letter, telephone.
Charges: Depends on workshop or event – see brochure.
Access: Car: on A488 between Knighton and Llandrindod Wells.

Lampeter

Cwrt y Cylchau
Llanfair Clydogau
Lampeter
Ceredigion SA48 8LJ   Tel: 01570 493526

Eco-spirituality
Started in 1998, this 5-acre smallholding is not a retreat centre as such but a
community building a new place. They offer board and camping to visitors
as a way of earning some income to continue developing Cwrt y Cylchau as
a place of therapeutic retreat for those in need of healing or a holiday to get
some rest. Meditation, world peace, connection with nature and care for each
other are a few of the major interests here. There is a strong focus on permaculture.

Llandrindod Wells

Dyffryn Farm
Llanwrthwl   Tel: 01597 811017
Llandrindod Wells   Fax: 01597 810609
Powys LD1 6NU   e-mail: retreat@dyffrynfarm.co.uk
           Website: www.dyffrynfarm.co.uk
Anglican – Inter-denominational
Situated in mid-Wales in a beautiful part of the Wye Valley, this seventeenth-
century house and farm of 20 acres has pastures, springs, old stone walls and
warm welcoming fires in the house in winter. Among the many compliments
from retreat guests have been these: 'Paradise found', 'A fabulous time',
'Wonderful hospitality', 'A beautiful day of prayer'.

Open: All year except Christmas. Receives men, women, groups, families.

Rooms: 10 singles, 5 doubles, plus self-catering.
Facilities: Conferences, garden, library, guest lounge, TV.
Spiritual Help: Personal talks, group sharing, spiritual direction, personal retreat direction. Ministry work appraised.
Guests Admitted to: Access to most areas.
Meals: Everyone eats together. Traditional, whole food. Vegetarian and special diets.
Special Activities: 3–4 weekend retreats a year.
Situation: In beautiful countryside.
Maximum Stay: 2 weeks, or 2 months if self-catering.
Bookings: Letter, fax, telephone.
Charges: Around £33 per person per day full board, £22–£26 B&B, self-catering rates on request.
Access: Train: Llandrindod Wells (8 miles away). Car: off A470.

Llandudno

Loreto Centre
Abbey Road
Llandudno   Tel/Fax: 01492 878031
Gwynedd LL30 2EL   e-mail: loreto.centre@llandudno42.freeserve.co.uk
                                    Website: www.loretollno.org.uk
Roman Catholic
The Loreto Centre is run by the Loreto Sisters and is located near the West Shore at the foot of the Great Orme. It is only a ten-minute walk from the town, the parish church and the East Shore. A lot of groups use the place as there are thirty-one bedrooms, but there are also eleven ensuite rooms and three self-catering apartments for individuals who are seeking to make a private or guided retreat, or want a quiet break. The programme, while a limited one, has at least one event or retreat each month. These have a strong Catholic basis. This is a big but comfortable place where quiet is fostered and group retreats usually maintain silence outside their meetings.

Open: All year except three weeks in September. Receives men, women, young people, groups, religious. Children welcome.
Rooms: 21 singles, 10 doubles (11 ensuite rooms). Fully equipped apartments, self-catering facilities.
Facilities: Disabled, conferences, garden, guest lounge, TV, guest phone (01492 878060).
Spiritual Help: Spiritual direction, personal retreat direction.
Guests Admitted to: Chapel, grounds, guest areas.
Meals: Everyone eats together unless in self-catering accommodation. Traditional food. Vegetarian and special diets by arrangement.
Special Activities: Programme of events including preached retreats – send for brochure.
Situation: Quiet, in countryside, by the sea. Spectacular views.
Maximum Stay: 2 weeks.
Bookings: Letter accompanied by SAE.
Charges: Wide range – about £30 per person per day full board on a retreat, £25 per day self-catering, £27 for a weekend (£24 students). Other charges in brochure. All charges are considered to be 'invited offerings' (as

in 'donations'), but there is a registration fee, which becomes part of your offering and is non-refundable. Currently this is £30 for individuals and £200 for groups.

Access: Train, bus and car all possible. Good directions in the brochure.

Llangunllo

The Samatha Centre
Greenstreete
Llangunllo
Powys LD7 1SP   Tel: 01348 811583

Buddhist – Theravada tradition
The Samatha Centre consists of a big farmhouse set in 88 acres of land. The setting is lovely, with views in all directions of green pastures and rising hills. There are streams and woods with secluded places where small huts have been built for use by those meditating who want solitude. Everyone is welcome here to learn this gentle and effective way of meditation. There are regular classes for the more experienced and some for beginners.

Open: During organised weekends and weeks. Receives men, women, young people.
Rooms: 9 singles, 4 in huts, camping.
Facilities: Garden, park, library, guest telephone.
Spiritual Help: Individual instruction on Samatha meditation, directed study. There is always an experienced teacher to whom a person can talk about their practice. This is an important aspect of the courses here.
Guests Admitted to: Unrestricted access. Work of community.
Meals: Everyone eats together. Traditional and whole food. Vegetarian and special diets within reason.
Special Activities: Send or telephone for brochure. Beginners can go to occasional introductory weekend courses in meditation practice.
Situation: Deep in the countryside on a green hill and very peaceful.
Maximum Stay: Length of course undertaken, usually a weekend or week.
Bookings: Letter, telephone.
Charges: £100 per week non-members.
Access: Train: Llangunllo (less than 1 mile away – an easy walk down a lane and up a small hill to the Centre). Car: from Knighton in Powys to Llangunllo, then through the village and the Centre will be seen on a hill to the left. The entrance is sign-posted.

Llandysul

Bach y Gwyddel
Cwmpengraig
Drefach Felindre
Llandyssul SA44 5HX   Tel/Fax: 01559 371427

Mind Body Spirit – Eco-spirituality
This centre is run by a couple who offer different but complementary skills to guests. Transpersonal therapy, the creation of personal rituals which assist

in moving through life changes, holistic massage, story-telling, group facilitation, instruction in developing low-impact alternative energy systems, and guided walks through old sacred sites and wildlife habitats are examples of what is on offer. A cat called Alice may be there to offer excellent pet therapy, including hugs, cuddles and deep stroking. Simplicity and a search for spiritual paths are important here. The family provides customised personal retreats. There are sacred site visits, hidden swimming places and special environmental sites too.

Open: All year, but varies according to type of accommodation you are using – some suitable for winter, others for summer. Receives men, women, young people, families, groups. Children welcome. No pets (Alice is not keen on strange dogs, particularly as she has a full diary of clients for her therapy work and needs to stay focused.)

Rooms: Yurt (Mongolian nomadic dwelling) for up to 6. It is 4.9 m (16 ft) in diameter, with wood burning stove, gas stove, water container and washing up kit, bedding supplied and a private garden area. Wood cabin for 2. Solar showers and toilet. Spring water supply to both types of accommodation. Camping.

Facilities: Garden, wood supplies, hot showers and toilet facilities, direct dialing phone, guest area. Books on women's issues, healing, spiritual development and sustainable living can be borrowed.

Spiritual Help: Personal talks, group sharing, spiritual direction, personal retreat direction, meditation, massage, psychotherapy, acupuncture, story-telling, sacred site visits and special environment site visits.

Guests Admitted to: Their own retreat and garden area of an acre, and by arrangement to the adjoining 18-acre permaculture farm owned by a trust that includes a pond, woodlands and a wildflower meadow.

Meals: Several options here, from self-catering to prepared meals on request.

Special Activities: None but the adjoining permaculture trust sometimes holds courses and camps on country craft skills, organic growing, alternative energy, building and permaculture design, and sustainable and holistic living.

Situation: Very quiet, in the countryside.

Maximum Stay: Usually a few weeks, otherwise by arrangement.

Bookings: Letter, fax, e-mail, telephone 8p.m.–11p.m.

Charges: Yurt and wood cabin £15 for 1 person, £25 for 2 people, more people by arrangement. 20% discount for 6 nights or more. Therapies are extra.

Access: Train: Carmarthen, then bus to Drefach Felindre (about 1 mile away). Details when you book.

Ceridwen
Penybanc Farm
Felindre
Llandysul
Ceredigion SA44 5XE   Tel/Fax: 01559 370211

Celtic spirituality – Pagan
This is a purpose-built residential centre for small groups at a farm in south-west Wales. It is a working organic farm and the site overlooks a beautiful

valley of trees. There are comfortable shared rooms and dormitories. Health and healing, and arts and crafts are subjects of interest here. Everyone is welcome, including children and families. Various alternative healing treatments can be arranged.

Llanidloes

Wilderness Trust
Waen Old Farmhouse
Llidiartywaen, Llanidloes
Powys SY18 6JT   Tel: 01686 413842

Interfaith
Open: March to December. Receives everyone. Children welcome.
Rooms: 1 single, 1 double, barn, camping site, 2 caravans, hermitages.
Facilities: Chapel, garden, guest lounge, payphone.
Spiritual Help: Personal talks.
Guests Admitted to: Unrestricted access.
Meals: Everyone eats together. Whole food. Vegetarian and special diets. Self-catering facilities.
Special Activities: None. Board is offered in return for smallholding work on restoring buildings, care for animals.
Situation: Quiet, in the countryside. A smallholding.
Maximum Stay: Unlimited for paying guests, others by arrangement.
Bookings: Telephone.
Charges: £15 per person per day full board or free to working guests. £50 per week.
Access: Train: Caersws. Bus: Llanidloes. Car: ask for travel details.

Llanpumsaint

The Community of the Many Names of God
Skanda Vale
Llanpumsaint   Tel: 01559 384421
Carmarthen SA33 6JT   Fax: 01559 384999
                                   Website: www.skandavale.org

Open spirituality – Timeless consciousness
Tucked away on a wooded hillside a few miles north of Carmarthen, Skanda Vale is something out of the ordinary. Indian temples, devotional chanting, a deer park, an elephant ... Step into this world and it's difficult not to be charmed, uplifted and deeply moved by the genuine love and inspiration that started the community nearly thirty years ago and which has seen it grow into a place of pilgrimage for thousands every year. The spiritual head of the community is a Sri Lankan known as Guruji, whose determination to set up and run a community where God comes first has meant a radical refusal to be bothered by the pressures of money. There are no charges here and the centre is financed solely through donation. The Community of swamis, monks and nuns live by strict rules. **Women visitors are requested to come in pairs unless they are already known by the community. There is caution towards single women, but everyone is welcome provided they respect the rules of this traditional monastic community. The custom of segregation**

in the temple is followed, and it is important to have eaten a vegetarian diet for three days before entering the temple. Prayers, or pujas, are joyful occasions and take place regularly throughout the day in one of the three temples. The most stunning of these, the Sri Ranganatha Temple, is constructed without a roof or walls as an outdoor water temple. A divine figure lies prostrate on a stone bed in the middle of a small lake. Around the lake, other figures – including Krishna, Shiva, and Buddha – remind us of the many forms of God. A short, but steep, walk up the hill through woodland and some of the wonders of God's creation await – Skanda Vale has its own deer park, bird sanctuary and elephant. Valli was an orphaned elephant given as a gift in the 1980s and is now a much-loved member of the community. The Maha Shakti Temple is where the community gathers for prayer three times a day. The community is actively involved in hospice work. Respite care in people's homes has been operating for several years, and they have just opened a day care centre and have plans for a residential hospice in the near future. Guests and retreatants are expected to work for four hours a day in exchange for their board and accommodation. Skanda Vale receives thousands of pilgrims and visitors every year and can be a very busy place, so don't come here if you want to get away from it all. But do come for any other reason. After all, a retreat is about stepping out of your ordinary life for a while, and The Community of the Many Names of God is surely just the place to do it. We confess that we could not resist a retreat with an elephant. She is a marvel of creation. **Highly Recommended.**

Llanrwst

Pencraig Arthur
Llanddoged
Llanrwst   Tel: 01492 640959
North Wales LL26 0DZ   e-mail: pencraig@madasafish.com

This centre has self-catering accommodation for five people as individuals or in a group. It is good for private retreats.

Llansteffan

Heartspring
Hill House
Llansteffan   Tel: 01267 241999
Carmarthen SA33 5JG   e-mail: info@heartspring.cco.uk
                                              Website: www.heartspring.co.uk
Open spirituality – Eco-spirituality
Guided individual retreats are available at Heartspring, which is a grand Victorian mansion with great views. Only organic vegetarian food is served here, and both full board and individual self-catering is possible. Children are welcome. Health and healing, environment-friendly and non-toxic living, meditation, counselling and inner process are concerns at Heartspring. B&B is about £24–£38 per person per night for a single room.

Monmouth

Society of the Sacred Cross
Tymawr Convent
Lydart, Monmouth
Gwent NP5 4RN   Tel: 01600 860244
                              Website: www.churchinwales.org.uk/tymawr

Anglican
Once a farmhouse, Tymawr has been home to the sisters of the Sacred Cross since 1923. Guests are made to feel at home here, sharing worship, simple good food and the spacious grounds with the community. There are nearby fields, woodland and even a reclaimed pond.

Open: Almost all year – enquire as to closed weeks. Receives men, women, young people, groups.
Rooms: 6 self-contained, 4 full-board singles, 2 self-contained doubles, 1 full-board double. This may seem a bit confusing, but different combinations are available so talk to the sisters.
Facilities: Disabled, chapel, garden, library, guest lounge, guest telephone.
Spiritual Help: Personal talks by arrangement in advance.
Guests Admitted to: Chapel. Work of the community sometimes.
Meals: Traditional simple food taken separately in nearby guest house. Vegetarian. Self-catering facilities.
Special Activities: None.
Situation: Very quiet, in countryside, in Wye Valley.
Maximum Stay: Generally 2 weeks.
Bookings: Letter, telephone 6.45–8p.m.
Charges: Guidelines are £25 per person per night full board, £15 per person per day self-catering.
Access: Car is best. House is 4 miles south of Monmouth.

Pantasaph

Franciscan Friary and Retreat Centre
Pantasaph   Tel: 01352 715030/01352 711053
Holywell   Fax: 01352 715349
Clwyd CH8 8PE   e-mail: eretreats@friarypantasaph.org
                                   Website: www.friarypantasaph.org

Roman Catholic
Private retreatants are welcome here at any time. There are preached retreats here as well as events, Franciscan workshops, and weekends on Padre Pio, *Growing in Holiness* and the Beatitudes.

Open: February to December. Receives men, women, young people, groups.
Rooms: 24 singles, 2 twins, 6-bedroom holiday house (Denbigh House).
Facilities: Garden, library, guest lounge, payphone.
Spiritual Help: Personal talks, preached retreats.
Guests Admitted to: Chapel, choir.
Meals: Everyone eats together in guest house. Traditional food. Self-catering facilities.
Special Activities: Planned programme of retreats.
Situation: Quiet.

Maximum Stay: By arrangement.

Bookings: Letter.

Charges: Various depending on whether for the night, the weekend or a 6-day retreat, so you need to ask.

Access: Train: Flint (London–Holyhead line). National coach: Flint. The Centre is 7 miles from Flint – pick-up possible if arranged in advance. Car: ask for directions.

Penmaenmawr

Noddfa Spirituality Centre
Conwy Old Road
Penmaenmawr
Gwynedd LL34 6YF

Tel: 01492 623473
Fax: 01492 622517
e-mail: noddfapen@aol.com
Website: www.noddfa.org.uk

Roman Catholic

Retreats at Noddfa, which means 'haven' or 'refuge', are open to members of all Christian denominations. Encounters with the Bible, and individually guided, preached, holistic, and Celtic retreats are all on offer here. There are retreats for women, and others taking a look at the future of religious life.

Open: All year. Receives men, women, groups, families, young people, those who care for others in their own home.

Rooms: 24 singles, 4 doubles/twins.

Facilities: Chapel, conferences, garden, library, guest lounge, TV.

Spiritual Help: Personal talks, group sharing, spiritual direction, personal retreat direction, circle dancing, massage.

Guests Admitted to: Unrestricted access except kitchen.

Meals: Everyone eats in dining room. Traditional food. Vegetarian and special diets.

Special Activities: Planned programme – send for brochure.

Situation: Quiet, in a village, near sea and mountains.

Maximum Stay: 2 weeks.

Bookings: Letter, fax, telephone.

Charges: £32 per person per day full board. Retreats are priced individually – see brochure.

Access: Train: Penmaenmawr (on Holyhead line). National coach: from London, Liverpool, Manchester or Birmingham. Boat from Ireland easy. Car: usually via A55.

Porthcawl

St Clare's Prayer Centre
Clevis Lane
Porthcawl
Glamorgan CF36 5NR

Tel/Fax: 01656 783701
e-mail: srbronach@onetel.net.uk
Website: www.stclares-prayercentre.co.uk

Roman Catholic – Inter-denominational

Hospitality and a place to reflect, meditate and pray is on offer here. The retreat centre is available for preached retreats, retreat days and quiet prayer days. The orientation of events on the short programme is Roman Catholic.

There is a pleasant walled garden, and the cottage available for accommodation is nice and may be used as a hermitage as well. There is Christian meditation every Wednesday evening.

Open: All year except mid-July to mid-August. Receives everyone.
Rooms: 3 singles, 4 doubles, caravan parking area, hermitage/cottage.
Facilities: Chapel, conferences, garden, library, guest lounge, TV, guest telephone.
Spiritual Help: Personal talks, group sharing, spiritual direction, meditation, reflexology, reiki.
Guests Admitted to: Unrestricted access.
Meals: Everyone eats together. Traditional food. Self-catering facilities in cottage. Ask about meals served when you book.
Special Activities: Some planned events.
Situation: Very quiet.
Maximum Stay: 1 month.
Bookings: Letter, fax, e-mail, telephone.
Charges: B&B £15, full board and guided retreat £35 per day, Quiet Day £6. Donations for therapies £10–£15 a session.
Access: Best by car. Good instruction in the information leaflet.

St Asaph

St Beuno's Spiritual Centre
St Asaph
Denbighshire
North Wales LL17 OAS

★

Tel: 01745 583444
Fax: 01745 584151
e-mail: StBeunos@aol.com
Website: www.home.aol.com/StBeunos

Roman Catholic
This is a leading Jesuit centre of spirituality for the teaching and study of the spiritual exercises of St Ignatius Loyola to Christians from all over the world. However, in its long tradition as a respected Roman Catholic Retreat Centre St Beuno's has always welcomed people of many denominations and also those who are unattached to any church. The famous Ignatian exercises are a series of scripture-based, Christ-centred meditations and contemplations designed to help each retreatant to discover his or her 'hidden self'. The Exercises have been the starting point for many forms of spiritual retreat in the Christian world since the sixteenth century. There are courses lasting six or eight days and others that are given in eight-day periods over three months, while the full course of spiritual exercises involves a continuous period of some thirty days. There are some Quiet Day retreats on offer as well. The Ignatian exercises are among the most famous and rigorous of all spiritual retreats. You should first read up about this form of retreat and perhaps discuss it with your spiritual adviser before deciding to go. This is a place for a serious *religious* retreat that is all about seeking God. **Highly Recommended.**

Open: All year except January. Receives men, women, groups.
Rooms: 45 singles. 2 nearby cottages are also used but are not suitable for those with walking difficulties.
Facilities: Disabled limited, but lift from ground floor to Chapel Gallery in main house planned for 2004. Garden, library, guest phone.

Spiritual Help: Personal talks, group sharing, spiritual direction, personal retreat direction, directed study, one-to-one retreats, 3-month courses in apostolic spirituality for Christians, 30-day retreats, 2-month training courses.
Guests Admitted to: Chapel, oratory, all guest areas.
Meals: Everyone eats together. Traditional simple food. Vegetarian and special diets.
Special Activities: Send for brochure.
Situation: Very quiet, in the countryside. Atmosphere of silence in the house and grounds.
Maximum Stay: Duration of planned or programmed retreat.
Bookings: Letter, fax, e-mail, telephone.
Charges: 8 days about £328, 6 days £294, weekends (2 days) £84.
Access: Rail: Rhyl, otherwise by bus or car.

St David's

St Non's Retreat Centre
St David's   Tel: 01437 720224/720161
Pembrokeshire SW62 6BN   e-mail: stnonsretreat@aol.om
                           Website: www.members.aol.com/stnonsretreat
Ecumenical
St. Non's is on the bay here and has a graceful little chapel. There is an Oratory, a library and eleven bedrooms. The programme is an interesting one, with subjects such as *Sacred Dance*, a six-day *Silent Dream Retreat* and *Walking Retreat*. Send for programme of events.

Tregaron

Gilfach Hermitage
Llandewi
Brefi, Tregaron
Cardiganshire SY25 6SB   Tel: 01974 298138
                           (between 7 and 8 p.m. please)
Inter-denominational
This is a little Welsh cottage set on a hillside with great views and offering three bedrooms for self-catering. Nice for a private retreat and rest.

Tywyn

Rainbow Rose Retreats
Tollgate Cottage   Tel/Fax: 01654 710310
Happy Valley, Tywyn   e-mail: stelyan@onetel.net.uk
Gwynedd LL36 9HU   Website: www.counserve.co.uk/rainbowrosecircle

Mind Body Spirit – Christian
In 8 acres of secluded woodland, this old farmhouse offers a warm if basic welcome. There are log fires and space for a relaxing time – but everything is being developed, so who can say what you will find? Working holidays, guided individual and group retreats, esoteric gardening, meditation, counselling, prayer and shamanic ritual are all possible.

Welshpool

Abhedashram
Camlad House
Forden
Welshpool
Powys SY21 8NZ

Tel: 01938 580499/01938 580311
e-mail: contact@abhedashram.org
Website: www.abhedashram.org

Yoga – Vedanta philosophy

Abhedashram was established in 1983 under the guidance of an Indian teacher and the Universal Confluence of Yoga-Vedanta Luminary Trust. *Abheda* is a Sanskrit word meaning 'devoid of all differences', and anyone, whatever their race, religion and age, is welcome here. The emphasis is on the practice and study of yoga and spirituality. The centre in Wales is a rather imposing but handsome red-brick Georgian building set in the rolling hills of the Welsh borderlands. There is ample space for retreatants as well as opportunities for people to live within the community in self-contained apartments. There is a daily rhythm of meditation and yoga classes most evenings of the week, as well as regular yoga sutra philosophy classes and talks – all of which are free. Yoga teacher training is also available for selected candidates. The spiritual purpose of the centre is to 'bring freedom to the individual from relative and phenomenal truths, based on love, service, sacrifice, right understanding and the spirit of adjustment'. There is an empowering emphasis on the individual's capacity to bring about peace – both internal and external – through his or her own efforts to engage in spiritual practice. This is a place for the serious study and application of an ancient Indian philosophy that has guided people towards liberation for hundreds of years.

Open: All year. Receives men, women. **Guests are expected to attend morning and evening meditation.**

Rooms: 1 single, 4 doubles, 5 family rooms, 3 dormitories. Can accommodate about 50 people in total. No smoking. No alcohol.

Facilities: Conferences, garden, library, payphone, book shop.

Spiritual Help: Guidance in practice of yoga and Vedanta, personal talks, spiritual direction, personal retreat direction, meditation, directed study, hatha yoga classes weekly and during planned programmes.

Guests Admitted to: All public and guest areas, outside grounds.

Meals: Vegetarian and vegan.

Special Activities: Programmes and course – send for information. Morning and evening meditation open to the public without prior notice. Meditation room (Satsanga Hall) available for meditation.

Situation: Quiet, in 29 acres in countryside.

Maximum Stay: 3 days or weekend on first stay here.

Bookings: Letter, e-mail, telephone daytime.

Charges: £10–£15 per person per night for retreat accommodation. Weekend programmes £50 plus in dormitories, £70 plus in twin or family rooms. Other programmes usually free. Donations welcome.

Access: Train: station 10 minutes away. National coach: ask for details. Car: one hour from M6/M56 and less from the M54.

Whitland

Holy Cross Abbey
Velfrey Road
Whitland
Dyfed SA34 0QX   Not available on telephone

Roman Catholic
This Cistercian community of nuns has only limited accommodation but
does receive guests. You must write to them.

Open: Most of year. Receives men, women.
Rooms: 1 single, 1 double.
Facilities: Chapel.
Spiritual Help: Personal talks on request sometimes possible.
Guests Admitted to: Chapel.
Meals: Self-catering plus very plain traditional food.
Special Activities: None.
Situation: Quiet, in the countryside.
Maximum Stay: 1 week.
Bookings: Letter only.
Charges: Donation according to means.
Access: Train: Whitland (½ mile away). Car: Whitland.

When a man surrenders
all desires that come to
the heart and by the
grace of God finds the
joy of God, then his soul
has indeed found peace.
THE BHAGAVAD GITA

Scotland

Aberdeen

St Margaret's Convent
17 Spital
Aberdeen AB24 3HT   Tel: 01224 632648
                    e-mail: ositewaleta@convent1fsworld.co.uk

Scottish Episcopalian – Anglican
There is only one guest room here, but the sisters have a really warm welcome for each person who visits this convent.

Open: All year except Christmas and Easter. Receives women, young people.
Rooms: 1 single. No smoking.
Facilities: Chapel, garden, library, lounge, TV.
Spiritual Help: Personal talks, personal retreat direction.
Guests Admitted to: Church, chapel, choir.
Meals: Taken together or in your room. Traditional, simple food. Vegetarian and special diets by prior arrangement.
Special Activities: None.
Situation: In a city but quiet.
Maximum Stay: 14 days.
Bookings: Letter, e-mail.
Charges: £20 per day if possible – but this is negotiable.
Access: Train then taxi. Car.

Banff

The Creative Centre
Apna Ghar
5 St Ann's Terrace
Banff   Tel: 01261 812276
Aberdeenshire AB45 1AW   e-mail: carla@thecreativeretreat.freeserve.co.uk
                    Website: www.creative-retreat.co.uk

Non-religious – Holiday creative retreat
At the Creative Retreat you can create, devise and think in a studio suitable for any number of activities, or simply relax in comfortable self-catering accommodation. There are wild seas on your doorstep, beautiful scenery, and the kids are welcome too. The centre is located in a small eighteenth-century fishing village clinging to the rocky north-east coast of Scotland, with a little shop, a pub and a good restaurant. This is a place to truly get away from the busy town and city life.

Boat of Garten

Avingormack Guest house and retreats
Jan and Mathew Ferguson   Tel: 01479 831614
Boat of Garten   Fax: 01479 831344
Inverness-shire PH24 3BT   e-mail: Avin.gormack@ukgateway.net
                                  Website: www.motivationretreats.co.uk

Mind Body Spirit – Healing spirituality
Set way up in the Spey Valley, this place is a nice simple house where the aim
is for you to discover where you want to go next by connecting with your
inner self. Counselling, inner process systems, group process methods, body
and breath work, and meditation are all used.

Open: All year. Receives everyone
Rooms: 9 beds. No smoking.
Facilities: Garden.
Spiritual Help: Meditation techniques, personal guidance, breath therapy,
  counselling, NLP.
Guests Admitted to: Guest area.
Meals: Traditional food. Vegetarian, special diets.
Special Activities: Planned events and courses – see website.
Situation: Quiet.
Maximum Stay: By arrangement.
Bookings: Letter, fax, e-mail, telephone.
Charges: B&B £25–£30 single. 2–3- and 5-day retreats from £275 all-inclu-
  sive. Group B&B rates available.
Access: Train: Aviemore, then taxi (4 miles).

By Beauly

Centre of Light
Tighnabruaich Struy
By Beauly   Tel: 01463 761254
Inverness IV4 7JU   e-mail: linda@centreoflight.co.uk
                                  Website: www.centreoflight.co.uk

Mind Body Spirit
This is a very beautiful and gentle place to stay, whether for quiet solitary
time, spiritual retreat or therapeutic work. Linda has been here for over thirty
years, and has developed a unique system and a loving environment for helping individuals to access deeper levels of consciousness and discern the light
and dark in themselves, and grow in wisdom and love. Among the techniques
used are meditation and resonance kinesiology. Visitors stay in a purpose-
built retreat cottage with a double bedroom, a gallery with two single beds,
a bathroom, a meditation space and a separate well-equipped cabin for cooking and eating. Further up the hill there is a secluded hermitage for private
retreats or extra accommodation. The Centre has five acres of woodland and
gardens, and from here you can explore the rivers, forests and mountains –
wonderful Highland country. **Highly Recommended.**

Open: All year. Receives everyone, including small groups.
Rooms: 2 singles, 1 double in own cottage, hermitage for 2 maximum.
Facilities: Garden, woods, park, library, lounge, TV.

Spiritual Help: Meditation techniques, personal guidance, kinesiology, colour and visual work, breath therapy.

Guests Admitted to: Unrestricted.

Meals: Everyone eats together in guest house or can be taken in your room. Vegetarian organic food. Special diets.

Special Activities: Planned events – send for brochure.

Situation: a safe and supportive landscape for a retreat in nature. Very quiet in remote countryside.

Maximum Stay: Usually 9 days or by arrangement for longer.

Bookings: Letter, e-mail, telephone early evening.

Charges: £60– £150. £400 per week for use of self-catering accommodation. Concessions available. Reduced rates for longer stays.

Access: Train: Inverness. Bus: Beauly-Struy. Coach: Inverness. Car: A9 from the south to Inverness – excellent map available.

Callander

Lendrick Lodge
Brig O'Turk
Callander
Perthshire FK17 8HR

Tel: 01877 376263
e-mail: enquiries@lendricklodge.com
Website: www.lendricklodge.com

Mind Body Spirit

Lendrick Lodge is one of those places where barriers come down and the power of spirit is palpable. Whatever your beliefs, you are welcome here: there is no specific religious tradition but respect for all and a strong commitment to love and acceptance. Managed by Stephen and Vicky Mulhearn, Lendrick Lodge focuses strongly on empowering individuals through the traditional tools and rituals of shamanism. In the course of programmes such as *Giant Steps* and *The Spirit of Shamanism*, there are opportunities to experience sweat lodges, journeying, and fire walking. Indeed Lendrick Lodge is now home to the world-renowned Sundoor International Fire Walking School, under the guidance of Peggy Dylan. Whether you are inspired to walk the path of the shaman or simply want to relax in the magnificent surroundings, you will be assured of comfortable accommodation – and very good vegetarian food. There is a beautiful meditation room, a light and spacious sitting room and a conference room where the real work is done. The grounds, set amidst the mountains and lochs of The Trossachs, are peaceful: trees and a meandering stream offer places to be alone and to reflect, whilst other areas have been set aside for the sweat lodge and fire walking ceremonies. There is a strong sense of continuity and spiritual heritage here. Once the gathering place of Druids from all over Celtic Britain, it is fitting that Lendrick Lodge should once again be offering ancient ceremonial initiations preserved by indigenous cultures throughout the world. For those who are interested in training in shamanic practices, there is a two- to five-year training. Modules can be taken individually as a one-off or as part of the Shamanism Practitioner training programme. Check the website for more details: www.gsteps.co.uk or e-mail Stephen at: s.mulhearn@virgin.net.

Crieff

St Ninian's Centre
Conlrie Road
Crieff Tel: 01764 653766
Perthshire PH7 4BG Fax: 01764 655824
e-mail: stninians@dial.pipex.com

Church of Scotland
A former church, St Ninian's has been adapted into a modern residential centre, providing a wide range of courses, retreats, renewal weekends and refreshment breaks. The little town of Crieff is situated in pretty countryside and has much to offer in the way of parks and nature trails for walking, as well as sports facilities, including fishing.

Open: All year except Christmas. Receives everyone.
Rooms: 22 singles, 14 doubles, 4 dormitories.
Facilities: Conferences, guest lounge, garden, TV, library, guest telephone.
Spiritual Help: Personal talks, group sharing.
Guests Admitted to: Unrestricted access.
Meals: Everyone eats together. Traditional food. Vegetarian and special diets.
Special Activities: Planned events – send for brochure.
Situation: Quiet, views across the hills.
Maximum Stay: Open
Bookings: Letter, fax, telephone.
Charges: £28 per 24 hours full board up to £160 per week (plus VAT).
Access: Train, bus or car via Perth and Stirling.

Dalmally

Family House of Prayer
Craig Lodge Tel: 01838 200216
Dalmally Fax: 01838 200622
Argyll PA33 1AR e-mail: mail@craiglodge.org
Website: www.craiglodge.org

Roman Catholic
This is an unusual family-based house of retreat and prayer. After a religious conversion at Medjugorje in 1985, the entire family converted their home into a centre of almost continuous devotional prayer and ministry. Several others have now joined them, and they are in the process of gaining official recognition from the Roman Catholic Church as a new ecclesial community, some of whose members will be under vows. The house, a traditional country one, sits on the banks of the River Orchy with mountains all around. It is a place of outstanding beauty. The community welcomes all-comers from all backgrounds and traditions for guided retreats and weekends of refreshment, healing and renewal. There are also youth conferences and private retreats for clergy and religious. The accommodation and food are homely and comfortable, in keeping with the family atmosphere. People of all generations ramble in and out, with teenagers as much involved in the domestic chores and the devotions as everyone else. There is a chapel where the Eucharist is exposed for adoration throughout the day. Divine Office is prayed morning and evening, and the Rosary three times a day.

Open: February to end November. Receives everyone.
Rooms: 4 singles, 18 doubles. Accommodation for up to 40 people, mostly shared rooms.
Facilities: Disabled, garden, library, guest lounge, TV, payphone.
Spiritual Help: Personal talks, shared prayer.
Guests Admitted to: Unrestricted access.
Meals: Whole food. Vegetarian and special diets.
Special Activities: Guided retreats, private retreats, healing weekends, youth conferences.
Situation: Very quiet, surrounded by mountains.
Maximum Stay: Open.
Bookings: Letter, fax, telephone 9–5p.m.
Charges: £30 per night full board. B&B £15.
Access: Train: Dalmaly Street (pick-up can be arranged). Bus from Glasgow. Car from Glasgow on A82 to Oban.

Dundonnell

Shanti Griha
Scoraig Peninsula
Dundonnell
Garve IV23 2RE

Tel: 01854 633260
e-mail: shantigriha@hotmail.com
Website: www.shantigriha.com

Eco-spirituality
This is a remote place that can only be reached on foot or by boat. Shanti Griha, which means 'House of Peace', is set in several acres of garden and is a restored and extended croft house. Spring water and electricity from a windmill tells you that this is where eco-spirituality is taken seriously. There is a bright and large meditation room, and there are regular courses in astanga yoga, Thai massage, meditation and Buddhism.

Open: Receives, men, women.
Rooms: 1 single, 2 twins, 1 double, 1 family room. No smoking.
Facilities: Workshops, meditation room, guest lounge.
Spiritual Help: Meditation, yoga, tai chi, massage.
Guests Admitted to: Everywhere in public guest areas.
Meals: Vegetarian. Special diets possible.
Special Activities: Guided group retreats, individual retreats, self-directed retreats all possible.
Situation: At the foot of Ben Ghobhlach, looking out onto Little Loch Broom towards the open sea.
Maximum Stay: By arrangement.
Bookings: Letter, e-mail, telephone.
Charges: Currently £30 per person per night full board. Groups self-catering.
Access: Bus to Ullapool, pick-up by arrangement.

> It is because Man is able to say 'No' that his 'Yes' is so full of resonance.
> PAUL EVDOKIMOV

Dunblane

Scottish Churches House
Kirk Street
Dunblane
Perthshire FKI5 OAJ

Tel: 01786 823588
Fax: 01786 825844
e-mail: reservations@scottishchurcheshouse.org
Website:www.scottishchurcheshouse.org

Inter-denominational – Ecumenical

This is a conference centre belonging to all the mainstream churches in Scotland, but daily retreats are organised for individuals. The centre consists of a row of converted and renovated eighteenth-century cottages and a church along two sides of the Cathedral Square. The atmosphere is quiet and homely.

Open: All year except Christmas and New Year. Receives everyone.
Rooms: 8 singles, 21 doubles.
Facilities: Disabled, conferences, garden, guest lounge, payphone.
Spiritual Help: Personal talks, spiritual direction, meditation, directed study during planned retreats – all as requested.
Guests Admitted to: Unrestricted access.
Meals: Everyone eats together. Whole food/vegetarian. Special diets.
Special Activities: Planned programme – send for details.
Situation: Quiet, in a Cathedral close.
Maximum Stay: Open.
Bookings: Letter, fax, telephone – best time 9.40a.m.–2.30p.m.
Charges: Programme ranges from about £20 to £100 plus. Ask for latest charges.
Access: Rail, bus or car.

Edinburgh

★

House of Prayer
8 Nile Grove
Edinburgh EH10 4RF

Tel: 01314 471772
Fax: 01314 469122
e-mail: nilegrove@rscj.freeserve.co.uk
Website: www.rscj.freeserve.co.uk

Roman Catholic – Inter-denominational

Located in one of Scotland's few moneyed and middle-class suburban areas, the House of Prayer embraces all denominations and tries to promote a non-sensational Christian spiritualism. Meditation is encouraged and there are two chapels. The community and the retreat team are members of the Society of the Sacred Heart of Jesus, an international congregation for women. Rooms are clean and bright, and surrounding the house is a fine garden. There are plenty of courses to choose from in the programme, such as 30-day retreats, women in scripture and tradition, Taize prayer days, work with icons, and a day on the Bhagavad Gita. Individually guided retreats in the tradition of the Ignatian Exercises are available. **Highly Recommended.**

Open: All year except Christmas, Easter, August. Receives men, women, young people.
Rooms: 5 singles, 1 double.
Facilities: Chapel, conferences, garden, library, guest lounge.
Spiritual Help: Personal talks, group sharing, meditation, directed study.

Guests Admitted to: Unrestricted except for community areas.
Meals: Taken in guest dining room. Home-cooked food. Vegetarian and special diets.
Special Activities: Planned programme. Day events. Brochure available.
Situation: Quiet suburb in a city.
Maximum Stay: 8 days.
Bookings: Letter, fax, e-mail, telephone.
Charges: Ranges from about £25–£30 per day full board to about £200 for an 8-day event. Concessions possible. See brochure.
Access: Train or car to Edinburgh. Local buses from Waverley Station.

The Salisbury Centre
2 Salisbury Road   Tel: 0131 667 5438
Edinburgh EH16 5AB   (10a.m.–7.30p.m. Monday to Friday)
e-mail: office@salcentre.ndo.co.uk

Mind Body Spirit – Holistic education
The Salisbury Centre was founded in 1973 with the aim of establishing a centre in the city where people could find opportunities for spiritual and psychological growth. A handsome Georgian house, set in organic gardens, the centre is a peaceful haven where classes run throughout the day, evening and over the weekend. There is a warm, homely feeling throughout the house – which has a bright, spacious first-level studio space, a pottery, smaller treatment/group rooms, a library overlooking the gardens and a kitchen where teas and coffees are available. Despite the busy programme, there is a real sense of peace and calm here, created in part by the small residential community that live and work in the centre. There are weekly classes in meditation, yoga, tai chi, creative writing, Pilates, pottery, stained glass, circle dancing and voice work. Weekend workshops vary but typically include astroshamanism, overtone singing, storytelling, healing and many other Mind Body Spirit topics led by experienced national and international teachers. Costs range from £35 to about £45 currently.

Elgin

Pluscarden Abbey
Elgin   Tel: 01343 890257
Moray IV30 8UA   Fax: 01343 890258
e-mail: monks@pluscardenabbey.org
Website: www.pluscardenabbey.org

Roman Catholic
Pluscarden is unique in being the only mediaeval monastery in Britain still housing a monastic community. The complete Benedictine Divine Office is sung in Latin to Gregorian chant – wonderfully well too. You can buy a CD to take home if you want. The monks do market gardening, book binding, and work with bees. Year by year the reputation of these most excellent men and their gifts of hospitality increases. If you are a man and want a retreat that is truly monastic with great depth in the prayer life, then go to Pluscarden. But if all you want is a rest from a troubled and busy world, then go here too for it *is* a place apart. As to coming here as a woman guest, the story is a little different. First of all, women guests are accommodated in a separate guest

house, St Scholastic's, where they cater for themselves in a smallish kitchen – the Abbey provides some basic foodstuffs, otherwise women have to bring in their own food and cook it. That can be a bit chaotic if more than three or four are trying to prepare supper at the same time! That said, most difficulties are overcome with flexibility and humour. Out of the twenty-six guests rooms, twelve are in the women's guest house, and two of those have two bunks in each. This can be unrestful, because if the other female guests are not in the mood to be silent, there is not much you can do about it. However, it would be fine if not many were staying or all were on quiet retreat. Nevertheless, the guest master monk is very solicitous and as concerned about the comfort of the women guests as about the men. With their dedication to prayer and meditative study, the monks are gentle of attitude and most welcoming. They are a lively group of men who have made a place of gladness and developed a beautiful liturgy in praise of God. Guests are admitted to the side chapels of the Abbey and to the ornamental garden in front of St Benedicts. Facilities include a quite well stocked shop. People who come here normally return. **Highly Recommended.**

Open: All year. Receives everyone (over 16 years of age unless accompanied by an adult).
Rooms: 26 singles, 2 doubles.
Facilities: Disabled, garden, library, guest lounge, guest telephone, house telephone in female retreat quarters (01343 890375).
Spiritual Help: Personal talks, spiritual counselling.
Guests Admitted to: Chapel, church.
Meals: Men eat together at lunch and supper, otherwise taken in guest house. Traditional food. Vegetarian and simple special diets. Women self-catering.
Special Activities: Some events.
Situation: Very far north and very quiet.
Maximum Stay: 2 weeks.
Bookings: Letter, fax, e-mail, telephone.
Charges: Donations.
Access: train: Elgin. Car: A96, B9010, follow signs.

Eskdalemuir

**Kagyu Samye Ling
Monastery and Tibetan Centre
Eskdalemuir
Langholm
Dumfries DG13 0QL**

Tel: 01387 373232
Fax: 01387 373223
e-mail: scotland@samyeling.org
Website: www.samyeling.org

Buddhist – Tibetan Kagyu tradition
Here is a very unusual and very peaceful place: a Tibetan monastery set in the rolling hills of southern Scotland. Founded in 1967, Kagyu Samye Ling was the first major Tibetan Buddhist centre in Europe and it is still regarded as the mother of the many Kagyu centres that have been established since. The temple is magnificent and is the heart of the community's life of daily prayer and practice. Guests are welcome to attend any of the meditation and prayer sessions, but some knowledge of the particular tradition of Vajrayana Buddhism is necessary to participate in the prayers. Vajrayana Buddhism

relies strongly on the visualisation of deities in transforming the mental poisons that cause us suffering. Learning such methods takes time and needs careful preparation and guidance. Lama Yeshe Losal is the Abbot and retreat master and he, together with the experienced sangha of ordained monks and nuns, undertakes such instruction and support. For those who are looking for a rest, Samye Ling offers a wide range of options. From working in the organic garden to helping out in the kitchens, from taking part in weekend courses to relaxing in the Tibetan tea rooms, there is plenty to do – or not do! There are lovely walks within the grounds and further away, and whether it's a meditative stroll around the stupa or a hearty stride into the hills, the benefits of a little exercise and fresh air are all part of life here. There is no expectation or pressure, and guests are free to choose their own programme of activity within the framework of the Five Golden Rules. These Rules safeguard the well-being of everyone and are: 'to protect life and refrain from killing; to respect other's property and refrain from stealing; to speak the truth and refrain from lying; to encourage health and refrain from all intoxicants; to respect others and refrain from sexual misconduct'. Less than a ¼ mile from the main centre is Purelands, a smaller independent centre where longer retreats are held and where groups may hire the space for their own work. Here the atmosphere is calm and peaceful, and more conducive to focusing inwards. It can get pretty busy at the main centre, especially in the summer. As well as the ongoing programme of building development and the continuing programme of courses, teachings, empowerments, there is a flourishing programme of humanitarian activity. The founder, Dr Akong Tulku Rinpoche, has set up initiatives to help the poor and homeless in the UK, Tibet and other countries. He also founded Tara Rokpa therapy, a system of psychotherapy that works with the principles of Buddhism to heal patterns of emotional and mental suffering. For those with more serious mental health problems, Lothlorien offers long-term support and residential care in a therapeutic community setting. Samye Ling welcomes people from all faiths in the understanding that Buddhism is a way of life rather than a religion. Nevertheless, there is a strong tradition of Tibetan Buddhism underpinning the work at this centre and a commitment to preserve the culture and heritage of Tibet. No one is expected to adopt Buddhism, but the opportunities to learn more about this profound philosophy and spiritual tradition are there for anyone who is open and interested. **Highly Recommended.**

Open: All year. Receives everyone but not families.
Rooms: 60 singles, 7 twins, 20 dormitories, camping. Bring bedding and
    equipment if you are camping, as these are not provided.
Facilities: Disabled, garden, guest telephone (01387 373227).
Spiritual Help: Personal retreat direction, weekend courses. Short retreats at
    Purelands Retreat Centre.
Guests Admitted to: Unrestricted access.
Meals: Everyone eats together. Simple vegetarian food only.
Special Activities: A big planned programme of events, courses and study –
    send for the brochure, which is among the best available.
Situation: Rather isolated, quiet but busy in summer. There can be lots of
    people visiting here.
Maximum Stay: No limit.
Bookings: Letter, fax, e-mail telephone 9a.m.–noon, 1.30–6p.m.

Charges: Dormitory bed £16, twin £21, single £27, camping with own tent £13. These rates are for accommodation per night and include meals. Weekend courses about £50 per person, including food and accommodation.
Access: Train: Carlisle, then bus. Bus: Hawick, then taxi. Car: via M6, A7.

Associated UK Kagyu Samye Dzongs and Rokpa Centres

KSD London	020 7928 5447
Tara Rokpa Edinburgh	0131 313 0304
Tara Rokpa Norfolk	01263 721493
Rokpa Glasgow	0141 332 9950
Rokpa Dundee	01382 872020
KSD Sandhurst	01344 762392
KSD Northamptonshire	01536 522395
KSD North West	01925 268322
KSD Cardiff	02920 306138

Falkland

Tabor Retreat Centre
Key House High Street
Falkland   Tel: 01337 857705
Fife KY15 7BU   e-mail: lynda@keyhouse.org
                                Website: www.keyhouse.org

Ecumenical
Tabor, a very pretty eighteenth-century house, is in the High Street next door to Falkland Palace, and situated in a garden with views of the Lemon Hills. It is an ecumenical house welcoming men and women of all traditions or none. The name of the centre comes from Mount Tabor, where Jesus chose to be apart for a time – a place of change. As the resident community is small, an informal atmosphere prevails and there is a mixture of silence and family-style life. This is a popular place, so you need to book well in advance.

Open: All year Tuesday to Sunday. Receives men, women, young people, groups.
Rooms: 4 doubles but can be booked as singles.
Facilities: Chapel, garden, guest lounge.
Spiritual Help: Personal talks, spiritual direction, meditation, personal retreat direction.
Guests Admitted to: Unrestricted access.
Meals: Everyone eats together – in the kitchen usually. Whole food, simple, mainly vegetarian. Special diets.
Special Activities: Planned programme – send for brochure.
Situation: Quiet, in a conservation village.
Maximum Stay: 5 nights.
Bookings: Letter, e-mail, telephone.
Charges: By donation – suggested £27.50 full board.
Access: Train, bus, and car are all possible – see brochure.

Firth

House of Living Water
6 Leaside
Firth
Mossbank
Shetland ZE2 9TF

Tel: 01806 242351/242081
e-mail: pat@pkpusniak.fsnet.co.uk
Website: www.livingwaterhouse.co.uk

Ecumenical Christian
In the lovely surroundings of the Shetland islands, this is a small, very quiet self-catering house. There is room for just three people. This is a good place to rest, be calm and let your heart open to God.

Forres

The Findhorn Foundation
The Park
Forres
Morayshire IV36 3TZ

Tel: 01309 690311
Fax: 01309 691301
e-mail: enquiries@findhorn.org
Website: www.findhorn.org

Mind Body Spirit – Non-denominational – Spiritual education centre
This is a well-publicised and famous place and can get very crowded in the summertime. The community was founded in 1962 by three people, who believed in the principle that the source of life, or God, is accessible to each person and that nature, including earth, is intelligence and part of a much greater plan. Nature spirits, or devas, are said to have allowed the community to raise vegetables and exotic flowers in a barren soil of sand and gravel. Today Findhorn is a large and highly organised operation and one of the largest private communities in Britain, maybe even in the world. Enthusiasm, harmony and love are the precepts by which the community tries to work, and there is a strong emphasis on meditation. The belief at Findhorn is that humanity is in an evolutionary expansion of consciousness, and they seek to develop new ways of creating a better world in which to live. Some 15,000 visitors are welcomed here every year, and the Findhorn reputation is known internationally. Courses of all descriptions, lengths and types run throughout the year. Subject specialities include alternative lifestyles and technology, meditation, food and gardening, health and healing, arts and crafts, inner process, prayer, and self-expression. Such is the popularity of this place that accommodation usually needs to be booked months in advance. It is definitely not a place for a private retreat as understood in the Christian or Buddhist traditions. New Bold House, part of the community, offers a live-work-meditate lifestyle for those who wish to share it. They have a separate programme and charges. There are also secondary island retreat centres of the Foundation, which are included in the brochure information. Visit their website to find out more details of what is on offer at this very popular place.

Open: All year. Receives men, women, families. Children welcome if supervised.
Rooms: About 130 bed spaces. Ask what is on offer when you book but there are singles and doubles, also chalets, caravans and campsites. No smoking.
Facilities: Many and varied facilities, including a visitors centre and shopping. Disabled, conferences, garden, park, library, payphone, large indoor space, several smaller working spaces.

Spiritual Help: Personal talks, meditation. Certain courses on offer to workshop participants.

Guests Admitted to: Most places, including the sanctuaries when on a programme.

Meals: Meals include vegetarian provision and certain special diets (wheat-free and sugar-free for example).

Special Activities: Planned programme of events – send for brochure.

Situation: Quiet but busy – those seeking silence may be out of luck here.

Maximum Stay: According to programme and by arrangement.

Bookings: Letter, telephone.

Charges: Vary and can run over £400 per week full board – but there is a fixed price system. Credit cards accepted.

Access: Train, coach, car, air all possible. See brochure for details.

Garvald

Sancta Maria Abbey and Abbey Guest House
Nunraw Garvald
Haddington
East Lothian EH41 4LW   Tel: 01620 830228

Roman Catholic

This is a very popular monastery. The accommodation is in a guest house some distance from the Abbey itself and is limited to about thirty people. Sometimes guests may be asked to share a room. The guest house is run in keeping with the contemplative nature of a monastic life. The surrounding countryside is very beautiful and the Abbey runs a large agricultural establishment. This is a place of silence and deep spirituality where you may truly put aside the burdens of everyday living and open yourself to the benefits of silence and solitude. The purpose in coming here is to seek God.

> Our hearts were made for you, O God, and will not rest until they rest in you.
> SAINT AUGUSTINE

Open: All year except February. Receives men, women, young people, families, groups, non-retreatants. Children welcome.

Rooms: 9 singles, 8 doubles, dormitory rooms, 4 family rooms.

Facilities: Park, library, guest lounge, payphone, direct dialing.

Spiritual Help: Personal talks, spiritual direction.

Guests Admitted to: Chapel, church.

Meals: Traditional simple food taken in the guest house.

Special Activities: None.

Situation: Very quiet, in the countryside. Woodlands, lakes, moorland, farm land.

Maximum Stay: 1 week.

Bookings: Letter, telephone.

Charges: Donation.

Access: Car.

Glasgow

Ignatian Spirituality Centre
7 Woodside Place
Glasgow G3 7QF

Tel: 0141 354 0077
Fax: 0141 354 0099

Roman Catholic – Ecumenical
Training courses, retreats and events based on the spiritual exercises of St Ignatius of Loyola for all who seek God in their lives are what this retreat place is about. There are day and evening events as well as longer courses. The centre is in the middle of a major city – but even here you can make a day retreat in peace. **This is a non-residential centre.**

Mount Carmel Retreat Centre
61 Hamilton Avenue
Pollokshields
Glasgow G41 4HA

Tel: 0141 427 0794

Roman Catholic – Inter-denominational
Run by Carmelites, this retreat centre is open to all denominations. There is a programme of retreats and spiritual direction, and counselling is available on request. With some thirty-three single rooms plus doubles, it is open to conferences and group retreats as well as individual private ones.

Hawick

Whitchester Christian Guest House and Retreat Centre
Borthaugh
Hawick
Roxburghshire TD9 7LN

Christian
Write for information on organised and private retreats here.

Isle of Arran

Holy Island
Lamlash Bay
Isle of Arran
Scotland KA27 8GB

Tel: 01387 373232 (extension 28)
Fax: 01387 373223
e-mail: office@holyisland.org
Website: www.holyisland.org

Interfaith
This is a very special place – an environmental and spiritual sanctuary that was once the home of the sixth-century Celtic hermit St Molaise and which is now under the guardianship of the Tibetan Buddhists of Kagyu Samye Ling Monastery (see entry in this section). Holy Island has been designated a UK Sacred Site and is home to a rich natural heritage of flora and fauna, including seabirds, wild ponies, Sanaan goats and Soay sheep. The coastal waters, warmed by the Gulf Stream, attract seals, dolphins and the odd basking shark – jellyfish too are common, so swimming is not advisable in many areas. St Molaise's cave still exists, marking the beginning of an informal pilgrimage

walk linking the two ends of the island. A healing spring and rock paintings depicting Tibetan Buddhist deities and saints bring the traditions of Christianity and Buddhism together in easy, harmonious relationship. The Buddhists acquired Holy Island in 1992 and have made every effort to protect the natural environment and to re-establish a living tradition of spiritual practice. At the south end of the island, lighthouse cottages have been refurbished as a cloistered retreat, and twelve women are currently participating in the traditional Tibetan Buddhist three-year, three-month retreat. Visitors to the island are asked to respect the privacy of this secluded area. At the north end of the island, new buildings have been added to an old farmhouse to form an attractive courtyard complex for the new Centre for World Peace and Health. So far the project has cost some £2.5 million and everything has been done to high standards. Still in its infancy, the centre offers retreat and conference facilities for interfaith, complementary health and environmental groups. Individuals are welcome for private retreat, but priority is given to groups during the summer months. Accommodation is spacious, modern, comfortable and light, and the vegetarian meals are delicious (some of the produce is grown on the island). There is a delightful Peace Garden, where rock paintings, a labyrinth peace walk, meditation corners, herbs and shrubs combine to soothe the senses and calm the mind. Guests and visitors are asked to respect the Five Golden Rules, which are there to protect the well-being of all sentient beings and the island's pure environment. These are: 'to protect life and refrain from killing; to respect other's property and refrain from stealing; to speak truthfully and refrain from lying; to encourage health and refrain from all intoxicants; to respect others and refrain from sexual misconduct'. Whether you come alone or as part of a group, for a day visit, a course or for a private retreat, Holy Island will not disappoint. Be prepared to wait to come on or off the island – weather conditions are renowned for disrupting ferry crossings! Lama Yeshe Losal, the Abbot of Samye Ling Monastery and director of this project, has said about this place: 'May every wonderful and wholesome thing arise here and may its goodness and happiness spread throughout the entire world.'

Open: All year except winter when ferry crossing is too difficult. Receives men, women, young people **over 16 years of age**, groups. No smoking. No alcohol. No drugs.
Rooms: 4 doubles, 30 singles, 24 dormitory places, camping.
Facilities: Camping. Conference. Library.
Spiritual Help: Personal retreat direction, meditation. **Read the programme brochure.**
Guests Admitted to: Unrestricted access.
Meals: Everyone eats together. **Vegetarian food only.**
Special Activities: Planned programme – send for brochure.
Situation: A beautiful sacred Scottish island.
Maximum Stay: Open.
Bookings: Letter, e-mail, telephone 9a.m.–12.30p.m. Monday to Friday.
Charges: Vary, but single about £40 per person per night, twin about £30 per person, single occupancy of a twin room in off-season about £25, dormitory about £20 per person per night. These rates all full board.
Access: Ask for instructions from the Monastery when you book.

Isle of Cumbrae

Cathedral of the Isles and College of the Holy Spirit   Tel: 01475 530353
Millport   Fax: 01475 530204
Isle of Cumbrae KA28 OHE   e-mail: tccumbrae@argyll.anglican.org
                                               Website: www.argyll-anglican.org

Scottish Episcopalian (Anglican)

The small but very beautiful island of Cumbrae enjoys wonderful views of the surrounding mountains and islands and is known for its marvellous bird life and wild flowers. Easily accessible by public transport, with a ferry crossing of only ten minutes, the College, built in 1851, is attached to one of Britain's smallest cathedrals. Cathedral and College stand in 8 acres of gardens, fields and woods, and present an appearance of tranquillity and peace. The somewhat ageing accommodation is undergoing extensive renovation to provide washbasins in all rooms and further bathroom facilities. Apart from a modest programme of themed retreats, people can come on private retreats, guided or otherwise, though there is more of a family guest house atmosphere in the summer months – for example, children banging up and down the corridors. There is a prayer-cabin in the grounds, and you can join in the daily rhythm of morning and evening prayer. Food is well prepared and cheerfully served in a refectory. The beds are reasonably comfortable. Recent programmes have included such themes as stress management, the hospitality of Jesus, and marriage renewal. In some ways, we felt the place was problematic as a spiritual retreat centre, as we felt it had rather a cool atmosphere and seemed somewhat uninterested in caring for guests. Admittedly there was extensive building renovation going on and also they run the place as a guest house in the summer, registered with the Scottish Tourist Board, and that probably gives it more of a commercial business-like flavour. The upgrading of many retreat places in more commercial times has, in some cases, resulted in a change in the nature of the welcome and care.

> Happiness cannot be found through great effort and willpower, but is already there, in relaxation and letting go.
>
> VEN LAMA GENDUN RINPOCHE

Open: All year except Christmas. Receives everyone.
Rooms: 19 bedrooms – singles, doubles, twins, family.
Facilities: Conferences, garden, library, guest lounge, TV, guest telephone.
Spiritual Help: Personal talks, spiritual direction. Personal retreat direction by prior arrangement only.
Guests Admitted to: Church, guest areas.
Meals: Taken in guest house. Traditional food. Vegetarian and special diets.
Special Activities: A short programme over the year – send for leaflet.
Situation: During the summer tourist months it can be quite busy here – otherwise quiet. 8 acres of grounds and only 5 minutes to the sea.
Maximum Stay: 10 days.
Bookings: Letter, fax, telephone. **Note: B&B guests who are not on retreat are received here during the school holidays.**
Charges: B&B £18–£20, half board £29–£30, full board £35–36. Courses £175–£235.
Access: Train, then ferry. Car: Glasgow/Largs, then ferry.

Isle of Erraid

Isle of Erraid Centre
Isle of Erraid
Fionnphort, Isle of Mull
Argyll PA66 6BN

Tel: 01681 700384
e-mail: bookings@erraid.fslife.uk
Website: www.findhorn.org/erraid

Non-sectarian spiritual community

A tiny island close to the ancient Isle of Iona, Erraid offers a mini-paradise of golden beaches, moorland and rocky shoreline. Here you can unwind for a week or two, living with the small resident community and participating in meditation, work, play and celebration. This is an island for the whole family – children will love the freedom and adventure of the natural world in an environment that is safe and contained. The Isle of Erraid belongs to the Findhorn Community but is an independent project. If you're looking for simplicity and a chance to live close to the elements, Erraid is very much a place to bear in mind.

Open: All year except mid-July–August. Receives men, women, young people, families, groups, non-retreatants.
Rooms: 10 singles, 2 doubles.
Facilities: Garden, lounge, TV, guest telephone.
Spiritual Help: Meditation, communal working.
Guests Admitted to: Unrestricted access.
Meals: Taken together. Organic food.
Special Activities: Mass often daily.
Situation: Isolated, beautiful.
Maximum Stay: 1 year.
Bookings: Letter, telephone about 6p.m.
Charges: £90–£260 – the level of contribution is chosen by the guest.
Access: From Mainland Oban to Isle of Mull to Fionnphort to Erraid.

Isle of Iona

Cnoc a' Chalmain
Roman Catholic House of Prayer
Isle of Iona
Argyll PA76 6SP

Tel/Fax: 01681 700369
e-mail: mail@catholic-iona.com
Website: www.catholic-iona.com

Roman Catholic

Founded in 1997 as a place of quiet retreat on Iona for pilgrims of all faiths, Cnoc a' Chalmain (which means 'The Hill of the Dove) is a small house up a rough track on a hillside overlooking the Sound of Iona. There is an oratory, where the Blessed Sacrament is reserved, and which is open to all for quiet prayer and meditation. By maintaining a Eucharist centre and reserved accommodation for visiting priests, Cnoc a' Chalmain ensures that there is daily Mass or Communion on Iona throughout the year. It collaborates with the Iona Community to offer these services at St Michael's Chapel in the Abbey on Sundays from Easter to October. This is a very peaceful house in a beautiful location away from the busy world. The welcome is warm and friendly.

Open: All year.
Rooms: Singles and twins, with shared bathroom facilities.

Facilities: Oratory, guest lounge.
Spiritual Help: Eucharistic services. Personal talks can be arranged.
Guests Admitted to: Whole house, oratory.
Meals: Taken together. Simple home cooking. Vegetarians catered for with advance notice.
Special Activities: None.
Situation: Quiet, on a hillside, overlooking Sound of Iona and Isle of Mull. Very beautiful.
Maximum Stay: By arrangement.
Bookings: Letter, e-mail, telephone.
Charges: £35 a day full board.
Access: Oban to Iona (2½ hours): ferry from Mull; then ferry to Iona; then 5-minute walk. (Glasgow to Oban 3 hours.) Good instructions in brochure.

Duncraig
Isle of Iona PA76 6SP　　　　　　　　　Tel: 01681 700202

Inter-denominational
This is a plain old house in a simple but historically spiritual setting offering a quiet and relaxing place for a private retreat.

Open: March–October. Receives men, women, groups.
Rooms: 2 singles, 2 doubles.
Facilities: Garden, library, guest lounge.
Spiritual Help: Personal talks, group sharing, meditation, opportunity to be quiet. Silence 10.30p.m.–9.15a.m.
Guests Admitted to: Unrestricted access.
Meals: Everyone eats together. Traditional/vegetarian food. Self-catering facilities.
Special Activities: None.
Situation: Very quiet and somewhat remote. A chapel, church and oratory are available on the island.
Maximum Stay: Minimum stay 3 days.
Bookings: Letter, telephone.
Charges: £30–£40 full board.
Access: Train: Glasgow to Oban, then ferry to Mull. Car: Oban, then ferry.

Iona Community
The Abbey
Isle of Iona　　　　　　　　　　　　　
Argyll PA76 6SN　　　　　　　　　Tel: 01681 700404
　　　　　　　　　　　　　　　　　Fax: 01681 700460
　　　　　　　　　　　　e-mail: ionacomm@iona.org.uk
　　　　　　　　　　　　Website: www.iona.org.uk

Christian – Ecumenical
On the remote and holy island of Iona stands the ancient monastic building of The Abbey, restored by the late Rev George Macleod and now home to the world-renowned Iona Community. The Iona Community is an ecumenical movement of ordained and lay Christians and welcomes more than 150,000 people to this ancient holy island every year. People come from all over the

world and from all walks of life to share in the daily work and worship of the community. The essence of Iona's approach is the integration of spirituality and social concern. With a strong emphasis on social justice, there have been controversial times in the community's history, but it continues to show courage and conviction. It was on this tiny, peaceful island in 563 CE that the Irish St Columba began his mission to bring Christianity to Scotland. A Benedictine Abbey was built here in the Middle Ages, and until the Reformation this offered hospitality to pilgrims. The present Iona Community began by rebuilding of the cloistral buildings of the Abbey – 'the place of the common life' – in the mid-twentieth century, then continued with a mission of work for political and social change and the renewal of the church. The Abbey itself is splendid: very little of the original Benedictine monastery remains, but the rebuilding of The Abbey in traditional style means that the cloisters, the refectory and the church itself are reminiscent of the lives of the monks who once lived here. The library is very special – rather like the cabin of a ship and full of interesting tomes. St Columba's Shrine, too, is a place for a moment of quiet prayer and reflection. Most of the members of the ecumenical Iona Community are dispersed throughout Britain pursuing their vocation in their daily lives. Celtic spirituality is a strong influence on the style of worship, which expresses the ecumenical and inclusive nature of the Community. Private retreats are possible in November, with the chance to join in daily worship in the Abbey, share chores and take turns in leading services. This is not a particularly quiet place. It is filled with many visitors and is an active facility, which involves everyone in all aspects of Community life, including daily chores. People come to join the Community for a minimum of three nights, which allows guests to get to know one another, eating together, doing chores and taking part in discussions. The Iona Community also runs the Camas Adventure Centre (see Isle of Mull entry) and the MacLeod Centre (see this section). In general, Iona is a place for finding a sense of belonging to God through community and shared activity. **Highly Recommended.**

Open: March–October and Christmas. Receives everyone.
Rooms: Total accommodation is for up to 45 people – twins, triples, etc.
Facilities: Library, guest telephone, common room.
Spiritual Help: Group sharing meditation. There is no individual support although care for one another is facilitated.
Guests Admitted to: Unrestricted access. Work of Community.
Meals: Everyone eats together. Vegetarian/whole food mainly. Special diets.
Special Activities: Planned programme. Lots going on here, from daily worship and Scottish-style social events to a pilgrimage around the island's sacred places.
Situation: Remote historic, sacred island with a small crofting population. A place of outstanding natural beauty.
Maximum Stay: Normally 6 nights.
Bookings: Letter, telephone weekdays.
Charges: Current weekly rate adults £210, low income/16–21 years of age £109. Daily rate adults £35.50, low income/16–21 years of age £20. Special rates for children.
Access: Train: Glasgow to Oban, then ferry to Isle of Mull, then bus or car across Mull (37 miles), then ferry to Iona.

Macleod Centre
Isle of Iona
Argyll PA76 6SN

Tel: 01681 700404
Fax: 01681 700460
e-mail: ionacomm@iona.org.uk
Website: www.iona.org.uk

Christian – Ecumenical

Run by the Iona Community and named after the Community's founder, the centre embodies the late Rev George Macleod's vision of building community among people of differing backgrounds, ages, abilities and attitude. It welcomes youth clubs, school classes, and church and community groups – all of whom live in dormitory accommodation and take part in the daily tasks of running the centre as well as in their own group work. Among the facilities are a multi-purpose community room, a craft room, sitting areas, a library and a quiet room. There are plenty of toys and games for younger visitors and sports equipment for the more active. This is a lively, spirited place, and fun and happiness are very much a part of the expression of a spiritual life here.

Open: Mid-March to mid-October and Christmas. Receives everyone.
Rooms: 2 singles for group leaders. Dormitories for up to 50.
Facilities: Library, guest lounge, craft room, payphone.
Spiritual Help: Group sharing, meditation, sharing in community life. Pastoral care where needed from in-coming group leaders.
Guests Admitted to: Unrestricted access. Work of Community.
Meals: Everyone eats together. Mostly vegetarian food. Special diets.
Special Activities: Planned programme – send for brochure.
Situation: Remote historic, sacred island with a small crofting population. A place of outstanding natural beauty.
Maximum Stay: 2 weeks.
Bookings: Letter, telephone during office hours.
Charges: See brochure. Current rates £190 per week adult, £99 per week low income/16–21-year-old.
Access: Train: Glasgow to Oban, then ferry to Isle of Mull, then bus or car across Mull (37 miles), then ferry to Iona.

Isle of Mull

Camas Adventure Camp
Ardfenaig
Bunessan
Island of Mull
Argyll PA67 6DX

Tel: 01681 700404 (Camas Co-ordinator)
Fax: 01681 700460
e-mail: ionacomm@iona.org.uk

Ecumenical

Camas is a stone-built salmon fishing station about 3 miles from Iona and a short walk over a moor. With no electricity, light comes from oil lamps, wood fires, sunshine and stars. Here is an opportunity to experience the simple life – with its challenges and rewards. 'The peace and beauty of Camas create an atmosphere where the mind can wander and the body revive – a special place.' The programme includes abseiling, rafting, camping, walks and other outdoor pursuits, as well as writing, the creative arts, music and ceilidhs. The centre is an ideal setting for team building, and there are weeks between May and October available for this work. Its commitment to inclusive spirituality makes for a welcoming place, but those committed to justice and peace issues will find it particularly inspiring.

Open: May to September. Receives men, women, young people, groups.
Rooms: Dormitories.
Facilities: Very simple lifestyle – see the brochure.
Spiritual Help: Group sharing, meditation, benefits of a simple lifestyle.
Guests Admitted to: Shared life and work of the Community.
Meals: Everyone eats together. Vegetarian whole food.
Special Activities: Planned programme – send for brochure.
Situation: Remote historic, sacred island with a small crofting population. A place of outstanding natural beauty.
Maximum Stay: 6 days.
Bookings: Letter, telephone.
Charges: See brochure for current rates.
Access: Train: Glasgow to Oban, then ferry to Isle of Mull, then bus or car across Mull (37 miles), then ferry to Iona.

Kilgraston

Garden Cottage
Kilgraston
Bridge of Earn
Perthshire PH2 9HN

Tel: 01738 812194
Fax: 01738 813585
e-mail: ssh-irs-bf@easynet.co.uk

Roman Catholic – Ecumenical
This small community of the Society of the Sacred Heart offers space for rest and spiritual refreshment in two small stone cottages run together, with the option of guided retreats, either in the Ignatian mode or inspired by the interconnectedness of Eastern and Western spiritualities. The community sees itself as ecumenical, aims to promote a holistic way of life and seeks to respond to the particular needs of individual retreatants. There are two small bedrooms and a shared bathroom for residents, as well as a little chapel where one can join in the morning and evening silent meditation periods. Eucharistic services can be arranged if desired. The accommodation is plain and comfortable; food is excellent and served in the community kitchen. For walks there is a formal garden in front, a large walled paddock with old fruit trees at the back, and rolling hills and woods over the road. At the end of the cottages there is a hermitage, and there is an activities centre along one side of the walled paddock. The intention is to create space for day and weekend workshops in yoga, meditation, dance and dance therapy, and body awareness. Professional counselling and reiki treatments will also be available. There is a profound spiritual peace about this centre; it would be a good place to go to. **Highly Recommended.**

Open: Most of year. Receives men, women.
Rooms: 2 rooms, hermitage.
Facilities: Comfortable rooms, sitting room, walks, garden, activities centre.
Spiritual Help: On-going spiritual direction, personal retreat direction, professional counselling, morning and evenings silent meditation periods.
Guests Admitted to: Everywhere except private community areas.

Meals: Taken together. Good honest food. Self-catering facilities.
Special Activities: Day and weekend workshops.
Situation: Secluded and peaceful.
Maximum Stay: 8 days or by arrangement.
Bookings: 9a.m.–5p.m.
Charges: Suggested donations: 8-day retreat £210, 6-day retreat £160, weekend retreat £55, day retreat with spiritual direction £20, spiritual direction £15 per session.
Access: Train or bus to Perth, where guests can be met. Car: ask for directions when booking.

Kilmuir

Coach House
Coach House Kilmuir Trust
Kilmuir
North Kessock
Inverness IVI IXG

Tel: 01463 731386
Fax: 01463 731386
e-mail: Coachhouse@kilmuir.fsbusiness.co.uk
Website: www.coachhousekilmuir.org

Christian-based open retreat centre
The Coach House is a lay retreat place where you can relax, reflect, study and recover some inner direction to face the strains of your ordinary life. We found it an extremely restful place, with spectacular views over the Moray Firth and marvellous woodland and beach walks – the wild flowers and bird life are renowned. The vision of the Coach House is to provide space for seekers exploring the interface between Christian and other faiths, and also the interaction between the psyche and the inner spirit. This approach offers a thoughtful bridge between Christianity and aspects of what we now call Mind Body Spirit spirituality. The work here is to provide the space and guidance for this to happen through individual retreats and workshops. Groups with an interest in these areas of spirituality also use the centre. Three types of retreat are usually available: an individually guided retreat based on the St Ignatius Exercises, a retreat based on spiritual or transpersonal counselling with one-to-one sessions, and a self-guided retreat with guidance if needed. On the retreat workshop side, there are a good variety of topics within the programme, ranging from topics such as *Celebrating Easter through Colour* to *Deepening Inner Wisdom, Sexuality and Spirituality, Working with Dreams, God's Creativity* and *The Mystic Heart of Scriptures*. Many people come here who cannot articulate exactly what it is they are searching for, as well as those with a particular faith tradition who wish to stretch the boundaries of their previous understanding of their beliefs. Individual direction is available if needed. Silence is observed during retreat times. This is an extremely caring and nurturing environment. **Highly Recommended.**

Open: March to December. Receives everyone.
Rooms: 4 singles, plus 1 single in cottage. 2 doubles.
Facilities: Garden, library, guest lounge.
Spiritual Help: Personal talks, group sharing, spiritual direction, personal retreat direction, meditation, directed study, workshops, bereavement and transpersonal counselling.
Guests Admitted to: Unrestricted access.

Meals: Everyone eats together. Traditional/vegetarian food. Special diets.
Special Activities: Planned programme – send for brochure.
Situation: Very quiet, overlooking the Firth, with woods, beach and hill walking at hand.
Maximum Stay: Open.
Bookings: Letter, e-mail, website, telephone 9.15a.m.– 8.30p.m.
Charges: Listed in current brochure. About £17 per day, £78 for two nights, £200 6-day residential retreat.
Access: Train, bus car and air all possible. Pick-up may be possible from arrival point.

Kilwinning

Smithstone House of Prayer
Dalry Road, Kilwinnning
North Ayrshire KA13 6PL

Tel: 01294 552515
Fax: 01294 559081

Roman Catholic – Ecumenical
This is a house and lodge built in the eighteenth and nineteenth centuries, and now a peaceful and beautifully situated retreat house of prayer run by the Sacred Heart Fathers. The aim here is to promote the spirituality of the heart. There is a programme of events that is available several times during the year. Accommodation is for up to forty people for a day event, while for overnight stays there are four singles and five twins.

Kinnoull

Redemptorist International Renewal Centre in Scotland
St Mary's
Hatton Road
Kinnoull
Perth PH2 7BP

Tel: 01738 624075
Fax: 01738 442071
e-mail: copiosa@aol.com
Website: www.kinnoull.org

Roman Catholic
This a large, rather institutional retreat centre overlooking Perth and enjoying peaceful seculsion. There is plenty of accommodation here, and a wide range of retreat and renewal courses are available, all of them firmly Christianity based. Some examples might be *The Bible in Liturgy*, *True Self-Esteem*, *Healing in the Spirit*, *Mercy and Forgiveness* and *Spirituality for the Third Age*. Individuals are welcome throughout the year.

Open: All year except Christmas. Receives everyone.
Rooms: 20 singles, 16 twins.
Facilities: Disabled, conferences, garden, library, guest lounge, TV, payphone (01738 636487/451813).
Spiritual Help: Personal talks, group sharing, meditation, directed study spiritual direction, personal retreat direction.
Guests Admitted to: Unrestricted access.
Meals: Everyone eats together. Traditional food. Vegetarian and special diets.
Special Activities: Planned programme – healing ministry, self-esteem development – send for leaflet.

Situation: Quiet, on edge of town.
Maximum Stay: Open.
Bookings: Letter, fax, e-mail, telephone 8a.m.–7p.m.
Charges: Enquire about charges when you book. Currently £38 per person per night full board.
Access: Train: Perth, then bus. Car: Perth, then via Hatton Road to the monastery.

Letterfourie

Letterfourie
Buckie
Banffshire AB56 2JP

Tel: 01542 832298
e-mail: Letterfourie1@sagainternet.co.uk

Inter-denominational
Letterfourie welcomes all people of all denominations or of none for self-organised retreats, conferences, workshops, church weekend, quiet restful breaks, renewal and just time for space and study. A residential Methodist preacher is willing to participate if needed. Letterfourie chapel is very handsome and seats sixty people. There are quiet rooms, and meeting rooms and suites. The place has quietness, harmony and a friendly way of hospitality. The house itself was built in 1773 and, since additions in 1806, has remained virtually unchanged except, of course, for the updating of necessary facilities. The house has connections with Bonnie Prince Charlie. This is altogether a 300-acre place, so there is plenty of space to walk – and find beauty and nature in abundance. In addition to the retreat programme, there is a programme for the Wool Works Studio at Letterfourie, so you may combine a workshop about things to do with wool with a retreat break – in fact the combination of manual work and prayer is a traditional way to reflect and find spiritual space within.

Open: All year. Receives everyone.
Rooms: 6 singles, 4 doubles. Family room with double and 2 singles.
Facilities: Chapel, conferences, garden, park, lounge, book stall, TV, guest telephone, extensive grounds.
Spiritual Help: Personal talks, group sharing, spiritual direction, personal retreat direction, directed study.
Guests Admitted to: Chapel, 300 acres of grounds, guest areas.
Meals: Traditional, whole food meals. Self-catering facilities.
Special Activities: Planned programme of events, plus spinning, natural dying, felting and beekeeping courses. Lots of walking if you like.
Situation: Adam mansion set in 300 acres, in countryside, on an organic farm.
Maximum Stay: None.
Bookings: Letter, fax, e-mail, telephone in evenings.
Charges: Currently £100 per person per week for accommodation, food extra at modest prices. Activity courses £48–£96 per week.
Access: Train: Keith. Bus: Keith. Coach: Aberdeen. Car: 2 miles south of A98/A942 junction.

Lochearnhead

Dhanakosa
Balquhidder
Lochearnhead
FK19 8PQ

Tel: 01877 384213
e-mail: dhanakosa@compuserve.com
Website: www.dhanakosa.com

Buddhist – Friends of the Western Buddhist Order
Situated on the shores of Loch Voil in a beautiful glen, Dhanakosa is in a haven of natural beauty and tranquillity. Formerly a small Highland hotel, Dhanakosa is now run by the Friends of the Western Buddhist Order as a retreat centre for Buddhists and non-Buddhists alike. Throughout the year, weekend and week-long courses offer opportunities to learn meditation and introductory Buddhism, and there is a special emphasis on integrating mind and body – through courses such as meditation and yoga, meditation and tai chi, shiatsu, massage, hill walking, painting and photography for example. There are also gay men's retreats, working retreats and the more informal open retreats. The atmosphere is very relaxed, warm and friendly: despite the fairly busy daily timetable, there is always time built in to allow retreatants to simply 'be' – and whether that means a stride up the hills, a swim in the loch, a quiet read or a snooze, it's all OK. Accommodation is comfortable: small dormitories with ensuite facilities provide an experience of community, which may or may not suit everyone! Dhanakosa itself is home to a small residential community of men, and this strong sense of spiritual community permeates the experience of being on retreat here, making it a very enriching stay indeed. Many of the retreats are suitable for beginners, but there are also retreats for 'regulars' – intensive meditation weeks, women's weeks, Buddhist festival retreats. These are particularly more suitable for people familiar with the practices and ethos of the FWBO.

Marydale

Cannich
Sancti Angeli Benedictine Skete
Marydale
Cannich
Inverness-shire IV4 7LTT

Tel: 01456 415218
e-mail: spc@santiangeli.org
Website: www.sanctiangeli.org

Roman Catholic
In the Highlands of Scotland, the Skete is a large hermitage dedicated to silence and prayer. Its activities are formation for prayer integrated into daily life and icon writing. All visitors live alongside in a monastic life with the community. Weekend monastic study breaks for students and young professional women are available, as well as long stays as helpers. A summer school and on-line course for icon writing is run. The website is excellent and informative and tells you about the Skete tradition and history in Christianity.

Open: All year except during house retreats. Receives women, young people, seekers of any faith or none.
Rooms: 2
Facilities: No disabled facilities.
Spiritual Help: Mass usually twice a week, confessions by prior arrangement.

All visitors do monastic studies and two to three one-to-one meetings regarding vocational discernment and the place of prayer in their lives.
Guests Admitted to: Choir; all guests join in monastic work and meals.
Meals: Vegetarian. Vegan and special diets possible if advance notice given.
Special Activities: Icon workshop, Gregorian chant studies, gardening.
Situation: In area suitable for walking. Fishing via local bus service to Loch Ness and Inverness.
Maximum Stay: Usually up to three months, otherwise by arrangement.
Bookings: E-mail preferred.
Charges: Recommended rate £25 per person per day inclusive of meals or a donation for students, long-stay guests and the low waged.
Access: Local bus from Inverness, request stop to be put off at Catholic Church in Cannich. By car from Drumnadrochit to Cannich.

Montrose

Boswell House
107 High Street
Montrose DD10 8QR   Tel: 01342 834249

Inter-denominational
This centre offers inter-denominational weekend retreats for a maximum of fourteen people in a seventeenth-century town house. There is a library, lounges, several kitchens for self-catering and a walled garden to sit in. A programme of retreats is available.

Musselburgh

Carberry Christian Conference Centre   Tel: 0131 665 3135
Musselburgh   Fax: 0131 653 2930
Midlothian EH21 8PY   e-mail: office@carberry.org.uk
                                        Website: www.carberry.org.uk
Inter-denominational
Carberry is a Scottish country house – big, grey, solid and granite – but with delightful public rooms, a good library and a Friends House, which has double bedrooms, mostly ensuite. The Carberry Trust, representing all Scottish churches, owns it. The programmes are most often group conferences and many do not appear to have much religious content, but it may include Alpha courses, youth weekends, Bible-related studies, and open and mid-week courses. Be warned, the centre can be literally swarming with people. It can also be a boisterous environment, with things going on like a charismatic youth conference, and does not give much spiritual atmosphere. So if you come, attend a course or workshop or come with a group. The volunteer staff live on site, and about twenty-five per cent of activities are about retreat work.

Open: All year. Receives everyone. Children welcome.
Rooms: Accommodates 16 singles, 13 doubles – modern, comfortable and up-to-date with some ensuite. Camping. Accommodation for up to 100 including camping.
Facilities: Disabled, conferences, garden, park, guest lounge, TV, guest pay phone (0131 653 5589).

Spiritual Help: Upon request only.

Guests Admitted to: All public areas.

Meals: Everyone eats together. Traditional food with vegetarian provision. Special diets.

Special Activities: Planned programme. Lots of activities – almost every weekend some event or course is going on here. Brochure available twice annually.

Situation: Very quiet, set in some 35 acres of park with fine trees, but busy with guests a lot of the time.

Maximum Stay: Open.

Bookings: Letter, fax, e-mail, telephone 9a.m.–5p.m.

Charges: See brochure. Currently single half board £44 per day, twins/doubles half-board £39 per day.

Access: Car is best. There is a good map in the brochure. Pick-up from public transport may be possible.

Orkney

Orkney Healing Retreat
The Belsair
Sanday
Orkney KW17 2BJ   Tel: 01857 600206
                                   e-mail: orkneyretreat@hotmail.com

Open spirituality – Spiritual healing

Orkney Healing Retreat is run by members of the National Federation of Spiritual Healers and offers to all a quiet refreshing and relaxing break away from busy lifestyles. Retreat time is according to your own plan but help is available if requested. Otherwise there are working meditations on the beaches, in co-operation with nature. Personal guidance is available if requested. The rates are B&B £25 per person per night ensuite, £18.50 standard. An à la carte menu is available, with meals ranging in price from £5 to £15. Snacks are available during the day. Individual healing sessions cost about £35 per hour, and group painting and meditation is about £5.50 per session. Other courses on offer from time to time are priced variously. This is a restful and healing place in a beautiful setting for a private retreat away from it all.

Woodwick House   Tel: 01856 751330
Evie   Fax: 01856 751383
Orkney KW17 2PQ   e-mail: mail@woodwickhouse.co.uk
                              Website: www.orknet.co.uk/woodwick

Non-denominational

Woodwick House is a guest house in a particularly lovely situation, which makes it a good place for a private retreat to get away from it all, but not if you are looking for a religious or particularly spiritual environment. The house is set in 12 acres of bluebell woodland, with its own burn and bay. This is a bit unusual in that Orkney is almost bare of trees, so Woodwick feels like a self-contained and enclosed space to be in. There are open fires and nicely prepared meals using local produce. Bird and seal watching, painting, walking or just sitting in front of the fire and reading a book from the house library are all possible here. This is a good place for small group retreats as well. There are six to ten concerts a year, mainly folk, jazz and other similar types of music. Poetry readings, plays and art expositions are also activities that may be on the programme.

Open: All year. Receives everyone.
Rooms: 8 rooms.
Facilities: Disabled, conferences, garden, library, guest lounge, TV, direct dialing.
Spiritual Help: None.
Guests Admitted to: Unrestricted.
Meals: Taken in guest house. Traditional food. Vegetarian and special diets.
Special Activities: Special music, literary and art events.
Situation: Unique situation of river and woodland, and near secluded bay.
Maximum Stay: No limit.
Bookings: Letter, fax, e-mail, telephone.
Charges: £28 per person per night B&B with shared bathroom facilities, £35 ensuite room.
Access: Ask for instructions when booking.

Roberton

Beshara School of Esoteric Education
Chisholme House
Roberton
Hawick
Roxburgh TD9 7PH

Tel: 01450 880215
Fax: 01450 880204
e-mail: secretary@beshara.org
Website: www.beshara.org

Non-denominational – Educational charity
Beshara means 'good news'. It is reputed to be the word the Angel Gabriel used when he announced the coming of Christ to Mary. The idea of the Beshara School is to strive towards an understanding of the unity of existence. This study of spiritual awareness here is quite demanding, as it encompasses many mystical traditions, especially sufism and in particular the works of Muhyddin Ibn Arabi. Residential courses of differing lengths, from a weekend to six months, are available. Courses consist of periods of meditition, work, study and devotional practices, and visitors are always welcome to partcipate in the daily rhythm. The whole thing is a spiritual mix of esoteric teaching, warm hospitality and love for the environment, which in this day and age strikes a chord with most people. The cooking, flower arrangements, bedrooms, kitchen gardens and reforestation programme all show love, care and impeccable taste. The house itself is Georgian, the accommodation almost luxuriously comfortable, and the food imaginatively prepared. In fact, the centre runs an organic kitchen garden and aims to produce about seventy per cent of its own food on its 200-some acres of land. The staff and students are helpful, relaxed and very welcoming. When we visited they immediately invited us into a study session and meditation period so we could share in their daily life. **Highly Recommended.**

Open: January to November. Receives everyone except groups.
Rooms: Single, doubles, dormitories. Up to 60 places, mostly shared.
Facilities: Garden, library, direct dialing (01450 880363).

Spiritual Help: Personal talks, meditation, directed study.
Guests Admitted to: Main building, work of the community.
Meals: Everyone eats together. Traditional and vegetarian food with a Middle Eastern influence. Special diets for medical conditions only.
Special Activities: Planned events – send for brochure.
Situation: Set in 200 acres of moorland and pasture – a very quiet place.
Maximum Stay: By arrangement.
Bookings: Letter, fax, e-mail, telephone 9.30a.m.–5.30p.m.
Charges: By donation according to means – suggested rate about £25 day for adults and lower for children. Weekend course £60, 9-day course £250, 6-month course £3,450.
Access: Train, bus and car all possible – ask for specifics.

Sandilands

Green Pastures
Sandilands
Near Lanark ML11 9TY
Tel/Fax: 01555 664711
Mobile: 0441 173902

Christian – Inter-denominational
This is a modern purpose-built retreat and equipping centre set between a town and a village. The pastoral ministry is to equip Christians to connect on a deeper level with Christ, themselves and others, and to enable Christians to use their gifts in service to their families, church and community.

Open: All year. Receives men, women, groups.
Rooms: 5 twins. Bring a Bible, notebook, towel and slippers if residential.
Facilities: Conferences, garden, guest lounge, TV.
Spiritual Help: Personal talks, spiritual direction, personal retreat direction, meditation, directed study. Discipleship counselling for those in personal and spiritual conflicts.
Guests Admitted to: Chapel, guest areas.
Meals: Taken in guest house. Traditional food.
Special Activities: Planned programme – send for information and leaflet.
Situation: Quiet, in countryside.
Maximum Stay: 4 days.
Bookings: Letter, telephone.
Charges: On request.
Access: Ask for directions when booking.

> Prayer is a matter of being more aware, of being more ready still to lift up one's heart.
> DOM EDMUND JONES

Tibbermore

The Bield at Blackruthven ★
Blackruthven House
Tibbermore
Perth PH1 1PY

Tel: 01738 583238
Fax: 01738 583828
e-mail: info@bieldatblackruthven
Website: www.bieldatblackruthven.org.uk

Christian

This centre is run by a wealthy Danish couple who got zapped by the Holy Spirit in the seventies, worked in Uganda for a number of years, then came back to Scotland to found a centre for rest, recovery, healing and growth – through worship, prayer, laying on of hands and art therapy. The Bield is a huge old estate with a spectacular Georgian house; a walled garden with vegetables, fruit trees and flowers; a swimming pool; and an orchard. Set up in 1997 as a centre of Christian spirituality, retreat and healing in the widest sense, it has a ministry team including an Episcopalian priest, a qualified counsellor, an art therapist and a horticultural/ecological specialist. Daily prayers and a Sunday Eucharist take place in the chapel, which is open at all times for prayer and meditation. Situated on a 370-acre organic farm, of which some 30 acres are parkland and paddocks, this place offers a large space for retreats and healing. The accommodation and conference rooms are in a converted steading, extremely comfortable and well-appointed. The food is mostly vegetarian, using organic produce from the garden when available. There is a separate smallholding project for people with learning disabilities. During the summer, the centre is used more as a quiet guest house. The Bield feels wealthy but do not let this detract from what it is offering. It seemed to us to be a loving and gentle place run by loving and gentle people. **Highly Recommended.**

Open: All year. Receives everyone.

Rooms: 9 rooms, used as singles and doubles.

Facilities: Conferences, garden, parkland, guest lounge, walled garden, payphone (01738 582153), heated indoor swimming pool, tennis courts, art room facilities, services in the chapel in the morning and evening, walking.

Spiritual Help: Personal talks, group sharing, spiritual direction, personal retreat direction, meditation, directed study, Ignatian retreat direction, art therapy.

Guests Admitted to: Unrestricted, except to private quarters of the owners.

Meals: Taken in guest house or room. Whole food/vegetarian/vegan/organic. Self-catering tea/coffee kitchen. Special diets. Arrangements available for silence during meals. You may also eat by yourself if you choose.

Special Activities: From time to time there are events.

Situation: Very quiet, in a beautiful setting, some four miles from Perth – a nice country town.

Maximum Stay: 6 nights.

Bookings: Letter fax, telephone 10a.m.–4p.m. Monday to Wednesday.

Charges: Suggested donation inclusive of all facilities: full board £35, half board £30, full day £15, half day with lunch £10, half day without lunch £5.

Access: Car: A85 from Perth to Crieff. Good directions in the brochure.

Channel Islands

Guernsey

Les Cotils Christian Retreat and Conference Centre
Les Cotils L'Hyureuse
St Peter Port
Guernsey
Channel Islands GY1 1UU

Tel: 01481 727793
Fax: 01481 701062
e-mail: lescotils@aol.com

Christian – Inter-denominational

This is a grand white place on a hill, with glorious views to the port and sea. In 12 acres, it offers first-class comfort, pretty furnished rooms and a coffee shop and tea room. This is retreating in luxury. For those on retreat peace and quiet is possible even if other non-retreatants guests are staying – there is an active management policy to maintain this balance. There is a programme of Ecumenical retreats and workshops. Send for details.

Open: All year. Receives everyone.
Rooms: 7 singles, 10 doubles, 2 family /large rooms.
Facilities: Conferences, garden, park, library, 3 guest lounges, TV, guest telephones.
Spiritual Help: Personal talks, group sharing. Spiritual direction and directed study on retreats. Morning and evening prayer.
Guests Admitted to: All public rooms.
Meals: Everyone eats together. Traditional and vegetarian food. Special diets.
Special Activities: They are expanding their programme so ask to see current brochure.
Situation: Situated above the port in a large garden and park with great views.
Maximum Stay: Open.
Bookings: Letter, fax, e-mail, telephone.
Charges: Various individual, group and conferences rates, but standard B&B with full English breakfast around £29 per night, half board £35 per night per person.
Access: Any south-coast airport or ferry port.

> There are two ways to go about getting enough – one is to continue to accumulate more and more. The other is to desire less.
> G.K. CHESTERTON

Ireland &
Northern Ireland

" May the road rise to meet you,
May the wind be always at your back,
May the sun shine warm upon your face,
The rains fall soft upon your field,
And until we meet again
May God hold you in the hollow of His hand. "
IRISH BLESSING

As you might expect of one of world's most deeply religious countries, Ireland offers an excellent choice of retreat centres and programmes. It is difficult to go to any of them without being in some of the most beautiful scenery in Europe. Most places are Roman Catholic but ecumenical in outlook, offering a warm welcome to all who seek to increase their spiritual awareness. The famed Irish hospitality and conviviality include the religious communities in all these places, and they are keen to develop retreat programmes that appeal to all ages and temperaments, from deeply traditional spiritual retreats to novel ones involving animals. From Donegal to the lakes of Killarney, the only problem will be which retreat centre to chose.

ANTRIM

Armoy

Corrymeela Knocklayd
The Corrymeela Community
28 Stroan Road
Armoy BT53 8RY

Tel: 02820 751521
e-mail: knocklayd@corrymeela.org.uk
Website: www.corrymeela.org.uk

Christian
A house and annexe set in pretty gardens high up a mountain about 8 miles from the Corrymeela Centre in Ballycastle. Accommodation is in singles and doubles, and there are kitchens. Self-catering and catered are both possible. Send for the programme of weekend retreats and quiet days.

Larne

Drumalis Retreat Centre
47 Glenarm Road
Larne
Co Antrim BT40 1DT

Tel: 02828 272196/276455
Fax: 02828 277999
e-mail: drumalis@btconnect.com
Website: www.drumalis.co.uk

Inter-denominational
The Drumalis Vision Statement says it all: 'Drumalis is a place of welcome, an oasis on the journey of life. A living community where all experience the power of God's love and compassion. Discover and value their gifts. Seek to be healers in a divided world. Grow in their relationship with God and all Creation. We draw our life and strength from sharing and prayer.' The house itself is a rambling late Victorian mansion with a view across Larne Harbour that has been called awe-inspiring. The house has recently been renovated. The programme here can include, for example, directed retreats, *Healing Touch Workshop, Celtic Spirituality, Yoga, Prayer and Painting, Dream Retreat* and *Reconnecting with the Passion of the Earth Retreat.*

Open: All year except Christmas and Easter. Receives men, women, young people, families, groups, non-retreatants.
Rooms: 54 singles, 10 doubles, 2 dormitories.
Facilities: Conferences, garden, library, guest lounge, payphone.
Spiritual Help: Personal talks, group sharing, meditation, personal retreat direction, spiritual direction. Reflexology sometimes offered.
Guests Admitted to: Almost unrestricted access.
Meals: Everyone eats together. Traditional food. Vegetarian and special diets.
Special Activities: Retreats for lay people, parishes, religious. Renewal courses, folk and prayer groups, inter-church work, Christian fellowship groups, Celtic spirituality, Cursillo weekends. Send for brochure.
Situation: Quiet, with spacious grounds, overlooking the sea.
Maximum Stay: By arrangement.
Bookings: Letter, fax, e-mail, telephone.
Charges: £40 per day full board. Brochures give course rates, which currently range from about £90–£230.
Access: Car: from Belfast take M2, leave at Exit A8, by station and harbour follow signs for the Coast Road. Drumalis is on right before Bankhands Lane just before leaving the town.

Portglenone

Our Lady of Bethleham Abbey
11 Ballymena Road
Portglenone, Ballymena
Co Antrim BT44 8BL

Tel: 02825 821211
Fax: 02825 822795
e-mail: kelley@unite.net
Website: www.bethleham-abbey.org.uk

Roman Catholic
This is a Roman Catholic monastery. Although it is in the countryside, it can be very busy, with many day visitors.

Open: Weekdays and sometimes weekends. Receives men, women, young people, non-retreatants.

Rooms: 2 singles, 8 doubles.
Facilities: Conferences, park, lounge, payphone. Book shop with books, crafts, religious objects.
Spiritual Help: Personal talks, personal retreat direction.
Guests Admitted to: Church, public areas.
Meals: Taken in guest house. Traditional food. Vegetarian and special diets.
Special Activities: None.
Situation: Rather busy, at edge of village, in countryside.
Maximum Stay: 5 days.
Bookings: Letter, telephone.
Charges: Suggested donation about £20 per day – or by other arrangement.
Access: Car and bus – ask for directions.

CAVAN

Jampa Ling Tibetan Buddhist Centre
Owendoon House
Bawnboy
Co Cavan

Tel: (0)49 952 3448
Fax: (0)49 952 3067
e-mail: jampaling@eircom.net
Website: www.Jampaling.org

Buddhist – Tibetan tradition

Jampa Ling was established in 1990 under the guidance and spiritual direction of Panchen Ötrul Rinpoche, and the patron is His Holiness the Dalai Lama. The Centre, a large Victorian house called Owendoon, is situated in 13 acres of meadow, woodland and gardens, and borders a lake. It is run by a small group of Panchen Ötrul Rinpoche's students and supported by many others scattered near and far across the world. It is open to visitors, both Buddhist and of other traditions. The name Jampa Ling means 'place of infinite loving-kindness'. The Aims of the Centre are: to preserve the Tibetan Buddhist tradition and culture through teaching meditation and Dharma practice; to assist in the re-establishment of monasteries in Tibet; to work for the re-establishment of Buddhism in Mongolia and relieve the difficulties of the Mongolian people; to promote interfaith dialogue at a deep spiritual level in the context of the work for peace in this island; to support Tibetan refugees and their monasteries in India; to work for peaceful co-existence between all living beings; to encourage conservation of earth's natural resources; and to develop an awareness of the interdependence of existence. There is an annual programme of events, courses and study. These have included the following: *White Tara Retreat* – a weekend retreat for those already having received initiation into the practice of Tara. Participants must arrive on Friday evening before 9p.m. in order to start early the following morning. This is a silent retreat and participants must stay at the centre. Cost 175€ including all meals and accommodation. *Saga Dawa* – a family day to celebrate the Buddha's birth, enlightenment and parinirvana, which occurs on the full moon. *Summer Solstice* – Tibetan Buddhist prayers to purify the environment. *Introduction to Buddhism and Meditation* – includes full lunch. Cost 50€. There is additional accommodation in Tara House, a restored nineteenth-century coach-house ideal for workshops and courses of all kinds. It is also fully equipped for self-catering family holidays. The building includes a beautiful timber-floored workshop room (6.7 x 6.0m/22 x 20ft), sleeping accommodation for twenty people (two bunk bed dormitories, a family room, a double and a single), a purpose-built kitchen and a dining room overlooking a 150-year-old walled garden.

CLARE

Sunyata Retreat Centre
Sixmilebridge
Clare

Tel: (0)61 367073
e-mail: Sunyata_ireland@hotmail.com

Buddhist – Open spirituality
Self-catering accommodation for personal retreats and Buddhist meditation retreats.

CORK

Castlemartyr

Carmel College
Castlemartyr, Cork

Roman Catholic
Until recently a school, this grand country house dating from 1720 enjoys wonderful views over vast lawns running down to waterways – just part of the 140 acres of lakes, pasture, forest and garden that surround the house. The chapel, full of light, is in the old ballroom and has magnificent plasterwork ceilings. Now used as a prayer centre for those wanting a restful and reflective day retreat, Carmel College is a good place to pause, recollect and reflect for a while.

Garranes Allihies

Dzogchen Bear and Rigpa Ireland
Garranes Allihies
West Cork

Tel: (0)27 73032 (administration),
(0)27 73147 (accommodation)
Fax: (0)27 73177
e-mail: info@rigpa.ie
Website: www.rigpa.ie

Buddhist – Tibetan tradition
This meditation and retreat centre for Buddhist study and practice is 400 feet up on the cliffs above Bantry Bay, with a vast panorama of the Atlantic Ocean. The centre is under the spiritual direction of Sogyal Rinpoche, and is affiliated to the Rigpa Fellowship. Sogyal Rinpoche was born in Tibet and raised as a son by one of the most revered spiritual teachers of this century, Jamyang Khyentse Choki Lodro. Rinpoche studied at university in Delhi and Cambridge and has been teaching in the West since 1974. He is the author of *The Tibetan Book of Living and Dying* and founder and spiritual director of

RIGPA, an international network of centres and groups that follow the teachings of the Buddha under his guidance. Sogyal Rinpoche and other Tibetan masters lead retreats at Dzogchen Beara several times a year. *Rigpa* is a Tibetan word meaning 'the innermost nature of the mind'. Rigpa International is a Buddhist organisation with centres in nine countries around the world, dedicated to practising the techniques of the Buddha under the guidance of Sogyal Rinpoche and to making these teachings available to benefit as many people as possible. Rigpa centres around Ireland (see below) offer a variety of courses based on *The Tibetan Book of Living and Dying*. The Centre also offers a range of retreats and courses on various aspects of Buddhism such as meditation, compassion and spiritual care for the dying, most of which are open to beginners. Visitors are also welcome at other times and may attend daily meditation classes or simply relax in this beautiful and peaceful environment. **Highly Recommended.**

Open: All year. Receives men, women, young people, families, groups, non-retreatants. Children welcome.
Rooms: Hostel, dormitories, self-catering cottages
Facilities: Conferences, garden, book and gift shop, payphone.
Spiritual Help: Meditation, directed study for students following the Rigpa Study and Practice Programme.
Guests Admitted to: Shrine room.
Meals: Self-catering.
Special Activities: Programme of planned events – send for brochure. Daily meditation classes to which beginners are welcome. Good walking, with sporting facilities in vicinity.
Situation: Very quiet, in countryside, with dramatic and beautiful views.
Maximum Stay: By arrangement.
Bookings: Letter, fax, telephone.
Charges: Ask for current rates.
Access: By bus from Cork City.

Rigpa Centres:
Cork
6 Sydney Place
Qwellington Road
Cork   Tel: (0)21 505949

Dublin
12 Wicklow Street
3rd Floor   Tel: (0)1 670 3358
Dublin 2   e-mail: dublin@rigpa.ie

Limerick
78 O'Connell Street   Tel: (0)61 332248
Limerick   e-mail: limerick@rigpa.ie

County Wicklow
Ballydonagh Cottage
Delgany   Tel: (0)1 287 7128

Cobh

St Benedict's Priory
The Mount
Cobh
Co Cork

Tel/fax: (0)21 481 1354

Roman Catholic
This Benedictine Community aims to provide
a place of silence and solitude where guests
can recollect and dwell within themselves at
peace. Rooms are a bit old-fashioned but
comfortable enough, and they have lovely
harbour views. Some even have balconies.
This is a peaceful and restful place.

> Silence of the heart
> practised with wisdom
> will see a lofty depth and
> the ear of the silent mind
> will hear untold wonders.
> HESYCHIUS OF JERUSALEM

Open: All year. Receives men, women, young
people, small groups up to 8.
Rooms: 6 singles, 2 doubles.
Facilities: No rooms on ground floor. Garden, Bible garden in 1½ acres with
pool and stream, library, guest lounge, direct dialing (021 481 1887).
Spiritual Help: Personal talks, directed study, daily Mass and exposition of
Blessed Sacrament, share in the liturgy of the community.
Guests Admitted to: Chapel. Helping in garden possible.
Meals: Everyone eats together. Self-catering facilities for breakfast.
Traditional food, some grown in own garden. Vegetarian and special diets.
Special Activities: None.
Situation: Very quiet, in a picturesque town on an island in Cork harbour.
All rooms have view of harbour, some also having balconies.
Maximum Stay: 2 weeks.
Bookings: Letter, telephone 10.30a.m.–12.30p.m.
Charges: Suggested donation 32€ per day.
Access: Train, car or ferry to Cobh. Train from Cork City. Air to Cork
Airport. Boat from France or England to Cork.

Leap

Myross Wood Retreat Centre
Leap
Co Cork

Tel: (0)28 33118/34078
Fax: (0)28 33793
e-mail: mscmyross@eircom.net

Roman Catholic
Missionaries of the Sacred Heart run this house set in lovely West Cork
among woodlands and streams, and near the sea. There is a programme of
individual and group retreats throughout the year. Private retreats are
welcomed. Accommodation is mostly in single rooms, with capacity for up to
thirty-eight guests.

Montenotte

St Dominic's Priory and Retreat Centre
Ennismore
Montenotte
Co Cork

Tel: (0)21 450 2520
e-mail: ennismore@eircom.net

Roman Catholic – Inter-denominational

Although located in an urban area of Cork, St Dominic's offers an oasis of green lawns and quiet views with much peace and quiet. A friendly old dog may be the first to greet you, and the warm welcome is continued inside by the housekeeping staff or a member of the community. The excellent food is prepared in an old-fashioned kitchen – the homemade chicken soup and bread are delicious. The gardens surrounding this large ambling house have plenty of benches and there is a charming old walled garden with box-hedge paths. All in all, a perfect place for a stroll and a good think. The facilities here are numerous and include an 1824 stable block converted into The Meditation House, consisting of two buildings with modern and comfortable bunk-bed facilities for youth retreats. Next to that, a separate hermitage is available sleeping up to six people. Nearby is a pottery, a specially designed meditation room, a lounge and a large conference area. Altogether this is a nice group of stone buildings around a pretty courtyard down the drive away from the main house. As to the retreat programme on offer, these lines of Scripture are good to bear in mind if you find a weekend course entitled 'pottery meditations' too unusual an approach for a retreat: 'Get up and make your way to the potter's house: there I shall let you hear what I have to say' (Jeremiah 18:2). Other stimulating courses on offer here from the resident Dominican community may include bio-spirituality focusing, Celtic spirituality, Meister Eckhart, Myers-Briggs, integrating sexuality, and celebrating creativity.

Open: All year. Receives men, women, young people, families, groups, non-retreatants.

Rooms: 38 singles, 2 doubles, hermitage, hostel.

Facilities: Disabled, simple chapel with lots of light, conferences, garden, library, TV, guest lounge and payphone.

Spiritual Help: Personal talks, group sharing, meditation, community prayers, personal retreat direction.

Guests Admitted to: Unrestricted access.

Meals: Taken in the guest house. Traditional/ whole food. Vegetarian and special diets. Self-catering available.

Special Activities: Planned programme of events – send for brochure.

Situation: Quiet, but can be rather busy. With 30 acres of grounds and spectacularly situated gardens, the centre feels as though it is in open countryside, but is only 3 miles from the city centre.

Maximum Stay: 2 weeks.

Bookings: Letter, telephone.

Charges: Ask for current charges – by length of course.

Access: Train: Cork. Bus: from city centre. Car: see map in brochure.

DONEGAL

Burnfoot

St Anthony's Retreat Centre
Dundrean
Burnfoot
Co Donegal   Tel: (0)77 68370

Roman Catholic – Open to all
This is a place of seclusion and peace amidst the rolling sheep-grazed hills that straddle the border between County Derry and County Donegal. Consisting of five hermitages discreetly placed beyond an old farmhouse, St Anthony's offers space, privacy, places to pray and long walks in the beautiful countryside. A pilgrim garden has been created in the immediate surroundings of the farmhouse, reflecting scriptural themes and the Celtic Christian tradition. The hermitages are simple and small. As this place develops and grows, things will change, including what retreat accommodation is available, so give them a call and find out exactly what is available at the time you would like to visit.

Open: All year except Christmas and New Year.
Rooms: 5 hermitages, equipped with ensuite toilet and stove.
Facilities: Communal kitchen/refectory, chapel, grounds, countryside.
Spiritual help: Individual spiritual direction, personal talks, Sacrament of Reconciliation, prayer and healing ministry, Eucharist several times a week.
Guests admitted to: Everywhere except community part of farmhouse.
Meals: Lunch and dinner provided by community members in the refectory. Breakfast self-catered in the refectory. Good, plain food. Special diets if requested in advance. Meals can be taken back to hermitages if desired.
Special activities: None.
Situation: Very quiet, in the hills, not far from the sea. Beautiful hill and beach walks.
Maximum stay: 8 days.
Bookings: Letter, e-mail, telephone.
Charges: 40€ full board, 10€ a day extra for spiritual direction (or according to means).
Access: Bus: to Derry (pick-up can be arranged). Car: on the Derry to Buncrana road, turn up the Upper Galliagh Road.

Creeslough

Capuchin Retreat Centre
Ard Mhuire
Creeslough   Tel: (0)74 913 8005
Letterkenny   Fax: (0)74 913 8371
Co Donegal   e-mail: grdmhuire@irishcapuchins.com
                                    Website: www.irishcapuchins.com

Roman Catholic
The Capuchin Friary, while running a busy programme, offers quietness and fresh air on the shore of Sheephaven Bay, beside Ards Forest Park and a stone's throw from the ocean. The programme includes Cursillo retreats, as

well as retreats for clergy, seminarians and religious, and various theme-based weeks; but individually directed retreats are also scheduled, and people can just book quiet time, with as much or as little spiritual guidance as desired. The Friars are extremely welcoming and a warm family atmosphere is created by the open kitchen, which dispenses homegrown potatoes, fresh fish and homemade jam and scones. Although there are many day visitors, it is possible to find solitude and peace here. **Highly Recommended.**

Open: February–December. Receives men, women, young people, groups, non-retreatants.

Rooms: 40 singles, 20 doubles, hermitage.

Facilities: Conferences, garden, park, guest lounge, TV, payphone, direct dialing (74 913 8013).

Spiritual Help: Personal talks, spiritual direction, personal retreat direction, meditation, directed study.

Guests Admitted to: Church, chapel, choir, oratory.

Meals: Everyone eats together in refectory. Simple, wholesome food, vegetarian if requested. Silence observed during silent retreats.

Special Activities: Special programme – write for details.

Situation: Very quiet, in the countryside, near seaside with forest walks.

Maximum Stay: By arrangement.

Bookings: Letter, fax, e-mail, telephone 9.30a.m.–1p.m., 2–5.30p.m.

Charges: About 38€ full board per day.

Access: Bus: McGinley Bus from Dublin to Creeslough (pick-up possible). Car: to Letterkenny, then N56 to Creeslough. The Friars will give you detailed directions when you book.

Pettigo

Lough Derg
St Patrick's Purgatory
Pettigo   Tel/Fax: (0)71 986 1518
Co Donegal   e-mail: info@loughderg.org
                                     Website: www.loughderg.org

Roman Catholic – Open to all

St Patrick's Purgatory has been a place of prayer and pilgrimage for at least 1,000 years. The pilgrimage to this holy place is one of the toughest in the Christian world. This island sanctuary located on Lough Derg challenges human frailty but may bring a deep and richly rewarding experience of spirituality, enabling participants to find peace of mind and giving them new strength for continuing their life's journey. A historic centre of Celtic spirituality, St Patrick's Purgatory remains a unique place of prayer and penance. The traditional pilgrimage is a three-day undertaking of fasting and incorporates a twenty-four-hour vigil, which means you do not go to bed for that period – it is meant to be penitential. The fast means just that too – a simple meal of dry toast and black tea each day. You must be in normal health, at least 15 years old and able to walk (including barefoot) and kneel unaided. You fast from the midnight prior to arriving on the island by boat. This type of pilgrimage, deeply Christian and Catholic in nature and also highly ritualistic, is not to be undertaken without great seriousness of purpose in the seeking of God. There is a less arduous one-day retreat, which does not require fasting or walking barefoot. As in all great places of spiritual pilgrimage, demand is great and prior booking is essential. With growing demand for retreats outside the traditional season, plans have been made to build a multi-purpose facility that can be maintained independently of the rest of the island. This centre, when finished, will provide amenities for school retreats, youth groups, and one-day retreats, and facilities for meditation and prayer during the traditional three-day pilgrimage retreat season.

Open: April to October. Receives men, women, young people over 15. Not suitable for children.

Rooms: 600 singles, 16 doubles, dormitories. No mobile phones. No chewing gum.

Facilities: Disabled, church, chapel, oratory, conferences, library, guest lounge, TV, guest telephone, payphone (71 986 1518).

Spiritual Help: Personal talks, group sharing, spiritual direction, personal retreat direction, meditation, Way of the Cross, Eucharist.

Guests Admitted to: Unrestricted access.

Meals: Everyone eats together. Traditional food. Vegetarian and special diets.

Special Activities: Brochure available in English, plus several other languages, explaining what is offered and details of pilgrimage retreats.

Situation: Isolated, very quiet, on an island.

Maximum Stay: 1 week.

Bookings: Letter, fax, e-mail, website, telephone. Book well in advance, as over 20,000 pilgrims come here every year.

Charges: Currently 40€ for 3-day pilgrimage. 25€ 1-day retreat. Other rates on application.

Access: Boat.

Rossnowlagh

Franciscan Friary and La Verna House
Rossnowlagh
Co Donegal

Tel: (0)72 51342/52035
Fax: (0)72 52206
e-mail: frbern@gofree-indigo.ie

Roman Catholic

This is a centre of peace and reconciliation with the emphasis on a Franciscan presence. The Friary tries to offer a quiet time to people burnt out and needing a listening ear. The buildings are modern, with all necessary facilities and close to the sea. The extensive grounds have been laid out to include several grottoes, peace gardens and an outdoor Way of the Cross. The view over the bay is quite dramatic. This centre is much used by religious orders, especially in summer. The programme of events includes *Dances of Universal Peace*; *One God, One Humanity, One Me*; *Peace and Reconciliation*, *Thinking and Praying with St Francis of Assisi* and *The Role of Spirituality in Addiction Recovery*. La Verna, the modern retreat house, situated over the road from the friary, is extremely comfortable – almost to the extent of being like a hotel, with tea-making facilities and a TV in every room – but we found the welcome warmer at the Capuchin place, Ard Mhuire at Creeslough (see entry in this section).

Open: All year except Christmas to first week January. Receives men, woman, supervised young adults, groups, small seminar groups of non-retreatants.

Rooms: 19 singles, usable as doubles.

Facilities: Garden, park, book shop, library, guest lounge, TV, guest payphone, direct dialing.

Spiritual Help: Daily Mass, RC Church, chapel, personal talks, group sharing, meditation, Sacrament of Reconciliation, Inter-denominational Julian meetings, healing and counselling services.

Guests Admitted to: Everywhere except community living quarters. Chapel, choir, shrine room, repository.

Meals: Retreat house has a kitchen and dining room for self-catering breakfasts; other meals are taken in the main friary refectory. Silence observed during silent retreats only, and not necessarily in La Verna even then. Vegetarian and special diets.

Special Activities: Planned programme.

Situation: Very quiet, in the countryside, with nearby swimming and surfing. Can be busy in summer.

Maximum Stay: 10 days.

Bookings: Letter or telephone, then in writing.

Charges: Private 24-hour retreat 47€, 6-day directed retreat 350€. See brochure.

Access: No public transport. Car: on coast road between Donegal Town and Ballyshannon (about 5 miles from Ballyshannon).

DOWN

Newry

Society of African Missions
Dromantine
Newry
Co Down BT34 1RH   Tel: 01693 821224

Roman Catholic
Only 70 miles from Dublin and 30 from Belfast, this large centre is situated in beautiful countryside with good walks at hand. While groups with their own programme usually come here, it is also open for a private retreat.

Open: All year except Christmas. Receives men, women, young people, groups, non-retreatants.

Rooms: 96 singles.

Facilities: Disabled, conferences, payphone.

Spiritual Help: Only by arrangement.

Guests Admitted to: Chapel.

Meals: Taken in guest house. Good plain food. Vegetarian and special diets.

Special Activities: None.

Situation: Quiet, in countryside, about six miles from nearest town.

Maximum Stay: By arrangement.

Bookings: Letter, telephone.

Charges: Depends on number in group and length of stay.

Access: Car route best, from either Dublin or Belfast.

Rostrevor

Christian Renewal Centre
44 Shore Road
Rostrevor
Newry
Co Down BT34 3ET

Tel: 02841 738492
Fax: 02841 738996
e-mail: crc-rostrevor@lineone.net
Website: www.crc-rostrevor.org

Inter-denominational

The community here was founded in 1974 as a group of Christians of a Charismatic approach drawn together to seek to demonstrate and proclaim the uniting and healing love of Christ. The first churches were Roman Catholic and Protestant, but since then membership has been drawn from the new Community and Fellowship Churches. Reconciliation, particularly in Ireland, revival and renewal are central to the work and prayer here. The place is large, part of it old but modernised, with new attached buildings. Renewal weekends and three-day break retreats are a speciality. Guests are invited to join in prayers, which are morning and evening daily. While this community has always had a charismatic flavour, it is now mostly focused on intercessory prayer for Ireland.

Open: All year except Christmas. Receives men, women, young people, groups. Children welcome.
Rooms: 5 singles, 3 doubles, large family room.
Facilities: Conferences, garden, library, guest lounge, TV, guest phone.
Spiritual Help: Personal talks, group sharing. Prayer ministry as requested.
Guests Admitted to: Gardens, prayer room, quiet room, lounge.
Meals: Everyone eats together. Traditional food. Vegetarian and special diets.
Special Activities: Special programme – send for brochure.
Situation: Very quiet, in a village, at the foot of the Mourne Mountains, with a glorious sweeping view of Carlingford Lough.
Maximum Stay: 1 week.
Bookings: Letter, fax, e-mail telephone 11a.m.–9p.m.
Charges: Suggested donation per person per day £12.50 B&B, £20 full board.
Access: Train: from Belfast or Dublin to Newry station, then bus. Bus: from Belfast or Dublin airport to Newry Courthouse, hence by bus to Rostrevor. Car: follow signs from Newry for Warrenpoint.

DUBLIN

Catholic Youth Council
20/23 Arran Quay
Dublin 7

Tel: (0)1 872 5055
Fax: (0)1 872 5010
e-mail: info@cyc.ie

Roman Catholic

The Catholic Youth Council offers a number of holiday centres for youth groups. Groups primarily use the centres for holidays and training as well as for retreat purposes. The centres in **Glendasan**, **Teach Chaoimhin** and **Teach Lorcain** are designed particularly for prayer and religious retreats. Groups make their own programmes. There are no resident staff except at

Coolure House, Co Westmeath, which is a fully staffed centre located near Lough Derraghvara with a wide range of services for retreats, plus extensive indoor and outdoor facilities and an equestrian centre. Most centres are in beautiful rural and coastal areas and some have planned activities in July.

Open: All year. Receives young people.
Rooms: Dormitories.
Facilities: See above.
Spiritual Help: Self-directed.
Guests Admitted to: Usually unrestricted.
Meals: Self-catering.
Special Activities: None.
Situation: See above.
Maximum Stay: None.
Bookings: Booking form.
Charges: Vary depending on centre and how long the stay will be – send for rate sheet.
Access: Ask for directions for centre booked.

Dominican Retreat & Pastoral Centre and St Joseph's Retreat Centre
Tallaght
Dublin 24 Tel: (0)1 404 8123/404 8191
Fax: (0)1 459 6080

Roman Catholic
Right in the middle of Ireland's fourth most populated area and surrounded by endless urban sprawl, St Joseph's is a surprisingly first-rate place for anyone going on retreat. The guest house is very comfortable, with its own big reading room, tea and coffee bar, book shop and all the other facilities one could want, from hair dryers to TV room. But the real delight is the gardens, with ancient walkways and many fine old trees. The community is fairly large and, unusually today in religious life, is composed of all ages from young to old. They are very hospitable and friendly in their welcome but mostly receive groups because of their catering set-up. However, it is sometimes possible for a person to visit on their own. Their combined voices rise up strong in choir and fill the large church, which was designed by one of Pugin's star pupils. The Friars run a number of educational and retreat programmes, as well as caring for some 7,000 parishioners in this densely populated area. As this is a major priory of the Dominican Friars, it is a place of prayer and contemplation.

Open: September to May. Receives men, women, small groups.
Rooms: 30 rooms, hermitage.
Facilities: Disabled for 1 person only. Conferences, chapel, garden, payphone, direct dialing. TV outside retreat times only.
Spiritual Help: Personal talks, group sharing, meditation, directed study.
Guests Admitted to: Chapel, choir, garden.
Meals: Everyone eats together. Traditional food. Vegetarian and special diets.
Special Activities: Planned programme – send for brochure.
Situation: In busy urban area, but a quiet and peaceful oasis.
Maximum Stay: 1 week.

Bookings: Letter only.
Charges: Ask for rates.
Access: Bus: No. 77 or 77a from Eden Quay in Dublin (easy access). Car: from M50.

Friends of the Western Buddhist Order – Ireland
23 South Frederick Street
Dublin 2

Tel: (0)1 671 3187

Buddhist
They will provide information on the activities of the organisation in Ireland.

Jesuit Centre of Spirituality
Manresa House
Clontarf Road
Dollymount, Dublin 3

Tel: (0)1 833 1352
Fax: (0)1 833 1002
e-mail: manresa@s-j.ie

Roman Catholic – Ecumenical
Situated on the north side of Dublin on the coast road, Manresa is set well back in its own extensive grounds, beside a 400-acre park with a glorious rose garden, and looking across to the wild bird sanctuary of Bull Island (accessible by bridge and causeway). An oasis in a busy metropolis where space, peace and a silent atmosphere help you touch base with yourself and with God, the centre has been providing Ignatian retreats and the Spiritual Exercises since 1968. Having recently completed refurbishments of the retreat house, Manresa is expanding its outreach to wider groups of lay people, offering retreats of differing lengths and seminars around such urgent themes as *Inter-faith Dialogue*, *Life-Threatening Illness* and *Faith and Justice*. The team of directors are seasoned, caring men and women who are used to accompanying others as they deepen their relationship with God. **Highly Recommended.**

Open: All year except Christmas.
Rooms: 41 singles ensuite, 1 with wheelchair bathroom access.
Facilities: Lift, tearoom, meditation chapel, main chapel, gardens, payphone, nearby park, bird sanctuary.
Spiritual help: Individual spiritual direction, Sacrament of Reconciliation, daily Eucharist.
Guests admitted to: Entire retreat house and outside grounds, excluding the Jesuit community house.
Meals: All eat together in communal dining room. Silence is maintained during retreats.
Special activities: Ignatian Spiritual Exercises, seminars on topical themes. Courses in spiritual accompaniment and direction, and in deepening faith and prayer.
Situation: Quietly hidden in trees, off a busy coast road north of the city, with views over the sea to the east.
Maximum stay: 30 days for the Exercises.
Bookings: Letter, e-mail.
Charges: 350€ for an individually guided 8-day retreat, all found.

Access: Bus: No. 130 from Lower Abbey Street – stops outside Manresa. Car: ask for directions. Dublin Airport is 30 minutes away.

Presentation Convent
Mount Saint Anne's
Dublin

This is a very charming convent set on a small grassy green hill, very quiet with pastures and parklands all around it. It is easy to find, off the main Route 7 Dublin Road. Write to Guest Sister.

The Sanctuary
Stanhope Street
Dublin 7

Tel: (0)1 670 5419
Fax: (0)1 672 8086
e-mail: enquiries@sanctuary.ie
Website: www.sanctuary.ie/images/space.gif

Mind Body Spirit

The Sanctuary is a holistic spiritual centre in the heart of the city of Dublin. It was designed to provide space and time to busy and stressed out people, so that they can develop balance and harmony between public and private selves in terms of their work and lifestyle. A beautiful contemplative space has been created both inside and outside the house, including a peaceful garden, where the team offer programmes, courses, workshops and individual treatments to nourish, illuminate and build inner strength and wisdom. While none of this is residential, the Sanctuary is offering the equivalent of what is often looked for in retreat settings – the chance to step back, take stock and find peace within one's everyday life. Contact the Sanctuary for brochures or visit their website. **This is not a residential centre.**

GALWAY

Athenry

Esker Retreat House
Athenry
Co Galway

Tel: (0)91 844549
Fax: (0)91 845689
e-mail: eskerret@indigo.ie
Website: www.eskercommunity.net

Roman Catholic

As you leave Athenry, you drive into a flat and unattractive valley dotted with houses and the stone walls so common in this part of Galway. Soon Esker Monastery looms in the distance, the only sizeable structure in sight. As you approach this formidable looking building, yet another suddenly appears – a nearby cement works. But do not be put off, for as you enter Esker's drive, the trees surround you and soon you are in a different world of rich greenery and grassy pastures. Close up the monastery is friendly if somewhat institutional at first sight. Rooms are comfortably furnished. Many members of the community are retired after long years of work, but one or more may join you in the lounge or for a meal. It is a friendly, old-fashioned place with activities, retreats and courses in its programme. Here, wisdom has prevailed and a completely separate Youth Village has been created and set aside solely for younger groups. There are garden walks and creative workshops, which include painting courses, woodcarving, and creative writing. Food is plentiful and traditional. There are Stations of the Cross in the garden along a bluebell walk through trees, where violets and primroses glow in the shade. The Stations are in an elegant Italian style. Esker is a prayerful place. **Highly Recommended.**

Open: All year. Receives men, women, young people, families, groups, non-retreatants. Children welcome.
Rooms: 8 singles, 27 doubles, dormitories, camp site.
Facilities: Conferences, gardens, woodland park, pitch and put course, lots of walks on grounds and in surrounding area, guest lounge, TV, payphone.
Spiritual Help: Personal talks, group sharing, spiritual direction, personal retreat direction.
Guests Admitted to: Church, chapel, choir, oratory.
Meals: Everyone eats together. Food by professional chefs with provision for vegetarians and special diets. Self-catering available.
Special Activities: Extensive planned programme – send for brochure.
Situation: Very quiet, in countryside.
Maximum Stay: Open.
Bookings: Letter, fax, e-mail, telephone 9p.m.–5p.m.
Charges: 90€ per day full board, 35€ B&B. Youth Village charges by arrangement.
Access: Train and bus possible. Good map in brochure. Pick-up possible if prior notice given. Car route easy.

Newcastle

An Díseart
Le Retraite Sisters
2 Distillery Road
Newcastle, Co Galway

Tel: (0)91 524548
Fax: (0)91 581312

Roman Catholic
This is a small community and usually only one person is received on retreat at a time. There is space and time for silence in a self-catering hermitage, which is a small two-bedroom house with its own kitchen/sitting room. A small oratory links this with the main house. There is no telephone in hermitage. You may join the community for prayer if you wish.

Open: All year. Receives women only.
Rooms: 2 bedrooms, self-contained hermitage.
Facilities: Chapel.
Spiritual Help: Personal talks, retreat and spiritual direction if requested.
Guests Admitted to: Chapel, oratory.
Meals: Self-catering.
Special Activities: None.
Situation: Town.
Maximum Stay: 8 days

Bookings: Letter, fax, telephone.
Charges: Suggested donation 20€ per 24 hours.
Access: By road. Ask for bus directions.

KERRY

Ardfert

Ardfert Retreat Centre
Ardfert, Co Kerry   Tel: (0)66 713 4276

Roman Catholic
This centre is staffed by Presentation Sisters and a priest director, and serves
many parishes. While this is a place for group bookings, individuals wishing
to join any Saturday or Sunday parish group retreat are welcome to do so by
prior arrangement with the secretary of the centre. There is a library service
for books and videos on Christian topics.

Open: All year except 4 weeks in summer – check dates. Receives men,
   women, young people, groups.
Rooms: 30 singles.
Facilities: A diocesan retreat centre in constant use by parish groups and
   schools.
Guests Admitted to: Almost unrestricted access.
Spiritual Help: Personal talks, spiritual direction, group sharing, meditation.
Meals: Available for groups but not for individual visitors. Traditional food.
Special Activities: Range from residential weekends of prayer and
   Enneagram workshops to days of support and prayer for dependants of
   those suffering from alcoholism. Send for brochure.
Situation: Very quiet, in the countryside.
Maximum Stay: According to the programme.
Bookings: Letter.
Charges: Suggested donation 32€ per person, 60€ per couple. Day rate avail-
   able for preached retreats and directed retreats.
Access: Train: to Tralee. Bus: to Tralee. Car: centre is 5 miles north of Tralee.

Inch

Lios Dána
The Natural Living Centre   Tel: (0)66 915 8189
Inch   Fax: (0)66 915 8223
Annascaul   e-mail: liosdana@gofree.indigo.ie
Co Kerry   Website: www.liosdana.foundmark.com

Mind Body Spirit – Holiday and healing – Yoga retreat
One of Ireland's leading holistic holiday centres for rest and renewal and the
practice of a new approach to life, Lios Dána is set in a wonderful location on
the southern shoreline of the Dingle peninsula in the south west of Ireland.
It has a large activity room with a huge floor area, a library, a lounge, a dining
room, conservatories, guest bedrooms and a garden – but the views and

setting are its greatest assets. A shiatsu practitioner, a macrobiotic counsellor and an artist who is a holistic interior designer run it. There are three-day programmes, including yoga and shiatsu massage, and group courses from March to October in a variety of holistic disciplines. Or you can come for a simple holiday break and use the centre's facilities. Country walks with sea and mountains and early Christian sites are here. **Highly Recommended.**

Open: All year. Receives everyone.
Rooms: 8 bedrooms, self-catering chalets.
Facilities: Large exercise room, excellent library, guest lounge, conservatories, hot and cool pool.
Spiritual Help: Creative and healing exercises and therapies, including yoga, shiatsu.
Guests Admitted to: Unrestricted in guest areas.
Meals: Vegetarian.
Special Activities: See above. Send for brochure and see website.
Situation: Quiet, by sea.
Maximum Stay: By arrangement.
Bookings: Fax, e-mail, online, telephone.
Charges: Tariff sheet available – rates vary according to course. Examples currently 40€ B&B per day or 950€ per week for self-catering groups.
Access: Train: to Tralee, then bus. Car: 2 hours from Cork or Limerick. Air: 20 miles from Kerry County airport (flights direct from London Stansted).

Killarney

Franciscan Prayer Centre　　　　　　　　　Tel: (0)64 31334
Killarney　　　　　　　　　　　　　　　　　Fax: (0)64 37510
Co Kerry　　　　　　　　　　　e-mail: friary@eircom.net
　　　　　Website: www.homepage.eircom.net/~franciscanprayercentre
Roman Catholic
Killarney is one of the most beautiful places in the world; surely no one can resist the beauty of its lakes, forests and mountains. The Franciscan Prayer Centre in the heart of this wondrous place of nature seems ideally placed for the search for God. It is also in the heart of the town of Killarney but set up from the road, above the noise. The present centre is only two years old, and there are many new activities going on and in the planning here, including a photographic retreat around the local beauty spots. Meals are taken with other guests or can be taken with the resident community. The rooms are clean and comfortable, and the beds are very good. The church has many wall and ceiling decorations combined with a stunning old-fashioned altar with various ornamentation and mosaics dating from circa 1917. A special feature is the sound of running water, which does move one to think of 'the living waters of faith'. This may help some with their contemplation – for others it will be a distraction. Overall, there is an atmosphere of friendly caring. The centre is only a few minutes from some of the glorious lakes of Killarney – not to be missed for true inspiration of the wonder of creation. You can take a cart and pony from near the centre and be driven to see it all.

Open: All year except Christmas, New Year, Easter season. Receives men, women, young people, groups.

Rooms: 6 singles ensuite.
Facilities: Church, garden, park, library, small book shop, guest lounge, TV.
Spiritual Help: Spiritual direction, group prayer, Friday evening Divine Office together with community in church, personal talks, meditation.
Guests Admitted to: Chapel, choir, oratory.
Meals: Guests usually eat together. Traditional food. Vegetarians catered for.
Special Activities: Planned directed retreats – send for information. Private retreats with spiritual direction if wanted. Shiatsu, counselling.
Situation: Quiet, in a village.
Maximum Stay: 30 days.
Bookings: Letter, fax, e-mail, telephone 10a.m.–4.30p.m.
Charges: Full board 50€, spiritual direction 5€ per session for guests. Spiritual direction for non-guests 30–35€ per hour
Access: Train, bus and car all easy.

KILDARE

Avelin
Ballymore Eustace
County Kildare

e-mail: begg@iol.ie
Website: www.celticretreat.com

Inter-denominational

At Avelin there is an experiential approach to Celtic spirituality, visiting ancient, prehistoric and early Christian sites. Each day ends with prayer in the Celtic tradition. There is a maximum of seven people for these courses, which are called *Celtic Journeys.*

Open: All year except Christmas. Receives men, women, young people, families, groups, non-retreatants.
Rooms: Accommodation for 7 guests.
Facilities: Garden, library, guest lounge, TV.
Spiritual Help: Personal talks, group sharing, spiritual direction, personal retreat direction.
Guests Admitted to: Unrestricted.
Meals: Everyone eats together. Traditional food. Vegetarians catered for.
Special Activities: 6-day Celtic journeys and pilgrims walks.
Situation: Quiet, in countryside, by lake and mountains.
Maximum Stay: Duration of course.
Bookings: Letter, e-mail.
Charges: B&B plus 3 evening meals about 530€ per 6-night event. No charge for transport involved in course.
Access: Bus: No. 65 from Dublin.

For the word of the Lord is faithful and all his works to be trusted.
PSALM 32

LIMERICK

Castleconnell

The Old School House　　　　　　　　　　Tel: (0)61 372777
Chapel Hill, Castleconnell　　　　　　　　Fax: (0)61 372713
Limerick　　　　　　　　e-mail: jharbison@harps.dnet.co.uk
　　　　　　　　　　　　　Website: www.irishharpcentre.com

Christian – Ecumenical

This place of retreat is a combination of several things as well as several places. First off, St Jospeh's Christian centre is a nineteenth-century former school house – hence the name The Old School House. The centre works on an ecumenical level for Christian development and also has an association with the Irish Harp Centre. Ecumenical work is done mainly, but not exclusively, through the medium of the arts. Accommodation is provided in a nearby village complex. There is a programme, which includes, of course, *Art and the Harp*, as well as retreats entitled *Exploring of the Creed*, *The Benedictine Experience* and *Celtic Christianity*.

Murroe

Glenstal Abbey　　　　　　　　　　　　　★
Murroe　　　　　　　　　　　　Tel: (0)61 386103
Co Limerick　　　　　　　　　　Fax: (0)61 386328
　　　　　　　　　e-mail: guestmaster@glenstal.org

Roman Catholic – Open to all

A long, elegant drive leads up to this great abbey of stone, but the large castle-like building houses the school run by the monks here. Their monastery and the guest area is much more modest – in fact it is fashioned from the old stable block. Rest assured, however, the monks are not deprived, for the monastery surrounds a pretty cloister away from students and visitors. The church standing to one side by itself is a stunner inside. The decorations of ceiling and altar are in vibrant colours and geometric designs with an oriental theme. Somehow this modernity combined with plain walls and simple furnishings works well. The gardens are large and have long walks through woods and by water, with azaleas blooming in the late spring. There is a walled and terraced early-seventeenth-century garden, which is usually locked, but ask if you can go inside. The monks are very hospitable, and a new guest house was opened in 1999, with extremely comfortable accommodation. The guest master is very attentive and is usually in the guest house to welcome guests and converse with them. Evening meals, which are taken in the monastic refectory with the monks, are quite solemn, graced with readings from something informative or enriching to the mind. Glenstal, founded in 1927 on ground owned by a medieval abbey, has a tradition of involvement in arts, crafts and liturgical renewal. One of the brothers currently produces beautifully turned wooden bowls. The annual ecumenical conference at Glenstal is a major event in Irish ecumenism. This is a large, active and growing religious community. **Highly Recommended.**

Open: All year except Christmas and the community's own annual retreat. Receives men, women. **Guests are expected to attend daily liturgy services in the church.**

Rooms: 10 singles, 2 doubles. Men and women accommodated in the same guest house.

Facilities: Disabled access, with one wheel-chair accessible bathroom. Small library, church, large grounds with long and varied walks through the surrounding woods.

Spiritual Help: Personal talks, spiritual counsel if requested, personal retreat direction.

Guests Admitted to: Church, most of the grounds.

Meals: Breakfast is self-catering in the guest house, lunch is served to guests in a small dining room, and dinner is in the monastery refectory with the monks. Traditional food. Vegetarian possible. Tea/coffee facilities.

Special Activities: None.

Situation: Very quiet, in the countryside.

Maximum Stay: 7 days.

Bookings: Letter, e-mail, telephone.

Charges: Average donation 50€ per day

Access: Train: from Dublin. No pick-ups, but taxis are available from Limerick. Car: 12 miles from Limerick, off the Dublin Road.

Ballintubber Abbey
Ballintubber
Claremorris, Co Mayo

Tel: (0)94 30934
Fax: (0)94 30018
e-mail: btubabbey@eircom.net

Roman Catholic – Ecumenical

Ballintubber is the thirteenth-century Abbey that refused to die – the surrounding community stubbornly continued to worship here long after the roof had been demolished in Penal times. The restoration of this simple but majestic old abbey was begun in the nineteenth century and completed at the end of the twentieth. The retreat and pilgrimage experience at Ballintubber includes the chance for a day of quiet on nearby Church Island (sacred from pre-Christian times), an optional 22-mile walk to the summit of Croagh Patrick, a day of prayer in the atmospheric grounds around the Abbey, and immersion in the Neolithic and Celtic roots of Irish Christianity at a nearby cultural heritage museum. As well as theme retreats for Confirmation groups, older students and adults, Ballintubber is used for private retreats in surroundings that deepen the sense of connectedness to the distant past.

Open: All year. Theme retreats not offered in June.

Rooms: Accommodation all in local B&Bs, with mostly good facilities, though not all ensuite or with disabled access. It is possible to accommodate up to 30 adults, though only 15 at a time can travel on the ferry to Church Island.

Facilities: Abbey, conference room, shop, video presentation, the Way of the Cross, the Way of Mary, the Way of Patrick, Celtic Furrow, Church Island (adults only).

Spiritual help: Spiritual accompaniment, personal talks, Sacrament of Reconciliation, daily Eucharist.

Meals: in local restaurant or café.
Special activities: The Ballintubber Experience (including Church Island, Croagh Patrick, Ballintubber Abbey and the Celtic Furrow), Passion Play in Holy Week, themed retreats for young people and adults.
Situation: Quiet village, 8 miles to the south of Castlebar, with views across to the Connemara mountains and Croagh Patrick.
Maximum stay: 5 days, or by arrangement for private retreatants.
Bookings: Letter, e-mail, telephone.
Charges: 31.50€ full board, plus 15€ if programme books are used.
Access: Train or bus to Castlebar (pick-up can be arranged). Car: N84 from Castlebar or Galway.

SLIGO

Holy Hill Hermitage
Skreen
Co Sligo

Tel: (0)71 66021
Fax: (0)71 66954
e-mail: holyhill@eircom.net
Website: www.spirituallife.org

Roman Catholic – Ecumenical
This group of men and women living as hermits in the Carmelite tradition, with a passion for God and His creation, is one of the foundations of the Spiritual Life Institute. As there are only five hermitages for retreatants, they tend to be booked well in advance, but it is worth checking if there are cancellations. For those who feel the need for complete silence and solitude, Holy Hill radiates peace amidst great natural beauty and some inspired gardens created or restored by the monks. The hermitage cabins are complete in themselves, very comfortable and simply furnished and equipped. From Holy Hill there is a magnificent view across the hills to Donegal Bay (the beach is only 4 miles away) and Ben Bulben, and there are wonderful hikes into the Ox Mountains. The old manor house and outbuildings have been lovingly and creatively restored. A couple of beloved dogs and cats roam around the grounds.

Open: All year. Receives everyone.
Rooms: 5 private hermitages, ensuite, with kitchenette. One is wheelchair accessible.
Facilities: Library, chapel, bicycles available.
Spiritual help: A conference with one of the monks available on request.
Guests Admitted to: Library, main house kitchen, some lounges, chapel, grounds.
Meals: Self-catered in one's hermitage. The makings of vegetarian meals are provided.
Special activities: Eucharist and Divine Office 3 times a week, Benediction, communal Sunday brunch after Mass.
Situation: 1½ miles up a steep hillside on the edge of the Ox Mountains, overlooking Donegal Bay. Very quiet and peaceful.
Maximum stay: 1 week, usually Friday to Thursday. Longer stays by arrangement.
Bookings: Letter, fax, e-mail.

Charges: By donation – check their most recent brochure for suggested offerings (which are very modest).

Access: Train or bus to Sligo, then bus to Skreen (pick-up may be possible from Skreen). Car: excellent set of directions available.

Kilsheelan

Rosminian House of Prayer
Glencomeragh
Kilsheelan
Clonmel
Co Tipperary

Tel: (0)52 33181
Fax: (0)52 33636
e-mail: theglen@rosminians.iol.ie
Website: www.iol.ie/~senan

Roman Catholic

The House of Prayer sits at the foot of the Comeragh Mountains looking out over the valley of the River Suir. This splendid refurbished nineteenth-century house has new and attractive rooms, tastefully decorated like a small, elegant country hotel, with pretty wallpaper and curtains. The bathrooms are sparkling clean and generously equipped. The community took professional advice on the decorating and it is a great success. With such outstanding attention to comfort and detail (even down to stationery in the desks) plus central heating, large dining room, library, church hall, spacious gardens, ornamental ponds, streams, hens and ducks, and a peacock wandering around to add a dash of colour, **Rosminian House must be one of the best retreat houses in Europe**. For exercise, there is a variety of forest walks, countryside rambles and mountain hills, all easily accessible. In addition to the main house, there is Glen Lodge, a separate modern and well-furnished self-catering house that is ideal for private retreats, groups and workshops. The small community of five makes everyone feel at home. There is a daily Mass, with a Taize one the last Saturday of each month; and both a Medjugorje evening and a Maranatha Rosary Group each week. This neat-as-a-pin place is the base for a spirituality and retreat programme that combines deep religious traditions and retreats with new thinking – for example the Eucharist may be celebrated outdoors by a waterfall in the hills. As to the food, it is honest and plain with homemade pies and other good dishes. It may well be, as the song says, a long, long way to Tipperary, but if you're headed to the Rosminian House of Prayer, the journey is worth it. **Highly Recommended.**

Open: All year except four days at Christmas. Receives men, women, groups, religious.

Rooms: 16 singles, 4 doubles, 2 twins, 4 hermitages.

Facilities: Disabled – 8 rooms on ground level. Conferences, garden with water ponds, library, TV, payphone, direct dialing.

Spiritual Help: Personal talks, personal retreat direction, spiritual direction, daily Mass (with a Taize Mass monthly), Sacrament of Reconciliation, massage, reflexology.

Guests Admitted to: Chapel. Residential guests have freedom of the house.

Meals: Everyone eats together. Whole food and traditional. Vegetarian, vegan and special diets.

Special Activities: Special programme including 12-Step Spirituality programme, De Mello weekend courses, preached retreats, creation retreats – send for brochure.

Situation: Very quiet, in the countryside.

Maximum Stay: By arrangement.

Bookings: Letter, e-mail, telephone 10.15a.m.–4p.m. Monday to Friday.

Charges: Full board 60€ daily, self-catering 30€ daily.

Access: Bus: ask for directions. Car: easy.

Roscrea

Mount St Joseph Abbey
Roscrea
Co Tipperary

Tel: (0)505 21711 (guest house)
Fax: (0)505 22198
e-mail: community@msjroscrea.ie
Website: www.iol.ie/~mtjoseph

Roman Catholic

This Cistercian monastery guest house is a large one with wide cool hallways and much silence. Compline with the community in the huge, grey stone, vaulted monastic church is a deeply enriching experience. The liturgy here is inspiring. The Abbey is set in quiet countryside and is conducive to prayer and relaxation. In this monastic splendour combined with simplicity, the atmosphere is friendly and warm from a community still busy seeking God and living out full lives in Christ.

> Glance at the sun. See the moon and stars. Gaze at the beauty of earth's greenings. Now, think.
>
> HILDEGARD OF BINGEN

Open: All year except 10 December to 10 January. Receives men, women, young people, groups, religious, non-retreatants.

Rooms: 20 singles, 30 doubles.

Facilities: Prayer room in guest house with Blessed Sacrament reserved, garden, nice walks in lovely park and grounds, guest lounge, guest phone.

Spiritual Help: Spiritual direction, personal retreat direction, meditation, daily Mass, Divine Office. Sacrament of Confession available.

Guests Admitted to: Church, chapel, oratory.

Meals: Everyone eats together in the guest house. Traditional, good, wholesome good food. Vegetarians catered for.

Special Activities: No planned programme but there is a brochure available.

Situation: Quiet, in countryside.

Maximum Stay: 7 days.

Bookings: Letter, fax, e-mail, telephone 4–9p.m.

Charges: Full board 45€, B&B 25€.

Access: Rail: from Dublin. Bus: to Roscrea town, then taxi (2½ miles). Car: from Dublin.

TYRONE

Tullycoll Trust Foundation
Tullycoll House
10 Tullycoll Road
Cookstown
Co Tyrone BT80 9QY

Tel: 028867 58785
Fax: 028867 58815
e-mail: Tully@hotmail.com

Mind Body Spirit – Spiritual development
This is a developing spiritual community set in the heart of Ulster with newly constructed bunkhouse accommodation for up to twenty-four people. The community is guided by the teachings of the book *A Course in Miracles* and is an open fellowship of people united by commitment to spiritual growth and a desire to support themselves and others in a loving environment, thereby creating a safer, more loving earth on which we may all live. The following retreat courses are typical of what is on offer: *Group Rebirthing Workshop, Sweat Lodge Ceremony, Men's Talking Circle, Intimacy in Relationships Workshop, Massage, Reflexology* and *Spiritual Mastery Training*. There is also a flotation tank.

WATERFORD

Waterford

Grace Dieu Retreat Centre
Sacred Heart Missionaries
Tramore Road
Waterford
Co Waterford

Tel: (0)51 374417/373372
Fax: (0)51 874536
e-mail: gracedieu@ireland.com
Website: www.Homepage.eircom.net/gracedieu.

Roman Catholic
This is a large and very busy place offering a wide variety of retreats, from scripture study weekends to exploring the inner child. It offers the opportunity for the development of profound insights in retreats such as those exploring male and female energies. The old house that is the retreat centre was built in about 1810, but there is an equally large modern addition. All the rooms are up to date, and all but two out of some thirty-four are ensuite with showers. The grounds are not extensive but offer mature trees, private sitting areas and a pleasant walk among trees and nearby pastures of almost a mile. All ages are catered for, with all kinds of retreat programmes. There is a chapel, simple in design, into which light pours from all sides. The resident community is friendly and has a wide range of interests. **There are good facilities for the disabled – sixteen disabled people with their own helpers were recently accommodated on a retreat.**

Open: Open all year. Receives men, women, young people, groups.
Rooms: 3 singles, 4 doubles, 26 twins.
Facilities: Disabled. Conferences, guest lounge, payphone.
Spiritual Help: Spiritual direction, personal retreat direction, guided meditation group. Aromatherapy massage in summer months.

Guests Admitted to: Chapel, work of community.
Meals: Guest dining room. Traditional food. Vegetarian and special diets.
Special Activities: Programme of retreats – send for brochure.
Situation: Quiet.
Maximum Stay: 7 days.
Bookings: Letter.
Charges: Charges from 28€ to 32€ per person per day – see brochure.
Access: Bus: ask for information when you book. Car: easy.

WICKLOW

Ballymore Eustace

Avelin Retreat
Poulaphouca
Bishopland
Ballymore Eustace
Co Wicklow

Tel: (0)45 864524
Fax: (0)45 864823
e-mail: begg@iol.ie
Website: www.avelin.hitsplc.com

Christian – Ecumenical
Avelin is a member of the Retreat Association (see Helpful Addresses) and the Methodist Retreat Group. The place is a warm and comfortable modern bungalow with four bedrooms ensuite. There are Celtic retreat programmes available with the Methodist minister and his wife who run Avelin. This retreat involves some walking – sometimes in the Irish mist. There are some lovely places to see on such a retreat and some beautiful works of art to contemplate.

Open: All year.
Rooms: 4 doubles ensuite.
Facilities: Garden, guest lounge, TV, quiet room. Guests may use e-mail and fax facilities.
Spiritual Help: Personal talks, group sharing, spiritual direction, directed study.
Guests Admitted to: Unrestricted access.
Meals: Everyone eats together. Traditional/vegetarian food. Special diets.
Special Activities: Programme – send for information.
Situation: Quiet, near lakes and mountains.
Maximum Stay: For the retreat or by arrangement.
Bookings: Letter, fax, e-mail, telephone.
Charges: Set charge for 6-day Celtic Pilgrimage Retreat, also B&B rates.
Access: Train: Dublin (pick-up available). Bus: No. 65 from Dublin. Car: N81.

Donard

Chrysalis
Donard
Co Wicklow

Tel/Fax: (0)45 404713
e-mail: peace@chrysalis.ie
Website: www.chrysalis.ie

Mind Body Spirit – Holistic centre
This centre, founded in 1989 for renewal and growth, is a former rectory dating from 1711 and now restored, specialising in residential courses in

personal growth and spirituality. The house is charming and welcoming. While the main concern here is Mind Body Spirit, there are Christian approaches such as de Mello exercises in the programme. This quiet sanctuary, which has now been running for some years, offers space for diverse spiritual traditions, with one of the most extensive programmes of residential courses, one-day courses and workshops on offer anywhere. These include *Search for Inner Freedom, Journey of Transition and Transformation, Touch and Relaxation, Facing Co-dependency, Searching for Inner Freedom, Journal Writing, Healing and Transformation* and *Inner Yoga and Imagery*. Vegetarian food and two hermitages add to the attractions of this place. **Highly Recommended.**

Open: All year except Christmas. Receives men, women, groups.
Rooms: 3 singles, 5 twins, 2 dormitories, 2 hermitages. Mobiles must be switched off.
Facilities: Conferences, lovely garden, park, library.
Spiritual Help: Personal talks, group sharing, meditation, directed study.
Guests Admitted to: Guest areas.
Meals: Everyone eats together. **Vegetarian food only.** Self-catering facilities.
Special Activities: Conferences, workshops, retreats. Planned programme – brochure available.
Situation: Very quiet, in the countryside.
Maximum Stay: Duration of course or event.
Bookings: Letter, fax, e-mail, telephone office hours.
Charges: All charges are listed in the extensive programme brochure – range from 20€ to over 200€.
Access: Bus or car.

Glendalough

St Kevin's Parish
Glendalough
Co Wicklow   Tel/fax: (0)404 45777

Roman Catholic
Glendalough, an ancient monastic site surrounded by the majestic splendour of the Wicklow Mountains, draws large numbers of visitors. However, it is also possible to make a peaceful hermitage retreat a little off the beaten track at St Kevin's Parish Church, which is up a quiet road overlooking the valley. There are five tastefully designed retreat hermitages, complete with bathroom, kitchenette and an open fire (there are also storage heaters) – and a bench outside on which to sit and gaze across the valley. Retreatants cater entirely for themselves, buying provisions locally. The monastic site is well worth lingering in, but go early in the morning or evening if you prefer to do it in a contemplative atmosphere. There are countless beautiful walks by lakes, streams, woods and hills.

Open: All year
Rooms: 5 self-contained, self-catering hermitages, one with disabled access.
Facilities: Converted coach-house with library, conference room, meditation room. Chapel, meditation garden, adjacent monastic site.

Spiritual help: Spiritual counsel with emphasis on Celtic spirituality, Sacrament of Reconciliation, Daily Eucharist.

Guests admitted to: Chapel, coach-house facilities.

Meals: Self-catered.

Special activities: Morning and evening prayer.

Situation: In quiet part of village, surrounded by forested mountains and close to two lakes.

Maximum stay: 6 days (minimum 2 days).

Bookings: Letter, fax, e-mail, telephone.

Charges: 35€ per night, exclusive of food.

Access: Bus: to St Kevin's – leaves twice daily from St Stephen's Green, Dublin. Car: ask for directions.

> God in his mercy looks on
> you not for what you are,
> nor for what you have been,
> but for what you wish to be.
> THE CLOUD OF UNKNOWING

France

There are many organised retreats available in France, although the majority of these are still Christianity-based, and Roman Catholic in particular. But there is an increasing number of retreats and places for rest and renewal that are of an alternative spirituality nature, with an emphasis on self-development and learning new skills. Some examples are herbal medicine and permaculture. In traditional retreat programmes there are still plenty of proven spiritually awakening themes, such as *Introduction to Bible Reading, Spiritual Meditation, Learning to Appreciate Prayer* and *Silence in the Carmelite Tradition*.

The response to changes in the religious life in France has been different to that in Britain. For this reason alone, the overall choice of retreats and courses on offer in France is narrower – although increasing in breadth and scope every year. Private individual retreats and group pilgrimages remain widely popular. Buddhist centres expect you to have spiritual intentions, although previous experience of meditation, while useful, is not always mandatory. There are plenty of beginners courses on offer now.

Do not think, however, that the French are less religious than the British or other European folk. A recent survey of France revealed that some 25 million people feel strongly about the role of religion in their lives. Some sixty-nine per cent of the French are Catholic; only two per cent are Protestant, and other religions account for seven per cent of the population. More than two-thirds of the French aged over 28 years old declare themselves Catholic. In Paris the figure is sixty-eight per cent, while outside the capital it ranges from forty-nine per cent to eighty-six per cent. Non-believers run a poor second place overall, with twenty-two per cent of the population believing God does not exist. This does not mean that such people do not go on retreats, because many of them do – in France as in Britain.

LANGUAGE

For most retreats you need an adequate understanding of French, but for some you may be able to manage without fluency in the language. It is also worth asking retreat centres if they offer retreats in English, which is now a growing possibility. This was bound to happen given the increasingly international profile of visitors to France (the world's number one tourist spot); the great rise in English language residents in France; and the common useage of English in commerce and on the internet. Some of the new English-language retreats are organised in France by non-French locals and others are organised in Britain. Some of the established retreat centres in Britain also run courses in France, often in lovely settings. Some French retreat house programmes are written partly in English, so it is worth sending for information if you spot a place that appeals to you.

From time to time, major Buddhist events are held in France at which English is available in instantaneous translation. For example, His Holiness The Dalai Lama recently gave a five-day programme of teaching on the theme of *The Road to Awakening* in the south-west of France, at which French, English and German translations were all available.

Most French people are tolerant and polite in accepting any attempt, no matter how inadequate, to speak their beautiful language. So if you want to go on retreat in France, you needn't necessarily be put off by the language. Just bear in mind that over seventy-five per cent of communication between people is in body language and not in words. *Bonne chance!*

Disabled An organisation worth contacting for the disabled is **Office Chrétien des Personnes Handicapées,** tel: (0)1 53 69 44 30, website: www.och.assoc.fr. The French are working hard to make facilities accessible to the disabled everywhere, but in general the level of awareness of such need does not seem to be as high among the general population as it is in Britain. Nevertheless, progress is being made, so it is always worthwhile discussing your requirements, even if we make no comment about disabled facilities in the listing for a particular retreat centre. Very often the welcome mat is out and waiting for the disabled – even if after it come steps to get inside.

Paris If you are staying in or near Paris for a while, there are plenty of evening talks and day retreats, some of which are good for taking inspiration back home and putting it into action for the benefit of others. For example, you may be able to catch a talk by someone from the l'Arche communities, the Faith and Light Movement or the Emmaus Movement. The French national daily newspaper *La Croix* usually has a brief listing of spiritual and religious talks being given. It is to be found near the end of the newspaper.

Buddhism Buddhism is the most rapidly expanding religion in France today, with some 5 million people claiming an interest in this spiritual path. Some Buddhist retreat centres are still in old buildings but many now are modern and purpose-built. For those keen on discovering and learning more about Buddhist teachings and retreats, the choice of places to go in France is wide – from traditional Tibetan establishments with ancient spiritual lineages to places where new teaching approaches to traditional Buddhism are being explored. There is an excellent guide in French, *Guide des Centres Bouddhistes en France* (Phillippe Ronce, Editions Noesis, Paris), which contains a fairly comprehensive listing of the various places by lineage and tradition.

Christian Many of the Christian religious communities have modern guest house facilities, which are often striking in design and concept and very comfortable. On the other hand, the oldest monasteries are huge buildings originally constructed to house big communities of men or women and, consequently, can strike one as very institutional and forbidding. But a large number of these rambling places have comfortable refurbished guest rooms, some ensuite. Many French Christian monasteries will expect your stay to be a spiritual one and not just for relaxation. In other words, if you are not there to be quiet and prayer, why have you come? However, this is much less the case today than in former years. Usually for reasons of earning income and putting to good use buildings that are too large for today's downsized communities, increasing numbers of monasteries have broadened their outlook on what retreats can be about in terms of spiritual journey. These days monastic retreat programmes often combine traditional Christian themes with modern spiritual modalities, making use of the arts, crafts, aspects of meditation, singing and inventive approaches to opening the heart to listen to God and the inner self.

Mind Body Spirit – Alternative spirituality Mind Body Spirit and Alternative spirituality facilities and programmes have increased exponentially in France. A quick look in any French newsagents will confirm the wide range of interests the French have in alternative spirituality and holistic health approaches. Mind Body Spirit centres and their programmes are often exciting, enabling and positive in terms of de-stressing, exploration of new horizons, self-improvement and discovering the inner person.

Yoga Yoga is now taught all over France and is as popular as in Britain. See Yoga in France section below.

Retreat Meals Do not expect the meals in monastic France necessarily to reflect the nation's reputation for cordon bleu cooking. By and large monks and nuns everywhere in the world cook simple, plain food. Some of it is great and some of it not so appetising. Vegetarians on retreat in France are in for a difficult time, as provision for them will be minimal unless they stay at a Buddhist or Mind Body Spirit centre. This has nothing to do with lack of Christian hospitality and everything to do with cultural differences in cooking and eating. However, time changes all, and the number of Christianity-inspired retreat guest houses now offering sufficient vegetarian food has increased somewhat. Vegan, fruitarian, dairy-free and gluten-free eaters are usually out of luck in France unless they are staying at an alternative healing centre or an English owned and managed establishment.

Retreat costs The charges for full board in France are usually 40€ or less per day, with lower rates for monastic hospitality and higher rates for places run more along commercial lines. Mind Body Spirit centres charge rates that roughly correspond with those you would expect in Britain.

RETREAT CENTRES AND PLACES

The first of the following listings is for a group of communities under the La Communauté Catholique des Béatitudes Foundation. These are listed separately because they have a number of centres and programmes, and the media in which they advertise their activities are not widely available to the general public. The subsequent, main body of the listings is organised by departments of France.

La Communauté des Béatitudes

Website: www.beatitudes.fr or www.institut.beatitudes.free.fr
Roman Catholic. The Communauté des Béatitudes now has houses in some thirty dioceses in France and thirty-five abroad (See St David's Monastery, Wales section). It runs many courses and retreats throughout France, and the following are just a few of its regular venues. While having a deep Christian basis, courses and retreats are wide-ranging in theme, including topics such as *The History of the Church*, *The History of Spirituality*, *Do Not be Afraid to Take Mary into Your Heart*, *Watercolour Painting* and *Saint Joseph Work* (in which you spend a week in prayer, sharing and work with the community), *Walking in the Desert of Sinai* (which takes place around the Red Sea area) and *Dance of Prayer, Dance of Healing*. There are also preached retreats. A number of workshop courses run by artists in the context of the spirituality of Communauté des Béatitudes are also available. In the recent past these have included *The Art of Illumination*, *Dances of Israel*, *Painting and Prayer* and *Singing and Interior Peace*. The Ateliers St Bernard at Abbaye Blanche, 50140 Mortain, tel: (0)2 33 79 47 47 is one place running such a programme. The Communauté des Béatitudes is a highly active, youthful and enthusiastic group of dedicated men and women whose development of a life in common for spiritual purposes is very exciting. **Highly Recommended.**

Cté des Béatitudes
Couvent Notre Dame
81170 Cordes sur Ceil

Tel: (0)5 63 53 74 10
Fax: (0)5 63 53 74 13
e-mail: cordes@beattitudes.org

Cté des Béatitudes
19, avenue Antoine Beguere
65100 Lourdes

Tel: (0)5 62 42 35 20
Fax: (0)5 62 42 32 66
e-mail: Lourdes.sessions@beatitudes.org

Cté des Béatitudes
60, avenue Général Compans
31700 Blagnac

Tel: (0)5 62 747 747
e-mail: blagnac@beatitudes.org

Cté des Béatitudes
1, rue du Petit Montauban la Chaume
85100 Les bales D'Olonne

Tel: (0)2 51 95 19 26
e-mail: Beautitudes.sables@wanadoo.fr

Cté des Béatitudes
Cœur Immaculé
2, avenue des Poiriers
76530 Les Essarts

Tel: 02 35 67 30 24

Cté des Béatitudes Marthe et Marie de Béthanie Burtin
41600 Nouan-le-Fuzelier

Tel: (0)2 54 88 77 33

Cté des Béatitudes
La Chasse
35750 Iffendic

Tel: (0)2 99 09 92 19

Cté des Béatitudes
18, Côte St Martin   Tel: (0)5 59 13 61 26
64800 Nay   Fax: (0)5 59 13 98 94

Cté des Béatitudes   Tel: (0)2 31 32 00 44
10, avenue Sainte Thérèse 14100 Lisieux Fax: (0)2 31 61 09 36
                    e-mail : Session.beatitudes.lisieux@wanadoo.fr

Cté des Béatitudes (for 14–18- and 18–30-year-olds)
Le Père des Miséricordes   Tel: (0)2 31 62 54 52
14100 Hermival-les-vaux   e-mail: Esperance.jeunes@beatitudes.org

---

AIN (01)

Bourg en Brese
Auris
6, rue Viala
01000 Bourg en Bresse   Tel: (0)4 74 22 48 86
Alternative spirituality, yoga, de-stressing, meditation, chanting, voice workshops and personal therapies. Send for brochure.

Le Plantay
Abbaye Notre-Dame-des-Dombes
Le Plantay   Tel: (0)4 74 98 14 40
01330 Villars-les-Dombes   Fax: (0)4 74 98 16 70
Roman Catholic. Trappist monks. Receives men, women, groups who desire
a retreat of silence and prayer. Accommmmodation for 40. Camping, woods,
dormitory and barn. Disabled facility for one. One-hour video on the
monastery, founded in 1863, is available. Monks make various products
including dried fruits and petits fours, and have a small shop.

Miribel
Centre Alain de Boismenu
Rue de La Chanal
BP 236   Tel: (0)4 78 55 31 47
01702 Miribel   Fax: (0)4 78 55 00 59
Roman Catholic. Welcomes men, women and groups who want a retreat of
reflection, recollection, and prayer. Close to the town, the guest house has a
private garden and offers peace and a spiritual atmosphere. Accommodation
for up to 100 guests, with a number of meeting rooms and equipment. Must
book in advance.

AISNE (02)

Brumetz
Maison de la Trinité
02810 Cerfroid   Tel: (0)3 23 71 41 85
Brumetz   Fax: (0)3 23 71 23 04
Roman Catholic. The community of sisters receives up to 30 men and
women guests. 30 singles, 1 double, guest lounges. Chapel, choir. Personal
talks with a sister if requested.

ALLIER (03)

Chantelle
Abbaye Bénédictine Saint-Vincent   Tel: (0)4 70 56 62 55
Rue Anne de Beauzier   Fax: (0)4 70 56 62 69
03140 Chantelle   e-mail: accueil@benedictines-chantelle.com
                             Website: www.benedictines-chantelle.com
Roman Catholic. Benedictine community. Receives men, women, accompanied disabled. 27 rooms, 5 conferences rooms, library, chapel, choir. Personal talks, meditation. 8 days maximum stay.

Dompierre-sur-Besbre
Abbaye Notre Dame de Sept-Fons
03290 Dompierre-sur-Besbre   Tel: (0)4 70 48 14 90
Roman Catholic. Men, religious, for religious retreats only. Personal talks possible.

Moulins
Monastère de la Visitation
65, rue des Tanneries
03000 Moulins   Tel: (0)4 70 44 27 43
Roman Catholic. Visitation nuns. 2 rooms for women, with enclosure for a silent retreat.

ALLIER (04)

Faucon de Barcelonnette
Couvent Saint-Jean de Matha   Tel: (0)4 92 81 09 17
04400 Faucon de Barcelonnette   e-mail: couvent.matha@wanadoo.fr
Roman Catholic. The community of religious men welcomes individuals or groups for stays of not more than 21 days. 14 singles, 9 doubles. About 30€ full board per day.

Ganagobie
Monastère Notre-Dame   Tel: (0)4 92 68 00 04
04310 Ganagobie   Fax: (0)4 68 11 49
                             e-mail: courrier@ndganagobie.com
Christian. This monastery has been restored to create an enterprise centre, which organises seminars on such things as management and ethics. Information available on courses.

ALPES-HAUTE (05)

Laragne
Terre Nouvelle
BP 52
05300 Laragne   Tel: (0)4 92 65 24 25
Alternative spirituality. A place like the Findhorn Community (see Scotland section). Many workshops in the summer. Send for course information and event charges.

Saint Etienne de Laus
Hotellerie Notre-Dame du Laus   Tel: (0)4 92 50 30 73
05130 Saint Etienne de Laus   Fax: (0)4 92 50 90 77
e-mail: accueil@notre-dame-du-laus.com
Roman Catholic. This is a very large establishment with accommodation for
upwards of 400. It is also very popular and bookings for summer need to be
made at least 4 months in advance. With a view of the mountains, this retreat
house offers disabled facilities, library, lounges, personal talks, conferences,
chapel, choir, masses, courses. Full board rates vary but are in 30€–40€ range.
Send for information.

ALPES-MARITIMES (06)

Carros
Communauté des Carmélites
06510 Carros-Village   Tel: (0)4 93 29 10 71
Roman Catholic. Carmelite nuns. Receives men, women, young people. In
rather isolated and very peaceful situation. 7 rooms for retreats of 10 days
maximum. Personal talks, prayers in chapel with community.

La Trinité   Tel: (0)4 93 41 09 60
Sanctuaire de Notre-Dame de Laghet   Fax: (0)4 93 41 21 78
06340 La Trinité   e-mail: sanctuairelaghet@free.fr
Roman Catholic. The sisters of the Sacred Heart receive men and women
retreatants and pilgrims. Some 60 rooms, guest lounges, library, personal
talks, conferences. Rates about 35€ full board per day.

ARDÈCHE (07)

Rochessauve
Aleph   Tel: (0)4 75 65 10 99
07210 Rochessauve   Fax: (0)4 75 65 08 02
Alternative spirituality. It is claimed that this centre is like no other. It is
certainly true that it is in a magical place in the Ardèche. Here is a setting of
gorges, mountains, prehistoric sites and sacred places. Aleph aims to help you
make contact with nature and, in turn, with your own nature. Send for information on their philosophy and courses.

Saint-Étienne-de-Lugdarès
La Père Hôtelier
Abbaye Notre dame des neiges
07590 Saint Laurent les Bains   Tel: (0)4 66 46 00 68
Roman Catholic. Open Easter to All Saints Day. Receives all, young people
in annexe. Group conferences. Setting high up in mountains. Much silence
and an austere life. Send for their brochure.

> He leads me beside the waters of peace.
> PSALM 23

AUDE (11)

Capendu
Monastère Sainte-Claire
Azille
11700 Capendu   Tel: (0)4 68 91 40 24
Roman Catholic. Open to men and women for retreats or just a short period
of reflection. Limited number of rooms. 8 days maximum stay.

Fanjeaux
Belvédère St Dominique
Rue de la Porte en Rivière
Prouilhe
11270 Fanjeaux   Tel: (0)4 68 24 72 36
Roman Catholic. This is an international cultural and retreat centre in a
village 360 metres up, with a panoramic view of the plain of Lauragais. It is
run in conjunction with the Dominicans, with a programme of events and
courses. Receives men, women, groups. 10 rooms several guest lounges,
library, personal talks, meeting rooms, chapel.

Rennes le Château   Tel: (0)4 68 74 23 21
Lavaldieu   Fax: (0)4 68 74 23 21
11190 Rennes le Château   e-mail: lavaldieu@aol.com
                                            Website: www.lavaldieu.com
Mind Body Spirit. Self-directed retreats and working holidays, which can also
be a form of retreat to get away from what you ordinarily do, all in a landscape which is inspiring. Yoga, breath work, earth mysteries, food and
gardening, healing and shamanic practice all take place here in this lovely part
of the world. About 20 bed spaces. Camping. Meals are vegetarian. No
smoking. Open to all ages, including children.

Seignalens
Agors Centre of Ayurvedic Medicine   Tel: (0)4 68 69 09 95
Agora Centre   Fax: (0)4 68 69 09 96
Le Lac   e-mail: Ayurved@fr.st
11240 Seignalens   Website: www.ayurved.fr.st
Ayurvedic and mind, body spirit. Seminars and relaxing holidays in the
foothills in the south-west of France. Nature, swimming in a lake in the
summer, mild winter weather, healthy Ayurvedic food. A range of courses
and workshops in Ayurvedic medicine for all. Self-healing, yoga, and other
healing and renewal subjects. Comfortable rooms with about 18 bed spaces.
Vegetarian food only. No smoking. Large indoor space. Easy from
Carcassonne, where flights arrive from London Stansted.

AVEYRON (12)

Espalion
Abbaye Notre Dame de Bonneval
Le Cayrol
12500 Espalion   Tel: (0)5 65 44 01 22
Roman Catholic. Cistercian nuns. Open to all for spiritual retreats. 32 single
rooms.

Mur-de-Barrez
Monastère Sainte-Claire
2, rue de la Berque   Tel: (0)5 65 66 00 46
12600 Mur-de-Barrez   Fax: (0)5 65 66 00 90
Roman Catholic. A community of Poor Clares welcoming women and families with children. Much peace and solitude. Chapel, personal talks and spiritual direction possible. Library, TV, meeting rooms. 13 singles, 17 doubles, 3 triples. About 28€ full board per day. Also self-catering.

Saint-Sernin-sur-Rance
Monastère Notre-Dame-d'Orient
12380 Saint-Sernin-sur-Rance   Tel: (0)5 65 99 60 88
Roman Catholic. Receives young and not so young, laymen and laywomen, priests, monks, nuns.

BOUCHES-DU-RHÔNE (13)

Aix-en-Provence
Carmel de Notre Dame de l'Assomption
4, Monteé Saint-Joseph
Route du Tholonet
13090 Aix-en-Provence   Tel: (0)4 42 21 40 58
Roman Catholic. Women and young women – two or three at a time – are received here by the Carmelite nuns.

Grans
Domaine de Petite
Union Culture et Promotion   Tel: (0)4 90 55 93 60
Route de Saint-Chamas   Fax: (0)4 90 55 87 74
13450 Grans   e-mail: domainedepetite@domainedepetite.com
Roman Catholic. Receives everyone for spiritual retreats, seminars and courses. An isolated house with a very large woodland park. 20 singles, 16 doubles, 4 dormitories. 7 meeting rooms, TV, pilgrim's way, chapel, library. Rates about 32€ full board, 22€ half board.

Jouques
Abbaye Notre-Dame-de-Fidélité   Tel: (0)4 42 57 80 17
13490 Jouques   Fax: (0)4 67 05 21
Roman Catholic. Benedictine hospitality for individuals and groups searching for peace and silence. Choir sings Gregorian chant.

Simiane-Collongue
Communautés Bénédictines de Sainte Lioba
Quartier Saint-Germain
13109 Simiane-Collongue   Tel: (0)4 42 22 60 60
Roman Catholic. Open all year to everyone. Receives those for a silent retreat in the convent, all others in guest housing. Hill walking nearby.

Tarascon   Tel: (0)4 90 90 52 70
Abbaye Saint-Michel-de-Frigolet   Fax (0)4 90 95 75 22
13150 Tarascon sur Rhône   Website: www.Frigolet.com

Roman Catholic. A magical place of herbs set in the beauty of Provence. Open to all, including pilgrims. 36 rooms. Restaurant (also open to day visitors), meeting rooms, TV, chapel, choir. Personal talks possible. About 35€ full board. Can sometimes be busy in summer, with lots of people coming and going – but it is well worth a visit even for the day.

CALVADOS (14)

Bayeux
Monastère des Bénédictines   Tel: (0)2 31 92 84 01/31 92 88 42
48, rue Saint-Loup – BP 219   Fax: (0)2 31 21 59 91
14402 Bayeux Cedex   e-mail: benedictines.bayeux@wanadoo.fr
Roman Catholic. Receives women and families. Open all year. Maximum stay 2 weeks. Accommodation for 35. Chapel. Personal talks possible. Quiet location and much silence.

Caen
Monastère de Carmélites
51, avenue Clemenceau
14000 Caen   Tel: (0)2 31 93 66 63
Roman Catholic. Welcomes all for private individual retreats. Longer stays for those considering a vocation.

Juaye-Mondaye
Abbaye St Martin de Mondaye   Tel: (0)2 31 92 58 11
14250 Juaye-Mondaye   Fax: (0)2 31 92 08 05
Roman Catholic. Open all year. Receives mostly men. Disabled. Special open door retreats in summer. Participation in Divine Office warmly welcomed. Accommodation for 60. Three lounges, 2 workshops, library, chapel. Personal talks possible. A popular place – you need to book several months in advance.

LISIEUX

Lisieux is a place of international Christian pilgrimage. Saint Thérèse de l'Enfant Jésus (1873–97), or The Little Flower as she is often called, was the daughter of a watchmaker. At the age of fifteen, she obtained permission to enter the Carmelite convent at Lisieux. She wrote about twenty prayers and an autobiography, *L'Histoire d'une âme* (*The Story of a Soul*), which has been translated into fifty languages and is the biggest-selling spiritual book after the Bible. She had little education, suffered grave and painful illnesses (from which she eventually died in agony) and sometimes faltered in her beliefs, yet she is one of the most famous and beloved saints in the world. Her popularity lies in her appeal to ordinary people. She believed, among other things, in a return to the word of God; the priority for all Christians of the virtues of faith, hope and charity in everyday life; the call of each baptised person to sanctity; and the need for brotherly affection for those of different beliefs and those who do not believe in God. She rose above the religious thinking of her time to show with inspired insight a new way to God based on the central message of the Gospels, which is love.

Accueil Providence
17, chemin de Rocques   Tel: (0)1 31 48 56 62
14100 Lisieux   Fax: (0)2 31 48 56 76
Roman Catholic. This is a very large place where a lot of groups and school parties come. Individual retreats are possible. All the facilities you would expect of such a large modern complex.

Ermitage Sainte-Thérèse   Tel: (0)2 31 48 55 10
23, rue du Carmel   Fax: (0)2 31 48 55 27
14100 Lisieux   e-mail: Ermitage-ste-therese@therese-de-lisieux.com
Roman Catholic. This is a centre for pilgrims open all year except 15 December to 15 January. There is a calendar of retreats, and both individuals and groups are received.

CHARENTE (16)

Ansac
Susan Gibbons Retreats
16500 Ansac   Tel: (UK) 020 8392 1905
Mind Body Spirit. A small house near the medieval town of Confolens, with wonderful views of the Vienne river from the back garden. There is single or twin accommodation. Susan Gibbons is a reiki master and teacher who gives guided retreats on a one-to-one basis or small group basis here at her house in France. She does only some 3 retreats a year, and arrangements must be made with her in Britain. Special activities include spiritual and reiki healing, meditation and personal talks. French lessons are also available. Meals are whole food and vegetarian. Well-behaved dogs welcome. Charges are by donation –about 15€–18€ per person per day full board suggested. Access is via London Stansted to Poitiers. Pick-up from the airport can be arranged.

Montmoreau-Saint-Cybard
Abbaye Sainte-Marie-de-Maumont Tel: (0)5 45 60 34 38
Juignac   Fax: (0)5 45 60 29 02
16190 Montmoreau-Saint-Cybard   e-mail: Acc.maumont@free.fr
Roman Catholic. Open to individuals or groups for stays of up to 8 days. Personal talks by arrangement. Chapel, choir. 23 rooms. Need to book 15 days in advance.

> *A partir de notre vécu, se découvre une voie d'éveil du cœur et de l'esprit, simple et universelle. Elle constitue le fond commun de tout cheminement authentique.*
> LAMA DENYS

CHARENTE-MARITIME (17)

La Rochelle
Carmel
1, rue Saint-Dominique
17000 La Rochelle   Tel: (0)5 46 41 47 02
Roman Catholic. Open to all women religious and young women. 3 rooms.

Saint Palais sur Mer
Béthanie, Monastère des Dominicaines
67, avenue de Courlay
17420 Saint Palais sur Mer   Tel: (0)5 46 23 12 19
Roman Catholic. Receives all individuals and groups of up to 20. Thirteen
rooms, guest lounge, TV, meeting room, chapel. Personal talks possible.
Guests are usually asked to help set the tables, wash up and change the beds
when they leave. If you want to come here in July or August you need to
book at least 3 months in advance.

CHER (18)

Saint-Doulchard
Monastère de Saint-Doulchard
115, route de Vouzeron
18230 Saint-Doulchard   Tel: (0)2 48 65 57 65
Roman Catholic. Receives individuals and groups for retreats. Maximum stay
8 days. About 20 rooms available. Chapel services in French. Mass every day.

CORRÈZE (19)

Aubazine
Monastère de la Théophanie
Le Ladeix, 19190 Aubazine   Tel: (0)5 55 25 75 67
Byzantine Catholic nuns. Religious services in French. Receives men, women,
young people, very small groups. One of the nuns speaks English. Great
hospitality from this community. The monastery is an old farmhouse, high up
in the Massif Central. Courses on Byzantine spirituality and the art and theology of icons are sometimes offered. Vegetarian food on request. 11 singles, 3
doubles. Central heating in winter. Guest lounge, library, chapel. Personal
talks possible. A busy place – for Easter and summer time you need to book
at least a month in advance.

CORSE (20)

Vico
Couvent Saint-François   Tel: (0)4 95 26 83 83
20160 Vico   Fax: (0)4 95 26 64 09
Roman Catholic. The community receives everyone for an individual or
group retreat. You may come for a few days or a weekend for reflection and
prayer. The convent is high up on the mountain with views. About 40 beds.
Cost about 38€ full board. Guest lounge, chapel, choir, meeting rooms,
library. Personal talks possible.

COTE-D'ÔR (21)

Flavigny-sur-Ozerain
Abbaye Saint-Joseph-de-Clairval　　　Tel: (0)3 80 96 22 31
21150 Flavigny-sur-Ozerain　　　Fax: (0)3 80 96 25 29
Roman Catholic. Open only to men for spiritual retreats of 5 days or for a
maximum stay of 1 week. 17 single rooms. Library, chapel, choir. Personal
talks possible.

Saint Nicolas les Cîteaux　　　Tel: (0)3 80 61 11 53
Abbaye de Cîteaux　　　Fax: (0)3 80 62 36 79
21700 Saint Nicolas les Cîteaux　e-mail: monastere@citeaux-abbaye.com
Website: www.citeaux-abbaye.com
Roman Catholic. Founded in 1098, this is the mother house of the order of
Cistercians. In it some 40 monks live a life of simplicity and austerity. The
Abbey is in a great park. The monks welcome individuals who want to make
a retreat of up to 8 days. 25 singles, 12 doubles, 5 family rooms. 2 guest
lounges, chapel, choir. Personal talks possible.

CÔTES-DU-NORD (22)

Saint-Brieuc
Carmel
55, rue Pinot-Duclos
22000 Saint-Brieuc　　　Tel: (0)2 96 94 22 95
Roman Catholic. Receives women for individual retreats.

Saint Jacut de la Mer　　　Tel: (0)2 96 27 71 19
L'Abbaye　　　Fax: (0)2 96 27 79 45
BP 1　　　e-mail: Abbaye.st.jacut@wanadoo.fr
22750 Saint Jacut de la Mer　　　Website: www.abbaye-st.jacut.com
Roman Catholic. Managed by the association La Providence, this retreat
house is open from September to the end of June to both individuals and
groups who wish to make a retreat. It runs a programme of courses, retreats
and events – send for brochure. The atmosphere is good for silence and time
to reflect. Disabled. 45 singles, 40 doubles, 7 family rooms. Meeting rooms,
guest lounges, tennis, library, TV, chapel, choir.

CREUSE (23)

Chatelus Malvaleix
Sabine Flury-Sanger
La Sagne
23270 Chatelus Malvaleix　　　Tel: (0)5 55 80 76 80
Mind Body Spirit, Ayurvedic. Courses of Ayurvedic massage, contact with
nature, and healthy eating are the themes of some of the workshops that
Flury-Sanger gives.

La Cellette
Le Blé en Herbe (The Ripening Seed)
Puissetier
23350 La Cellette

⭐

Tel: (0)5 55 80 62 83
Fax: (0)5 55 80 62 83
e-mail: maria-sperring@gofernet.com

Alternative spirituality, eco-spirituality. Holistic retreats. Open from February to December. Receives men, women, children, groups. Set in the rolling foothills of the Massif Central, this well-established place run for many years by Maria Sperring has an 8-acre organic garden with wild flower fields and is surrounded by unspoiled countryside. The lifestyle here is one of simplicity and closeness to nature. No smoking indoors. No excessive alcohol. Mobiles not to be used in grounds. These restrictions are to maintain the quiet and peaceful haven that has been created. There is time for reflection into self and nature, and space for solitude or group sharing. A variety of options for a get-away-from-it-all retreat are on offer. Programmes, which are given in English and/or German, may include *Holistic Massage, African Dancing, Meditation of Dance, Transformational Breathing Seminar, Easter Celebrations, Shiatsu and Healing, Sacred Space for Women* and *Herbal Medicine*. There is a 1-week *Barefoot Herbalist* course introducing the theoretical, practical and intuitive skills of herbal medicine with Ben Edwards (3 Place Farm Cottages, Fairlight Place, Hastings, Sussex TN35 5DT, tel: (UK) 01424 812761), which costs about £300 including camping and organic food. In addition there is a programme of garden activities during the different seasons of the year. Personal talks, group sharing. 3 singles, 5 doubles, camping, caravan site. Vegetarian organic food. B&B 18€, full board 32€, self-catered camping 5€ (per day), camping with meals 25€. Courses 90€–500€ depending on duration and type of activity. There is a wonderful Rose Cottage, which is self-catering and self-contained. This centre is roomy, cosy, a hide-away to delight you. Send for brochure. **Highly Recommended.**

DORDOGNE (24)

Bergerac
Carmel du Sacré-cœur
79, rue Valette
24100 Bergerac

Tel: (0)5 53 57 15 33

Roman Catholic. Open only to those who are making a retreat or families of the religious. Open May and June. 5 singles.

Echourgnac
Abbaye Notre-Dame-de-Bonne-Espérance
Echourgnac
24410 Saint-Aulaye

Tel: (0)5 53 80 82 50
Fax: (0)5 53 80 08 36
e-mail: m.echourgnac@wanadoo.fr

Roman Catholic. Trappist nuns. Open all year. Receives all for spiritual retreats of up to 10 days. A very peaceful place with 25 rooms, 2 guest lounges, chapel.

Monestier
Centre d'études et de prière
Sainte Crois, 24240 Monestier

Tel: (0)5 53 63 37 70

Christian. A study and prayer centre run by an Orthodox priest and his wife. There are some workshops organised by outside people. Send for brochure.

Montignac
Dhagpo Kagyu Ling Tel: (0)5 53 50 70 75
Saint-Léon-sur-Vézère Fax: (0)5 53 50 80 54
24290 Montignac e-mail: dhagpo.kagyu.ling@wanadoo.fr
Buddhist, Karma Kagyu, Tibetan. This is one of three international centres, the others being in Sikkim and America. The property was given by Bernard Benson in 1977 and is a place of silence near the famed Lascaux caves. Practice is in Tibetan, but information is available in English. 3-year, 3-month and 3-day retreats are all on offer. Day membership is possible. Accommodation ranges from dormitories at about 4€ a night to singles and doubles at 10€ a night. Meals 3€–4€.

Saint-Léon-sur-Vézère
La Bicanderie Tel/Fax: (0)5 53 50 75 24
24290 Saint-Léon-sur-Vézère e-mail: chanteloube@wanadoo.fr
Buddhist, Vajrayana, Tibetan. Situated in a green valley, not far from Brive, in the direction of Bordeaux. Spiritual practices are in Tibetan, but information is available in English and French. 3-year guided retreats are possible here, as well as various programmes of study, which cost about 7€ a day. Single and double rooms about 3€ a day, and food 2.50€ a day.

St Crépin Carlucet
Centre Eviel
Les Granges Tel: (0)5 53 28 93 27
24590 St Crépin Carlucet Fax: (0)5 53 28 81 17
Mind Body Spirit. This is a centre for personal development and awakening the spiritual in you. Courses on offer may include workshops with titles such as *Opening the Heart, The Inner Clown, Truth through Painting, Intuitive Massage, Relaxation Techniques* and *Bio-Dance*. Send for information on current year's programme and rates.

DOUBS (25)

Besançon
La Roche D'Or
25042 Besançon Tel: (0)3 81 51 42 44
Roman Catholic. This place has become quite famous for giving retreats, and it is worth sending for their annual programme.

Nans sous Sainte Anne
Prieure Saint-Benoît
Nans sous Sainte Anne
25330 Amancey Tel: (0)3 81 86 61 79
Roman Catholic. The nuns receive women, religious, priests and couples for private retreats and to take part in the community prayers. 3 singles, 5 doubles. Workroom, chapel, choir. Personal talks possible.

DRÔME (26)

Aiguebelle
Abbaye Notre-Dame d'Aiguebelle
Montjoyer
26230 Grignan　　　　　　　　　Tel: (0)4 75 98 52 33
Roman Catholic. Trappist monastery. Guest house for retreats.

Chateauneuf de Galaure
Foyer de Charité
BP 11　　　　　　　　　　　　　Tel: (0)4 75 68 79 00
26330 Chateaneuf de Galaure　　　Fax: (0)4 75 68 66 91
Christian. A place for individual and group retreats – send for brochure.

Crest
Monastère de Sainte-Claire　　　　Tel: (0)4 75 25 49 13
53, rue des Auberts　　　　　　　　Fax: (0)4 75 25 28 80
26400 Crest　　　　　　　e-mail: crest.clarisse@wanadoo.fr
Roman Catholic. Receives all for retreats of up to 8 days. Disabled. 25 rooms.
Garden, library, chapel, choir. Personal talks possible. Book at least 15 days
in advance.

Grignan
Prieuré de l'Emmanuel
26230 Grignan　　　　　　　　　Tel: (0)4 75 46 50 37
Roman Catholic. Receives everyone looking for peace and reflection.
Retreats and courses on biblical subjects. Brochure available. 8 rooms,
dormitories, possibility of camping. Guest lounge. Woods and lavender
fields all around.

Saint-Bonnet de Valclérieux
Château de Valclérieux
Saint-Bonnet de Valclérieux
26350 Crépol　　　　　　　　　Tel: (0)4 75 71 70 67
Alternative spirituality. A beautiful and popular place, which organises
yoga and various health therapy courses and workshops for both individuals and groups. Send for information about current year's programme,
along with fees.

Saint Jean en Royans
Atelier Saint-Jean Damascene
Centre d'Enseignement Icone-Fresque-Mosaique
La Prade　　　　　　　　　　　Tel: (0)4 75 48 66 75
26190 Saint Jean en Royans　　　Fax: (0)4 75 47 70 77
Christian. An information centre on icons, frescos and mosaics that welcomes
all for a spiritual stay to study these three artforms from an artistic and religious viewpoint. There is a park and swimming pool nearby, and a number
of other local attractions worth a visit. 4 doubles. Chapel, TV. Personal talks
possible. About 12€ per night.

Triors
Monastère Notre-Dame de Triors
Triors BP 1
26750 Chatillon St Jean Tel: (0)4 75 71 43 39
Roman Catholic. Receives everyone for retreats. Respect requested for the silence. Simple and austere place and life. 9 singles, 9 doubles, dormitory. Men eat in refectory; women self-catering.

EURE (27) ★

Le Bec-Hellouin
Abbaye Notre-Dame-du-Bec
Le Bec-Hellouin Tel: (0)2 32 44 86 09
27800 Le Bec-Hellouin Fax: (0)2 32 44 96 69
Roman Catholic. This is a grand monastery of the Benedictine Olivetan Order. Set in green pastures and near to the Channel ports, Le Bec is open to all. Men stay with the monks individually or in groups and take meals in the refectory. There are about 30 rooms available in 2 areas – one is inside the monastery for guests who wish to join the community in their silence and prayer, while the other is outside the monastery and reserved for groups and young people on retreat or on courses. Women guests stay at the convent 2 km away, **Monastère Sainte-Francoise-Romaine**, tel: 0(2) 32 44 81 18, fax: (0)2 32 45 90 53, and may join the Abbey's religious services, such as Vespers and Mass. The Divine Office is sung in Gregorian chant and in French. If you would like to go on retreat in France and want something not too far from home, these two communities will welcome you warmly and offer you peace and sanctuary. For either the Abbey or the Convent, write and ask what their charges will be – and for the Convent what accommodation is available when you want to stay. Car access is easy and train is possible on the Paris Saint-Lazare–Évreaux line, which stops at Bec-Hellouin.

FINISTÈRE (29)

Plounéventer
Monastère de Kerbenéat Tel: (0)2 98 20 47 43
29400 Plounéventer Fax: (0)2 98 20 43 03
Roman Catholic. Receives everyone. A tree-lined lane leads to the church, while the monastery is near woods, with fields on most sides. A quiet place with the possibility of visiting a hermitage nearby. 10 singles, 2 family rooms. Meeting room, 2 guest lounges, library, chapel, choir. Personal talks possible. Wide range of charges, so enquire. Write well in advance to book.

Le Relecq-Kerhuon
Carmel de Brest
88 bis, boulevard Clemenceau
29219 Le Relecq-Kerhuon Tel: (0)2 98 28 27 93
Roman Catholic. 3 rooms for women only for private retreat. Self-catering.

GARD (30)

Congénies
La Maison Quaker de Congénies
11, avenue des Quakers
30111 Congénies   Tel: (0)4 66 77 19 72

Les Tois Puits
12, avenue des Quakers
30111 Congénies   Tel: (0)4 66 77 19 72
Christian – Quaker (La Société Réligieuse des Amis Association). Open to all.
This is the oldest Quaker Meeting House in France and unique in that it is
the only one ever purpose-built. It has now been restored and turned into a
centre for retreats, as well as cultural, leisure, educational and other related
activities. Both the facilities and the events programme are still developing
and will grow as the centre establishes itself. There is a meeting room, workshops, a few bedrooms and a self-contained area of four rooms that can be let
weekly. Camping is sometimes permitted in the grounds. Les Tois Puits
across the street is a private house that puts up retreat and events guests –
B&B about 25€ per person per night for a double, 30€ for a single. An
evening meal is available for about 12€.

Uzès
Carmel
7, avenue Louis-Alteirac
30700 Uzès   Tel: (0)4 66 22 10 62
Roman Catholic. Open only for individual retreats. Uzès is a wonderfully
restored small town with graceful arches around the market square. Full of
tourists in the summer, with many foreigners owning local holiday homes,
this small town is, nevertheless, a gem of a place.

GARONNE (HAUTE) (31)

Blagnac
Monastère Notre-Dame-des-Sept-Douleurs
et de Sainte-Catherine-de-Sienne
60, avenue Général-Compans
31700 Blagnac   Tel: (0)5 61 71 46 48
Roman Catholic. Dominican nuns. Open to all. Guest accommodation is
separate from the monastery. Guest lounges, library, chapel, choir. Individual
or groups retreats with own leaders for reflection and prayer. Beautiful
setting, in a quiet place by the river.

Bellegarde-Sainte-Marie   Tel: (0)5 61 85 61 32
Abbaye Sainte-Marie-du-Désert   Fax: (0)5 61 85 04 32
31530 Bellegarde-Sainte-Marie   e-mail: abstemariedesert@wanadoo.fr
Roman Catholic. Cistercian monks. 25 rooms for retreatants, for up to 8
days. There is an annual pilgrimage in September for the Nativity of the
Virgin Mary.

Muret
Carmel
La Combe-Sainte-Marie
67, chemin Lacombe
31600 Muret   Tel: (0)5 61 51 03 67
Roman Catholic. Carmelite nuns who receive guests for individual retreats in solitude.

Toulouse
Scandinavian Yoga and Meditation School
46, rue de Metz
31000 Toulouse   Tel: (0)5 61 25 17 69

GERS (32)

Auch
Sœurs Dominicaines d'Auch
10, rue de la Somme   Tel: (0)5 62 05 07 37
32000 Auch   Fax: (0)5 62 63 67 25
Roman Catholic. Welcomes young women for a private retreat of prayer and life with the community. If you go, take time to see the remarkable carved wood choir stalls in Auch Cathedral, which are one of the great heritages of France. Information is available about them in English.

Saramon
Monastère Cistercien de Sainte-Marie-de-Boulaur
32450 Boulaur   Tel: (0)5 62 65 40 07
                                                      Fax: (0)5 62 65 49 37
Roman Catholic. Receives women, young people, groups, families only. Open May to September. Groups in winter only. 53 beds.

GIRONDE (33)

Auros
Abbaye de Sainte-Marie-du-Rivet   Tel: (0)5 56 65 40 10
33124 Auros   Fax: (0)5 56 65 44 18
                             e-mail: Cellerie.rivet@wanadoo.fr
Roman Catholic. Cistercian nuns. One of the oldest monasteries in France, with a 13th-century church surrounded by 9th-century fortifications. Guest accommodation for individuals in search of calm and repose. 26 rooms. Personal talks possible, Guest lounge, large park, nice garden, much peace. Choir offices in French and Gregorian chant.

Bordeaux
Centre Louis-Beaulieu
145, rue de Saint-Genés   Tel: (0)5 56 96 57 37
33082 Bordeaux Cedex   Fax: (0)5 56 96 88 12
Roman Catholic. Retreat house that welcomes individuals and groups. It is on the Lourdes–Compostelle route, so it is also a centre for pilgrims. Situated in the town. 30 rooms, 6 of which have 4 beds in each. Guest lounge, meeting rooms, library, park, sports facilities. About 30€. per day full board.

Monastère de la Visitation
47, cours Marc-Nouaux
33000 Bordeaux Tel: (0)5 56 44 25 72
Roman Catholic. Receives women only. If possible, write in the first instance.

Rions
Monastère du Broussey Tel: (0)5 56 62 60 90
33410 Rions Fax: (0)5 56 62 60 79
Roman Catholic. Receives everyone for silence and prayer. May join the community in their life of prayer. 18 rooms. Guest lounge, garden, chapel, library. Personal talks possible. Write in first instance and include a SAE. Suggested donation about 25€ per day.

HÉRAULT (34)

Le Bousquet-d'Orb
Monastère Orthodoxe Saint-Nicolas
La Dalmerie, 34260 Le Bousquet-d'Orb Tel: (0)4 67 23 41 10
Orthodox – Eastern Rite. Receives men, women. Open Easter to October for spiritual retreats only. Up to 7-day stay. 8 beds, camping. Guest dining room. Orthodox only for holy sacraments.

Montpellier
Espace Manrése – Centre de Spiritualité Ignatienne
21 bis/23 rue de la Garenne Tel: (0)4 67 04 38 60
34090 Montpellier Fax: (0)4 67 04 38 79
Roman Catholic. Jesuit-run guest house attached to their community building. Individual retreats for a few days; longer stay possible for undertaking the spiritual exercises of St Ignatius. Disabled possible, but ask about exactly what is on offer. 7 rooms. Library, chapel, choir. Personal talks and spiritual direction possible. Pilgrims welcome. About 30€ per day full board.

Roqueredonde
La Borie Noble, 34650 Roqueredonde Tel: (0)4 67 44 09 89
Ecumenical Christian. The main house of the charitable organisation La Communauté de l'Arche. It is high up in the mountains and not easy to find or get to. A community of about 100 live an austere life here (for example, without electricity), based on Gandhian principles. Open all year. Receives men, women, young people, families, groups. Visitors join in the community work and routines. If you do not know about the work of l'Arche, which has houses in Britain and elsewhere, it may be rewarding to find out, especially if you are young and want to help people less fortunate than yourself within the context of community life – even if only for a short time.

Saint-Mathieu-de-Tréviers
Communauté Dominicaine
34270 Saint-Mathieu-de-Tréviers Tel: (0)4 67 55 20 62
Roman Catholic. Open to men, women, families, groups. 40 rooms, some doubles, many ensuite. Library, guest lounges. Personal talks possible. Situated between sea and mountains, among trees. A place of deep silence and prayer.

ILLE-ET-VILAINE (35)

Plerguer
Notre-Dame-de-Beaufort   Tel: (0)2 99 48 07 57
35540 Plerguer   Fax: (0)2 99 48 48 95
                                    Website: www.ndbeaufort.free.fr
Roman Catholic. Dominican nuns. Open to all for the purposes of retreat. 20
rooms, plus annexe and dormitory. Maximum stay 10 days. 2 guest lounges,
library, chapel. Personal talks possible. To book write to the Guest Sister at
least 8 days in advance. The monastery is among trees, near a lake.

INDRE (36)

Fontgombault
Abbaye Notre-Dame-de-Fontgombault   Tel: (0)2 54 37 12 03
36220 Fontgombault   Fax: (0)2 54 37 12 56
Roman Catholic. Benedictine monks. Receives guests in an 11th-century
abbey where retreats are in silence and austerity is the rule. Retreatants are
expected to be present at the principal Divine Offices. If you are would like
to experience a religious life of silence and contemplative reflection, try this
place.

Pellevoisin
Monastère des Dominicaines
3, rue Notre Dame   Tel: (0)2 54 39 00 46
36180 Pellevoisin   Fax: (0)2 54 39 04 66
Roman Catholic. Open to all. Accommodation for 8 for religious retreats.
Guest lounge, meeting room, chapel, choir. Personal talks possible.
Pellevoisin has been a place of pilgrimage since 1815, when there were
apparitions of the Virgin Mary here.

ISÈRE (38)

Biviers
Centre Saint Hugues   Tel: (0)4 76 90 35 97
38330 Biviers   Fax: (0)4 76 90 35 78
                         e-mail: st.hugues.de.biviers@wanadoo.fr
Roman Catholic. At the entrance to Grenoble and near the mountains, this
Jesuit community offers a place for silence and reflection.

Voiron
Monastère de la Visitation
Notre-Dame-du-May
38500 Voiron   Tel: (0)4 76 05 26 29
Roman Catholic. Visitation nuns. Receives individuals and groups for silent
retreats and participation in prayer. Women may make a retreat within the
enclosure for deep silence, meditation and prayer. Spiritual guidance in the
tradition of St Francis de Sales is available if desired.

Voreppe
Monastère des Clarisses
94, chemin Sante-Claire
38340 Voreppe

Tel: (0)4 76 50 26 03
Fax: (0)4 76 50 03 44

Roman Catholic. The community of sisters welcomes individuals and groups for 8- to 10-day retreats. There are retreat courses in meditation and others based on the Durckheim School of body and meditation exercises for interior unification and deep renewal. Chapel, choir. Personal talks possible. A small monastery and guest house in a setting of trees and mountains. **Highly Recommended.**

JURA (39)

Vitreux
Abbaye D'Acey
Vitreux
39350 Gendrey   Tel: (0)3 84 81 04 11

Roman Catholic. Cistercian monks. Open to all. 15 rooms. Groups do their own catering. A popular place, so book several months in advance.

LANDES (40)

Moustey
Ressoruce-Stage
La Vigne
40410 Moustey

Tel: (0)5 58 07 79 29
Fax: (0)5 58 07 79 90
e-mail: Cmrf.marie@wanadoo.fr

Roman Catholic community. Courses and weekend workshops are held here under the general title of *Sources of The Living Waters*, with the theme of 'know yourself for understanding others'. The day is divided up into periods of prayer, teaching, and exercises, with a Mass in the evening. Spiritual accompaniment is possible if requested. The centre is near Bordeaux, so flights are easy from the UK. Course prices are modest – about 550€ full board, with a couple rate of around 850€ for the 2.

Mugron
Abbaye Notre-Dame de Maylis
40250 Mugron

Tel: (0)5 58 97 72 81
Fax: (0)5 58 97 72 58

Roman Catholic. Benedictine monks of the Olivetan Order as at Le Bec (see above). The monastery is situated in lovely country in the midst of this vast department of France, which has very many trees. The community organises retreats, usually for groups, but individuals who want a retreat for spiritual reasons are welcomed. Many ancient churches in the area. At the nearby hilltop town of St Sever there is an annual summer exhibition (with demonstrations) of the work of outstanding artisans, including bookbinders, woodturners, and weavers.

Saint Vincent de Paul
Oeuvre du Berceau de Saint-Vincent de Paul
40990 Saint Vincent de Paul

Tel: (0)5 58 89 90 01
Fax: (0)5 58 89 97 77

Roman Catholic. This is the birthplace of St Vincent de Paul, the founder of an Order that serves the poor throughout the world. There is a retreat guesthouse, which welcomes individuals and groups for retreats and courses. There are a number of tourist sites in the area. Disabled possible. Accommodation for 50. Meeting rooms, guest lounge, library, TV, chapel. Personal talks possible. Pilgrims welcome.

LOIRE (42)

Pradines
Abbaye Saint-Joseph-et-Saint-Pierre de Pradines
42630 Pradines

Tel: (0)4 77 64 80 06
Fax: (0)4 77 64 82 08
e-mail: Resins.42.cdi@wanadoo.fr
Website: www.ensignement-loire.com

Roman Catholic. Receives individuals or groups for retreats in silence. Maximum stay 7 days. Disabled. 2 dining rooms, 2 guest lounges, meeting room, library, chapel, choir. Personal talks possible. Donations towards cost of room and board.

HAUTE-LOIRE (43)

Langeac
Monastère de Sainte-Catherine de Sienne
2, rue de Pont
43300 Langeac

Tel: (0)4 71 77 01 50
Fax: (0)4 71 77 27 61

Roman Catholic. Dominican nuns. Receives individuals and groups for retreats. Maximum stay 2 weeks. 13 rooms. Central heating, chapel. Personal talks possible. Write to the Guest Sister at least 1 week in advance.

Le Puy en Velay
Saint-Georges Retreat House
4, rue Saint Georges
43000 Le Puy en Velay

Tel: (0)4 71 09 93 10
Fax: (0)4 71 09 93 17

Roman Catholic. Receives everyone. This is a place of pilgrimage, and Saint Georges is a very large complex and a grand seminary building where people are welcomed all year as individuals or in groups. Massive amount of accommodation. Park, gardens, disabled facilities, library, TV, chapel, choir. Personal talks possible. Pilgrims welcome. If you want to stay in Le Puy and cannot stay here, then ask about other places, because there are a number in the vicinity.

LOIRE-ATLANTIQUE (44)

La Meilleraye-de-Bretagne
Abbaye Notre-Dame-de-Melleray
44520 La Meilleraye-de-Bretagne

Tel: (0)2 40 55 27 37
Fax: (0)2 40 55 22 43
e-mail: melleray@wanadoo.fr
Website: www.citeaux.abbaye.com

Roman Catholic. Cistercian Trappist monks. Receives men for spiritual retreats and visits for peace and reflection. Retreats are in silence.

LOIRET (45)

Orléans
Château du Yoga Sivananda
Neuville au Bois
Orléans 45000　　　　Website: www.sivananda.org/orleans/indeng.htm
Mind Body Spirit – yoga. The Château du Yoga Sivananda is one of the
International Sivananda Yoga Vedanta centres (see Paris entry) whose aim is
to spread the ancient teachings of yoga to all. This place, formally an ashram,
is located about 100 km south of Paris and very close to the city of Orléans.
It is a large property in a calm and peaceful setting near one of France's
largest forests. Activities take place throughout the year. You can book your-
self into the ashram and take part in the normal daily timetable or you can go
on a course or organised retreat. Some examples of recent ones include
Karma Yoga Weekend; *Nana Yoga – Inner Awakening through the Power of
Sacred Sounds with Live Music*; *Yoga and Hiking*; *Yoga and Stress
Management*; *Fasting Weekend*; *Yoga, Sport and Nature*; *Yoga and the
Family*; and *A Festival of Yoga and the Sacred Arts*.

Saint-Jean-de-Braye
Monastère des Bénédictines de Notre-Dame-du-Calvaire
65, avenue de Verdun
45801 Saint-Jean-de-Braye　　　　　　　　Tel: (0)2 38 61 43 05
Roman Catholic. Benedictine nuns. Religious retreats only. Receives women.
Weekends within cloister for young women considering a religious life. Not
a particularly quiet situation, as it is in a busy town.

LOT (46)

La Buissiére
Lot Valley　　　　　　　　　　　　Website: www.yogafrance.com
Mind Body Spirit – yoga. Yoga and walking in rural France, based at a
comfortable house with 2 acres of private parkland and pool.

Montcuq
Le Chartrou
Belmonet
46800 Montcuq　　　　　　　　　　　　Tel: (0)5 65 31 90 23
Mind Body Spirit – alternative therapies. A naturopathy retreat for de-stressing and increasing your energy by means of diet, nutrition and revitalisation
to maximise the natural biological forces of your body. Brochure available
with events and courses plus charges.

Rocamadour　　　　　　　　　　　　　　　　　　　　
Centre d'Accueil Notre-Dame
Le Château　　　　　　　　　　　　　　Tel: (0)5 65 33 23 23
46500 Rocamadour　　　　　　　　　　Fax: (0)5 65 33 23 24
Roman Catholic – Ecumenical. This centre is run by the Diocesan of Cahors
and is open all year for individuals or groups on retreat. Rocamadour
possesses a church dating from the Middle Ages in which there is a sanctuary
considered by Christian pilgrims to be a holy place – try to visit it if you stay
here. In it is an ancient wooden statue of Mary holding the Child Jesus that

is simple yet deeply dramatic. This is a mysterious and spiritual place set in a rugged and equally mysterious countryside. 46 rooms. Guest and meeting rooms, library, TV, chapel choir, disabled facilities (but the sanctuary has steps and the centre itself is steep and not very easily accessible). Personal talks possible. Rates on demand. Lots of tourists about in the summer, but the atmosphere inside is peaceful. **Highly Recommended.**

LOT-ET-GARONNE (47)

Agen
Foyer Valpré le Lido
500, avenue Léon Blum   Tel: (0)5 53 47 47 73
Route de Cahors, 4700 Agen   Fax: (0)5 53 66 59 72
Roman Catholic – Ecumenical. Located 170 km from Lourdes and only 100 km from Toulouse, this centre welcomes everyone, individuals and groups, for days of reflection and rest, and prayer retreats. 20 rooms, 4 family rooms. Disabled facilities, conferences, library, TV, chapel, choir. Personal talks possible.

Loubes-Bernac
Le Village des Pruniers (Plum Village)
Buddhist – Mahayana (Vietnamese), Unified Buddhist Church. Plum Village is a group of several rural retreat places located in three departments of France – the Dordogne, the Gironde and the Lot-et-Garonne. **Hameau du Bas, Meyrac, 47120 Loubès-Bernac,** tel: (0)5 53 94 75 40 is a community which receives men, women and married couples. **Hameau du Haut, Le Pey, 24240 Thénac,** tel/fax: (0)5 53 58 48 58 is a monastery receiving men only. **Hammeau Nouveau, 13 Matineau, 33580 Dieulivol,** tel: (0)5 56 61 66 88) is a convent receiving women. More than 400 people a year visit these places for meditation. Plum Village is a big, busy and serious place with at least three major organised retreats each year. About 175–200€ each week. Meals are vegetarian. Send for information (available in English), as Buddhist centres have different requirements as to meditation and other experience. You will need to book 3 months in advance.**Highly Recommended.**

MAINE-ET-LOIRE (49)

Angers
Prieuré de Notre-Dame-du-Calvaire
8, rue Vauvert
49100 Angers   Tel: (0)2 41 87 76 28
Roman Catholic. Benedictine nuns. Individuals or small groups for retreats. Retreats within the enclosure possible for women religious and young women who want to participate more fully in the community's life of prayer.

Bégrolles-en-Mauges   Tel: (0)2 41 63 81 60
Abbaye de Bellefontaine   Fax: (0)2 41 75 60 46
49122 Bégrolles-en-Mauges   Website: www.bellefontaine-abbaye.com
Roman Catholic. Cistercians. Receives men and mixed groups for retreats only. 50 singles, 15 doubles. Guest lounge, disabled facilities, library, chapel. Personal talks possible. Men may be able to help with some work of community.

MANCHE (50)

Avranches
Monastère du Carmel
59, boulevard du Luxembourg
50300 Avranches   Tel: (0)2 33 58 23 66
Roman Catholic. Receives men and women retreatants. 4 rooms. A place for
a prayer and reflection retreat. Set between a busy road and quiet countryside.

Le Mont-Saint-Michel
Communauté de l'Abbaye
BP 3   Tel: (0)2 33 60 14 47
50170 Le Mont-Saint-Michel   Fax: (0)2 33 60 31 02
Roman Catholic. Benedictine monks. Receives men and women **for spiritual
retreats only**. 12 beds. Guests must attend all Divine Offices. This is a
famous abbey and place, and still one of the greatest tourist attractions of
Europe. However, a stay with the community here does not guarantee you a
visit to the monument. Visit it before or after your retreat. A magnificent site.

Mortain
Ateliers St Bernard
Abbaye Blanche
50140 Mortain   Tel: (0)2 33 79 47 47
A number of workshop courses run by artists in the context of the spiritual-
ity of the Communauté des Béatitudes (see this section). Programmes in the
recent past have included such courses as *The Art of Illumination*, *Dances of
Israel*, *Painting and Prayer* and *Singing and Interior Peace*.

Saint-James
Prieuré Saint-Jacques
50240 Saint-James   Tel: (0)2 33 48 31 39
Roman Catholic. This community of nuns receives women individuals and
religious who want a private retreat and perhaps to participate in the community's life of prayer. 9 rooms, chapel. Pilgrims welcome. Personal talks sometimes possible.

Saint-Pair-sur-Mer
Carmel
213, route de Lézeaux
50380 Saint-Pair-sur-Mer   Tel: (0)2 33 50 12 00
Roman Catholic. Receives individual for religious retreats.

MARNE (51)

Arcis-le-Ponsart
Abbaye Notre-Dame-d'Igny
51170 Arcis-le-Ponsart   Tel: (0)3 26 78 08 40
Roman Catholic. Open for spiritual retreats only, for stays of up to 1 week.
Participation in the Divine Office with help from one of the community in
this Cistercian abbey. Brochure available.

Reims
Monastère Sainte-Claire
11 bis, avenue Roger-Salengro
51430 Tinqueux Tel: (0)3 26 08 23 15
Roman Catholic. St Clare nuns. Open to women, religious, priests, married couples. 55 beds, including annexe, barn and dormitory. Closes last 2 weeks of July.

Saint-Thierry
Monastère des Bénédictines Tel: (0)3 26 03 10 72
51220 Saint-Thierry Fax: (0)3 26 03 15 49
Roman Catholic. Receives individuals and groups for retreats. 22 rooms. 3 guest lounges, library, chapel, choir. Personal talks possible. Maximum stay 8 days. Write 15 days in advance to the Guest Sister.

MAYENNE (53)

Craon
Monastère des Bénédictines du Saint-Sacrement
15, rue de la Libération Tel: (0)2 43 06 13 38
53400 Craon Fax: (0)2 43 06 03 80
Roman Catholic. Receives women, young women, families, group retreatants. 14 rooms (some facing the road, some facing the garden), plus other accommodation. Library. Divine Office in Latin Gregorian chant. Women may apply to make a retreat within the enclosure.

MEURTRE-ET-MOSELLE (54)

Art sur Meurthe
Villa Chaminade
1, rue du Chateau
54510 Art sur Meurthe Tel: (0)3 83 56 97 44
Roman Catholic. A Marianist community that welcomes all persons, groups and families for stays of 1–8 days. Spiritual direction for a retreat on request. Accommodation for 25. Library, guest lounge, chapel. Personal talks possible.

MORBIHAN (56)

Bréhan
Abbaye Notre-Dame-de-Timadeuc Tel: (0)2 97 51 50 29
Bréhan Fax: (0)2 97 51 59 20
56580 Rohan e-mail: timadeuc.abbaye@wanadoo.fr
Roman Catholic. Cistercians. Receives men and women for stays of up to 8 days. Near the monastery are 2 further guest centres for young people. The atmosphere is peaceful and you join the community in much silence. 41 rooms. Full board available – charges on request. 2 guest lounges, disabled facilities, library, chapel, choir. Personal talks possible.

> Tout comprendre,
> c'est tout pardonner.
> VOLTAIRE

Campénéac
Abbaye la Joie Notre-Dame   Tel: (0)2 97 93 42 07
Campénéac 56800   Fax: (0)2 97 93 11 23
Roman Catholic. Cistercian nuns. Receives men, women, groups for confer-
ences. 30 rooms, 2 dormitories, camping. Library, chapel, choir, meeting
room, guest lounges. Personal talks possible. Very quiet, in the heart of
Brittany and close to the Forest of Broceliande. The nuns have an exhibition
on the monastic life.

Plouharnel
Abbaye Sainte-Anne de Kergonan
56340 Plouharnel   Tel: (0)2 97 52 30 75
Roman Catholic. Benedictine monks. Receives men individually for retreats
or study. 15 singles. Meals in refectory. Divine Office in Gregorian chant.
Quiet location close to the sea.

MOSELLE (57)

Gorze
Béthanie
Prieuré Saint-Thiébault   Tel: (0)3 87 52 02 28
57680 Gorze   Fax: (0)3 87 69 91 79
Christian – Orthodox. Centre of meditation run by an Orthodox priest.
Individual retreats possible. Write and ask what can be arranged for you,
explaining what you are looking for.

NORD (59)

Le Mont-des-Cats
Abbaye Sainte-Marie-du-Mont
Le Mont-des-Cats   Tel: (0)3 28 42 52 50
59270 Godewaersvelde   Guest House: (0)3 28 42 58 22
Roman Catholic. Open to all. 30 rooms. Meals taken in silence. Countryside
location.

Moustier-en-Fagne
Prieuré Saint-Dodon
59132 Moustier-en-Fagne   Tel: (0)3 27 61 81 28
Roman Catholic. This is a Benedictine Olivetan community of nuns, so you
will be assured of a warm welcome in a very homely and peaceful atmosphere.
Closed September and October. Receives men, women, young people,
groups. 5 rooms, plus separate self-catering annexe for groups with own
leader. Stays of up to 15 days. There is a Byzantine chapel, and icon painting
is a speciality of the community. Byzantine liturgy once a week. A very quiet
setting near a small river with lots of trees and much peace. It is possible to
walk into Belgium from here. **Highly Recommended.**

Mouvaux
Centre Spirituel du Hautmont   Tel: (0)3 20 26 09 61
31, rue Mirabeau BP 19   Fax: (0)3 20 11 26 59
59420 Mouvaux   e-mail: hautmont@wanadoo.fr
Roman Catholic. A centre run by the Jesuits, open all year for individuals and groups. Set in a large park. 46 rooms. 2 meeting rooms, 10 guest and course rooms, 8 work rooms, disabled, chapel, choir. Personal talks possible. Full board about 27€ per day.

ORNE (61)

Alençon
Monastère Sainte-Claire
7, rue de la Demi-Lune
61000 Alençon   Tel: (0)2 33 26 14 58
Roman Catholic. St Clare nuns. Receives men, women. 12 rooms for retreatants. A fairly noisy location in town – but within, the life is peaceful.

Soligny-la-Trappe   Tel: (0)2 33 34 50 44
Abbaye Notre Dame de la Trappe   Fax: (0)2 33 34 98 57
61380 Soligny-la-Trappe   e-mail: la.trappe@wanadoo.fr
Roman Catholic. Trappist monks. Receives men only, individually or in groups, for retreats of up to 8 days. 30 beds. Library, chapel, choir. Personal talks available. Full board. Retreats in silence. A very quiet location in a forest.

PAS-DE-CALAIS (62)

Boulogne-sur-Mer
Monastère de la Visitation
9, rue Maquétra
62220 Saint-Martin-Boulogne   Tel: (0)3 21 31 35 88
Roman Catholic. Receives religious, women. Retreats in silence. Participation in Divine Office.

Wisques
Abbaye Saint-Paul
Wisques   Tel: (0)3 21 12 28 50
62219 Longuenesse   Fax: (0)3 21 12 28 72
Roman Catholic. Benedictine monks. Receives men individually or in groups for retreats. Spiritual direction and personal talks possible. 23 rooms. Camping possible for young people. Brochure available.

PUY-DE-DOME (63)

Chamalières
Monastère des Clarisses-Capucines
11, avenue de Villars
63407 Chamalières Cedex   Tel: (0)4 73 37 73 11
Roman Catholic. One of only three Capucine monasteries remaining in France. The nuns are enclosed. Franciscan spirituality. Receives everyone for individual retreats. 8 rooms. Brochure available.

Randol
Abbaye Notre-Dame-de Randol Tel: (0)4 73 39 31 00
63450 Saint-Amant-Tallende Fax: (0)4 73 39 05 28
Roman Catholic. Benedictine monks. Receives men. A new monastery opened in 1971 of very modern architectural design, dramatically set on the very edge of a steep gorge in an isolated position. A similar looking place to Prinknash Abbey in England, but much grander and more imposing. 5 days maximum stay. Retreatants must respect the silence and attend services if possible. Library, chapel. Personal talks possible. No preached retreats but spiritual direction is sometimes possible.

PYRÉNÉES-ATLANTIQUES (64)

Anglet
Convent des Bernardines Notre Dame de Refuge
Avenue de Montbrun
64600 Anglet Tel: (0)5 59 63 84 34
Roman Catholic. Bernardine nuns. Receives women only, for silent retreat. 5 singles. Meals with community. The food is from their fields and gardens.

Orthez
Monastère Sainte-Claire
35, rue Saint-Gilles, 64300 Orthez Tel: (0)5 59 69 46 55
Roman Catholic. The nuns have a few rooms for self-catering stays. Participation in prayers of the community.

Urt
Abbaye Notre-Dame-de-Belloc
64240 Urt
Tel: (0)5 59 29 65 55
Fax: (0)5 59 29 44 08
e-mail: belloc.abbaye@wanadoo.fr
Website: www.perso.wanadoo.fr/belloc
Roman Catholic. Benedictine monks. Receives men, married couples, small groups of men for day retreats and retreat stays up to 1 week. An isolated monastery in one of the loveliest parts of France, with mountains and valleys lush with wildflowers and trees. Sheep abound, as do tiny villages where life seems to continue much as it has for centuries. It is possible here to imagine that indeed all *is* well with the world. This has not always been so – the abbot and his prior were sent to Buchenwald and Dachau concentration camps during the Second World War because of the help they gave to refugees and resistance fighters. After the war, the Abbey community was awarded the honour of the Cross of War. Today the Abbey continues to offer hospitality to all in accordance with the Rule of Saint Benedict that all guests should be received as if Christ himself. 18 singles, 10 doubles, 4 dormitories. Guest lounges, library, chapel choir, conferences. Personal talks possible. Programme of activities sometimes available – ask for brochure. The monks are attentive to the needs of busy modern people who are looking for a time and place in which to seek the spiritual. There are Benedictine sisters nearby at the **Monastère Sainte-Scholastique, 64240 Urt**, tel: (0)5 59 70 20 28. Write to them for details of their hospitality. **Highly Recommended.**

Laslades
La Seve
40 Route de Tarbes
653560 Laslades   Tel: (0)5 62 35 08 34
Mind Body Spirit. A programme of healing courses and an experience of self.
Topics include discovering your relationship through the Zodiac, essential oil
therapies, and rediscovery of the senses of taste, sight, hearing, touch and smell.

LOURDES

Lourdes is one of the greatest places of religious pilgrimage in the world. It
is visited by millions of people every year, so it is always very crowded. The
history of this great Christian shrine is a simple one. A fourteen-year-old
peasant girl, Marie-Bernarde Soubirous (1844–79) received eighteen apparitions of the Blessed Virgin Mary at the Massabielle Rock in Lourdes over a
period of months. During this time, a spring appeared in the grotto of the
rock, the waters of which are believed to be miraculous. Almost from the
beginning people visited the grotto to seek cures for their illnesses and
fulfillment of their prayers. The girl later became a nun and is known today
as Saint Bernadette. The Catholic Church is medically and ethically
extremely rigorous in deciding if any claim of a cure is authentic. There have
been a small but impressive number of cases declared so over the years, and
you may read about these in detail. The grotto itself is filled with candles and
has remained relatively simple. People here are quite silent and all attention
is on spiritual intentions – the atmosphere is unique and conducive to prayer
in spite of the number of people gathered together. However, an enormous
church has been built on the site, with religious chapels and sanctuaries, plus
a museum and all the various facilities related to handling millions of visitors
each year. Many of these are ill, infirm, in wheelchairs or on stretchers.
Indeed, those suffering from illnesses and handicaps come by the coach- and
plane-load each year. At all times, there are visitors who may not be
Christians or who have doubts about the existence of God but have been
attracted to Lourdes by its global fame. Along with many Christians, they
may be appalled by the commercial aspects of Lourdes – the streets lined
with shops and stalls selling religious trinkets such as rosaries, statues and
bottles of holy water from the grotto spring. They may also be distressed by
the plight of of ill pilgrims and by the harsh realities of how men and women
sometimes behave when driven by their religious yearnings. But all great
religious shrines and places of pilgrimage through the ages, whether
Christian or not, have suffered this kind of commerce. A visitor, who is not
a pilgrim or believer, needs to put to one side the human economic foibles
and think about the spirituality that draws pilgrims here by the millions. All
have taken time to devote a few days to prayer and God. And is it such a bad
thing that some hope, no matter how faint, may be given to the sick and the
incurable when nothing else has given it? So the shrine at Lourdes and its
huge church are well worth a visit. Forget the commerciality and concentrate on the prayerful atmosphere of the shrine with its many candles radi-
ating inspiring light. Afterwards you might take a picnic lunch to Lourdes
Lake nearby and drift in a pedal-boat. This is the kind of day retreat that lifts
the heart.

There are many hotels and guest houses in all price ranges in Lourdes and, of course, a number of religious houses, some of which take guests. The Lourdes tourist information office will help you find accommodation. The Lourdes website **www.lourdes-France.com** gives details about the place and has some good photos.

Carmel Notre-Dame-de-Lourdes
17, route de Pau
65100 Lourdes   Tel: (0)5 62 94 26 67
Roman Catholic. Receives men and women for day retreats and in the summer months for longer stays.

Foyer Familial
2, avenue Saint-Joseph   Tel: (0)5 62 94 07 51
65100 Lourdes   Fax: (0)5 62 94 57 14
Roman Catholic. Run by the Dominican sisters. The house, with a garden, is situated in town, not far from the shrine and sanctuary area. 12 singles, 9 doubles, 5 family rooms.

Le Bosquet
Maison Familiale
Les Grange Juloa   Tel: (0)5 62 94 29 72
65100 Lourdes   Fax: (0)5 62 42 09 80
Non-religious. Situated about 3 km from Lourdes, this large establishment is open all year for seminars or retreats. In a village on the mountain, with beautiful views of the Pyrénées.

Résidence de la Pastourelle
34 rue de Langelle   Tel: (0)5 62 94 26 55
65100 Lourdes   Fax: (0)5 62 42 00 95
Ecumenical. This large residence is in the centre of Lourdes and has all facilities, especially for the disabled, with physical care available. Although near the shrine, it is a peaceful place.

Maison Sainte-Thérèse   Tel: (0)5 62 94 35 16
32-34 rue du Sacré-cœur   Fax: (0)5 62 94 70 13
65100 Lourdes   e-mail: emmalourdes@wanadoo.fr
Roman Catholic. The Community of Emmanuel receives guests for up to 7 days, who may participate in the life of the community. It is about quarter of an hour's walk from the shrine. Accommodation for up to 60. Full board about 20€ per night. Languages spoken include English.

Monastère des Dominicaines
Route de Pontacq   Tel: (0)5 62 46 33 30
65100 Lourdes   Fax: (0)5 62 94 89 76
Roman Catholic. The sisters here offer monastic hospitality to individuals and groups. Maximum stay is 15 days. Private retreats possible. 22 rooms. Full board about 28€ per day. Languages spoken include English.

Maubourguet
Église Protestante Évangélique
138 Place Libération
65700 Maubourguet   Tel: (0)5 62 96 32 22
Evangelical Christian. For those travelling or buying a holiday home in the
increasingly popular Southwest, there is a welcome for all Christians on
Sundays at 10.15 am at the Evangelical church in Maubourguet. Just park in
the central market square and walk in. The first Sunday of the month service
usually makes provision for English language speakers as there are number of
regular members who speak English.

St Pé de Bigorre
Monastère du Désert de L'Immaculée   Tel: (0)5 62 41 88 49
65270 St Pé de Bigorre   Fax: (0)5 62 41 88 61
Roman Catholic. Nuns of the Community of Bethlehem, Assumption of the
Virgin, and Saint Bruno, a religious community in the Carthusian tradition,
have made and built a small monastery high above the town. You drive up
through trees and hills until you turn into the drive, where all is peaceful and
silent. This is an enclosed order in the hermit tradition, so you are unlikely to
meet more than the guest sister if you are staying here. **This monastery is
not run as a retreat house** but offers a simple hermitage at the gate for a
single person – usually a priest, nun or monk. However, it is well worth the
detour for its charm and setting, and you might like to take an hour out to
pray and be silent during your travels in south-west France. The chapel is
absolutely beautiful and all of limed timber. You may join in the Offices or
Mass by entering a door and sitting above the sisters, who come in below to
form the choir. Mass is sometimes said in Spanish, otherwise in French or
Latin. You are usually welcome to help with the trees and hedges outside and
around the monastery, and the nuns make delicious jams and jellies, which
are on sale in a small open-door room next to the visitor's door to the chapel.

Tourney
Abbaye Notre-Dame
65190 Tournay   Tel: (0)5 62 35 70 21
Roman Catholic. Benedictine monks. Receives men, women. Services in
French. 30 singles for men, plus dormitories. 12 rooms for women. Men take
meals in refectory, women guests eat separately. Quiet location, close to a
river. Lovely area of south-west France and regularly visited by local people.
Highly Recommended.

PYRÉNÉES-ORIENT (66)

Le Perthus
Laure Saint-Antoine
Monastère des ermites
St Jean des Alberes
66480 Le Perthus
Roman Catholic. This is a hidden isolated community of women hermits, living
a solitary life and joining together for prayers and some work. It is a place to
go to only if you are already experienced in the eremitical solitary life of
contemplation and prayer and now need complete seclusion and reclusion for

a period of silent retreat. A hermitage for a guests is available from time to time, but you must write in advance and in French to the Guest Sister to discuss the possibility of your being received. This is a serious religious place for a particular kind of private solitary retreat in the style of the early Desert Fathers.

Maureilla
Fédération Internationale de Yoga Himalayen
c/o Stephane-Jean
Les Ilipotiers
Las Illas Village   Tel: (0)6 11 51 47 53/(0)4 68 83 04 76
66480 Maureillas   Website: www.membres.lycos.fr/himalaya/program
Mind Body Spirit – yoga. Hatha Yoga programmes including *Yoga, Ayurveda and Psychotherapy* workshop. Suitable for both beginners and advanced practitioners. Diet and personal schedule with individual instruction. Location for workshops varies but has been in the beautiful Luberon area in Provence, with local accommodation at a good hotel. Price for workshop, meals and accommodation around 500€ (travel not included).

Prades
Star of Light Mountain Retreat Centre
Maison Bird
Conat   Tel/fax: (0)4 68 96 04 80
66500 Prades   e-mail: bird.conat@easynet.fr
Mind Body Spirit. Programme includes hatha yoga, reiki healing and workshops with titles such as *Men, Stress, Health and Well-being* and *The Zodiac of Your Soul*. Charges start at £100 per person for the course, plus shared accommodation at £210 per person per week.

The Sun Centre   ★
Prades   Tel: (0)4 66 45 59 63
66160 St Martin de Boubaux   Website: www.thesuncentre.net
Mind Body Spirit – yoga. A yoga and Ayurveda therapy centre recently set up by Alex Duncan and his wife Sharon. Morning yoga practice is on a large outdoor deck in the woods in a beautiful setting. The food is organic vegetarian and cooked according to Ayurvedic principles. The accommodation is simple, in twin-bedded rooms, but comfortable. 'Uncluttered comfort' is how one guest described it. The Sun Centre is located halfway up a mountain overlooking a deserted valley – quiet, unspoiled, very green, with lots of woodland walks round about. Sounds like the sort of place the famous spirituality writer Thomas Merton, who was born at nearby Prades, would have liked. The centre itself is in a tiny hamlet with no through road, so the setting is very peaceful. Comments from guests are full of praise for this place: 'I came away refreshed, revitalised and rested. Had a wonderful stay.' 'Alex's knowledge of his subject was faultless.' 'First rate teaching.' 'Great food!' 'Very good value for money.' 'All in all, very spiritually uplifting.' With afternoons largely free, additional activities include walking, river swimming or sunbathing in the gardens, and every other night there is some kind of evening activity – star gazing, chanting, even group foot massage. The cost is about £285 excluding travel. Pick-up possible from N'mes Airport, about two hours away by car. **Highly Recommended.**

RHIN – BAS (67)

Kuttolsheim
Sakya Tsechem Ling
Institut Européen de Bouddhisme Tibétain
5, rond-point du Vignoble   Tel: (0)3 88 87 73 80
67520 Kuttolsheim   Fax: (0)3 88 60 74 52
Buddhist. Tibetan Vajrayana. About 20 minutes drive from Strasbourg. Daily practice. Languages used include French, English, German and Tibetan. There are courses and a library. Accommodation about 6€ per night, meals about 3.5€ each. Everyone eats together.

Rosheim
Monastère Notre Dame du Sacre Cœur   Tel: (0)3 88 50 41 67
Hôtellerie Notre Dame de la Source   Fax: (0)3 88 50 42 71
3, rue Saint-Benoît   e-mail: Benedictines@media.net.fr
67560 Rosheim   Website: www.benedictines-rosheim.com
Roman Catholic. Benedictine nuns who receive men and women all year round and organise retreat programmes. 15 rooms plus dormitories. Very modern in newly converted farm buildings. Divine Office in Gregorian chant. Courses are available during the year in Gregorian chant. Walks in forest and countryside. Full board about 32€ per day. Brochure available.

Strasbourg
Centre Zen de Strasbourg
21, rue des Magasins
6700 Strasbourg   Tel: (0)3 88 75 06 50
Buddhist. Soto Zen. This centre was created in 1970 by a number of groups in France and southern Germany. Three weekends a year are organised, including a beginner's one. Send for programme. There is regular practice of Zazen, using English, German and French.

RHIN – HAUT (68)

Landser
Monastère Saint Alphonse
68440 Landser   Tel: (0)3 89 81 30 10
Roman Catholic. The nuns receive everyone for retreats. 8 days maximum. Located in the heart of the village, high up in the mountains, with a large park. 6 rooms. Guest lounge, TV, meeting room, chapel, choir. Personal talks possible. Full board about 25€. Write a month in advance.

Oelenberg
Abbaye de Notre-Dame d'Oelenberg
Oelenberg
68950 Reiningue   Tel: (0)3 89 81 91 23
Roman Catholic. Receives men and women individually or in groups for retreats. 26 rooms.

Sigolsheim
Monastère des Clarisses-Capucines
5, rue Oberhof
68240 Sigolsheim   Tel: (0)3 89 78 23 24
Roman Catholic. Receives women and religious only. 3 rooms available all
year. Maximum stay 10 days. Guest lounge for the daytime.

RHONE (69)

L'Arbresle
Centre Thomas More
La Tourette
BP 105   Tel: (0)4 74 26 79 70
69591 L'Arbresle   Fax: (0)4 74 26 79 99
Roman Catholic. Designed by Le Corbusier, the centre is in the Dominican
convent of La Tourette. Weekend retreats of reflection on religion and society.

Lyon
Terre du Ciel   ★
BP 2050
69227 Lyon cedex 02   Tel: (0)4 72 41 07 51
Mind Body Spirit. The Terre du Ciel organisation have a centre, **L'Espace,**
8 rue Henri IV, 69002 Lyon, where a large number of events are run.
These cover a wide range of practices, including sadhana yoga, oriental dance,
finding the inner self, and Ayurveda massage. The leaders of the courses and
workshops are usually well known and established leaders in the Mind Body
Spirit field. Terre du Ciel also organises courses and retreats at other venues
outside Lyon. Send for information. **Highly Recommended.**

SAÔNE-ET-LOIRE (71)

La Boulaye
Kagyu Ling
Centre Bouddhique Vajrayana
Chateau de Plaige   Tel: (0)3 85 79 43 41
71320 La Boulaye   Fax: (0)3 85 79 43 09
Buddhist. The monastery here is known as The Temple of a Thousand
Buddhas and was founded in 1974 by the Tibetan master Kalou Rinpoche. A
number of courses are held here and in other places on Tibetan meditation,
spirituality, yoga, philosophy and language. Send for annual programme of
what is on offer and the charges.

Mazille
Carmel de la Paix   ★
71250 Mazille BP 10   Tel: (0)3 85 50 80 54
Cluny   Fax: (0)3 85 50 83 83
Roman Catholic. Carmelite nuns. For over 30 years, the 31 sisters of this
monastic community near famed Cluny have fulfilled the double vocation of
silence and ecumenical inter-religious dialogue. Open to both men, women,
families. Accommodation in small chalets and hermitages. For families on
retreat it is sometimes possible to organise childcare by someone in the

monastery for some of the time. Participation in Divine Office. The sisters raise cows and sheep, and help with farming chores is always welcomed. A good place for a deeply peaceful retreat. **Highly Recommended.**

Maison sur Le Monde
Centre Jacques Vidal
71250 Mazille   Tel: (0)3 85 50 82 89
Ecumenical. Situated about 7 km from Cluny in an old presbytery. This is a good place to seek prayer in a Christian ambience.

Paray le Monial
Foyer du Sacré-cœur   Tel: (0)3 85 81 11 01
14, rue de la Visatation   Fax: (0)3 85 81 26 83
71600 Paray le Monial   e-mail: foyers@club-internet.fr.
Roman Catholic. Various retreats and courses are held here, led by different priests and retreat facilitators. It is very traditionally based, with retreat themes such as *So You Know the Gift of God, The School of the Virgin Mary* and *Show Me God's Way*. Send for annual or monthly programme.

Taizé   ★
Communauté de Taizé   Tel: (0)3 85 50 30 30
71250 Taizé   Fax: (0)3 85 50 30 16
                                                    e-mail: meetings@taize.fr
                                                    website: www.taize.fr
Ecumenical. In founding the Taizé Community, Brother Rogers sought to create a way to heal the divisions between Christians and through reconciliation of Christians to overcome certain conflicts in humanity. In his own words he felt that 'the Church can be a leaven of community and peace in the entire family'. Today the community includes some 80 brothers, both Protestant and Catholic, from over 20 countries. This is one of the most popular retreat places in the Western world – in some years there have been over 6,000 visitors in a single week. Taizé receives men, women, families and especially young people, among whom it is a very popular place. 30 rooms, dormitories, camping, caravans. While all activities take place in Taizé itself, most adult accommodation is in villages nearby. Disabled facilities. Personal talks, meditation, group discussions. Special meetings for different age groups – for example, activities for younger people and events for the over-sixties. Everyone eats together. Very simple food. No provision for vegetarians or special diets. Send for information, which lists the various meetings and gives important details, which you need to know before deciding to come here. You must write at least two months in advance and wait for a reply before making any firm arrangements. The centre is so crowded in summer that older people are advised to come outside the season. In spite of this, Taizé remains a place where you may find inner peace and joy. **Highly Recommended.**

SARTHE (72)

Solesmes
Abbaye Saint-Pierre de Solesmes   Tel: (0)2 43 95 03 08
72300 Sablé-sur-Sarthe   Fax: (0)2 43 95 68 79
e-mail: hospes@solesmes.com
Website: www.solesmes.com
Roman Catholic. Founded in 1010 and occupied until 1790, the Abbey was
again opened in 1833 and later refurbished and rebuilt. The guest house is
in the enclosure and receives men only for retreats of a few days to a maximum of 1 week. The work of the monks here is divided between prayer,
manual labour, and intellectual endeavour and study. This is a silent place.
There is an outstanding collection of Gregorian music.

SAVOIE (73)

Albertville
Abbaye Notre-Dame de Tamié
Plancherine   Tel: (0)4 79 32 42 01
73200 Albertville   Fax: (0)4 79 37 05 24
e-mail: tamie.abbaye@wanadoo.fr
Website: www.abbaye-tamie.com
Roman Catholic. The monks receive men and women. Accommodation for
about 30 guests. Families are also welcome but stay in a separate chalet.
Disabled, library, chapel, choir, conferences. Personal talks and directed
retreats possible. You may participate in the Divine Office, and help with the
work of the community is appreciated. Beautiful location in the mountains.
Peaceful and calm setting. **Highly Recommended.**

Arvillard
Institut Karma Ling
Ancienne Chartreuse de Saint-Hugon   Tel: (0)4 79 65 64 62
73110 Arvillard   Fax: (0)4 79 25 78 08
Buddhist. This is a centre for Buddhist study and meditation. Men, women
and families are welcome. High up in Savoie, the centre is a place for awakening your heart and spirit and experiencing authentic living. Retreats for individuals may be from 10 days to 6 months in duration. Variety of accommodation from single rooms to dormitories. Vegetarian food. Send for brochure.

Saint Pierre de Curtille
Hautecombe Abbey
73310 Saint-Pierre de Curtille   Tel: (0)4 79 54 22 14
Christian. A Charismatic community now lives here and receives guests.
Monastic communities tend to be slow to change, but other groups can
change more quickly and radically, so it a good idea to write in the first
instance and ask what is on offer at the time you are thinking of staying here.

Saint-Pierre-d'Albigny
Monastère de la Visitation
Clos Minjoud, 73250 Saint-Pierre-d'Albigny   Tel: (0)4 79 28 50 12
Roman Catholic. The sisters receive up to 3 women within the enclosure,
where there is a large park. Individual retreats outside the enclosure are

possible for both men and women – one person or one couple at a time. There is a small garden with mountain walking near at hand.

SAVOIE–HAUTE (74)

Saint Gervais les Bains
Fleur des Neiges
287, chemin des Granges d'Orsin   Tel: (0)4 50 93 41 96
74170 Saint Gervais les Bains   Fax: (0)5 50 93 49 56
Roman Catholic. Beautifully situated in the mountains, with Mont Blanc only 2 km away. Welcomes all to join in the community's life of prayer and the monastic Offices. 20 singles, 5 doubles, camping by arrangement. Library, guest area, TV, chapel, small conferences. Personal talks and directed retreats possible. Full board from about 30€ per person per day.

SEINE (PARIS) (75)

Paris
Abbaye Sainte-Marie
3, rue de la Source
75016 Paris   Tel: (0)1 45 25 30 07
Roman Catholic. Benedictine monks. It has a well-known library that is open by arrangement for study purposes. Receives men only, for spiritual retreats in silence and solitude – not for tourist stays. Men and women together accepted for a few hours of silence and reflection or for a day retreat. Personal talks possible, sometimes courses. Good library. Everyone eats together. This is a sanctuary of peace in the midst of a rushing, noisy and beautiful city.

Centre International Sivananda de Yoga Vedanta
123, boulevard de Sébastopol   Tel: (0)1 40 26 77 49
75002 Paris   Fax: (0)1 42 33 51 97
       Website: www.sivananda.org
Mind Body Spirit – yoga. With centres and ashrams around the world, this organisation has trained over 8,000 yoga teachers. Send for information on courses and study available in France. See also entry under Department 45 in this section. Swami Vishnudevananda founded the centre. It is run as a non-profit organisation whose purpose is to propagate the teachings of yoga and vedanta as a means of achieving physical, mental and spiritual well-being and self-realisation.

Monastère de Bethléem
Notre-Dame de la Présence de Dieu
2, rue Mesnil
75116 Paris   Tel: (0)1 45 01 24 48
Roman Catholic. The sisters receive men and women who want to participate in silent prayer or in the liturgy of the community. There is no guest accommodation at the monastery. The community lives as much as possible in the spirit of the desert in the middle of this great city. From Sunday night to Monday noon they observe this special spiritual practice, and the church is closed during this period.

Monastère de l'Adoration-Réparatrice
39, rue Gay-Lussac
75005 Paris   Tel: (0)1 43 26 75 75
Roman Catholic. Receives men and women for individual retreats except
during July and August.

Monastère de la Visitation
68, avenue Denfert-Rochereau
75014 Paris   Tel: (0)1 43 27 12 90
Roman Catholic. Receives up to 5 women at a time in the enclosure to join
the nuns in silence, solitude and Divine Offices.

Mont Thabor – Myriam-Salomé
c/o Leonore Gottwald, Secrétariat
105, rue de la Convention
75015 Paris   Tel: (0)1 45 58 00 11
Christian – alternative spirituality. An association formed by the Marianist
priest Bernard Rérolle. Christian and Eastern spirituality, meditation, tai chi,
sacred rituals and body in spirit exercises are on offer. There is a good
programme of weekends. Prayer groups. Send for season's brochure.

SEINE-MARITIME (76)

Rogerville
Fraternité du Père Arson
14, rue du Père Arson   Tel: (0)2 35 20 42 57
76700 Rogerville   Fax: (0)2 35 55 58 84
Roman Catholic, Franciscan sisters and friars welcome all to this retreat
house, which is open all year. 15 rooms. Conferences rooms, guest lounge,
TV, chapel. Personal talks possible. Full board about 30€.

Saint-Wandrille-Rançon
Abbaye Saint-Wandrille
76490 Saint-Wandrille   Tel: (0)2 35 96 23 11
Roman Catholic. The monks receive men, women, young people, groups.
Up to 8-day stays. 35 rooms. Men eat with the community; women and
couples eat separately. Personal talks, group discussion. A quiet location in a
village. Must book 1 month in advance.

SEINE-ET-MARNE (77)

Brou-sur-Chantereine
Prieuré St Joseph   Tel: (0)1 60 20 11 20
1, avenue Victor-Thiebaut   Fax: (0)1 60 20 43 52
77177 Brou-sur-Chantereine   e-mail: pr.stjoseph.brou@club-internet.fr
Roman Catholic. Receives women, religious, couples in guest house for individual or group retreats in silence and prayer. 9 singles, 3 doubles, 2 family
rooms. Guest lounge, disabled facilities, library, chapel, choir. Personal talks
possible. Write in the first instance to the Guest Sister.

Faremoutiers
Abbaye Notre-Dame-et-Saint-Pierre
1, rue Fénélon Desfourneaux   Tel: (0)1 64 04 20 37
77515 Faremoutiers   Fax: (0)1 64 20 04 69
Roman Catholic. Benedictine contemplative nuns. Receives women and groups
of up to 15 in self-catering accommodation. Chapel, choir, garden, library.
Personal talks possible. Some liturgy is in Gregorian chant but the psalms are
usually in French. Brochure available. Approximately 55 km from Paris.

Jouarre
Abbaye Notre Dame de Jouarre
6, rue Montmorin   Tel: (0)1 60 22 06 11
77640 Jouarre   Fax: (0)1 60 22 31 25
Roman Catholic. The sisters receive women, families and small groups. 40
singles, 9 doubles. Library, meeting room, chapel, choir. Personal talks possible. Guests eat evening meal in silence. There is a Merovingian crypt of
special interest. Brochure available. Quiet village setting.

YVELINES (78)

Bonnelles
Monastère des Orantes-de-l'Assumption
Chemin de Noncienne
78830 Bonnelles   Tel: (0)1 30 41 32 76
Roman Catholic. Receives men and women individually or in groups for
retreats. 32 rooms. Guest lounge, library, disabled facilities, TV, meeting
room, chapel. Personal talks possible.

Versailles
St Mark's English Church   Tel: (0)1 39 02 79 45
31, rue du Pont Colbert   Fax: (0)1 39 50 97 29
78000 Versailles   e-mail: stmarks@wanadoo.fr
Anglican. This is an Anglican Church in the Diocese in Europe and under the
patronage of the intercontinental Church Society. All English speakers are
welcomed. Regular Sunday worship, a crèche, children's and teenagers'
groups. During the weekdays Bible study, social events, and a mother and
toddlers group. There are also services at St Paul's Church, Chevry, and Gif-
sur-Yvette on Sunday afternoons. The Chaplain is Rev David Marshall and
the Assistant Chaplain Rev Angela Marshall.

SEVRES–DEUX (79)

Niort
Monastère du Carmel
157, rue de Strasbourg   Tel: (0)5 49 24 18 72
79000 Niort   Fax: (0)5 49 33 59 39
Roman Catholic. Carmelite nuns who receive women only. 3 beds. Retreats
in silence and prayer. Participation in Divine Office. Chapel open to the
public. A town location.

TARN (81)

Dourgne
Abbaye Saint-Benoît-d'en-Calcat
81110 Dourgne

Tel: (0)5 63 50 32 37, Guest house: (0)5 63 50 84 10
Fax: (0)5 63 50 38 78, Guest house: (0)5 63 50 34 90
Website: www.encalcat.com
Guest house e-mail: hotellerie@encalcat.com

Roman Catholic. We very much like this place for a private individual retreat. Between 60 and 70 monks live a life of contemplation and prayer in this abbey, and are also involved in many different activities and programmes. The monastery receives everyone, including non-believers, the non-baptized, divorced people and people of other faiths. The monks do not organise retreats themselves, but groups do come on retreat here with their own leaders. Open to men in the monastery, all others in the guest house. 26 singles, 39 doubles. Guest lounge, TV, chapel, choir, meeting rooms. Guest house visitors eat separately from the community. A quiet location in the countryside. There is a library open to the public, and a special library of over 100,000 volumes open under certain conditions. The monks make a form of zither called a Psalterion (Cithare), which is now used in monasteries and churches throughout the world, as well as for private accompaniment of the psalms. They also produce delicious honey and CDs of their Gregorian chant, and have glass and pottery workshops. This is a highly popular place to visit, with numbers often exceeding 60,000 in a year. More than 4,000 guests are received annually too. This is a hard-working community of men who extend a warm welcome, and a restful, comfortable and beautiful place in which to pray, reflect, and be at peace. And all in *belle France* too! Could you want anything more? **Highly Recommended.**

Montredon
Labessonnie
Castelfranc   Tel: (0)5 63 75 62 84
81360 Montredon   Fax: (0)5 63 75 63 14

Alternative spirituality. Provides space and encouragement for the stressed and weary – all who are in need of rest and recuperation. B&B. Cultural events and concerts. To enquire about what is on offer and charges this season contact them on the **UK number: 020 7538 5633.**

TARN-ET-GARONNE (82)

Mas-Grenier
Abbaye Saint-Pierre
82600 Mas-Grenier   Tel: (0)5 63 02 51 22

Roman Catholic. Benedictine nuns. Receives individuals and groups in next door guest house, Acceuil St Pierre, for silent day or longer retreats. 35 rooms.

VAR (83)

Cogolin
Trimurti
Chemin du Val Périers   Tel: (0)4 94 54 44 11
83310 Cogolin   Fax: (0)4 94 54 63 31
Alternative spirituality. Trimurti is a centre for courses, workshops, resources
for knowing yourself, and personal development. Situated in the south of
France in the countryside beyond St Tropez. There is much on offer here,
with good facilities for guests. Send for information on the current year's
programme.

Cotignac
Monastère La Font Saint-Joseph du Bessillon   Tel: (0)4 94 04 63 44
83570 Cotignac   Fax: (0)4 94 04 79 78
Roman Catholic. A place of peace on a hillside with distant views, only 90 km
from Marseille. An enclosed community, the nuns receive women only, for
retreats. 6 singles. Central heating.

VAUCLUSE (84)

Avignon
Centre Atma
50, rue des Liuces
84000 Avignon   Tel: (0)4 90 27 35 14
Alternative spirituality – yoga. The centre is open all year for courses and
workshops in yoga and massage. They also organise a group expedition to
India each year. Write for brochure.

Le Thor
Le Petit Trentin
84250 Le Thor   Tel: (0)4 90 33 85 04
Roman Catholic. Run by the Companions of Trentin. Retreats are offered to
all for 5 to 12 days duration. Accommodation for 12. Two guest lounges,
library, TV, chapel, choir. Personal talks possible. Pilgrims welcome.

Montfavet
Monastère Sainte-Claire-de-Notre-Dame-des-Miracles
La Verdière
BP 28
84141 Cedex Montfavet   Tel: (0)4 90 31 01 55
Roman Catholic. 5 km from Avignon. Receives men and women for retreats
of up to 8 days. A very peaceful atmosphere.

VENDÉE (85)

Chavagnes en Paillers
Centre spirituel Ursulines de Jésus   Tel: (0)2 51 42 36 38
Rue de la Petite Maine BP 8   Fax: (0)2 51 42 36 98
85250 Chavagnes en Paillers   e-mail: chacspi@wanadoo.fr
Roman Catholic. The community offers retreats, weekend retreats of prayer,
and other events. Welcomes men and women in a climate of prayer and

peace. 60 singles, 23 doubles. Park, guest lounge, meeting rooms, disabled facilities, TV, chapel, choir. Personal talks and directed retreats possible. Full board about 30€ per day.

VIENNE (86)

Ligugé
Abbaye Saint-Martin   Tel: (0)5 49 55 21 12
86240 Ligugé   Fax: (0)5 49 55 10 98
Roman Catholic. Benedictine monks. Open to all. Guest house near monastery of about 20 singles, 15 doubles, dormitories and camping. Gregorian chant in Divine Office.

Poitiers
Abbaye Sainte-Croix
Saint-Benoît
86280 Poitiers   Tel: (0)5 49 88 57 33
Roman Catholic. Benedictine nuns who receive women, young people, families, and groups for spiritual retreat and prayer only. 30 rooms. 2 guest lounges.

Saint-Julien l'Ars
Monastère de l'Annonciation
11, rue du Parc
86800 Saint-Julien l'Ars   Tel: (0)5 49 56 71 01
Roman Catholic. Benedictine nuns. Receives women for retreats of up to 8 days. Young women may participate in life of community. Chapel. Personal talks and group discussions. Pilgrims welcome. Quiet in a country village.

VOSGES (88)

Ubexy
Abbaye Notre-Dame de Saint-Joseph   Tel: (0)3 29 38 25 70
88130 Ubexy   Fax: (0)3 29 38 05 90
                                     e-mail: Uy.compt@wanadoo.fr
Roman Catholic. Cistercian nuns. Receives men and women for retreats of up to 8 days. 15 rooms, dormitory. 3 guest lounges, library, chapel, choir. Personal talks possible.

YONNE (89)

Saint-Léger-Vauban
Abbaye Sainte-Marie de la Pierre-Qui-Vire   Tel: (0)3 86 32 24 06
89630 Saint-Léger-Vauban   Fax: (0)3 86 32 24 06
                        e-mail: info@abbaye-pierrequivire.asso.fr
                        Website: www.abbaye-pierrequivire.assoc.fr
Roman Catholic. Open all year except January. Receives men, women, groups for individual retreats of up to 1 week. 7 singless, 12 doubles, dormitories. Participation in Divine Office and guests may help with work of the community. There is a library, a church and two oratories for private prayer. Personal talks possible. Guests eat separately, with some meals taken in

silence. A very peaceful location in the woods. Write to the Guest Brother 2 weeks in advance.

Sens
Monastère de la Nativité
105, rue Victor-Guichard   Tel: (0)3 86 65 13 41
89100 Sens   Fax: (0)3 86 65 73 49
Roman Catholic. Dominican nuns. Receives men and women for retreats. Situated in town, near the cathedral. Accommodation for 80. Charges for room and board vary, so ask when you contact the Guest Sister. Vegetarian food sometimes possible. Library, meeting rooms, chapel, choir. Personal talks possible. Brochure available.

Vézelay
Fraternités monastiques de Jérusalem   Tel: (0)3 86 33 39 53
Secrétariat Jérusalem Vézelay   Fax: (0)3 86 33 36 93
Presbytere   e-mail: Jerusalem.vezelay@wanadoo.fr
89450 Vézelay   Website: www.vezelay.cef.fr
Roman Catholic. A wonderful place high on a hill with a magnificent basilica, the town itself little changed from the Middle Ages with tiled roofs, cars hardly allowed in, and streets where monks, nuns, pilgrims, tourists and town folk all intermingle. Truly a step into another world. Retreat programme and excellent accommodation.

TERRITOIRE DE BELFORT (90)

Lepuix-Gy
Prieuré Saint-Benoît de Chauveroche   Tel: (0)3 84 29 01 57
90200 Lepuix-Gy   Fax: (0)3 84 29 56 80
                              e-mail: chauveroche@wanadoo.fr
Roman Catholic. Receives men, women, and groups for individual retreats in a small guest house of 7 rooms. Meals taken with the community in silence. There is also a chalet for groups close by the priory with accommodation for 25 in 6 rooms.

ESSONNE (91)

Évry
Maison Sainte Geneviève
Notre Dame de Sion
2m, avenue Ratisbonne   Tel: (0)1 60 77 31 45
91000 Évry   Fax: (0)1 69 36 49 90
Roman Catholic. This guest house of the Sisters of Our Lady is only 30 km from Paris. They welcome individuals and large and small groups for retreats. The guest house is situated in a park near the Seine. 24 rooms. Camping possible for young people. Lots of lounges and other rooms, library, TV, chapel. Write to the Director.

Vauhallan
Abbaye Saint-Louis-du-Temple
Limon   Tel: (0)1 69 85 21 00

91430 Vauhallan   Fax: (0)1 69 85 28 96
                                                 e-mail: liman@wanadoo.fr
Roman Catholic. Benedictine nuns. The Abbey was founded in memory of
the French royal family, who were imprisoned in the temple tower during the
revolution. Stained glass windows designed by Maire Genevieve Gallois
(1888–1962). Receives men, women, small groups under guidance of one of
the sisters. Accommodation for 40 in a number of buildings. Dormitory.
Conference rooms, library, chapel, choir. Personal talks possible. Peaceful
village location. **Highly Recommended.**

HAUTS-DE-SEINE (92)

Fontenay aux Roses
Résidence Universitaire Lanteri
7, rue Gentil Bernard   Tel: (0)1 41 13 36 00
92260 Fontenay aux Roses   Fax: (0)1 43 50 88 45
Roman Catholic. This retreat and guest centre is open from the beginning of
July until mid-September to anyone who wants to spend time alone. Groups
organising their own retreat are also received for an unlimited period.
Accommodation for 160 in singles, doubles, family rooms. 2 guest lounges,
parking, library, TV, church, chapel, meeting rooms. Personal talks possible.
Full board 35€. Accommodation without meals also available. Reduced
charges for groups. Enquire in writing a month in advance.

EVANGELICAL CHURCHES IN FRANCE
(Églises Évangéliques en France)

There are a number of evangelical fellowships throughout France. **La
Fédération Évangélique de France** will provide information.

Fédération Évangélique de France
40, rue des Réservoirs   Tel: (0)4 69 49 06 21
91330 Yerres, France   Fax: (0)4 69 48 17 89

Evangelical Centres for Holidays
(Centres Évangéliques de Vacances)
The Federation above also runs the Centres Évangéliques de Vacances. Write
to them for details of these centres.

Arles
L'Etoile du Matin
Centre Évangélique de l'Espérou
5, rue de la Madeleine
13200 Arles   Tel/Fax: (0)4 90 93 55 77

Chamrousse
Centre Évangélique Le Belledonne   Tel: (0)4 76 89 90 17
38410 Chamrousse   Fax: (0)4 76 89 94 27

Boug d'Oisans
Le Camp des Cimes
La Rivoire
38520 Bourg d'Oisans   Tel: (0)4 76 80 07 20

Le Champ prés Froges
Centre de Vacances Champfleuri   Tel: (0)4 76 71 41 07
38190 Le Champ prés Froges   Fax: (0)4 76 71 38 44

Sondernach
Centre de Vacances Landersen   Tel: (0)3 89 77 60 69
68380 Sondernach   Fax: (0)3 89 77 74 31

Munster
Centre Évangélique Chrischona
13, chemin de la foret Hohrodberg   Tel: (0)3 89 77 31 35
68140 Munster   Fax: (0)3 89 77 05 37

Houlgate
Maison Évangélique
4, passage Évangélique   Tel: (0)2 31 28 70 80
BP 30 – 14510 Houlgate   Fax: (0)2 31 24 60 46

St Lunaire
Centre des Jeunes
Le Pont St Lunaire
35800 St Lunaire   Tel: (0)2 99 46 33 94

St Albain
Château de St Albain
71260 St Albain   Tel: (0)3 85 33 12 95/85 33 14 28

YOGA IN FRANCE

Yoga is taught all over France, in venues as diverse as village community centres, leisure centres, fitness clubs and fully equipped yoga centres. There are regular weekly classes as well as retreats and courses.

A national organisation for further information is **La Fédération Nationale des Enseignants de Yoga (FNEY)**. Contact: Yse Masquelier, 3 rue Aubriot, F-75004 Paris, tel: (0)1 42 70 03 05.

The following places offer yoga. Those marked # have a detailed entry in listing of retreat places above, organised by department of France.

> *L'homme debout est la gloire de Dieu.*
> IRÉNÉE DE LYON

#Auris, 6 rue Viala, 01000 Bourg en Bresse, tel: (0)4 74 22 48 86.
#Centre Atma, 50 rue des Lices, 8400 Avignon, tel: (0)4 90 27 35 14.
Centre de Yoga Iyengar de Lyon, Clos de Fourviere II, 40 rue Roger Radisson, 69005 Lyon, tel: (0)4 78 36 03 84.

#**Centre Eviel**, Les Granges, 24590 St Crépin Carlucet, tel: (0)5 53 28 93 27, fax: (0)5 53 28 81 17.

#**Centre International Sivananda de Yoga Vedanta**, 123 boulevard de Sébastopol, 75002 Paris, tel: (0)1 40 26 77 49, fax: (0)1 42 33 51 97.

#**Château de Valclérieux**, Saint-Bonnet de Valclérieux, 26350 Crépol, tel: (0)4 75 71 70 67.

#**Château du Yoga Sivananda**, Neuville au Bois, Orléans 45000, website: www.sivananda.org/orleans/indeng.

Ecole Francaise de Yoga du Sud-Est, 18 rue Victor Leydet, 13100 Aix en Provence, tel: (0)4 42 27 92 20.

#**Fédération Internationale de Yoga Himalayen,** c/o Stephane-Jean, Les Ilipotiers, Las Illas Village, 66480 Maureillas, tel: (0)6 11 51 47 53/(0)4 68 83 04 76, website: www.membres.lycos.fr/himalaya/program.

Fédération Inter-Régionale de Hatha-Yoga, 322 rue Saint Honoré, 75001 Paris, tel: (0)4 42 60 32 10.

Kaivalyadhama-France, Lozeron, 26400 Gigors-et-Lozeron, tel: (0)4 75 76 42 95.

L'Association provençale de Hatha Yoga, 12 rue J. Daret, Aix-en-Provence, tel: (0)5 42 64 18 54.

#**La Buissière**, Lot Valley, website: www.yogafrance.com

La Fédération Tantra Kundalini Yoga, Château Laroque, 33890 Juillas.

La Fédération des Yogas Traditionnels, André Riehl, 65 rue des Cèdres, 84120 Pertuis, tel: (0)4 90 09 65 27.

#**La Seve**, 40 route de Tarbes, 653560 Laslades, tel: (0)5 62 35 08 34.

La Val Dieu, Pyrénées, contact: Annette Tolson, tel: (UK) 01225 311826.

La Yoga Thérapie, Christine Campagnac-Morette, 5 place du Général Beuret, 75015 Paris.

#**Le Chartrou Belmonet**, 46800 Montcuq, tel: (0)5 65 31 90 23.

#**Le Blé en Herbe**, Puissetier, 23350 La Cellette, tel: (0)5 55 80 62 83.

#**Scandinavian Yoga and Meditation School**, 46 rue de Metz, 31000 Toulouse, tel: (0)5 61 25 17 69.

#**Star of Light Mountain Retreat Centre**, Maison Bird, Conat, 66500 Prades, tel/fax: (0)4 68 96 04 80, e-mail: bird.conat@easynet.fr.

#**Terre du Ciel**, BP 2050, 69227 Lyon cedex 02, tel: (0)4 72 41 07 51.

#**The Sun Centre**, Prades, 66160 St Martin de Boubaux, tel: (0)4 66 45 59 63, website: www.thesuncentre.net

CREATION SPIRITUALITY IN FRANCE
(Mouvement Création Spiritualité en France)

Followers of Mathew Fox's Creation Spirituality theology may find courses, seminars, and workshops in France by writing to:

**Francis Gohard
Mouvement Creation Spiritualité
76, rue de Margnolles
69300 Caluire**
Tel: (0)4 72 27 01 63

HERMITAGE RETREATS IN FRANCE
(L'expérience de poustinia en France)

It is possible to have a hermit experience of silence and solitude in France. Some hermitages are in the heart of towns and others situated in the silence of remote places. Here are two addresses to start you off. The first deals with hermitages in Paris and Lyon, the second is a community of Roman Catholic nuns who live as hermits in the mountains in south-western France.

Madonna House
1, rue de l'Abbé Migne   Tel: (for Paris) Myriam (0)1 42 72 16 04
75004 Paris   (for Lyon) Jacqueline (0)4 72 34 61

Laure Saint-Antoine
Monastere des ermites
St. Jean des Alberes
66480 Le Perthus

BUDDHIST FACILITIES AND PROGRAMMES

Association Zen en Mouvement
55, boulevard Stalingrad
06300 Nice

Association Un Pas vers les Tibétains
26, Chaussée de l'Etang
94160 Saint Mandé   Tel/fax: (0)1 43 28 47 24

Friends of the Western Buddhist Order – France
c/o 21, Place de la République
11300 Limoux   Tel: (0)4 68 31 78 02
Information available on centres and activities in France.

Institut Karmappa
35, chemin rural de la Ferriére   Tel: (0)4 93 60 90 16
06750 Valderoure   Fax: (0)4 93 60 48 75

Nyima Dzong
Institut Européen de Bouddhisme Tibétain   Tel: (0)4 94 76 90 88
Château de Soleils   Fax: (0)4 94 85 68 27
04120 Castellanne   e-mail: nyima@wanadoo.fr

FURTHER INFORMATION ON FRANCE

The following publications cover houses of retreat, places that receive pilgrims, retreat programmes of courses and workshops, and monastic hospitality in France. They may prove helpful to those who are keen to explore their spirituality across the Channel. These books are in French and published in France, but they can usually be ordered from larger British book shops.

Alternatively, you can obtain them from **The English Language Bookshop,** **5 rue du Bourg, 65100 Lourdes,** tel/fax (0)5 62 42 27 94. The staff here speak English and will post the books to you. Regrettably, many of the great number of books published in France on spiritual subjects are never translated into English.

Centre d'Information et de Documentation Religieuses (CIDR), 6 Place du Parvis de Notre Dame, 75004 Paris, tel (0)1 46 33 01 01. This is an organisation that publishes a monthly brochure, *Calendrier des retraites spirituelles*, listing retreat programmes, including courses and workshops, on offer at various monasteries and retreat houses in France.

***Des outils pour un changement*, Editions Terre du Ciel, BP 2050, 13 rue Henri IV, 69227 Lyon cedex 02,** tel (0)4 72 41 07 51, fax (0)4 78 37 65 44. The organisation Terre du Ciel is one of the best sources in France for information about aspects of Christian, Judaic, Buddhist, and Sufi spirituality; yoga; holistic health methods; and many of the leading as well as the somewhat obscure mind, body spirit approaches to self-awareness and harmony with others and with planet earth. The aim of Terre du Ciel is to create and bring together invitations to change and renewal of self. They publish a bi-monthly journal with articles and listings of workshops and courses that reflect this aim.

***Bouddhisme – Actualités*, Nice Premier, 455 Promenade des Anglais, 06199 Nice cedex 3.** A monthly magazine with information about what is happening in the various places of Buddhist practice in France, with lots of addresses for forthcoming programmes and ads for courses and visiting teachers. It is on sale in most large newsagents.

***Guide des monastères*, Maurice Colinon, Pierre Horay Éditeur, Paris.**
In addition to listing various monasteries in France, Belgium, Switzerland and Luxembourg, this guide also gives a short history of monasticism and includes directories of the Catholic religious orders in France and of those monasteries that make and sell artisan products. It is usually possible to stop and buy such products without staying as a guest. Maurice Colinon also publishes a guide to monasteries in Europe for those interested in retreats outside French-speaking countries.

***Guide des Pèlerinages de France*, Bernard Iselin, Dervy, Paris.**
There have been Christian pilgrims almost since the beginning of Christianity itself – and the tradition of walking along a sacred way, stopping to pray at holy sites, and finally arriving at a great and famous holy place is, of course, not unique to Christians. In Europe, the pilgrimage of the way of St Jacques de Compostelle has been famous for centuries. It takes the pilgrim through France and Spain from sacred place to sacred place on a specific route. Today, it is an increasingly popular spiritual journey whether you do it on foot, which is the traditional and authentic way, or by bicycle, motorcycle, car or horse. This guide is an excellent reference, including sections on the history of Christian pilgrimages, route directions, holy and sacred sites, and places of sanctuary and welcome for pilgrims along the way. An illustrated book, *Les chemins de Saint-Jacques de Compostelle*, **BP 20, 65502 Vic-en-Bigorre** is also very good.

Guide Saint-Christophe, **Association Saint-Christophe, Paris Cedex 05.** This guide covers many retreat houses in France and some other European countries – it is particularly good on places in Belgium and Italy, but Hungary, Switzerland, Spain, and Portugal are also included. In addition there is information on the pilgrim way of Saint Jacques de Compostelle (see above) and on places for peaceful holidays.

Guide des Centres Bouddhistes en France, **Philippe Ronce, Éditions Noesis, 12 rue de Savoie Vie Paris**. This guide lists centres all over France, many listings with illustrations of the sites, and gives good details of facilities, practices and spiritual schools. There is also a helpful index.

> The words of holy prophets can be sacred arrows that come in the form of words but change within you to burning arrows that pierce your heart and shake your beliefs. They wake you up to the fact you are a spiritual being and make you realise your heart can be touched by the idea of the divine – no matter how little conscious attention you may have previously paid to the spiritual. This can be a revelation, one that can transform your entire life.
>
> LIVING THE SACRED

Italy

Italy, eternally a treasure house of beautiful monasteries and churches, is taking on a new aspect for people in Britain wanting a spiritual retreat. Where we once went to this exciting and wonderful country to visit the famed religious sites of Assisi and Rome, we are now booking onto pilgrimage tours and monastic retreat events and courses. Italy is one of the most thoroughly Roman Catholic nations in the world, and non-Catholic retreat centres are much less numerous than in even Ireland, another very Catholic country. There are many excellent guides to such religious places in Italy and a great many travel agencies who know about touring and staying in monasteries or making a group pilgrimage to Italy. Here are just a few ideas to get you thinking about making a retreat in Italy.

The Monastic Community of Bose (Comunità Monastica di Bose)
I-13887 Magnano (BI)   Tel: 051 679185
                                                              Fax: 051 679290
The Monastic Community of Bose, founded by Fr Enzio Bianchi in the late 1990s, is an Ecumenical community with each member retaining his or her own church membership after joining Bose. Living under the Rule of Saint Benedict, the Community remains close to the ideals and spiritual values of the early Desert Fathers. Among other activities, they run a small publishing house, which enjoys an excellent reputation. The Community has gone from strength to strength in a very few years and is now opening a second house in Assisi. The Community produces a brochure with full details about their life and how to travel directions. The monastery is 65 km from Turin and 115 km from Milan. Car, continental train or bus, and air from Britain are all possible.

Reading Retreats in Rural Italy
Castello di Galeazza
Via Provanone 8585
40014 Galeazza di Crevalcore (BO)   Tel: 051 985 170
                                      e-mail: mailto:%20info@galeazza.com
                                      Website: www.montefano.com
Now here is something really new in retreats. It is funky, fun, unpredictable, sometimes noisy and over-the-top, often so quiet you could hear a pin drop, both super-efficient and madly disorganised – a real treat for tired souls, a beautiful spot to just be, and a happy place to let go of your worries and chill out. So leave behind your mobile phones, laptops, stereos, video cameras, arguments with your partner or parents, and the mad rush of your busy life and join small groups of people from around the world who gather here in this castle for a personal reading retreat sojourn. That's right! You live in a castle and reading a book is what you do – as well as sleep a lot, eat well (and share in the cooking too), listen to music, hold conversations, make new friends, go for a

bike ride or just sit around doing nothing. You may want to discuss the book you are reading or books in general with someone, but then again you may not bother at all and no one will care. If you are a person who needs the reassurance of structured days or fidgets when things don't happen exactly on time, forget this place. If, on the other hand, you enjoy great hospitality and a house party atmosphere, and thrive on a mix of excitement and calm, book in now!

Reading Retreats in Rural Italy, started in 1996 by a brilliant and cultured American, Clark Lawrence, satisfies everyone's reading appetite by letting them read as much, whatever and whenever they want. The library here is growing steadily, and many guests donate the books they bring to the castle to Reading Retreats in Rural Italy's library. Some people come alone, some as couples, and others in small groups. There are often local Italian members in the castle, who come from Bologna, Ferrara or Modena for dinner or to attend concerts, art exhibits or other events. The unique mix of foreign and local friends of the Castle is a pleasure for both, because there are always familiar faces around but always new people to meet as well. Many visitors enjoy trying out their Italian, while the Italians take the opportunity to practise their English.

The oldest part of the Castle of Galeazza is the tower, which was built in the late fourteenth century. After climbing 122 steps from the ground floor to the terrace of the tower, the visitor is rewarded with impressive views of the fertile surrounding countryside and a bird's eye view of the brick and terracotta roof tiles of the castle. On clear days one can see the Apennines to the south and the Alps to the north, as well as other towers and campanili of the plains here and there on the horizon. Although the castle was built in several phases through the centuries, the most recent and obvious additions were all made in the second half of the nineteenth century. Around 1870, Signor Alessandro Falzoni Gallerani, a gentleman from the nearby town of Cento who was known for his exquisite taste and appreciation of art and culture, bought the tower. Falzoni Gallerani wanted to create a luxurious summer residence for his very large family, so he added to the tower an impressive castle with harmonious, neo-gothic details. Reading Retreats in Rural Italy moved to the castle in the spring of 2003. It does not occupy all of the castle's one hundred or so rooms, but shares with the owners of the property the most beautiful part of the castle, near the main entrance. This area includes high-ceilinged frescoed rooms of varying size, which serve as library, sitting rooms, and guest rooms. Concerts and receptions are held on the ground floor, in the main entrance hall and the rooms on either side of the central foyer. The garden and park of the castle are noteworthy for their size and design, and the variety of trees, plants and animals found in them.

The Castle is open all year round. **Bookings are by letter only (FAO Clark Lawrence).** There are four guest rooms (for a maximum of eight guests). Each room is furnished with antiques and has frescoed ceilings (shown on the website). There are no rooms with private bathrooms. Facilities include the library, CD collection, three pianos, a small fleet of old bicycles and free parking. Everyone prepares meals and eats together. (Usually traditional Italian food and local wine.) Guests who want a steady stream of fancy cocktails and after-dinner drinks are asked to bring their own. Children of any age are allowed to stay in the castle if their parents make reservations before other guests, and then those who want to come during that period are warned there will be children around. If other guests already have rooms reserved in the castle, children are not allowed. Families should therefore make reservations early to avoid disappointment. Pets are not allowed on the property. The castle has a large garden and acres of private woodland. Galeazza is located in the plains of north-eastern Italy, about 40 minutes due north of Bologna, 40 minutes east of Modena, and 40 minutes west of Ferrara. **Highly Recommended.**

(Historical information about the castle was taken from *Castelli e Ville Bolognesi*, Umberto Beseghi, Tamari Editori, Bologna 1957.)

Podere Fiorli
Centre for Peace and Community
Via Poggilamo
I-56048 Volterra

Tel: 0588 33193
Fax: 0588 33235
e-mail: poderefiorli@friedensgasse.ch
Website: www.friedensgasse.ch

Podere Fiorli in Tuscany is the Italian House of the Kommunitat Friedensgasse of Basel, Switzerland, a spiritual and social community composed of celibate men and women and married and committed same gender couples who live together in a life of spiritual practice in peace and caring for others, including the disabled and disadvantaged. They have several houses in Basel, which are quiet and welcoming places, open to everyone. Meals are taken together. Each community house has its own chapel room where the community says prayers together several times each day. Urs Mattmann, former head of the community, founded **C-Queer, an organisation for Gays and Lesbians in Christian Spirituality**, website: www.friedensgasse.ch/C-Queer. He organises and leads retreats for gay and bisexual men at Podere Fiorli. These are usually co-facilitated by someone who is not a member of the community. Such facilitators are established retreat leaders and speakers, and have included James Alison, the Catholic priest, theologian and author. Urs Mattmann, who is a qualified social worker and a Psychosynthesis therapist with a background in mediation, recently published a book on Christian spirituality for lesbians and gays entitled *Coming In*. First published in German, it is soon to be issued in English. **Highly Recommended.**

The Community address in Switzerland is:
Friedensgasse Diakonische Kommunitat
Friedengasse 72
4056 Basel
Switzerland

Tel: 61 383 12 59
Fax: 61 383 12 58
e-mail: adm@friedensgasse.ch
Website: www.friedensgasse.ch

Convento San Silvestro
00040 Monte Compatri
Rome   Website: www.beatitudes.fr, www.institut.beatitudes.free.fr

A former Carmelite monastery, now a house of the Roman Catholic Communauté des Béatitudes, which has houses in some 30 dioceses in France (see France section) and 35 abroad (See Wales Section, St David's Monastery). Apart from hospitality, the main aims of the house are parish missions, weekend retreats and retreats for youth groups.

ITALIAN MONASTIC RETREATS AND STAYS

The following monastic houses, most of which take private retreat guests and may have annual retreat programmes for both individuals and groups, are available in detail online. Almost all the sites have photos of the monastery and its setting. Some are so ravishingly beautiful you will want to jump on the next flight out. If you have difficulty in accessing them through your search engine, then go to the website for Italian monasteries **www.cattolici.org/monasteriositalia.**

Abbazia Benedettina Santa Maria di Finalpia
Abbazia Benedettina San Pietro dei Sorres, Borutta
Abbazia Cistercense di Cadamari (silent Order)
Abbazia del Santi Nazzario e Celso
Abbazia del Goleto
Abbazia di Borzone
Abbazia di Chiaravalle di Fiastra
Abbazia di Monte Oliveto Maggiore (among the greatest of Italian historic places and still a Benedictine Community of the Olivetan Order (See Turvey Abbey in East and East Anglia section).
Abbazia di Novacella
Abbazia Sacra di San Michele
Abbazia di San Bertolo
Abbazia di San Benedetto
Abbazia di Sant'Agata
Abbazia di San Benededetto Po
Abbazia di Sant Egidio
Abbazia di San Giovanni Evangelista, Parma
Abbazia di San Martino di'Bocci
Abbazia di San Paolo, Rome
Abbazia di Santa Giustina
Abbazia di Sassovivo, Foligno
Abbazia di Vallombrosa
Abbazia di Villanova di San Bonifacio, Verona
Carmelo S. Anna di Carpineto, Rome
Clonard Monastery
Comunità monastioca di Germagno
Comunità Trappiste di Valserena (silent Order)
Famiglia Monastica Fraternita di Gesù
Fraterinta Monastica della Trinità
Monache Agostiniane, Schio
Monasteri Benedettini di Subiaco (see also Quarr Abbey, South and Southeast section).
Monastero Camaldolese (eremetical Order)
Carmelo Santa Anna (enclosed Order)
Cistercense Dominus, Piemonte (silent Order)
Della Clarissse St Marioa delle Grazia Franese
Monastero di Lanuvio
Monastero di Pra'd Mill
Monastero di Sant' Anna, Salerno
Monastero di San Biagio Mondovi
Monastero di San Domenico Abate, Sora

Monastero di San Paolo, Fuori Le Mura
Monastero di Santa Chiara
Monastero di Vitorchiano, Rome (Trappist – silent Order)
Monastero Eremo San Silvestro in Monefano
Monastero Silvestrina
Monastero Carmelo, Sorano
Monastero Di Bastia Capuchins (English and Spanish languages on website)
Monastero Certosa di Pavia
Monache Domenicane Santa Maria della Neve
Nostra Signora di San Giuseppe (Trappiste – silent Order)
San Benedetto, Modica
Saint Anthony Monastery (Capuchins)

> We all love the comforts of our habits, but such a state of living ignores the nature of the universe. It causes illusions and desires to flourish and the ego loves this state of affairs because it stops your pilgrimage of spiritual discovery. Accepting change is that important.
> LIVING THE SACRED

Spain

Buddhist – Mind Body Spirit In recent years, there has been an increase in the number of alternative spirituality and Buddhist centres in Spain. The warm weather and the relaxed atmosphere of this country provide a restful setting for many healing and renewal programmes, including de-stressing courses, yoga, relaxation techniques, complementary health methods, and self-realisation and self-development courses – many of which are set in sunny holiday sites such as Granada or the Malaga area. The programmes are much the same as you would find in Britain, the core aim frequently being to encourage relaxation and renewal within a holistic context. **Cortijo Romero** (see below) is one of the older and still among the most successful centres. **Guhyaloka** (see below), hidden away in the mountains of Valencia, is a Buddhist centre owned and run by the Friends of the Western Buddhist Order (FWBO) – booking and information through the Padmaloka Buddhist Retreat Centre for Men in Britain (see East and East Anglia section). **Tara Samye Dzong** (see below) is organised by the Kagyu Samye Ling Tibetan Centre in Scotland (see Scotland section). Write either directly to the centre in Spain or to Scotland.

Monastic retreats Spain is a treasure house of peaceful and welcoming monasteries gradually becoming known to tourists and those seeking a retreat. The Spanish tourist offices (see below) now supply details of those offering hospitality. Many of these only receive guests of one gender and the accommodation can be simple and the food plain. They are not hotels, and the monks and nuns are inspired by values of simplicity, silence and seclusion. While you will be expected to respect their way of life, your personal religious beliefs will not normally pose any problem. Such places would not normally expect to accommodate unmarried couples in the same room. Charges are usually modest, at about 8€ to 12€. You could try combining hotel accommodation with monastery visits, staying at one of the Spain's hotel-type paradores, such as the **Parador de Santo Domingo de la Calzada, Plaza del Santo No. 3, Santo Domingo de la Calzada** (Tel: 941 340 300), and venturing out from there to visit famous but peaceful monasteries, for instance the **Monastery of Santo Domingo de Silos**, south of Burgos, and the **Monastery of San Millan de la Cogolla**, which is east of Burgos and a place that those interested in art and architecture will greatly enjoy. These places are in or near Spain's wine growing area of La Rioja.

Pilgrim's route to Santiago de Compostela The pilgrim's route to Santiago de Compostela is tremendously popular these days, with thousands of people from all over the world and of all ages from teenagers to the seniors walking from the interior of France to the Spanish border and on down to Santiago de Compostela They follow ancient roads and enjoy themselves, most realising by the end that the spiritual nature of a pilgrimage is not in the arrival but in the journey itself. They usually stay in hostels, refuges or monasteries along the way, often located in some of Spain's loveliest countryside. Many of the historic places and churches contain great works of art. Given the limited number of rooms in such guest places and the number of people doing the pilgrimage, try to book well in advance. If, like most pilgrims, you fall behind in your walking schedule and just happen to discover a nearby monastery as night falls, a knock on their door will probably find you both a bed and a meal. After all, the monks on this route have been dealing with pilgrims for hundreds of years.

Organised travel retreats and pilgrimages For those wanting an organised retreat in Spain, there are travel operators who specialise in such programmes. If you are Catholic look in the *Catholic Herald* or if Anglican try the *Church Times* for advertisements, particularly for pilgrimages. Retreats in recent years have included a Holy Week retreat in Valladolid, north of Madrid, which is famous for its Holy Week processions. Group leaders have included several well-known British retreat facilitators. Another has taken place in Poio, a Mercedarian monastery south of Santiago, with excursions to Santiago de Compostela and the Trappist monasteries of Galacia.

Yoga in Spain More and more yoga retreats are being held in Spain by British yoga teachers. These are often not established programmes but are arranged on a year-by-year basis. Information on programmes can quickly go out of date, so if you are looking for a yoga holiday in Spain, it is best to discuss it with your local yoga teacher and then surf the net. See the websites listed in this book in the Yoga section (under Yoga on the Web). In addition, you might like to try the following websites and search names:
www.yogaholidays.net
www.bodyworkposters.com/Yogalinks.htm
www.holistic-online.com
www. yogadirectory.com/Retreats_and Vacations
Ashtanga Yoga and Ayurveda Retreats in South Spain
Astanga Yoga and Ayurvedic Retreats in Ibiza

The following offer yoga holidays in Spain:

Duncan Hulin Holistic Yoga   e-mail: devonschoolyoga@eclipse.co.uk
Duncan Hulin, who holds regular yoga classes in Exeter and Sidmouth, also organises yoga holidays in Southern Spain (and in Kerala, South India). There are a number of other yoga retreats and events on offer from time to time in his programmes.

Yoga Space
Basement Studio
35/37 Thomas Street
Manchester M4 1NA   Tel: 0161 288 6918
Yoga retreats are planned for a residential centre in Spain, so get in touch to find out the programme. Founded in 2001, Yoga Space is relatively new and the first yoga centre in central Manchester. Evening and day classes and courses in many style of yoga are on offer here. All teachers are accredited,

and the director of the studio invites only those teachers who have a strong understanding of the spiritual dimension of yoga as well as a high proficiency in the postures. It is expected that this standard will be used for any yoga courses held abroad.

SPAIN – GENERAL

Spanish Tourist Office
22/23 Manchester Square
London W1M 5AP

Tel: Brochure request line 09001 669920
(calls cost about 60p per minute)

Alicante
Guhyaloka
c/o Padmaloka Buddhist Centre
Surlingham
Norwich NR14 7AL

Tel: 01508 538112

Buddhist. Guhyaloka is a magical place of peace and austere simplicity for men. It is set high up in a remote place in the Spanish mountains not far from Alicante. The deep silence here offers a chance for you to deepen your meditation experience. The full time community are committed to creating a monastic Vihara devoted to study, meditation and work in this place. You can enjoy a summer retreat here, a solitary retreat in one of the little chalets dotted around the valley nearby, a winter semi-working retreat or a working retreat led by Yashodeva and members of the Guyaloka community. This working retreat gives you a chance to spend an extended period away from the ordinary busy life of towns and cities. There is ample time for exploring the valleys and mountains around the centre. Prices for accommodation and board range from £12 per night for a solitary chalet to £30 per week for a working retreat to £77 for a semi-working retreat. There is usually an Open Retreat of 2–3 weeks, which costs about £250 and is most suitable for focussing purely on Buddhist practice. **Highly Recommended.**

Barcelona
Abadia de Montserrat
Montserrat
Barcelona

Tel: 938 777 779
Website: www.abadiamontserrat.net

Roman Catholic. A Benedictine community receiving men, women and children in a guest house situated in the marvellous mountain setting of Monserrat Natural Park, 50 km north-west of Barcelona. There is a lot to discover here – a wonderful view, a library of over 300,000 books and a museum rich in treasures, including paintings by El Greco. Many day visitors come here. There are concerts and various cultural events during the year. 48 singles and 4 doubles available, and a place to eat. Charges are reasonable for accommodation and board at about 20€, but see website for current prices. **Highly Recommended.**

Karma Lodro Gyamtso Ling
Pau Claris No. 74
2-008010, Barcelona Tel/fax: 933 015 472
Buddhist. A place organised in association with the Kagyu Samye Ling Tibetan Centre in Scotland. Write either to Barcelona or to Scotland (see Scotland section) for information.

Burgos
Abadia de Santo Domingo de Silos
Santo Domingo de Silos
Burgos Tel: 947 390 049
Roman Catholic. Benedictine abbey receiving men only. 21 rooms, which are much above the average in comfort, with individual bathrooms and central heating. There is a peaceful and serious atmosphere here. Divine Office in Gregorian chant. The Holy Week religious services are impressive and justly famous. **Highly Recommended.**

Abadia de San Pedro de Cardena
Burgos Tel: 947 290 003
Roman Catholic. Founded in 899, this was the first Benedictine monastery in Spain. It has had a colourful history, surviving through invasions and wars. A Cistercian abbey, it receives men only who wish to share in the spiritual life of the community. Stays of up to 8 days. 24 rooms within the monastery. Full board offered. Much silence and an atmosphere of contemplation prevail here.

Monasterio de Las Huelgas
Burgos Tel: 947 206 045
Roman Catholic. Receives women in an annex guest house.

Monasterio de Palacios de Benaver
Palacios de Benaver
Burgos Tel: 947 451 009
Roman Catholic. Receives both men and women. A convent with 4 guest rooms. Gregorian chant at the services.

Caceros
Monasterio de Yusto
Cuacos, Caceros Tel: 927 480 530
Roman Catholic. Receives men for stays of up to 1 week.

Cantabria
Abadia de Via Celis
Corbreces
Cantabria Tel: 942 725 017
Roman Catholic. Cistercian community receiving men only, for stays of up to 1 week. This is a place to stay if you are going on a serious religious retreat and not just to rest and relax. The atmosphere is strict, silent and deeply spiritual.

Estercuel
Monasterio de Nuestra Senora del Olivar
44558 Estercuel
Teruel   Tel: 974 753 144
Roman Catholic. Founded in 1627. Situated at 700 m. You can take the train
to Alcaniz and get a bus from there. 23 rooms. Men, women, groups, children with their parents welcome. Costs are very modest at about 15€ per
person per day full board. Camping is possible.

Diego de Leon
Sivananda Yoga Vedanta Centre
Clerao 4
Diego de León   Tel: 913 615 150
Yoga. Part of the international Sivananda Yoga Vedanta Centres of France.
Yoga courses, teachings and workshops.

Ibiza
The Garden of Light   ★
School for Yoga and Human Development   Tel: 971 334 644
Apdo 1126   Fax: 971 334 644
07800 Ibiza   e-mail: thegardenoflight@hotmail.com
Alternative spirituality. Yoga. Open May to October to men, women and
groups. A spacious place in a forest about 2 km from the beach. Not much
luxury here but lots of beauty, with the emphasis on creativity and simplicity.
Accommodation for 32 in dormitories and 1 double room. Conferences, nice
garden, guest lounge, guest telephone. Everyone eats together. Vegetarian
food. Open also to groups who arrange their own programme. Check out
current year's rates, as charges everywhere are going up fast. Currently about
30€–37€ per day all inclusive. **Highly Recommended.**

Iznate
Maggie Levien
Calle Malaga 41
Iznate, 29792   Tel: 952 509 603/630 718 204
Home of yoga teacher Maggie Levien, who teaches beginners one-to-one
and couples while they stay for a holiday in her self-contained apartment in a
traditional old house in a white-washed Spanish village. She helps you
discover what is suitable for you in yoga practice and will cater for any physical limitations. This is yoga at a gentle pace for the beginner. Beautiful views,
lovely walks, close to both mountains and a nature reserve, and only about
20 minutes from the coast.

Javea Port
Javea Port
Costa Blanca
Ecumenical. A retreat apartment owned and run by the Grace and
Compassion Benedictine sisters in Britain (see South and South-east section).

The self-catering apartment is in a little fishing port near the harbour, the church and a number of restaurants. Three bedrooms accommodating 6 people. Central heating, well equipped and open all year round. Write to **The Superior, St Benedict's, 1 Manor Road, Kemp Town, Brighton BN2 5EA.**

La Coruna
Monasterio de Santa Maria de Sobrado
Sobrado
La Coruna   Tel: 981 787 509
Roman Catholic. Receives men only.

La Vid de Aranda
Monasterio de Santa Maria de la Vid
09491 La Vid de Aranda   Tel: 947 530 510
Burgos   Fax: 947 530 429
Roman Catholic. This monastery was founded in 1162 in an imposing position above the village among trees, and has many styles of architecture, ranging from Roman to Baroque. Men, women and children with their parents are received. 54 single and double rooms. Meals taken with the community. About 18€–20€ per day per person full board.

Leon
Monasterio Santa Maria de Carrizo
Carrizo de Ribera
Leon   Tel: 987 357 055
Roman Catholic. Cistercian nuns. Receives men and women. 4 rooms. Maximum stay of eight days. The convent closes early in the evening and guests are expected to respect the religious timetable.

Monasterio de San Pedro de las Duenas
Sahagun
Leon   Tel: 987 780 150
Roman Catholic. Benedictine nuns. Receives both men and women in a guest house. Visitors may come here just to relax and rest or for a retreat – for which the charges are lower.

Leyre
Abadia de San Salvador de Leyre
31410 Leyre
Yesa   Tel: 948 884 011
Roman Catholic. High in the mountains, the abbey looks down on the plain. Mass and religious offices in Gregorian chant. Men only are received – but fathers may bring their children if over 7 years. Stays of 3–10 days. 8 rooms within the monastery. Modest charges at about 15€ per person for a room and meals. There is a 3-star guest hotel outside the monastery itself, which is charming and very comfortable. A double room is about 66€.

Madrid
Abadia de Santa Cruz del Valle de los Caidos
28029 Valle de los Caidos   Tel: 918 905 411
Madrid   Fax: 918 905 594
Roman Catholic. Situated near the huge monument to the Civil War built by
General Franco. The monks have made this abbey a prayerful place of
welcome. Men and woman are received in two different facilities. One is in
the monastery itself and is reserved for men wishing to join in the spiritual
life of the community. Full room and board per person per day here is about
14€. The other accommodation is outside the monastery and has 110 rooms
with bathrooms. Full board from around 30€ per day per person. **To
communicate direct with the guest house telephone 918 905 492.**

Monasterio de El Paular
Rascafria
Madrid   Tel: 918 691 425
Roman Catholic. Receives men for stays of up to 10 days.

Malaga
Montana Palmera SC   Tel: 952 536 506
El Canuelo   Fax: 952 536 506
29710 Periana   e-mail: montpalmera@hotmail.comn
Malaga   Website: www.andalucia.co.uk/monmtana_palmera/index.html
Yoga – open spirituality. A rural mountain retreat in Alta Axarquias near
Malaga where you can escape and relax for a week or so. Walking is at hand,
mountain bikes are provided, and horseriding is also possible. Otherwise laze
around the pool, which has marvellous distant views. 9 bedrooms. B&B
about 24€–45€ depending on season; full board, again depending on season,
about 400€–550€. There is a regular programme of residential yoga courses
with qualified teachers priced at around £600 all in, excluding travel.

Manresa
Taras Samye Dzong
Place Major No.6-1
08240 Manresa   Tel: 938 720 254
Buddhist. A place organised together with the Kagyu Samye Ling Tibetan
Centre in Scotland. Write direct or to Scotland (see Scotland section) for
information.

Navarre
Monasterio de La Oliva
Cascastillo
Navarre   Tel: 948 725 065
Roman Catholic. Receives both men and women in a wonderful example of
Cistercian architecture. Peaceful but busy and hard-working atmosphere.
Highly Recommended.

Órgiva
Cortijo Romero
Apartado de Correos 31
18400 Órgiva
Granada   Tel: 958 784 252

Alternative spirituality – yoga. Receives everyone over 16. Groups and individuals welcome. Cortijo Romero has been established for many years now and is justly popular. It is set in an inspiring location in a wonderful climate. The courses here are designed for personal rest and renewal and the enrichment and discovery of self. Examples of what may be on offer are: *Movement and Stillness* for learning to be grounded in who you are, *Yoga for Form and Feeling*, and *Forgiveness, Gratitude and Grace* for dealing with issues of human development. Facilities include swimming pool, orchard, 3 singles, some 11 doubles, guest lounge, guest telephone. Personal talks, group sharing, meditation, directed study may all take place. Costs per week, including courses, excursions, accommodation and meals, about £350–£400 a week, but check out the current year's prices with them. **Information and Bookings tel: (UK) 01494 765775, e-mail: bookings@cortijo-romero.co.uk, website: www.cortijo-romero.co.uk. Highly Recommended.**

Palencia
Monasterio de San Isidro de Duenas
Venta de Banos,
Palencia   Tel: 988 770 701

Roman Catholic. A Trappist monastery open to men, woman and married couples seeking a retreat.

Salamanca
Convent de Carmel Dascatros
Las Mostas
La Alberca
Salamanca   Tel: 923 437 133

Roman Catholic. A strictly religious place where men only may go for spiritual retreat and then only by prior request and permission. **It is not open to tourists.** The film director Luis Bunuel stayed here once and fell in love with the beautiful Las Batuecas valley where the monastery is situated. He called it 'a paradise on earth'. Remember that you must write first to this monastery to make arrangements to stay.

Segovia
Monasterio de Santa Maria del Parral
El Parral
Segovia   Tel: 911 431 298

Roman Catholic. Receives men seeking a spiritual retreat for stays of up to 1 week. 3 ensuite rooms. Guests can either follow the monks' routine and take meals with them or be independent.

Monasterio San Juan de la Cruz
Alameda de la Fuencisla
40003 Segovia

Tel: 921 431 349
Fax: 921 431 650

Roman Catholic. Renaissance style monastery. Receives men and women in a retreat centre of 40 rooms. There are gardens and a large library.

Soria
Monasterio de Santa Maria de la Huerta
Santa Maria de Huerta
Soria

Tel: 975 327 002

Roman Catholic. Cistercian monks receiving men only. 8 rooms. Best to write first and not just show up.

Tarragona
Abadia de Santa Maria de Poblet
Espluga de Francoli
Tarragona

Tel: 977 870 089

Roman Catholic. Receives men only within the abbey itself. Guests are expected to keep to the community's monastic timetable. Everyone eats together in the refectory.

Valencia
Centro Budhista de Valencia
Calle Ciscar 5, apt 3a
46005, Valencia

Tel: 963 740 564

Buddhist. Run by the Friends of the Western Buddhist Order (see London section). They will provide information on this place and others in Spain.

> If tomorrow was the legendary Day of Judgement, what evidence of your love would you place before the angels?
> LIVING THE SACRED

Yoga Centres

Yoga is a spiritual practice that involves the body, the mind and the spirit. It is a spiritual traditon that is thousands of years old. Many people go to yoga classes to keep fit, but yoga is much more than that – it can calm you and help heal you, and ultimately is a tool designed to lead you to enlightenment. There are many local yoga classes as well as clubs and groups throughout Britain and across Europe. Most of these do not own a centre of their own and meet in various venues from halls to community and local leisure centres and health and fitness clubs. Educational authorities now commonly include yoga classes in their adult and evening education programmes.

If you want more details about yoga and yoga centres, have a look at *Best Yoga Centres and Retreats* **(see Selected Reading.)**

The British Wheel of Yoga (BWY) is the recognised information centre for yoga in Britain. It can give you information about British Wheel trained teachers, courses and classes. It has a nation-wide network of teachers and representatives who are available to help you at a local level. It has been recognised by the British Sports Council as the governing body for yoga in Great Britain and is a non-profit making charity.

British Wheel of Yoga
1 Hamilton Place
Boston Road
Sleaford   Tel: 01529 306851
Lincs NG34 7ES   Website: www.bwy.org.uk

The following is a selection of places around Britain and abroad where you can find yoga courses and retreats.

ENGLAND – LONDON

Always at the heart of things, London has classes and courses in yoga centres, dance studios, gyms, alternative therapy centres, health associations, church halls and private homes.

LONDON GENERAL
Art of Health and Yoga Centre, tel: 020 8682 1800, contact Nell Lindsell.
City Yoga Centre, tel: 020 7253 3000, contact Paul Lurenson.
School of Yoga Westminster and Croydon, tel: 020 8657 3258.
Yoga Mosaic Association of Jewish Yoga Teachers, website:
    www.yogamosaic.org.
Yoga Shakti Mission London, website: www.yogashakti.org/london.

LONDON NORTH

Yoga Therapy Centre/Yoga Biomedical Trust, 90–92 Pentonville Road, London N1, tel: 020 7689 3040, website: www.yogatherapy.org.

Yoga for Gay Men, 255 Liverpool Road, London N1, tel: 020 7625 4521, website: www.gn.apc.org/gayyoga.

LONDON NORTH-WEST

Bikram Yoga College of India, 173 Queens Crescent, London NW5, tel: 020 8692 6900, website: www.bikramyoga.co.uk.

Hamish Hendry at Ashtanga Place, Diorama, 34 Osnaburgh Street, London NW1, tel: 020 8342 9762, website: www.ashtangayoga.co.uk.

Soho Gym, 193 Camden High Street, London NW1, tel: 020 7482 4524, website: www.sohogyms.co.uk.

LONDON WEST CENTRAL

Central YMCA Club, 112 Great Russell Street, London WC1B, tel: 020 7343 1700, e-mail: theclub@centralymca.org.uk, website: www.centralymca.org.uk/club.

LONDON WEST

Bikram Yoga Centre, 260 Kilburn Lane, London W10, tel: 020 8960 9644, website: www.bikramyoga.co.uk.

Danceworks, 16 Balderton Street, London W1, tel: 020 7629 6183, website: www.danceworks.co.uk.

Innergy Yoga Centre, Acorn Hall, East Row, Kensal Road, London W10, tel: 020 8968 1178, website: www.innergy-yoga.com.

Iyengar Yoga Institute Maida Vale, 223a Randolph Avenue, Maida Vale, London W9, tel: 020 7624 3080, e-mail: office@iyi.org.uk, website: www.iyi.org.uk.

LONDON EAST CENTRAL

Barbican YMCA, Fann Street, London EC2, tel: 020 7628 0697. In the YMCA tradition: qualified instructors and simple, clean facilities. Let's go!

Champneys Citypoint, 1 Ropemaker Street, London EC2, tel: 020 7920 6200, website: www.champneyscitypoint.com. Fresh, sparkling, never too full. Everything laid on. Careful yoga classes.

LONDON EAST

Bodywise Natural Health Centre, 119 Roman Road, London E2, tel: 020 8458 4716. Associated with the nearby London Buddhist Centre, this alternative health centre is managed by a staff of Buddhist women. Drop-in yoga classes. Calm, peaceful place.

Yoga Place E2, First Floor, 449 Bethnal Green Road, London E2, tel: 020 7739 5195, website: www.yogaplace.co.uk Two studios, many teachers. Some workshops led by well-known teachers. Regular programme.

LONDON SOUTH-EAST

Camberwell Leisure Centre, Artichoke Place, London SE5, tel: 020 7703 3024, website: www.fusion-lifestyle.com. Gym club, with pool.

Yoga at Globe House, 2A Crucifix Lane, London SE1, tel: 020 7378 1177, website: www.lordshiva.net. Peaceful venue, good staff. No-frills place. Popular.

LONDON SOUTH-WEST

Earls Court Gym, 254 Earls Court Road, London SW5, tel: 020 7370 1402, website: www.sohogyms.co.uk. Dance and yoga studio. Great atmosphere. Buzzy and busy.

Sangam Yoga Centre, 80A Battersea Rise, London SW11, tel: 020 7223 2899, website: www.sangamyoga.com. Morning and evening classes in a dynamic yoga centre devoted to ashtanga yoga. Beginners given a warm welcome.

Sivananda Yoga Vendanta Centre, 51 Felsham Road, London SW15, tel: 020 8780 0160, e-mail: London@sivananda.org, website: www.sivananda.org/ london. This place is spiritual home to those living the Sivananda yoga lifestyle.

SOUTH-WEST ENGLAND

CORNWALL

PENZANCE Mounts Bay Health Studio, Queens Hotel, The Promenade, Penzance, Cornwall TR18, tel: 01736 369460.

PORTH Trevelgue Hotel, Watergate Road, Porth, Cornwall TR7, tel: 01637 872864, e-mail: trevelguehotel@btinternet.com, website: www.trevelguehotel.co.uk/health.html.

REDRUTH Carn Brea Leisure Centre, Station Road, Redruth, Cornwall TR15, tel: 01209 714766,

SALTASH Aero Sport, Health and Leisure Club, St Mellion International Hotel, Golf and Country Club, St Mellion, Saltash, Cornwall PL12, tel: 01579 351351, website: www.st-mellion.co.uk. Yoga classes plus a gym, pool, sauna, steam room and jacuzzi. Café-bar.

TRURO Ananda Yoga Centre, Truro. Tel: 01872 530317, contact Nandini Devi.

DEVON

GENERAL Devon Yoga Teachers' Federation, tel: 01837 54880, contact Angela Blezard.

ASHBURTON The Ashburton Centre, 79 East Street, Ashburton, Devon TQ13, tel: 01364 652784, e-mail: stella@ashburtoncentre.freeserve.co.uk, website: www.ashburtoncentre.co.uk.

AXMINSTER Axe Valley Sports Centre, Chard Street, Axminster, Devon EX13, tel: 01297 35235. Facilities include a gym, pool and sunbeds. Good basic centre.

BARNSTAPLE North Devon Leisure Centre, Seven Brethren Bank, Sticklepath, Barnstaple, Devon EX31, tel: 01271 373361. Yoga and body balance classes. Facilities include a pool, good gym, sauna, steam room and jacuzzi. Restaurant and bar.

COMBE MARTIN The Wild Pear Centre, King Street, Combe Martin, Devon EX34, tel: 020 8341 7226/01271 883086.

EXETER Jenny Kane, tel: 01884 252940, e-mail: bearfacelies@yahoo.com.

SIDMOUTH Devon School of Yoga, Sidmouth, tel: 01395 512355, contact Duncan Hulin.

TORQUAY The Kevala Centre, Hunsdon Road, Torquay, Devon TQ1, tel: 01803 215678, e-mail: info@kevala.co.uk, website: www.kevala.co.uk/yoga/.

DORSET
BOURNEMOUTH Astanga Yoga, 87 Gladstone Road, Bournemouth, Dorset BH7, tel: 01202 398269, e-mail: jwebster66@hotmail.com.
DORCHESTER Thomas Hardy Leisure Centre, Coburg Road, Dorchester, Dorset DT1, tel: 01305 266772.
POOLE Yoga with Christopher Gladwell, Poole Yoga Centre, Poole, Dorset BH15, tel: 01179 244244, website: www.yogawithchris.co.uk. Monthly class. See website or telephone for current times and dates. Telephone for a lift.

SOMERSET
BATH Viniyoga Britain, Bath, tel: 01225 426327, contact P. Harvey.
BISHOPSTON Yoganjali Yoga Teaching and Therapy Centre, Princes Place, Bishopston, Avon BS7, tel: 0117 944 2994, e-mail: info@ yoganjali.co.uk, website: www.yoganjali.co.uk.
BRISTOL Yoganjali Yoga Centre, tel: 01225 426327, e-mail : paul@viniyoga.co.uk, website : www.viniyoga.c o.uk/yoganjali.

WILTSHIRE
CHIPPENHAM Sheldon Sports Hall, Hardenhuish Lane, Chippenham, Wilts SN14, tel: 01249 651056.
SWINDON Fitness 2000, Hobley Drive, Lower Stratton, Swindon, Wilts SN3, tel: 01793 333666, e-mail: jane@lanefamily.freeserve.co.uk.

BERKSHIRE
GENERAL Yoga Teachers' Circle, tel: 0118 989 3345, contact Raye Lomax.
MAIDENHEAD Meridian Health and Fitness Club, Crown Lane, Maidenhead, Berks SL6, tel: 01628 544044.
READING David Lloyd Club, Thames Valley Park Drive, Reading, Berks RG6, tel: 0118 966 2904, website: www.davidlloydleisure.co.uk
WINDSOR Living Yoga, Clewer St Stephen's Church Hall, Vansittart Road, Windsor, Berks SL1, tel: 020 8898 0978, e-mail: tuesday@yoga.greatxscape.net or tuesdaymcneill@yahoo.co.uk.

HAMPSHIRE
ALTON Satchidananda Wholistic Trust, tel: 01420 561054, contact Swami Satchidananda Ma.
BASINGSTOKE Basingstoke Sports Centre, Porchester Square, Basingstoke, Hants RG21, tel: 01256 326331, website: www.bassports.co.uk.
FARNBOROUGH Farnborough Recreation Centre, Westmead, Farnborough, Hants GU14, tel: 01252 370411.
SOUTHAMPTON Karuna Yoga School, 79 Clarendon Road, Southampton SO16, tel: 01703 632881, contact Fiona Ashdown.

KENT
ASHFORD Contours Fitness Studio, Stour Leisure Centre, Tannery Lane, Ashford, Kent TN23, tel: 01233 664660.
BROMLEY LA Fitness, 31–33 East Street, Bromley, Kent BR1, tel: 020 8460 3725, website www.lafitness.co.uk.
CANTERBURY Jackey Thurston Yoga, Canterbury, Kent CT1, tel: 01303 893911.

DOVER Dover Leisure Centre and Swimming Pool, Woolcomber Street, Kent CT16, tel: 01304 201145 reception/225050 gym direct.

ROCHESTER Moores Health and Fitness Club, 671 Maidstone Road, Rochester, Kent ME1, tel: 01634 400003.

TUNBRIDGE WELLS Victoria Health Club, 4 Market Square, Royal Victoria Place, Tunbridge Wells, Kent TN1, tel: 01892 513444.

WEST MALLING Inner Light Yoga and Health Company, West Malling, Kent ME20, tel: 01622 715576, e-mail: rms@globalnet.co.uk.

MIDDLESEX

GENERAL Yoga-Dham, Middlesex, tel: 020 8428 6691, contact Tara Patel.

HOUNSLOW Yoga Shakti Mission Trust, Hounslow Yoga Centre, 74–76 Hibernia Road, Middlesex TW3, tel: 020 8572 8273, e-mail: info@yogashakti.co, website: www.yogashakti.co.

SOUTHALL Dormers Wells Leisure Centre, Dormers Wells Lane, Southall, Middlesex UB1, tel: 020 8571 7207.

SUDBURY Vale Farm Sports Centre, Watford Road, Sudbury, Middlesex HA0, tel: 020 8908 6545, website: www.leisureconnection.co.uk.

UXBRIDGE Virgin Active, The Arena Club, Stockley Park, Uxbridge, Middlesex UB11, tel: 0845 130 1777, website: www.virgin.com/active.

SURREY

CAMBERLEY British Wheel of Yoga and Bihar School of Yoga, Glenbarry, 53 Blackdown Road, Deepcut, Camberley, Surrey GU16, tel: 01252 834240, e-mail: kate@yogasankhya.freeserve.co.uk.

EPSOM Ruth White Yoga Centre, 99 College Road, Epsom, Surrey KT17, tel: 020 8644 0309, website: www.ruthwhiteyoga.com.

KINGSTON The Yoga Practice, United Reformed Church, Eden Street, Kingston-upon-Thames, Surrey KT1, tel: 07775 900020/020 8398 1741, e-mail: turiya@yogamatters.fsnet.co.uk or richardsjudith@hotmail.com.

RICHMOND-UPON-THAMES Studioflex, 26 Priests Bridge, Richmond, Surrey SW14, tel: 020 8878 0556. A dance studio with yoga and fitness classes. If yoga is not enough for you, you can enroll in belly-dancing.

SUTTON Surrey Iyengar Yoga Centre, Cheam, Sutton, Surrey SM3, tel: 020 8644 0309.

WOKING Chekira Wholistic Trust Yoga and Therapy Centre, Beech Lawn, Beech Grove, Mayford, Woking, Surrey GU22, tel: 01483 870064.

SUSSEX

GENERAL: Institute of Iyengar Yoga (Sussex Branch), website: www.iiya.org.uk.

GENERAL: Viniyoga in Sussex, tel: 01293 536664, contact Gill Lloyd.

BATTLE Patanjali Yoga Centre and Ashram, Battle, Sussex, tel: 01424 870538, contact Sri Indar Nath.

BRIGHTON Yoga Plus, 177 Ditchling Road, Brighton, Sussex BN1, tel: 01273 276175, website: www.yogaplus.co.uk.

HOVE Bikram Yoga Brighton and Hove, Old Perfume Factory, Fonthill Road (just behind Hove train station), Sussex BN3, tel: 01273 721944, e-mail: bikramyogabrightonandhove@hotmail.com, website: www.bikramyoga.com.

UCKFIELD Yoga for All, Ukfield Civic Centre, Bell Lane, Uckfield, Sussex TN22, tel: 01825 768010.

WORTHING Bihar School of Yoga, Flat 2, 33 Winchester Road, Worthing, Sussex BN11, tel: 01903 820525, contact Swami Ramdevananda.

EAST AND EAST ANGLIA

BEDFORDSHIRE
GENERAL: Bedfordshire Yoga Association, tel: 01234 852756, contact Ann Davenport.
DUNSTABLE Dunstable Leisure Centre, Court Drive, Dunstable, Beds LU5, tel: 01582 6043307/01582 608107, e-mail: dunstable@leisureconnection.co.uk, website: www.leisureconnection.co.uk
DUNSTABLE R-3 Leisure Club, 71–73 High Street North, Dunstable, Beds LU6, tel: 01582 477500.
LEIGHTON BUZZARD Leighton Buzzard Working Men's Club, Garden Hedge, Leighton Buzzard, Beds HP22, tel: 01525 210553, e-mail: yogalison@hotmail.com.

CAMBRIDGESHIRE
CAMBRIDGE Cambridge Iyengar Yoga Centre, 59 Norfolk Terrace, Cambridge CB1, e-mail: info@cambridgeyoga.co.uk.
CAMBRIDGE Yoga Biomedical Trust, Cambridge, tel: 01223 36730, contact Dr Robin Monro.
ST NEOTS St Neots Recreation Centre, Barford Road, St Neots, Cambs PE19, tel: 01480 388700.

ESSEX
GENERAL Outdoor Yoga in South-east Essex Countryside, tel: 01702 200386, e-mail : yogacoach@hotmail.com.
GENERAL Shanti Bhakti Sangha, tel: 020 8549 2754, contact Vera.
BASSINGBOURN Dharma Yoga Centre, Bassingbourn, tel: 01763 249957, contact Mary Demetriou.
CHELMSFORD Iyengar Yoga Centre for Essex, Chelmsford, tel: 01224 5421496, contact Susan Long.
COLCHESTER Feering Yoga for Pregnancy, Prested Hall, Prested Chase, Feering, Colchester, Essex CO5, tel: 07739 559276, e-mail rnb@breathemail.net.
COLCHESTER Satyananda Yoga Centre, Colchester, tel: 01206 823383, contact Swami Yogaprakash.
DAGENHAM London Borough of Barking and Dagenham Leisure Services, Ripple Road, Dagenham, Essex RM9, tel: 020 8984 7694.
LOUGHTON School for Living Yoga, Loughton, tel: 020 8502 4270, contact Ernest Coates.
ROMFORD Romford YMCA, Rush Green Road, Rush Green, Romford, Essex RM1, tel: 01708 766211, website: www.romfordymca.org.

HERTFORDSHIRE
BISHOPS STORTFORD Sivanada Yoga (Affiliated), Parsonage Community Hall, Bishops Stortford, Herts, tel: 01279 834670.
HEMEL HEMPSTEAD Hemel Hempstead Hatha Yoga with Cynthia

Collisson, Hemel Hempstead, Herts HP1, tel: 01442 391617.
ST ALBANS Hertfordshire Yoga Workshop, St Albans, tel: 01727 760067, contact Kerstin Elliot.
ST ALBANS Kundalini Yoga and Meditation, St Albans, tel: 01727 826183, contact Valerie Crawford.
WARE Ware Centre for Yoga Arts and Healing, Sucklings Yard, Church Street, Ware, Herts SG12, tel: 01920 466567, e-mail: brigid@yogaware.fsnet.co.uk, website: www.wareyoga.co.uk.

LINCOLNSHIRE
GENERAL Sally Worth Yoga, tel: 01522 543985, e-mail: sally_worth@lineone.net.
SLEAFORD Sleaford Fitness and Leisure Station, Tamer Court, Church Lane, Sleaford, Lincs NG34, tel: 01529 304770.

NORFOLK
GENERAL: Norfolk Iyengar Yoga Institute, c/o John and Ros Claxton, The Farmhouse, Booton, Near Peepham, Norfolk NR10.
GENERAL Norfolk Yoga Group, tel: 01603 436659, contact Bob Camp.
AYLSHAM Aylsham Meditation Group, Aylsham, tel: 01263 732426, contact Cherry Cooke.

SUFFOLK
BURY ST EDMUNDS Return to Top Dome Leisure Centre, Bury Road, Mildenhall, Bury St Edmunds, Suffolk IP28, tel: 01638 717737.
IPSWICH Clarice House, Bramford Road, Bramford, Ipswich, Suffolk IP8, tel: 01473 463262, e-mail: cdk@netcomuk.co.uk, website: www.clarice.co.uk.

CENTRAL ENGLAND

WEST MIDLANDS
BIRMINGHAM Birmingham and District Institute of Iyengar Yoga, Birmingham, tel: 0121 743 8143m contact Jayne Orton.
BIRMINGHAM Satyananda Yoga Centre, Birmingham, tel: 0121 444 5976.
SUTTON COLDFIELD Wyndley Leisure Centre, Clifton Road, Sutton Coldfield, West Midlands B73, tel: 0121 464 7742.
WOLVERHAMPTON The Parkdale Yoga Centre, 10 Parkdale West, Wolverhampton WV1, tel: 01902 424048, e-mail: info@heartyoga.org.uk, website: www.heartyoga.og.uk.

BUCKINGHAMSHIRE
GENERAL Buckinghamshire Iyengar Yoga, tel: 01753 882112, e-mail: moni@alt128.co.uk.
AYLESBURY Spirit Health and Fitness Club, Aston Clinton Road, Weston Turville, Aylesbury, Bucks HP22, tel: 01296 399220.
BEACONSFIELD Beacon Centre, Holtspur Way, Beaconsfield, Bucks HP9, tel: 01494 677764.

MILTON KEYNES Woughton Leisure Trust, Woughton Centre, Rainbow Drive, Leadenhall, Milton Keynes, Bucks MK6, tel: 01908 660392.

DERBYSHIRE
GENERAL Derbyshire Yoga Teachers' Association, Chesterfield. Tel: 01773 822033, contact Russell Brown.
ILKESTON Albion Leisure Centre, East Street, Ilkeston, Derbyshire DE7, tel: 0115 944 0200. General yoga class but so popular that you must book in advance.

GLOUCESTERSHIRE
GENERAL Gloucestershire Integral Yoga, Redmarley, tel: 01531 820354, contact Brenda Judge.
CIRENCESTER Viniyoga Cotswolds, Cirencester, tel: 01285 750293, contact Mary Harris.
STROUD Hawkwood College, Painswick Old Road, Stroud, Glos GL6, tel: 01453 759034, e-mail: hawkwoodcollege@cs.com.

HERTFORDSHIRE
BROMYARD Bromyard Leisure Centre, Cruxhall Street, Bromyard, Herefords HR7, tel: 01885 482195.
HEREFORD Hereford Leisure Centre, Holmer Road, Hereford HR4, tel: 01432 278178. Community sports centre plus yoga classes during the week.

LEICESTERSHIRE
GENERAL Leicestershire Area Yoga, tel: 01162 706399.
GENERAL Leicestershire Yoga Circle, tel: 01162 793594, contact Brenda Kirby.
ASHBY-DE-LA-ZOUCH Springs Health Farm, Arlic Farm, Gallows Lane, Packington, Ashby-de-la-Zouch, Leics LE65, tel: 01530 273873, e-mail: enquiries@henlowgrange.co.uk, website: www.healthfarms.co.uk.
MELTON MOWBRAY Viniyoga East Midlands, Melton Mowbray, tel: 01664 464852, contact Sheila Baker.

NORTHAMPTONSHIRE
BRACKLEY Brackley Recreation Centre, Springfield Way, Brackley, Northants NN13, tel: 01280 701787.
GREAT HOUGHTON YogaNorthants, Willow Cottage, 28 Willow Lane, Great Houghton, Northants NN4, tel: 01604 766760.
RUSHDEN Harpers Fitness Club, H E Bates Way, Rushden, Northants NN10, tel: 01933 411635, website: www.harpersfitness.co.uk. Yoga classes plus Pilates and other courses. Dance studio, gym, cardio-vascular fitness equipment, sauna, sunbeds and crèche. Bar too.

NOTTINGHAMSHIRE
GENERAL Friends of Yoga Society, tel: 01159 7335435, contact Pauline Mainland.
NOTTINGHAM Expanded Yoga, Digby Avenue, Mapperley, Nottingham, Notts NG15, tel: 0115 955 0444.
NOTTINGHAM Yoga for Men, Claremont School, Claremont Road, Carrington, Nottingham, Notts NG15, tel: 0115 955 0444.

OXFORDSHIRE
BANBURY Banbury Yoga Group, Spiceball Park Sports Centre, Spiceball Park, Banbury, Oxon OX16, tel: 01295 257522.
HENLEY-ON-THAMES Henley Indoor Sports Centre, Gillotts Lane, Henley-on-Thames, Oxon RG9, tel: 01491 577909.
OXFORD Chinese Wu Hsing Buddhist Yoga, Oxford, tel: 01865 245095, contact Christopher Jones.
OXFORD Hugh Poulton Yoga, Oxford, tel: 01865 340335, e-mail: hughpoulton@btconnect.com. Ashtanga yoga classes for all levels.
OXORD Oxford Yoga Group, tel: 01865 841018, contact Gillian Webster.
OXFORD The Yoga Garden, 4 South Parade, Summertown, Oxford OX2, tel: 01865 311300, e-mail: mail@yogagarden.co.uk, website: www.yogagarden.co.uk.

SHROPSHIRE
BROSELEY Bodylife Centre of Massage and Yoga, Spout Lane, Benthall, Broseley, Shrops TF12, tel: 01952 883135.
SHREWSBURY Fitness First, 112 St Michael's Street, Shrewsbury, Shrops SY1, tel: 01743 270272, website: www.fitnessfirst.com.

STAFFORDSHIRE
CANNOCK Chase Leisure Centre, Stafford Road, Cannock, Staffs WS11, tel: 01543 504065, website: www.cannockcouncil.gov.uk.
LEEK Brough Park Leisure Centre, Ball Haye Road, Leek, Staffs ST13, tel: 01538 373603, e-mail: ghall@parkwoodleisure.co.uk.

WARWICKSHIRE
LEAMINGTON SPA Mark Freeth Yoga, Leamington Spa, tel: 01926 888556.
RUGBY Midland Yoga Centre, Rugby, Warwicks CV21, tel: 01788 330056, e-mail: maurice_yoga@web-sights.co.uk, website: www.web-sights. co.uk/yoga/

WORCESTERSHIRE
WORCESTER Malvern Hills Yoga Centre, tel: 01684 310884, contact Gail Reeves.

NORTHERN ENGLAND

CHESHIRE
GENERAL Cheshire Yoga Teachers' Association, tel: 0161 973 8319, contact Christine Royle.
GENERAL Susan Rennie Yoga, tel: 01606 888324/558252, e-mail: susaniyengaryoga@yahoo.com. Iyengar yoga.
GENERAL The Yoga Circle, tel: 0161 904 0588, contact M. Priestner.

CUMBRIA
BURTON-IN-KENDAL You and Me Yoga Centre, Burton-in-Kendal, tel: 01524 782103.

ULVERSTON South Lakes Yoga Teachers' Club, Ulverston, tel: 01229 861134.

DURHAM AND TYNE AND WEAR
NORTH SHIELDS Kripalu Yoga Support Group, North Shields, tel: 0191 257 0988.
SEABURN DENE North East Institute of Iyengar Yoga, Seaburn Dene, tel: 0191 548 7457.

LANCASHIRE
GENERAL Lancashire Yoga Teachers' Association, Oswaldtwistle, tel: 01254 381325, contact Irene O'Meara.
LANCASTER St Leonardsgate Yoga Studios, 98 St Leonardsgate, Lancaster LA1, tel: 01524 34054, e-mail: dreamyoga@freeuk.com.

GREATER MANCHESTER
CHORLTON Ananda Marga Centre, 42 Keppel Road, Chorlton, Manchester M21, tel: 0161 282 9224, e-mail: Anandamarga.mcr@gmx.net, website: www.anandamarga.org.
MANCHESTER Manchester Buddhist Centre, 16–20 Turner Street, Northern Quarter, Manchester M4, tel: 0161 834 9232, e-mail: info@manchesterbuddhistcentre.org.uk, website: www.manchesterbuddhistcentre.org.uk.
MANCHESTER Manchester and District Institute of Iyengar Yoga
MANCHESTER YogaSpace, Basement Studio, 35–37 Thomas Street, Manchester M4, tel: 0161 288 6918, website www.yogaspace.org.uk.

MERSEYSIDE
GENERAL Merseyside Yoga Association, tel: 0151 652 6343, contact Janet Irlam.
NEW BRIGHTON Comprehensive Yoga Fellowship, tel: 0151 639 9402, contact Gordon Smith.

NORTHUMBERLAND
GENERAL Northumberland Yoga Group, tel: 01670 787423, contact Betty Websell.
PRUDHOE The Buzz Factory, Swalwell Close, Prudhoe, Northumberland NE42, tel: 01661 831002.

YORKSHIRE
EASINGWOLD Crayke Yoga Club, Easingwold, tel: 01347 23004, contact Jane Cluley.
HARROGATE Amanda Latchmore Yoga, York Place, Harrogate HG1, tel: 01423 561173, e-mail: amanda@harrogateyoga.com.
HUDDERSFIELD Charmony Yoga Circle, Huddersfield, tel: 01484 535298, contact June Morella.
THIRSK Holy Rood House, 10 Sowerby Road, Sowerby, Thirsk, N Yorkshire YO7, tel: 01845 522580, email: holyroodhouse@centrethirsk.fsnet.co.uk, website: www.holyroodhouse.freeuk.com
YORK Yoga for All, York, tel: 01904 423340.

WALES

BRECON BEACONS Yoga Holidays, Cambridge Iyengar Yoga Centre, 59 Norfolk Terrace, Cambridge CB1, email: sashaperryman@yahoo.com, website: www.cambridgeyoga.co.uk/holiday/holiday.html

CARDIFF Drop-in Yoga, Community Centre, Merthyr Tydfil, Cardiff, South Glamorgan CF48, tel: 01685 384182.

LLANDEILO Mandala Yoga Ashram, Pantypistyll, Llansadwrn, Llandeilo, Carmarthenshire SA19, tel: 01558 685358.

SOUTH WALES Claire Senior Yoga, South Wales area, e-mail: Clairesenior@yahoo.com.

WELSHPOOL Abhedashram, Camlad House, Forden, Welshpool, Powys SY21, tel: 01938 580499.

SCOTLAND

GENERAL Scottish Yoga Teachers' Association, 16 Hilltop Crescent, Gourock, Inverclyde, Scotland PA19, tel: 01475 633967, e-mail: info@yogascotland.org.uk, website: www.yogascotland.org.uk.

AYRESHIRE

LARGS Connections, 48 Gallowgate Street, Largs, Ayrshire KA30, tel: 01475 675533, e-mail: manager@well-connected.biz, website: www.well-connected.biz.

LOTHIAN

EDINBURGH Brahma Kumaris World Spiritual University, 20 Polwarth Crescent, Edinburgh, Lothian EH11, tel: 0131 2297220, e-mail: mail@bkwsuedin.org.uk, website: www.bkwsuscotland.com.

EDINBURGH Edinburgh and Lothian Yoga Association (ELYA), tel: 0131 441 7214.

EDINBURGH The Salisbury Centre, 2 Salisbury Road, Edinburgh EH16, tel: 0131 667 5438, e-mail: office@salisburycentre.org, website: www.salisburycentre.org.

INVERCLYDE

WEST SCOTLAND West of Scotland Yoga Teachers' Association, 43 Roman Road, Bearsden, Glasgow G61, tel: 0141 943 0597.

FIFE

FIFE Yoga Group, Jill Travers, e-mail: jill.travers@talk21.com.

GLASGOW

GLASGOW Allander Sports Centre, Milngavie Road, Glasgow G61, tel: 01412 942 2233.

GLASGOW Leisure Drome, 147 Balmuildy Road, Bishopbriggs, Glasgow G64, tel: 0141 772 6391.

GRAMPIAN
ABERDEEN Brahma Kumaris, 66A Hamilton Place, Aberdeen, Grampian AB15, tel: 01224 639105, e-mail: aberdeen@bkwsu.com, website: www.bkwsuscotland.com.

HIGHLANDS AND ISLANDS
ALNESS The Perrins Centre, Alness, Highlands & Islands IV17, tel: 01349 880682, e-mail: sylvia.middleton2@btopenworld.com.
ISLE OF SKYE Quiraing Lodge, Staffin, Isle of Skye IV51, tel: 01470 562330, website: www.quiraing-lodge.co.uk.

INVERNESS
Shanti Griha, Scoraig, Dundonnell by Garve, Wester Ross IV23 2RE, tel: 01854 633 260, e-mail: shantigriha@hotmail.com, website: www.shantigriha.com

MORAYSHIRE
FORRES Findhorn Foundation, The Universal Hall, The Park, Forres, Morayshire IV36, tel: 01309 691170, e-mail for yoga: celia@diamondcoaching.com.

TAYSIDE
GENERAL Yoga Association Tayside, Lower Lesser Caird Hall, Dundee DD1, website: www.yogascotland.org.uk/index.html.

WIGTOWNSHIRE
STRANRAER Johnny Glover Yoga, 84 Eastwood Avenue, Stranraer DG9, tel: 01776 704994, e-mail: yogafolk@aol.com.

IRELAND AND NORTHERN IRELAND

GENERAL Irish Yoga Association, (0)86 807 5379, contact Liam, e-mail: info@irelandyoga.org.
GENERAL Yoga Centre of Ireland, The Field of Doves, 10 Clanbrassil Road, Cultra BT18. Tel: 02890 428370, e-mail: norma.yoga@btconnect.com.
GENERAL Yoga Therapy and Training Centre, 16 Kinghill Road, Cabra, Nr Rathfriland Newry, County Down BT34, tel: 02840 630686, e-mail: info@yogateachers.net
GENERAL Yoga Fellowship of Northern Ireland, 19 Elsmere Park, Belfast BT5, tel: 02890 705913, e-mail: info@ynfi.co.uk, website: www.yfni.co.uk.

ANTRIM
BELFAST Yoga Therapy and Training Centre.
LARNE Drumalis Retreat Centre, Glenarm Road, Larne, Antrim BT40, tel: 02828 272196, e-mail: drumalis@dial.pipex.com.

GALWAY
BURREN Yoga Meditation Centre, Lig do Scith, Cappaghmore, Kinvara, Galway, tel: (0)91 637 680, e-mail: burrenyoga@yahoo.com, website: www.burrenyoga.com

KERRY

INCH Lios Dana, The Natural Living Centre, Inch, Annascaul, Kerry, tel: (0)66 915 8189, website: www.holistic.ie/liosdana.

CORK

WEST CORK An Sanctoir, Bawnaknockane, Ballydehob, West Cork, tel: (0)28 37155, e-mail: sanctoir@eircom.net, website: www.westcorkweb.ie.

DUBLIN

GENERAL Viniyoga Ireland, Dublin, tel: (0)1 288 9012, e-mail: hannegillespie@eircom.net.

WICKLOW

WICKLOW Rani Sheilagh Dunn, County Wicklow, tel: (0)45 867202, e-mail: info@prana.ie, website: www.prana.ie.

DOWN

NEWRY Emmet Devlin, 23 Cairnhill, Newry, Down BT34, tel: 02830 264865, e-mail: emmetdevlin@ireland.com.

BALLYMENA

BALLYMENA Claire O'Neill, 9 Farmlodge Avenue, Ballymena BT43, tel: 02825 647091

YOGA HOLIDAY RETREATS

FRANCE

La Fédération Nationale des Enseignants de Yoga (FNEY), Yse Masquelier, 3 rue Aubriot, F-75004 Paris, tel: (0)1 42 70 03 05.

Centre Atma, 50 rue des Lices, 8400 Avignon, tel: (0)4 90 27 35 14.

Centre de Yoga Iyengar de Lyon, Clos de Fourviere II, 40 rue Roger Radisson, 69005 Lyon, tel: (0)4 78 36 03 84.

École Francaise de Yoga du Sud-Est, 18 rue Victor Leydet, 13100 Aix-en-Provence, tel: (0)4 42 27 92 20.

Fédération Inter-Régionale de Hatha-Yoga, 322 rue Saint Honoré, 75001 Paris, tel: (0)4 42 60 32 10.

Kaivalyadhama-France Lozeron, 26400 Gigors-et-Lozeron, tel: (0)4 75 76 42 95.

L'Association Provençale de Hatha Yoga, 12 rue J. Daret, Aix-en-Provence, tel: (0)5 42 64 18 54.

La Fédération des Yogas Traditionnels, André Riehl, 65 rue des Cedres, 84120 Pertuis, tel: (0)4 90 09 65 27.

La Val Dieu Pyrenées, tel: (UK) 01225 311826, contact Annette Tolson.

La Yoga Thérapie, Christine Campagnac-Morette, 5 place du Général Beuret, 75015 Paris.

Château du Yoga Sivananda, Neuville au Bois, Loiret, Orléans 45000, website: www.sivananda.org/orleans/indeng.htm.

Lot la Buissiére (Lot Valley), website: www.yogafrance.com. Yoga and walking in rural France, staying in a comfortable house with 2 acres of private parkland and pool.

The Sun Centre, Prades, 48160 St Martin de Boubaux, tel: (0)4 66 45 59 63, website: www.thesuncentre.net.

Maureillas Féderation Internationale de Yoga Himalayen, c/o Stephane-Jean, Les Ilipotiers, Las Illas Village, 66480 Maureillas, tel: (0)6 11 51 47 53/ (0)4 68 83 04 76, website: www.membres.lycos.fr/himalaya/program.

Star of Light Mountain Retreat Centre, Maison Bird, Conat, 66500 Prades, tel: (0)4 68 96 04 80, e-mail: bird.conat@easynet.fr.

SPAIN

Sivananda Yoga Vedanta Centre, Clerao 4, Diego de Leon, tel: 913 615 150.

Cortijo Romero, 18400 Orgiva, Granada, tel: 958 784 252; information and bookings: (UK) 01494 782720, UK address: Little Grove, Grove Lane, Chesham HP5 3QQ.

Maggie Levien, Calle Malaga 41, Iznate 29792, tel: 952 509 603/630 718 204.

Holistic Holidays, Villa Isis, Los Topes, 35572 Tias, Lanzarote, Canary Islands, tel: 928 524 216, brochure line (UK) 020 7692 0633, e-mail: enquiries@hoho.co.uk, website: www.hoho.co.uk.

HELPFUL JOURNALS

Spectrum, Journal of the British Wheel of Yoga, 123 Bear Road, Brighton, East Sussex BN2 4DB, tel: (editorial) 01273 698560.

Resurgence, Ford House, Hartland, Bideford, Devon EX39 6EE, tel: 01237 441293, e-mail: (editorial) ed@resurge.demon.co.uk, (subscriptions) subs.resurge@virgin.net.

Love solves all problems, opens all closed doors.
SHEIKH MUZAFFER, SUFI MASTER

Open Centres

Open Centres are concerned with interfaith work, meditation, movement, healing and spiritual awareness. They are, in essence, centred in open spirituality and healing within the Mind Body Spirit context and include religious and spiritual approaches. The following organisation provides a link between the centres:

Open Centres
Avils Farm
Lower Stanton St Quintin
Chippenham
Wiltshire SN14 6PA   Tel: 01249 720202

Open Centres publishes a bi-annual non-profit-making newsletter. It includes a directory listing meditation groups around the country, Julian meetings devoted to the practice of Christ-centred contemplative meditation, Open Centres and regional addresses for the National Federation of Spiritual Healers. **Send to the above address for details of Open Centres and how to obtain your copy of this newsletter.**

Here are a few Open Centres to get you started:

The Abbey, Sutton Courtney, Abingdon, Oxon OX14 4AF,
   tel: 01235 847401.
Amrit Hermitage, Helland Cottage, Ladock, Cornwall TR2 4QE,
   tel: 01726 883811.
The Barn, Lower Sharpham, Ashprington, Devon, TQ9 7DX,
   tel: 01803 732661.
Beacon Centre, Cutteridge Farm, Whitestone, Exeter EX4 2HL, tel:
   0139281203.
Beech Lawn, Beech Grove, Mayford, Woking, Surrey GU22 OSX,
   tel: 01483 747519.
Bournemouth Centre CM, 26 Sea Rd, Boscombe, Bournemouth,
   tel: 01202 36354
Caer, Rosemerryn, Lamorna, Penzance, Cornwall TR19 6EN,
   tel: 01773 672530.
Centre of New Directions, White Lodge, Stockland Green Rd,
   Speldhurst, Kent TN3 OTT.
Centre of Unity, 6 Kings Grange, 46 W Cliff Rd, Bournemouth, Dorset
   BH4 8BB.
Christian Meditation Centre, 29 Campden Hill Rd, London W8 7DX,
   tel: 020 7912 1371.
The Coach House, Kilmuir, N. Kessock, Inverness IV1 1XG.
Centre of Truth, Suite 4, Carlton Chambers, 5 Station Rd, Shortlands,
   Kent BR2 OEY.

Coombe Quarry, Coombe Hill, Keinton Mandeville, Somerset TA1 1DQ, tel: 01458 223215.

Croydon Healing Centre, Kesborough, 16 Bisdenden Rd, Croydon, Surrey CR0 6UN, tel: 020 8688 1856.

The Core Centre, Cark in Cartmel, Grange-over-Sands, Cumbria LA11 7PQ, tel: 01395 59328.

Easter Centre, 16 Bury Rd, Hengrave, Bury St Edmunds, Suffolk IP28 6LR, tel: 01284 704881.

Ellbridge, Broadhempston,Totnes, Devon TQ9 6BZ, tel: 01803 813015.

Fellowship of Meditation, 8 Prince of Wales Rd, Dorchester, tel: 01305 251396

Flint House, 41 High St, Lewes, E Sussex BN7 2LU, tel: 01273 473388.

Gaia House, Woodland Rd, Denbury, Devon, TQ12 6DY, tel: 01803 813188.

Grail Centre, 125 Waxwell Lane, Pinner, HA5 3ER, tel: 020 8866 2195.

Grail Retreat Centre,Tan-y-Bryn St, Abergynolwyn, Gwynedd LL36 9WA tel: 01694 782268.

The Grange, Ellsmere, Shropshire SY1 9DE, tel: 01691 623495.

Hawkwood College, Old Painswick Rd, Stroud, Glos. GL6 7QW, tel: 01453 759034.

Home Farm Workshops, Burley on Hill, Oakham, Rutland LEA15 7SX, tel: 01572 757333.

Lifeways, 30 Albany Rd, Stratford on Avon, Warwicks CV37 6PG, tel: 01789 292052.

Living Centre, 12a Durham Road, Raynes Park, London SW20 0TW, tel: 020 8946 2331

Middle Piccadilly, Holwell, Sherborne, Dorset, tel: 01963 23468.

Minton House, Forres, Moray IV36 0YY, tel: 01309 690819.

The Mudita School of Healing, 82 Freshfield Bank, Forest Row, E Sussex RH18 5HN, tel: 01342 823099.

Newbold House, St Leonard's Road, Forres, Moray IV36 0RE, tel: 01309 72659.

Associated with the Open Centres are a number of regional members of the National Federation of Spiritual Healers. You can obtain a list of the names and addresses of the fifteen regional associations together with a brochure of their annual courses from:

National Association of Spiritual Healers
Old Manor Farm Studio
Church Street
Sunbury-On-Thames
Middlessex TW16 6RG   Tel: 01932 783164

Appendix

A SPIRITUAL NOTEBOOK

THOUGHTS FROM A MONASTERY

(Gregory van der Kleij, OSB is a Benedicine monk and priest of the Roman Catholic Olivetan Congregation and Superior of the Monastery of Christ Our Saviour at Turvey (See East and East Anglia section). Fr Gregory, with his community, is the founder of the Turvey Centre for Group Psychotherapy and of the Emmaus Centre near Bedford, both of which are now independent charitable trusts.)

A Little Homily, by Gregory van der Kleij, OSB

The seed has been sown but are we fertile soil? Have we experienced the freedom of the children of God in our lives, standing free in our openness to God's grace?

We think in terms of status and importance. Saint Benedict warns us in the Rule about that: be especially attentive to the poor because the rich get enough respect as it is.

Every perfect gift is from above, coming down from the father of lights. Life as a gift, but not a gift we possess and own and do with what we want: a gift to be shared

Once we dare to free ourselves from our own culture and all its value judgements, then we can also descend, as it were, into our own minds and be freed from all the judgements passed upon us in the past – and they are many.

AN EXPERIENCE OF A BUDDHIST RETREAT

(The following is a personal account of a retreat visit to Holy Island by Anna Howard of *The Good Retreat Guide* research team. She also explains Buddhism in a personal but authoritative manner, giving a feminine slant to her experience. (You can read details of what's on offer at Holy Island in the Scotland section of the guide and find out more about Buddhism at www.thegoodretreatguide.com.))

Holy Island, by Anna Howard

As I sailed across the waters towards the Isle of Arran, Holy Island stood proud – a huge rugged rock rising up from the seabed. It may have been the light, but if it had moved, turned over to reveal its soft underbelly to the sky, I wouldn't have been surprised. It looked alive.

Journeys are often as interesting as destinations, and journeys to a retreat take on the flavour of a pilgrimage in my experience. Transitions across water have a peculiar effect. It has something to do with breaking away from land and losing contact with the solid earth beneath my feet. In Buddhism, a great deal of attention is paid to the elements. The elements – earth, water, fire, air and space – constitute physical reality, our own and that of the planet we inhabit. When we come into contact with that reality, we are reminded of the impermanence of our bodies, of the illusory existence of a separate self. This fictitious self to which we are attached and which is the cause of our suffering. When we feel the deep connection we have with these five basic elements, we enter a bigger picture, and the hard edges of our separating ego begin to soften.

Buddhism teaches that when we die the physical process involves the dissolution of the elements one by one. The earth element is the most substantial and the one with which we most readily identify. This element dissolves into the water element as we begin the process of physical death. When we go on retreat, we have the opportunity to leave behind our worldly responsibilities and daily habits; we let go a little and that letting go is similar to the process of letting go when we die. We let go in order to enter into our spiritual self more fully. A journey across water to go on retreat is a powerful mirroring of the biggest, and for many the most frightening, journey we have to make.

These thoughts accompanied me on my journey to Brodick, where the ferry docked an hour after leaving the mainland – a short journey south to the pretty village of Lamlash and to the boat that would ferry me over to Holy Island itself. The sun was shining, the sea was calm – it wasn't far from idyllic. The boat goes to the north end of the island, where the new Centre for World Peace and Health has just been completed. Climbing off the boat onto the old jetty, I walked up to the centre past eight small stupas. Stupas are common all over Tibet and Nepal: they are built according to strict geometrical principles that create a balanced, symmetrical form which is said to help balance the elements and alleviate the particular sufferings of war, poverty, pollution, famine and drought. Each of the eight stupas represents a major event in the life of the Buddha.

The Centre itself is an attractive restoration and expansion of the original farmhouse. It's designed around a courtyard with accommodation for up to sixty people in single and twin rooms, with dormitories overlooking the bay. The main conference building is set slightly apart and is spacious, light and airy. Great attention has been paid to creating a centre that is in harmony with the natural environment and that respects the importance of building with ecological sensitivity.

Whilst Holy Island itself is now owned and managed by the Buddhists of Samye Ling, the new Centre for World Peace and Health is an interfaith initiative that seeks to bring people of all faiths together. With the exception of the room names (you stay on the Wisdom Wing or the Compassion Wing) – there is nothing to suggest the centre has anything to do with Buddhism. It is deliberately free from religious identification and has been created as a space that would make anybody feel comfortable and welcome.

During my three days at the centre, I had time to explore this powerful, magical island. After morning meditation, I spent a couple of hours helping the community with practical work – which in my case involved cleaning rooms after the very first course had been run. I then spent the rest of the day walking and talking to various members of the community. I even did a healing exchange with one of the community. It was a quiet few days – and this was in part due to the sudden and dramatic change in the weather. Gale-force winds whipped up the night I arrived and the boat was unable to cross.

And what a wind! Walking along the north path became a battle to put one foot in front of the other – the wild wind, the bracken that swayed like underwater seaweed, the white horses racing across the grey sea, seagulls and oystercatchers hanging in midair before being swept violently into a slipstream of air. It was magnificent – invigorating, fantastic. I was protected by and trapped on the island at the same time.

A gentler day followed, and I chose to take a meditative walk along the coastal path that links the north and south ends of the island. It's a walk that is lined with reminders of the past, a walk that brings to attention the spiritual significance of this island and its vision for peace in the world and the unity of all people – in particular through the deepening bond between Buddhism and Christianity.

Holy Island was once the home of a sixth-century Christian hermit, St Molaise. He is said to have lived and prayed within one of the many natural overhangs of rock that form caves. The particular cave he used is still here and is a site of pilgrimage for many Christians. At its foot is a spring and well, reputed to have healing properties. Further along, the first of a series of rock-paintings catches the eye, White Tara. The most famous of all the female deities, Tara is the 'liberating woman', the embodiment of dynamic compassion, the Mother of all the other buddhas. She represents the feminine aspect of wisdom, the innate wisdom that is the understanding of the true nature of the mind, of reality. Tara is most commonly depicted in her green form, as a young girl, but of the twenty-one Taras that are recognised, the white form is also well-known. White Tara is associated with health and long-life, and it is appropriate perhaps that she should come before the rock painting of Green Tara on this particular island.

Beyond the two Taras, paintings of various Tibetan saints – from Milarepa, who lived as a yogi on nettle soup and wrote inspirational songs, to Marpa, who lived as a householder with wealth, livelihood and a family – reminded me of the many paths to enlightenment. The path of the ascetic who takes him or herself off to isolated places is perhaps the most romantic but is certainly not necessarily the superior way. The path of the ordinary mystic is no less valid or valuable. Yet Holy Island is a remote environment, removed from the secular world, protected from its modern ways and exposed to the elements in such a way that our wills must yield to the will of nature. And it is this combination that makes this a very special place, naturally and spiritually; a place where the veils do grow thin and the mind can expand and open; a place where God was found by the sixth-century Christian hermit and is found still by whatever name those who come to this island are familiar with. The name that is pure experience ... beyond form and beyond concept.

AN EXPERIENCE OF A MEN'S SPIRITUALITY RETREAT

(The following is a personal account of attending a Men's Rites of Passage Retreat at Launde Abbey (see Central section) by Adrian Scott, who has opened The Listen Centre in Sheffield (see North section).)

Launde Abbey Retreat for Men, by Adrian Scott
This retreat – attended by sixty men from England, Wales, Scotland, Ireland, The Czech Republic and Austria – was a profound journey for me into the

quest and questions that generations of men have wrestled with. It was led by Father Richard Rohr and a team of British men who have attended the same experience in New Mexico and have been trained to deliver these rites. The retreat took the form of a five-day immersion into the patterns and themes of male initiation drawn from Father Rohr's research and study of primitive people's rites and the theology of initiation of the Gospels and the early Christian church. It was deeply experiential, with rituals and prayer services that engaged me as the *whole man*. It ended with a Eucharist on the hills above Launde Abbey under two spreading oak trees, where we partook of a sacred meal in commemoration of the New Adam, Jesus Christ. The whole event was an amazing experience for all of us. Men's spirituality work in the UK has been given a very good platform from which to grow and flourish in the years to come.

THE NEED FOR A MASCULINE SPIRITUALITY

(Richard Rohr, OFM is a Franciscan of the New Mexico Province. He was the founder of the New Jerusalem Community in Cincinnati, Ohio in 1971, and the Centre for Action and Contemplation in Albuquerque, New Mexico in 1986, where he presently serves as Founding Director (see www.cacradicalgrace.org). He considers the proclamation of the Gospel to be his primary call, and uses many different platforms to communicate that message. Scripture as liberation, the integration of action and contemplation, community building, peace and justice issues, male spirituality, the Enneagram, and eco-spirituality are all themes that he addresses in the service of the Gospel. Fr Rohr is largely responsible for raising awareness in Europe of the need for a masculine spirituality based in rites of male passage.)

Masculine Spirituality, by Fr Richard Rohr OFM

The battle of the spiritual man is always with himself. Today we are seeing the sad results of our failure to prepare men for this battle. When great religion no longer teaches and defines our deepest soul, we face life unprepared for the trials that will surely come our way. The effects are all around us: legitimated and even glorified violence, compulsive addiction, breakdown of foundational relationships, projection of shame and blame, and a common inability to believe in ourselves, others and life in general.

It seems that we do not have the time or the skill to learn the great patterns for ourselves. They are learned over generations and passed down through what first seem like empty aphorisms, rituals and commandments. From popular aphorisms, such as 'What goes around comes around', to religious proclamations, such as 'Christ has died, Christ has risen, Christ will come again', the soul must imbibe the truths that it will not learn or is unable to learn by logic, computer or mere intelligence. We Christians call it 'divine revelation'; Jews call it 'Torah' and 'Talmud'. Most native peoples searched for such truth in myths, taboos, and consistently repeated feasts and ceremonies. Often operating on a subliminal and unconscious level, great religion grounds, names, and liberates us for great truth. For God.

For a dozen different reasons, many people – men and women – are unable or unwilling to hear these great truths through the mediation of Western religious institutions. The language of personal trust, divine union and living presence is not even considered because it does not appear to tap into, or even recognise, our first longings. Many of us have to go back to those primordial images and words in the presence of which we first opened our eyes to God: mother love; nature; silence; religious ceremony that *worked*; childhood pictures that evoked awe; our first true love; the negative experiences of fear, betrayal, abandonment and grief. Masculine and feminine spirituality are both trying to rebuild the gender foundations so that a grounded church can rise again.

There is a need to rediscover the great truths of life for ourselves. Hopefully we can see it is the same truth that our ancestors were talking about and that the church is desperately trying to proclaim. It is called tradition and along with scripture is one of the two fonts of good theology. We need to go back to both of these fonts, in which we can drink long and deep. We need to follow suggestions for process and containment where men can grieve, rant and sit in the belly of the whale without needing someone to blame or attack. That is precisely the mystery of church. Finally it leads to shared contentment and even rejoicing.

In this post-modern era we need a spirituality that appreciates the non-rational cyclic meanings instead of mere linear progress, the importance of the dark side of our spiritual education, which is also the importance of the outcast, the poor and the failure in our lives. We need to move away from the false individualism of modernism back to social connectedness, to communal religion that is accountable for what it says it believes. Modern worldviews separated religion and science, the feminine from the masculine. Women have rightly become mistrustful of technology and power; men have unfortunately become mistrustful of religion and spirituality. Externalisation and innerness can no longer operate on different tracks. We need a language and experience that connect rather than react. We need some fundamental teaching that begins in union and aims towards further union. That will only come from great religion.

Our religious leaders have largely found themselves incapable of writing a pastoral letter on women, but it has never even occurred to them to write one on men. We seem to have resigned ourselves to church meetings where men are largely absent, to church ministry that is mainly run by women but overseen by a clerical caste, to an often soft devotionalism that attracts only a specific male clientele. Often the men who do become involved in church are subservient and not the risk-takers, leaders and missionary personalities that attract other men. This is increasingly apparent in minority neighbourhoods of the world, where the men with religious ire invariably move towards evangelical churches and community service projects. We cannot continue to lose such men under a false banner of orthodoxy when the issue is in fact usually one of control. It must be significant that Jesus chose working men, independent types, even a Zealot and a would-be betrayer to get this whole thing started. We are choosing our religious leaders in an increasingly narrow category. We can do much better.

Helpful
Addresses

Retreat Association　　　　　　　　　　Tel: 020 7357 7736
The Central Hall　　　　　　　　　　　Fax: 020 7357 7724
256 Bermondsey Street　　　　　　e-mail: info@retreats.org.uk
London SE1 3UJ　　　　　　　　Website: www.retreats.org.uk
The Retreat Association is a very important national organisation which makes available the programmes of many of the Christian retreat houses in Britain. It has grown in scope and excellence of work over the last few years and comprises the following Christian retreat groups: the Association for Promoting Retreats (mainly Anglican), the National Retreat Movement (mainly Roman Catholic), the Methodist Retreat Group, the Baptist Union Retreat Group, the United Reformed Church Silence and Retreat Group, and the Quaker Retreats and One-to One Ministry (Q-ROOM). The Retreat Association aims to foster and develop the rich and diverse expressions of Christian spirituality. There are no individual members. It provides information and resources, maintains networks, co-ordinates new initiatives and publishes an annual journal *Retreats*. The journal lists retreat houses and their programmes in Britain and Ireland. There are articles about retreats and the journal is available by post from the Association or from Christian book shops. Do ask also in your local book and magazine shop, as it may be available there. You may send an SAE for a list of courses. If you are looking for a spiritual director, the Retreat Association can help by putting you in touch with a contact person in your area.

Amaravati Buddhist Centre
Great Gaddesden
Hemel Hempstead　　　　　　　　　Tel: 0144 842455
Herts HP1 3BZ　　　　　　　　　　Fax: 0144 843721

Baptist Union Retreat Group
42 Coniston Road
Chippenham, Wilts SN14 OPX
Occasional papers which are very helpful: *Personality and Prayer, Patterns of Evangical Spirituality, Prayer in Midlife and Praying with Scripture.*

Bahá'í Community of the UK
27 Rutland Gate
London SW7 1PD　　　　　　　　Tel: 020 7584 2566

Brahma Kumaris World Spirituality University
Global Co-operation House　　　　Tel: 020 8459 1400
65 Pound Lane　　　　　　　　　　Fax: 020 8451 6480
London NW10 2HH　　　　e-mail: bk@bkwsugch.demon.co.uk

British Association of Iconographers
Prior of Our Lady of Peace
Turvey Abbey, Turvey, Beds MK43 8DE
Courses, retreats and study for all interested in icons.

British Buddhist Association
11 Biddulph Road
London W9 1JA   Tel/Fax: 020 7286 5575

Buddhist Society
58 Ecclestone Square   Tel: 020 7834 5858
London SW1 IPH   Fax: 020 7976 5238

Catholic Charismatic Renewal Network   Tel: 020 7352 5298
International Office   Website: www.portsmouth-dio-org.uk/charisma

Catholic Marriage Centre
Oasis of Peace
Penamser Road   Tel: 01766 514300
Porthmadog LL49 9NY   Fax: 01766 515227
Courses for marriage healing, retreats for marriage, prayer and teaching
workshops and counselling.

Christian Life Community
St Joseph's
Watford Way   e-mail: clcew@iname.com
London NW4 4TY   Website: www.clcew.org.uk
A worldwide community composed of small local groups inspired by Ignatian
spirituality.

Community of the Hermits of St Bruno
St Bruno's Hermitage
38 Helmshore Walk
Chorlton-on-Medlock
Manchester M13 9TH
International community following ermetical traditions. Information of
interest to Catholics who feel called to the hermit life.

Creative Arts Retreat Movement
136 London Road
Gloucester GL1 3PL   Website: www.carmretreat8.org

Council of Churches for Britain and Ireland
Inter-church House
35–41 Lower Marsh   Tel: 020 7620 4444
London SE1 7RL   Fax: 020 7928 0010

Evangelical Alliance UK
Whitefield House
186 Kennington Park Road   Tel: 020 7207 2100
London SE11 4BT   Fax: 020 7207 2150

**Faith and Light
82 Dereham Road
Norwich NR2 4BU**
Movement for those with learning difficulties and their parents and families. Offers support for their faith and opportunities to go on pilgrimage to various sites and take part in other activities.

**Fellowship of Contemplative Prayer
202 Ralph Road
Solihull
West Midlands B90 3LE** Tel/Fax: 0121 745 6522

**Fellowship of Solitaries
Coed Glas
Talgarth Road
Bronllys, Brecon** Website: www.solitaries.org.uk
Powys LD3 OHN e-mail: solitaries@onetel.com
An association for all seeking a spiritual life in prayerful solitude, including those who work and are married.

**Focolare Movement
Centre for Unity
69 Parkway
Welwyn Garden City
Herts AL8 6JG** Website: www.focolare.org
International Roman Catholic lay movement, founded by Chiara Lubich, whose spirituality centres on love and unity. It has many members and is growing all the time. The Movement runs a publishing house, New City, and produces the free publication *Word of Life*. The website gives detailed information and inspiring and helpful commentaries. Focolare runs annual retreats in Britain.

**Friends of the Western Buddhist Order
London Buddhist Centre
51 Roman Road** Tel: 020 7981 1225
Bethnal Green Fax: 020 8980 1968
London E2 OHU e-mail: lbc@alanlbc.demon.uk

FTM Network Helpline: 0161 4321 1915
BM Network (Wednesdays 8–10.30p.m. only)
London WC1N 3XX Website: www.ftm.org.uk
Offers advice and support to female-to-male transsexual and transgender people and to families and professionals.

Gender Trust Tel: 01273 424024 (offices hours only)
PO Box 3192 Helpline: 07000 790347
Brighton BN1 3WR Website: www.3.mistral.co.uk/gentrust/
A UK charity offering help with gender issues to adults who are transsexual (especially male-to-female), gender dysphoric or transgenderist. Also offers advice and support to partners, families, carers and professionals.

Hindu Cultural Trust Centre
55 Manor Road
Hounslow
Middlesex TW4 7JN   Tel: 020 7230 0571

Inter Faith Network for the United Kingdom
5–7 Tavistock Place   Tel: 020 7387 0008
London WC1H 9SN   Fax: 020 7387 7968

Inter Faith Resource Centre
91 Mantilla Drive
Styvechale
Coventry CV3 6LG   Tel: 01203 415531

Islamic Centre England
140 Maida Vale   e-mail: ice@ic-el.org
London W9 1QB   Website: www.ic-el.org

Iyengar Yoga Institute
223a Randolph Avenue
London W9 1NL   Tel/Fax: 020 7624 3080

Julian Meetings
The Rectory, Kingstone
Hereford HR2 9EY   Website: www.julianmeetings.org
Silent contemplative prayer groups. Christian, ecumenical with some 350 groups
around Britain. Fellowship, quiet days, and retreats. See website for details.

L'Arche
Bradbury House
51A Aldwick Road   Tel: 01243 863426
Bognor Regis   Fax:01243 840383
W Sussex PO21 2NJ   e-mail: bognor@larche.org.uk
An international group that aims to build community among people with and
without learning disabilities. It is interfaith but largely based on the Christian
ethics of the Gospel. Its members range from those for whom a L'Arche
community is a lifetime home to those living outside but working at the
community house.

Lesbian and Gay Christian Movement   Tel/Fax: 020 7739 1249
Oxford House   Counselling Helpline : 020 7739 8134
Derbyshire Street   e-mail: lgcm@churchnet.ucsm.uk
London E2 6HG   Website: www.members.aol.com/lgcm

Open Centre
Third Floor
188 Old Street
London EC1 9FR   Tel: 020 7251 1504
Now running for over twenty years, The Open Centre offers a programme to
increase your awareness of yourself and others and to help you take a look at your
relationships, your assumptions and your decisions about life and work. The key

ideas are centred in therapy, movement, healing and growth. Courses on offer may include primal integration, bio-energetics and transactional analysis. A brochure is available on request and, as a guide, prices range from individual sessions at £30–£35 per hour to intensives and residential courses at £110–£305.

Pagan Federation
BM Box 7097
London WC1N 3XX   Tel/Fax: 01691 671066

Quaker Retreats and One-to-One Ministry
80 Lock Street, Abercynon
Glamorgan CF45 4HU

The Quiet Garden Movement
Stoke Park Farm   Tel: 01753 643050
Park Road   Fax: 01753 643081
Stoke Poges   e-mail: quiet.garden@ukonline.co.uk
Bucks SL2 4PG   Website: www.quietgarden.co.uk

Roman Catholic Church in England and Wales
Catholic Communications Centre   Tel: 020 7233 8196
39 Eccleston Square   Fax: 020 7933 7497
London SW1V 1BX   e-mail: 101454.103@compuserve.com

Salvation Army
101 Queen Victoria Street   Tel: 020 7236 5222
London EC4P 4EP   Fax: 020 7236 6272

Spirituality of Ageing Resource Centre
St Monica's
62 Headingley Lane   Tel/Fax: 0113 261 8059
Leeds LS6 2BU   e-mail: pam.kent@mha.org.uk

St George Orthodox Information Service
The White House
Mettingham   Tel/Fax: 01986 896708
Suffolk NR35 1TP   e-mail: StGeorgeOIS@aol.com
Public relations office serving the Orthodox (Russian, Greek, etc) Churches in Britain. Publications and books by mail order, and information.

Vedanta Movement (Hindu)
13 Elsenham Street
Southfields, London SW18 5UN   Tel: 020 8874 6100

World Congress of Faiths
2 Market Square   Tel: 01865 202751
Oxford, Oxon OX1 3EF   Fax: 01865 202746

World Sikh Foundation
88 Mollison Way, Edgware
Middlesex HA8 5QW   Tel: 020 8257 0359

Helpful Publications

Christian (Ecumenical)
Retreats
Retreat Association
The Central Hall
256 Bermondsey Street
London SE1 3UJ

Tel: 020 7357 7736

Christian (Baptist)
Baptist Times
PO Box 54
129 The Broadway
Didcot, OX11 8XB

Christian (Anglican)
Church Times
33 Upper Street
London N1 OPN

Tel: 020 7359 4570
Fax: 020 7226 3073

Christian (Evangelical)
Evangelism Today
320 Ashley Down Road
Bristol B57 9BQ

Tel/Fax: 0117 924 1679

Christian (Roman Catholic)
The Tablet
Great Peter Street
London SW1P 2HB

Buddhist
Tricycle: The Buddhist Review
Sharpham Coach Yard
Ashprington
Totnes
Devon TQ9 7UT

Tel: 01803 732082
Fax: 01803 732037
e-mail: buddhist.publishing@dial.pipex.com

Buddhist
Middle Way and The Buddhist Directory of Buddhist Groups and Centres in the UK
The Buddhist Society
58 Eccleston Square
London SW1V 1PH

Hindu
Hinduism Today
1b Claverton Street
London SW1V 3AY

Tel: 020 7630 8688
e-mail: 100700.513@compuserve.com

Jewish
Jewish Chronicle
25 Furnival Street
London EC4A 1JT

Tel: 020 7415 1500
Fax: 020 7405 9040
e-mail: jacdmin@chron.co.uk

Mind Body Spirit
Kindred Spirit Quarterly
Foxhole
Dartington
Totnes
Devon TQ9 6EB

Tel: 01803 866686
Fax: 01803 866591
e-mail: kindred@spirit.co.uk

Mind Body Spirit
Parabola
PO Box 3000
Denville
New Jersey 07834
USA

Website: www.parabola.org

Muslim
Islamic Times
Raza Academy
138 Northgate Road
Edgeley
Stockport SK3 9NL

Tel: 0161 477 1595

Retreats in the USA
Sanctuaries by J. & M. Kelly
Bell Tower, N.Y.
ISBN 0517 885174

Yoga
Spectrum
The Journal of the British Wheel of Yoga
123 Bear Road
Brighton
E Sussex BN2 4DB

Tel: (editorial) 01273 698560

Travel Organisations

Bicycle Beano
Erwood
Builth Wells
Powys LD2 3PQ
Biking around Wales – what a way to get relaxed! Fresh air, lovely landscapes, great local folk ... Since we can pray anywhere because God is everywhere, why not try a personal bike retreat? You could call it: *My Pedal and Prayer Retreat*. This is a well-known bike holiday organiser. Send for their brochure.

Baobab
Alternative Roots to Travel
Old Fallings Hall
Old Fallings Lane
Wolverhampton WV10 8BL
Tel: 01902 558316
Fax: 01902 558317
e-mail: inf@baobabtravel.com
Website: www.baobabtravel.com

Dolphin Connection
Second Floor
46 Osmond Road
Hove
E. Sussex BN3 1TD
Tel: 01273 882778
e-mail: Dolphin.connection@virgin.net
Website: www.dolphinconnectionexperience.com
Holidays encountering wild dolphins and whales. Believe it when you are told this is a spiritual adventure!

Footprint Adventures
5 Malham Drive
Lincoln LN6 OXD
Many different locations on offer from this alternative holiday operation. Send for programme.

Head for the Hills
The Hexagon
Garth
Builth Wells
Powys LD4 4AT
Tel: 01591 620388
e-mail: hfth@the-hexagon.co.uk
Website: www.the-hexagon.co.uk
Based in Wales but runs walking adventures throughout Britain. Ancient sites, meditation, formal pilgrimages.

Neal's Yard Agency
BMC Neal's Yard
London WC1N 3XX

Tel: 0870 444 2702
e-mail: info@nealsyardagency.com
Website: www.nealsyardagency.com

Neal's Yard Agency produces an excellent *Holiday Events Guide*, usually every six months or so. This contains a wealth of information on programmes running at places in the UK, plus a host of others abroad, and even outside Europe. Just a few of the sites that have been listed are Greece, Turkey, France, Spain, Egypt, the Grand Canyon Arizona and Nepal. The range of spiritual approaches is wide, encompassng Buddhism; Mind Body Spirit; and Dru yoga among others. **Highly Recommended.**

Retreats Beyond Dover
St Etheldreda's Church
14 Ely Place
London EC1N 6RY

Tel/Fax: 020 7831 2388
e-mail: retreats@dircon.co.uk
Website: www.retreats.dircon.co.uk

This is our favourite creator of retreats abroad. The founder and director, Anthony Weaver, puts together exciting, unusual and interesting retreat projects – for example, a retreat at the Benedictine Monastery of Montserrat in Spain, a retreat at the Rosminian Sacro Calvario in Italy, and another Italian one lead by Bishop Christopher of St Albans. Gracefully fluent in a number of languages, Anthony Weaver is now creating an entirely new kind of retreat abroad, designed especially for busy young men in the City of London – or for that matter any other men feeling wound up and stressed out by their careers. If you are one of these guys, then contact him and find out what his plans are. You may be surprised and delighted to discover a retreat full of imagination and adventure on distant shores. Retreats Beyond Dover are always informative for the mind and inspirational for the spirit. There are not many held each year, so ask early what is going to be on offer. **Highly Recommended.**

Tangney Tours
Pilgrim House
Station Court
Borough Green
Kent TN15 8AF
Tel: 01732 886666
Fax: 01732 886885

Christian pilgrimages, mainly to Roman Catholic sites such as Lourdes (see France section).

VegiVentures
Castle Cottage
Castle Acre
King's Lynn
Norfolk PE32 2AJ
Tel: 01760 755888
e-mail: holidays@vegiventures.com
Website: www.vegiventures.com

Exclusively vegetarian holidays in Europe and South America. Local culture, ancient sites, arts and crafts, yoga, meditation.

Selected Reading

People often wonder what to take on a retreat for reading outside any material that may be provided. A religious retreat centre will usually have available literature centred around its beliefs. Other places may leave you to browse in their library or book shop, where with so many books on offer choosing can be difficult. Regardless of whether you follow a particular spiritual path or not, reading that widens your understanding of spirituality and the inner self can often prove helpful. It may lead to reflection on your lifestyle and your present values while you are taking time out from ordinary living – or even give you a greater vision of humanity and God than you had before. It is for this reason that this very short list is not organised according to religion or spiritual path.

Books by Stafford Whiteaker, author of *The Good Retreat Guide*:
Best Yoga Centres and Retreats, Stafford Whiteaker, Rider, London 2003.
Little Book of Inner Space, Stafford Whiteaker, Rider, London 1998.
Living the Sacred, Stafford Whiteaker, Rider, London 2000.

Other books:
A Journey with Jonah: the Spirituality of Bewilderment, Paul Murray OP, The Columba Press, Dublin 2002.
A Thirst for God: Daily Readings with St Francis de Sales, DLT, London 1985.
Bhagavad Gita: Chapters 1–6, Mahrarishi Mahesh Yogi, Penguin, London 1969.
Confessions of Saint Augustine, trans R.S. Pine-Coffin, Penguin Books, London 1961
Crossing-Reclaiming the Landscape of Our Lives, Mark Barrett, DTL, London 2001.
The Desert Fathers, Helen Waddell, Vintage Books, New York 1998.
Essential Rumi, trans Coleman Barks, HarperSanFrancisco, USA 1995.
Essential Gay Mystics, Andrew Harvey, HarpersCollins, New York 1997.
Faith beyond Resentment: Fragments Catholic and Gay, James Allison, DTL, London 2001.
Golden Age of Zen, John C.H. Wu, Image Books, Doubleday, New York 1996.
Good News Bible, The Bible Society, HarperCollins. London 1994.
In Search of Nature, Edward O. Wilson, Island Press, Washington DC 1996.
Interior Prayer: Carthusian Novice Conferences, Darton, Longman & Todd, London 1996.
Introducing The New Testament, John Drane, Lion Books, Oxford 1986.
Introducing the Old Testament, John Drane, Lion Books, Oxford 1987.

Koran, trans N.J. Dawood, Allen Lane 1978.

Meister Eckhart, The Essential Sermons, Paulist Press, New York 1981.

Muhammad: A Short Biography, Martin Forward, Oneworld, Oxford 1998.

Native American Spirituality, Dennis Renault & Timothy Freke, Thorsons, London 1996.

New Jerusalem Bible, Darton, Longman & Todd, London 1990.

New Seeds of Contemplation, Thomas Merton, New Directions Books 1972.

Path of Life, Cyprian Smith, Gracewing 1995.

Paths in Solititude, Eve Baker, St Pauls 1995.

Practice of the Presence of God, Brother Lawrence, Mowbray, London 1980.

Souls on Fire, Elie Wiesel, Touchstone, USA 1972.

Teachings from the Silent Mind, Ven Ajahn Sumedho, Aamaravati Buddhist Centre 1987.

Way of the Shaman, Michael Harner, HarperCollins, New York 1990.

Western Buddhism, Kulananda, HarpersCollins 1997.

> I will not look for perfection in another person until I have attained perfection for myself. Since I know this will never be, let me learn to accept things as they are, and stop manipulating them into changing. Let me look for a wiser approach to life from myself, not from other people.
>
> AL-ANON, IN ' ONE DAY AT A TIME'

Glossary

Alexander Technique: Gentle posture work that guides the body into a more natural stance and relaxed state, bringing awareness of how to do the same by yourself. It is of particular help to those with back, postural and tension-related problems.

Aromatherapy: A holistic treatment that enhances well-being, relieves stress and helps the body to restore its energies. Many conditions can be helped. Essential oils are selected for the individual person's needs and gently massaged into the skin.

Bahá'': This Faith began in Persia in 1844. Bahá'' members believe their scriptures to be the revealed word of God. Key beliefs are in one God, the unity of mankind, independent investigation of truth, the common foundation of all religions, the harmony of science and religion, equality of opportunity for men and women, elimination of all prejudices, universal education, abolition of the extremes of poverty and wealth, establishment of world peace, and progressive revelation.

Buddhism, Buddha: Buddhism has no personal deity. It makes no claim to have a divinely inspired book and it has no central organising authority. The teachings of Buddhism are an inheritance from Siddhartha Gautama's own search for truth. He was believed to be *enlightened*, that is to be a Buddha. Thus the emphasis for Buddhists is on a tradition of teachings. While they begin by learning about these teachings, in the end each individual must discover their own experience of truth and what it has taught them. The *Noble Eightfold Path* in Buddhist teachings is concerned with wisdom, morality, concentration and meditation. Central to Buddhism is meditation, of which there are various methods.

Charismatic retreat: Christian healing retreat which usually involves praying in tongues and prophecy.

Choir: A body of singers assisting at Divine Office. Lay singers are usually the choir at church services, but the choir in a monastery consists of the religious of that community, who come together for the Divine Office. They may or may not invite guests to join them.

Christianity, Christian life: The common focus of Christianity is on the person of Jesus of Nazareth. He is seen as the criterion by which all of life is to be evaluated. The universal significance of Jesus is always asserted. The name *Christians* was originally given to early followers of Jesus who believed him to be the *Christ*, or Messiah. Christian life is the living out of the command by Jesus to 'love one another as I have loved you', so Christians try to base their lives on the pattern of his life, which was characterised by sacrificial and self-giving love.

Community: In the Christian sense, a group of people who live together under a common rule, usually but not always with obedience to one person, who worship together and whose lives are devoted to seeking God. It is traditional for communities to be of men only or women only, but this is not always the case (see Burford Priory). Sometimes men and women religious in separate communities will work and worship together (see Turvey Abbey). Buddhist monks and nuns also live in communities, working and sharing a life devoted to Buddhist practices. There are lay people (see Omega Order) who also live together with much the same purpose.

Compline: The last prayer at night in the Catholic and Anglican liturgy of the hours (see *Divine Office*).

Contemplative: A person devoted to religious meditation and who gives his or her life to seeking God as the primary purpose and aim.

Contemplative prayer: The prayer of stillness or contemplative prayer, has been a recognised way of praying for thousands of years. It is silent and based not on knowing about God, but on knowing God. The message of Psalm 46 best sums it up: 'Be still and know that I am God.'

Counselling: A method of helping people with various personal or relationship problems through understanding, and empathic and uncritical listening. This approach is combined with helping the person to clarify the problem and decide what action to take.

Cursillo: A renewal weekend retreat for Christians to try to experience their religion from new perspectives.

De Mello retreats: Anthony de Mello SJ was born in Bombay and died in New York in 1987. He was a popular spiritual guide who wrote a number of books of methods and practices for prayer and meditation, exercises for deepening the inner self, and stories for reflection. He drew heavily on the Ignatian Exercises (see that entry), and his work is very scripture orientated.

Dharma: Dharma is the intrinsic property of something, the thing that holds it together, that which sustains it. Thus it is the essential, final character of something, including a person. For example, the dharma of water is its wetness. Used in both Hindu and Buddhist traditions to represent the truth or spiritual teachings.

Directed retreat: A six- to eight-day retreat consisting of silent prayer and deep inner reflection, and including a daily meeting with a spiritual director. An Ignatian retreat is usually a directed one.

Divine Office, Canonical Hours, Liturgy of the Hours, Offices: All these terms are used to describe the official daily prayer cycle of the Catholic Church, which is an adaptation of the liturgy of the synagogue that has evolved over the centuries. The *hours* consist of seven periods of prayer which may be chanted, sung or spoken together, in a group or individually. These are called Virgils, Lauds, Terce, Sext, None, Vespers and Compline. A version is used by the Anglican Church, usually referred to as Morning Prayer and Evensong. The liturgy is built around psalms, songs and words from scripture. The Divine Office provides the prayer structure for monastic life.

Eco-spirituality: A spirituality based on relating our inner self and the way we live to earth, the natural world and all other creatures. Through realising our connection to earth, we may deepen the universality of our spirituality. Eco-spirituality, while essentially a Mind Body Spirit spiritual approach, can also be found mirrored in Christian retreats and in Celtic spirituality. For example, on Nature Retreats use may be made of walks in woods, wild flowers, fields, mountains or the sea to enhance inner awareness.

Ecumenical, Ecumenical movement: The movement in the Christian church towards the visible union of all believers in Christ. This aspiration for unity is an old one and widely popular today. A retreat house or retreat programme that is *ecumenical* is open to all of Christian faith no matter to which church they belong.

Enclosure: The practice of taking religious vows and remaining within a religious house without excursions into the outside world. Enclosed communities are sexually segregated. Today some Communities are semi-enclosed; that is, the members leave the convent or monastery only rarely and for specific necessary purposes, such as a visit to the dentist.

Enneagram: A very ancient method, using a circular diagram with nine points, of discerning a person's spiritual disposition and activity (see Introduction).

Eucharist: The word means thanksgiving and is the term applied to the central act of Christian worship, instituted by Christ who *gave thanks,* and because the service is the supreme act of Christian thanksgiving to God. Other names used are *Holy Communion, The Lord's Supper,* and the *Mass.* Bread and wine are used in an act of sacred consecration and prayer to form the service of thanksgiving.

Evangelical: Christians who try to live according to the Christian scriptures viewed as the supreme authority for Christian life. They feel strongly called to bring others into the Christian church by means of evangelism (meaning 'good news') by means of sharing what Christians believe God has done in and through Jesus Christ.

Guided retreat: A retreat that is guided from time to time by a spiritual director but not on a daily basis as for a directed retreat (see above).

Hermitage retreats, Poustinia, Poustinia experience: *Poustinia* is a Russian word meaning 'hermitage'. These were originally little isolated huts, located deep in the forests of Russia. They offered total silence, solitude, and uninterrupted time to seek God. They are ususaly in the form of a self-catering cottage or a small caravan parked outside the monastry in a field.

Hinduism, Hindus: The Hindu tradition allows the use of various symbols, names, terms and images that may help people to discover the divine. Within the religion there are both those who believe in one God and for whom there is a distinction between God and the world, and those who believe that God is simultaneously both one and many. A number of central values are shared by most Hindus, although in practice they may differ in interpretation. These key ideals and values include respect for parents and elders, reverence for teachers, regard for guests, vegetarianism, non-violence, tolerance of other races and religions, the sanctity of marriage, the discouragement of all pre-marital and extra-marital sexual relationships, the sacredness of the cow, and an appreciation of the equality and sanctity of all living beings.

Icon: A painting or enamel that represents a saint or other sacred person. Icon painting retreats use the painting of the icon as a structure and centring for prayer.

Inter-denominational: Common to several religious denominations.

Inter-faith: Common to several different religions. An Inter-faith retreat would be one held with members of two or more faiths.

Ignatian Exercises, St Ignatius of Loyola: St Ignatius (1491–1556) was founder of the Society of Jesuits. He wrote *Spiritual Exercises*, which has remained one of the great Christian spirituality practices for deepening faith and inner awareness of God. Ignatian retreats are usually eight, ten or thirty days in duration and have recently regained much of their popularity. A spiritual director is assigned to guide you through. There is much solitude and silence so that time and space is given over to meditation and reflection.

Islam, Muslim: Islam is monotheistic and its God is all-merciful, all-powerful and all-present. He controls and sustains the universe, and, although humans may choose which path of life to follow, all eventually return to God, to whom they are accountable. Islam rests on seven basic beliefs: the oneness of God, the books revealed by God, the existence of the prophets, the existence of the angels, a Day of Judgement, life after death, and that all power belongs alone to God. Muslim practice is based on the *Five Pillars of Islam*. The first is the declaration of Faith or *Shahadah*, which is that there is no God except God, and Muhammad is his messenger.

Laity, lay man, lay woman: Members of the Christian church who do not belong to the clergy.

Massage: Massage counteracts stress by bringing deep relaxation of the body and person. As the muscles relax, the breathing improves and the circulation strengthens. It helps restore harmony and balance to the mind and body. It also strengthens the body itself.

Meditation: In Christian meditation, the term denotes mental prayer. Its method is devout reflection on a chosen, often biblical, theme to deepen spiritual insight. In Buddhist and Hindu practice, meditation is a way towards personal development by directly working on the mind to transform it. Although there are hundreds of approaches to meditation, these divide into two main streams of practice. One is to calm and refresh the mind, relax the body and relieve psychological tensions so that a deeply contented state is achieved. The other aims at developing wisdom in the context of self, others and the nature of all things. Breathing techniques are often part of the meditation method.

Monks, nuns, religious: Monks are men and nuns (or sisters) are women who have undertaken to live a life, usually together in a community, devoted to seeking God or enlightenment. Christian monks and nuns may make promises of poverty, chastity and obedience. Buddhism also has monks and nuns living in communities.

New Kadampa Mahayana tradition (NKT): The New Kadampa tradition is a sect founded by a Tibetan Buddhist monk named Geshe Kelsang Gyatso It is now the fastest-growing Buddhist sect in England. (See Manjushri Buddhist Centre in North section of listings.)

Non-religious: Belonging to no established religion or faith.

Non-retreatant: A description often used by those running retreat houses and also in this guide. It refers to a person who is staying at a retreat centre for rest and relaxation in the form of a short, quiet holiday and is not planning to attempt anything of a spiritual nature. Many places do not invite visitors who desire only a holiday, and this is understandable. Other places actively encourage this type of guest.

Order: Monks, nuns and religious belong to Orders that dictate the type of life they lead. Among the best known Orders in Western Christianity are the Society of Jesus, noted for teaching and missionary work; the Benedictines, with an emphasis on prayer, work and study of scripture and holy books; the Dominicans, known for intellectual study; the Carmelites, who lead a life centred on silent prayer and meditation; and the Franciscans who follow the rule of St Francis of Assisi.

Pilgrim, pilgrimage: Journeys to holy places motivated by personal devotion, with the aim of obtaining supernatural help or as an act of penance or thanksgiving. Lourdes has acquired world fame as a place of pilgrimage (see France section). Pilgrims are those who are in the process of a pilgrimage.

Poustinia: The word *poustinia* is Russian for 'desert'. In the West it is now used interchangeably with the word 'hermitage'. In the spiritual sense, both terms designate a quiet, solitary place that we retreat to in order to find God who dwells within. The number of *poustinias* available at retreat centres is increasing every year.

Preached retreat: A group retreat in which a speaker or facilitator gives talks each day, usually on a particular theme and with scripture at their core.

Private retreat: A retreat period of solitude and usually much silence without guidance or direction from anyone.

Psalm: Although their origins are lost in primitive religion, the Psalms in the Old Testament are a legacy from Hebrew and have become a part of Christianity's very fabric. Jesus himself quoted the Psalms as his own prayers. The Psalms are often said to be the perfect prayers.

Reflexology: This ancient healing therapy originated in China centuries ago. It is a form of compression massage of the feet and hands in which energy pathways in the body are activated, enabling self-healing and generating a feeling of well-being. It is also used to treat specific areas of illness or blocked energy.

Refectory: Monastery dining room.

Reiki: An Asian healing technique in which an energy transfer occurs between the therapist and the patient by the laying on of hands. This may promote healing, a sense of well-being and the reduction of stress.

Sacrament: A sacrament is an outward and visible sign of an inward and spiritual grace given to Christians by Christ. In Christian theology the term has wide variations. Three sacraments, Baptism, Confirmation and Orders, are held to be non-repeatable. The Eucharist (see entry above) is a sacrament.

Scripture, Holy Scripture: The sacred writings of the Old and New Testament, together known as the Bible.

Shamanism, Shaman: One of the primitive religions, in which all the good and evil of life is thought to be brought about by spirits which can be influenced only by Shamans. The native religions of the North American Indians and the people of the Ural region in Siberia are shamanic. A Shaman is a priest or medicine-man, a *master of ecstasy* in touch with the realm of experience or reality that exists outside the limited, narrow state of our normal waking consciousness. By performing certain acts and rituals a Shaman is able to influence the spirits and change consciousness to bring about a greater state of wholeness. Shamanism is widely used for the discovery of the inner person and for healing. Shamanism, particularly that of the Indians of the Americas, has greatly increased in popularity in the West, especially in Britain and France (see Eagle's Wing Centre for Contemporary Shamanism in London section). Programmes of many Mind Body Spirit places include courses and workshops with shamanic themes or practices, for example sweat lodges, chanting, drumming and dancing.

Shiatsu: A powerful Japanese healing therapy. *Shiatsu* means finger pressure, which is applied on specific areas to release blocked energies, with increased circulation, improved health and enhanced flexibility resulting.

Sufism: Sufism is a commitment to the practical and accessible aspects of Islam but emphasises the inner or mystical aspects of the faith. The members of Sufi Orders may use various aids to spiritual development, including meditation, chanting and ritual dancing.

Tai chi (chuan): Ancient Chinese method of meditation through movement, involving in a series of extremely graceful, slow, flowing and gentle movements. These exercises are intended to quiet the inner self, mind and body. The movements also actively exercise most of the muscles of the body. They can be done by people of any age.

Vipassana meditation: Insight meditation, originating in Southeast Asia and now popular in Europe, practised to attain mindfulness and understanding of the nature of self and others. It assumes that kindness, compassion and generosity of spirit may be cultivated by any person.

Virgin Mary, the Blessed Virgin Mary, Mary: The mother of Jesus Christ. In the Bible, Mary figures prominently in the stories of Jesus' birth. Belief in Mary's intercessions as a result of direct prayer to her is probably very old, dating back to the third or early fourth century. The most famous shrines to Mary are at Lourdes (see section on France) and Fatima, where there were apparitions of the Virgin. Mary's presence in the New Testament stories is marked by her obedience to God and her humility.

Zen: a transliteration of the Sanskrit word *Dhyana*, meaning 'meditation'.

> Riches are not from abundance but from a contented mind.
> HADITH, *SAYINGS OF THE PROPHET MOHAMMED*

Visit the Good Retreat Guide

Visit www.thegoodretreatguide.com where you can learn about:

Selected retreat places
Going on retreat
Different kinds of retreats
How to find your retreat
Buddhism
Christianity
Mind Body Spirit
Healing retreats
Yoga today
Prayers and praying
Types of meditation
The way of the desert
Gateways to heaven
Obtaining spiritual help
Soul companionship
Books by Stafford Whiteaker
Recommended spirituality books
Getting in touch with us

Website design by Nicky Trulsson (nicky.t@telia.com)

REPORTS WELCOMED

The Good Retreat Guide welcomes reports on places of retreat whether your opinion is favourable or not. If you discover a new retreat place, let us know please. There is a Report Form on page 403 at the end of the guide or you may send an email to staffordwhiteaker@compuserve.com or via our website www.thegoodretreatguide.com

REPORT FORM

To: The Good Retreat Guide
        Rider Books
        Random House
        20 Vauxhall Bridge Road
        London SW1V 2SA

Or go online to reach us at www.thegoodretreatguide.com

If you want to email Stafford Whiteaker directly:
staffordwhiteaker@compuserve.com
or staffordwhiteaker@thegoodretreatguide.com

I have visited the following retreat on .... 20.........

Establishment name:...

Address:..

....

....

Post code:................................... Telephone:....................................

In the space below, please describe what the retreat was like and give any other details you feel to be relevant. For example, include what you thought of the rooms and meals, the situation, atmosphere, spiritual help offered, special activities and charges. (Please continue on the reverse of this sheet if necessary.)

From my personal experience I recommend this retreat centre for inclusion in/exclusion from future editions of The Good Retreat Guide.

I am not connected in any way with the retreat centre other than as a guest.

Name and address (BLOCK CAPITALS, PLEASE):

....

....

....

Signed:...